THE TRAVEL CATALOGUE

CATALOGUE

by
Karen Cure

A Gladstone Book
Holt, Rinehart and Winston
New York

ABOUT THE AUTHOR

Karen Cure, former associate editor of *Holiday*, is a free-lance travel writer who spends a lot of time seeing the places she writes about. A graduate of Brown University, Ms. Cure's previous book was *Mini-Vacations USA*. Her travel articles have appeared in such publications as *Better Homes and Gardens, Travel and Leisure, Newsday, Family Circle*, and *Good Housekeeping*. She makes her home in New York City.

Many thanks are due to the countless tourism office people, festival directors, museum curators, hoteliers, and innkeepers, whose generous assistance and encouragement over the last five years put this project within my reach to begin with. Their kindnesses and enthusiasm have always made my work a delight.

And to Nanette Rainone, Maria Martin, Jessica Greenbaum, Jennifer Crewe, Laura Ellin, and Emily Schaffer, who kept on working hard and stayed cheerful even when the going was rough.

Acknowledgements

page 95. Quoted from *Landforms* by George F. Adams and Jerome Wyckoff © 1971 by Western Publishing Company, Inc. Used by permission.

Published simultaneously in Canada by Holt, Rinehart and Winston of Canada, Limited.

Library of Congress Cataloging in Publication Data

Cure, Karen.
  The travel catalogue.

  Includes index.
  1. Travel. 2. Voyages and travels—1951- —Guide-books. I. Title.
  G151.C87 910'.202 77-21276
  ISBN Hardbound 0-03-020711-8
  ISBN Paperback 0-03-020706-1

First Edition
Back flap photo by Jane Hamborsky, New York

Printed in the United States of America
10 9 8 7 6 5 4 3 2 1

Contents

Arts and Crafts, Music and Dance/74

Shakespearean festivals • film festivals • pageants • Chautauquas • summer dance • Jamaica dance • square-dancing resorts, clinics, and contests • a polka festival • a country-dancing camp • learning decorative arts • a museum of television • jazz festivals • summer concerts from symphonic to folk • music in the mountains • music in the vineyards • marching-band festivals • concerts on the green • summer opera • barbershop-quartet music • fiddle music • the Grand Ole Opry • country-and-western music • voodoo in Haiti and Puerto Rico • the big crafts fairs and festivals • mountain crafts • Pennsylvania Dutch crafts • Canadian crafts • Caribbean crafts • Renaissance crafts • learn-a-craft vacations • crafts museums • American Indian crafts

A Potpourri of Vacation Ideas and Activities/94

Reading highway signs • an FM radio guide • books on tape • truck stops • a diesel directory • appreciating and understanding landforms • a guide to the roads of the Canadian Rockies • twenty-eight super-scenic drives • how to find covered bridges • the longest and highest bridges • a circus museum • circus collections • a circus in a casino • a circus festival • a clown school • where and when to see the great parades • where to gamble • magic—festivals, conventions, stores, and restaurants • the great amusement parks • the great roller coasters • museums and collections—air guns, archery artifacts, barbed wire, beer memorabilia, buttons, tureens, pottery, clocks and watches, decoys, dollhouses, fire apparatus, comic strips, glass, guns, cameos, coins, Kewpie dolls, miniatures, music boxes, paper, pharmacopeia, tools, totems, toys, world records, Americana • learn-a-language vacations • alpine chalets in the United States • the Caribbean in Canada • Chinatowns • Czech fests • Florida's little Cubas • the Danes in America • Dutch treats • a Basque festival • France in Missouri • German restaurants, festivals, and settlements • Greek culture • Iceland West • Little Italy • some outposts of Japan • a Lithuanian museum • Mexican fiestas • a Polish museum • Norwegian celebrations • the Scots' gatherings • Swisstowns and Swiss festivals • melting-pot festivals • state fairs • the Canadian National Exhibition • the last camptown fair • Mardi Gras and other carnivals • Christmases—elegant, quaint, citified, historical, with foreign influences, or on skis • learn-to-cook vacations • big feeds and food festivals—apple butter, bananas, beans, black walnuts, blueberries, barbecued buffalo, cereal, Swiss cheese, cherries, chili, chitlins, citrus fruit, wild game, corn, crawfish, eggs, grapes, ham, huckleberries, molasses, pancakes, peaches, peanuts, pumpkins, wild rice, sassafras, salmon, sauerkraut, seafood, strawberries, sugar cane, watermelon, wurst, popcorn, chocolate • some places to watch food being made • how to find America's vineyards • some wine guides • wine-country tours • wine museums • grape-harvest festivals • wine seminars • where to buy grape vines • distillery tours • brewery tours • some spectacular gardens • resort gardens • a butterfly garden • some arboretums • Caribbean gardens • Caribbean wildlife • snorkeling and scuba diving in the Caribbean • Florida's underwater park • organized scuba trips • places to learn about undersea life • where to see American wildlife—birds, elk, bison, alligators, snakes, fishes • a bird-watching ranch • a listing of wildlife refuges • tours and camps for wildlife watching • caribou-watching • whale-watching • bear-watching • the largest alligator farm in the world • a worm-fiddling contest • rattlesnake roundups • frog jumps • a burro race • turkey races • a chicken museum • a buzzard festival • some perfect beaches in the Caribbean, on the Pacific rim, the Atlantic Coast, the Gulf islands, and the Great Lakes • some nude beaches • sand-castle-building contests • beach camping • shell collecting • the great swimming holes • some of the world's best surfing • running the rivers—tubing, canoeing, kayaking, and rafting

Introduction

This book is a sampler designed to set you dreaming about the vast assortment of travel and recreation possibilities that exist all over the United States, Canada, and the Caribbean today. It's a book for thrill-seekers, for outdoors people and indoors people, for sybarites and dedicated sightseers, as well as for people whose idea of the best of all possible vacations is simply to sit around and sip a tropical punch on a palm-scattered crescent of sand.

Flip through the pages and you'll find raft trips on streams wild enough to frighten a daredevil, vacation-length canoe trips that even beginners can handle, and tales of those rare and marvelous streams that are exactly deep, clean, and fast enough that you can float them safely in an inner tube. There are enchanting country inns and supersophisticated resorts, farms where you can stay for a vacation, and dude ranches where you can help with the chores—or just loaf.

Look some more and you'll come on places where you can rattle across a covered bridge, or learn (once and for all) the difference between Sheraton and Duncan Phyfe furniture. There's a restaurant where the world's most famous magicians get together to lunch and to trick each other from soup to nuts; a casino where acrobats soar through the air on the flying trapeze; an amusement park where you can see what it's like to walk a real tightrope and fall into the net below. The best parades and roller coasters in the United States are here, plus some truly magnificent drives, some festivals where you can let your hair down and some others where gorging on local food specialties is the order of the day. You'll find places where you can see masses and masses of flowers (more than you ever thought you'd see in one place in your life) or millions of birds making a spectacle so overwhelming that you don't have to be a birdwatcher to enjoy it. There's information about scuba diving—not just in the Caribbean but also in Maine, Kentucky, the Pacific Northwest; about shopping for Shaker antiques; about following in the footsteps of America's earliest explorers; and about visiting some other spots so historic you won't be able to keep down the goosebumps. When a subject has been treated in a thorough-going fashion in another book, I've referred you to it.

All this material is slotted into four main categories—one devoted to lodging places and other spots to enjoy a stay-put vacation; another to historic sites and attractions; another to vacations that will involve you in crafts, music, dance, and other arts; another to a wildly varied lot of subjects from the circus and clocks to ethnic doings and wine-tasting tours.

To get ideas for a trip, all you've got to do is browse through these four sections.

If you're interested in a specific subject or a particular place, check out the index. Though last in the book, it's far from the least important.

When you get ready to plan your trip, you'll want to read the first chapter, which deals with the mechanics of traveling: how to shave expenses, why you need to insure your luggage, where to find the best seat on the plane and how to wangle a really great meal, and so on. At the same time, be sure to write to the chamber of commerce directors, hoteliers, museum personnel, and other sources to whom I've referred you; they can brief you on any changes that have taken place and tell you what will be happening at the time you intend to visit. Also check out the guidebooks I've mentioned; I've tried to inform you about the kind of publications that will enhance your enjoyment of your trip—which is, in the end, what it's all about. I only hope you have as much fun reading, dreaming—and seeing for yourself—as I have had putting the book together.

Practicalities

How to Stretch Your Travel Dollars

Other than saving on air fares by taking advantage of charters and special rates, the easiest way to shave the most dollars from your travel budget is to travel when other people are staying home. Go to Florida or the Caribbean in the summer or the fall. (It's not that hot and you will have the beaches nearly to yourself.) Visit foliage country or a ski resort in the summer. Visit the big summer attractions in the winter. Go to a popular weekend resort midweek. Most of the time the pleasant hostelries and good restaurants will be open at off-times, but the prices will be lower by far.

But what if you want to ski, or do the foliage, or see the summer glories of the parks and forests? What if you can't travel midweek? Then you've got to save just a little in several ways. Here are some possible ways to trim expenses.

Use a Travel Agent

There are over thirteen thousand of them in the United States; annually they sell some $8 billion worth of travel goods and services. And they can be helpful—even if you don't live in a community so small that using one is the only way to book an airline reservation without making a long-distance telephone call. Travel agents can arrange for a cruise or tour, or plan a multistop independent trip from beginning to end, using up-to-the-minute data on airlines. They can reserve your plane seat, find you hotels, rent you cars, suggest things to see and do. Travel agents can advise you about special fares for buses, trains, and planes, and can tell you when charters are cheapest—and when they aren't. They can tell you how to change your travel plans and save money. They can make sure that you get the room with the view if that's what you want.

The charge? In some cases you might be asked to pay for some long-distance telephone calls. Most of the time, however, travel agents make their money from the commissions paid by the airlines, the cruise lines, the tour operators, hotel management. You don't pay more: the travel-service suppliers collect less. The amount of the commission would figure in your bookings only if you were dealing with a less-than-scrupulous travel agent or if you were vague about exactly what you wanted.

You will, in other words, seldom do worse with an agent than you would on your own—and you can do a lot better, provided that you go to the right person. How to find the right one? Membership in the American Society of Travel Agents is at least an indication that the agent has been in business for at least three years; the initials C.T.A. after the agent's name indicate that he's successfully completed a special course sponsored by the Institute of Certified Travel Agents.

As for the agent's ethics—you've got to judge them as you would a doctor's or a lawyer's or an interior decorator's. Get recommendations from friends whose judgment you trust and whose tastes you share. Check out their recommendations with the Better Business Bureau. Then go around and talk to a few. You want an agent who is not only ethical but also able to understand what you're looking for in a vacation; you want someone with whom you can talk because a good portion of the success of your relationship, as in any relationship, will depend on how well the two of you can communicate about what you're after. A travel agent is no mind reader.

Finally, when the time comes to get down to brass tacks, do some research on your own—find out what there is to see and do in the area you want to visit, about the lodgings situation and the price structure thereof, and about the various types of transportation and fares available to get you there. You'll enjoy your trip more for having put just that much more effort into it and, should the travel agent you've picked be somewhat less than knowledgeable, you may even save yourself some money.

Save on Lodgings

Tent camping is of course cheapest. However, when you want a roof and a bathtub, there are ways to shave.

Membership in the Travelers Directory (6224 Boynton Street, Philadelphia, Pennsylvania 19144). A sort of mutual hospitality exchange you can join for $10. The directory you get when you join lists people who will put you up for free; but to receive you must be available to give. You're not obligated, however, to put up someone who makes you feel strange or to have a guest when you have other commitments.

Tourist homes and inns where you can get a bath down the hall. Generally quite inexpensive for couples. For a list, write the Tourist House Association of America, P. O. Box 355, Greentown, Pennsylvania 18426.

Hostels. Also good for couples. Hostels are operated by the American Youth Hostel Association as well as by church groups and so on. A good listing can be found in *Where to Stay USA,* available both in bookstores or from the publisher—the Council on International Educational Exchange, 777 United Nations Plaza, New York, New York 10017—for $2.95 plus 50c for postage and handling.

Budget motels and chains. Modern chain places that go easy on such amenities as luxurious furnishings, carpets, swimming pools, and restaurants on the premises can also be good deals, again especially for couples. A few of the bigger names: Motel 6, Days Inns, Scottish Inns, Chalet Susse, Econo Travel. A listing of the chains is contained in the *National Directory of Budget Motels,* an annual publication of Pilot Books, 347 Fifth Avenue, New York, New York 10016 ($2.95, postpaid). This booklet also lists a few mom-and-pop operations.

However, more comprehensive in this area are the *Gomer's Guides* by Gomer Lewis. The intended audience is senior citizens, but the listings of motels where the maximum double rate is $15 (or, in areas where all lodging places charge more than that, the listing covers the least expensive ones) are useful no matter what your age. There are two volumes, one for the states east of the Mississippi, one for those to the west. Both contain suggestions for cutting expenses in other ways, mileage and climate charts, maps, and so on. ($3.95 each, from Hammond, Inc., Maplewood, New Jersey 07040.) Also, see the directory of Budget Hotels and Motels of America, Inc. ($1 from the publisher at 1115 East Hennepin Avenue, Minneapolis 55414).

When you're traveling with children, it's often true that the large nonbudget chains will be cheapest because these establishments don't charge extra for children who share a room with parents and use existing facilities. Further, remember that each chain defines *children* differently. To the Holiday Inns of most of the world, children are human beings under 12 (sometimes under 18); to Howard Johnsons, usually under 18; to Imperial 400s, mostly under 12; to the Marriotts, your off-spring of any age qualifies as a child. At Quality Inns, the cutoff age is 17; at Ramada Inns, 19; at Rodeways, 17; at Sheratons, 18; and at Stouffers, 17. If you're trying to shave dollars when traveling with your youngsters, staying at a large chain motel is one way to do it.

Home exchanges. Home exchanges are the cheapest for stay-in-one-place vacations, no matter how you cut it. You do have to plan in advance, however. First, you have to register with one of the home exchange clubs, all of which publish directories of members' homes. This can cost anywhere from about $10 to $15 (sometimes more) annually. Then you write to any families whose house appeals to you and to whom you think, based on the information given, your own home might appeal—ten to fifteen letters altogether. Some business executive, long since transferred to another city, is bound to want to take his kids back to the city he started in to see old friends; some fond grandparents long since moved to Florida are bound to want to come back and visit their children without giving up their privacy. If there's no response from your first batch of letters, try again. You might end up with a Georgian house in New England, a seashore concrete-and-glass palace, a plantation dwelling in the South, a ski country condominium. Some owners may leave their maids and gardeners. Some may let you use their cars—which will make

the savings just that much larger.

Some house-swapping clubs are the Vacation Exchange Club, 350 Broadway, New York, New York 10013; the Holiday Home Exchange Bureau, P. O. Box 555, Grants, New Mexico 87020; Adventures-in-Living, P. O. Box 278, Winnetka, Illinois 60093; the International Hospitality Service, Suite 3, 1377 Ninth Avenue, San Francisco, California 94122; and, in Canada, the Canadian Holiday Home Exchange, P. O. Box 826, Ganges, B.C. VOS 1EO, Canada. An organization called Inquiline, another home exchange service, will also check on the family you exchange with (for about $50) and give you details on the home you plan to use (for about $25); the charge for the two services together runs about $60. The address is Box 208, Katonah, New York 10536.

Save on Meals

If all you want is a hot meal, try a cafeteria instead of a restaurant. If you want a fine and fancy meal, try the restaurant of your choice at noon instead of in the evening. Remember that local food specialties can be found in groceries and delicatessens as well as in restaurants. In California, for example, the fruits and vegetables in the supermarkets and the seafood in the fish markets make it well worth your while to go to the trouble of getting a housekeeping unit; the markets there are far and away one of the state's most underrated tourist attractions. In New York, delicatessens are an institution. At places like Zabar's at 81st Street and Broadway or Balducci's at 424 Sixth Avenue in the Village, you can pick up exotic fixings for a real gastronomical orgy of a picnic. The cheeses from around the world, the sausages, smoked ducks, and salads and condiments do not come cheap—

and you may end up with leftovers that you can't store. But even then, you'll spend less than you would for a comparable adventure in a restaurant and have a real New York experience at the same time. Chicago, another city where you might expect to have to spend a lot on food, is full of Greek, Chinese, Serbian, Argentinian, Polish, and other ethnic restaurants where you can get a whole meal for the price of an appetizer in someplace fancy. Some are the type of formica-topped-table coffee shops that in other communities would probably be serving meat-loaf-and-mashed-potatoes blue-plate specials; some of them are a good deal more genteel. But the variety of kinds of food available is one of the things that makes Chicago unique, and if you miss the cheap food, you'll be missing half the city's fun.

On driving trips through parts of the country where you expect to find a culinary desert, you will often discover the most interesting food in the plainest places—the barbecue stands in storefronts in tiny towns in South Carolina or the Midwest, for example. For good cheap eating, your best advice will often come from local policemen; motel clerks will almost always direct you to the most expensive place in town, and only if you're really lucky, will the menu offer anything beyond standard steak-and-potatoes fare and the decor be anything more interesting than plastic baroque. If you have the time and the energy and if the terrain lends itself to a picnic, you can probably eat just as well by picking your meal off the shelves at the local grocery. At least then the decor (a surrounding wood) and the show that goes with the meal (a sunset or a babbling brook) will be first rate and the prices right.

How to Travel without Being Rich
by Norman D. Ford

Ford starts by making a distinction between a tourist—a person who has put himself in the hands of the commercial travel industry and lets himself be guided and babied and wooed—and the traveler, who makes his own plans and goes his own way. Tourists, says Ford, are on the outside looking in. Travelers are on the inside looking out.

"In those hotels and inns which lie between the deluxe tourist palaces and the second rate, you will meet the intelligentsia, the upper middle class people . . . who can . . . show you their countries to a degree impossible on guided tours. . . . Time was when the object of travel was defined as broadening the mind . . . satisfying your curiosity about other people . . . You'll find that the more expensive commercial travel you buy, the farther you will be from the goal of satisfying your curiosity. To put it bluntly, the more you spend on travel, the less you get out of it in fun and education."

How to Travel without Being Rich tells you how to spend little on travel. The information is mostly relevant to people who have big chunks of time to spend and are interested in circumnavigating the globe. However, sandwiched between the chapter on the Pan American Highway (which details such matters as trips down the Amazon) and the one on transatlantic trade routes are six fascinating pages about island hopping by boat and plane through the West Indies from Miami to Jamaica, Hispaniola, Puerto Rico, Trinidad. Ford gives three itineraries, describes the islands, quotes fares, and suggests side trips that sound a long sight more interesting than spending a week at the beach and that, in the end, would show you a Caribbean more interesting than most tourists can even imagine. Harian Publications, Greenlawn, New York 11740; $2.95.

Going My Way: A Travel Editor's Guide to Getting More for Less
by Georgia Hesse

This isn't so much a tome on how to travel on a budget (as the title suggests) as it is a guide to being a traveler rather than a tourist. The point is driven home again and again in dozens of different ways, as the author talks about money and health; makes a case for travel agents and tells you when they can be of help; and encourages you to pack lightly, to drive through foreign countryside, and to use public transportation when in cities; to stay in small hotels and eat in small restaurants and sometimes go for picnics. Nothing Hesse says has not been said before—but here it is said better. And there are nice anecdotes, briefly told, of friends' experiences and strangers' complaints and inquiries that are fun to read and have the effect of making you feel comfortable about seeing the world. She is brisk, sympathetic, and never condescending; and even though most of the tales and tips pertain to destinations in Europe, the thoughts behind them are also valid for trips of only a weekend or so. Chronicle Books, 870 Market Street, San Francisco, California 94102; $3.95.

Travel Sense: How to Make the Travel Industry Work for You
by Ruth Lana

The travel coordinator for the National Retired Teachers' Association and the American Association of Retired Persons has put down a wealth of interesting—and very useful—details to save you headache and heartache whenever you take a package tour. The author talks about transportation; accommodations (whose reservations will the hotel honor if they've overbooked?); meals ("traveling takes energy and energy takes food; people who think they can economize on food rarely manage"); sightseeing; conducting the trip (checking in and out of hotels, getting to the airport, doling out tips, complaining about baggage and rooms when necessary; and beginning and ending the trip. Perhaps most interesting are the author's comments on how to read a brochure and about the reality behind some of the catch phrases you'll find.

Some examples:

"What's the difference between a hosted tour and an escorted tour?" (An escort takes you from beginning to end while hosts change from stop to stop.)

"Is it really a bargain?

"What portion of the price are they talking about?

"Who is really responsible for the tour and its operation?

"Are there any exceptions? Are there any supplements?

"Does the package offer as 'special attractions' items that are standard in any trip or free to any traveler?

"Does the package offer too many 'extras,' forcing you to pay far more than the package price for items necessary to a good trip?

"Do you understand the flight pattern and time. . . . Will you have to wait in an airport for a plane to get you to your destination?

"Hotel: What does the grade mean? And does it apply to your room? . . . What appliances are there in the room?

"Is there too much [sightseeing] in too short a time?

"What is the quality [of the sightseeing bus]?

"Meals: where—and is there a choice of dishes?

"Tour management: are you getting the service you're paying for? . . . Who is in charge of what?"

Dolphin Books, Doubleday & Company, 245 Park Avenue, New York, New York 10017; $2.95.

How to Rent a Car and Not Get Rooked

When you're going to rent a car, either because you don't own your own wheels or because, timewise, it makes more sense to fly where you're going, it can pay you to shop around. While the car-rental companies offer roughly competitive rates, some will be cheaper than others, depending on your plans. The size of your car, when you rent it, when and where you return it, and how far you drive it will all figure into the cost.

Some companies offer special packages for five days, some for four, some for three, some for weekends, some only for the business week. Most companies have at least an approximation of the unlimited mileage rate, and it almost always works out to be cheaper than the old daily-rate-plus-mileage-charge game. But often there's a point at which additional miles start to cost 10c to 20c apiece extra. Depending on how far you plan to drive, you may be better off paying a higher daily-rate rental that has a higher mileage limit.

To complicate matters further, not all rates are available at all locations. Generally, the smaller the town in which you rent, the less common the lower bargain rates will be and the fewer small (and therefore cheaper) cars will be available. The more flexible you can be, the better deal you can get: if you're going to spend a week in a small town in Colorado, you may be better off renting a car in Denver and driving it to your destination even if you could fly all the way and rent a car once you got there. The smaller town probably wouldn't have the choice of cars or the range of bargain rates that Denver would. Then, too, some places will quote you rates on subcompact cars but won't promise you that they'll be available. Would you be better off with that agency's compact (the next-larger car size) or with the competition's compact? Do you want to take the chance?

One last word. If you don't have a credit card, be prepared to stop by the rental office ahead of time for a credit clearance. The agents may ask you to prove your employment, give a bank reference and a listed telephone number, and put down a deposit, in cash.

Driveaways

Corporations that are transferring their executives use driveaways. Finance companies repossessing cars use driveaways—and so do just plain folks

who don't like long drives. Car delivery companies, which earn their keep by collecting fees from the people who want their cars delivered, got their start in the fifties when car manufacturers needed help in getting new models across the country. For ordinary people who just need an inexpensive way to get from A to B, they're a godsend.

Making arrangements to get one of these cars—generally recent models and sometimes really fancy ones—is not the simplest thing in the world first time around. You have to pass a stiff security check; present references; give names and addresses of your relatives and of people with whom you'll be staying at your destination; show identification such as a passport, employee ID, Social Security card; hand over a couple of passport-sized photographs—and get fingerprinted. After you've got a car (but not before), you may have to plunk down a $50 to $350 security deposit, which will be refunded by the car's owner unless you're to blame for an accident—in which case you may or may not get it back. Also you can take only two passengers; they must also sign the car application. No children or pets are allowed.

A couple of other limits to your freedom—you're given a time and mileage allowance for delivery, which means you can't dawdle along the way. Also, you may not get a car the day you want it.

To locate a driveaway company, check the Yellow Pages of your phone book for "Automobile and Truck Transporters" or "Driveaway Companies." It's a good idea to check with several to find one whose plans and procedures are most convenient—and, at the same time, to check with the Interstate Commerce Commission, who certifies the companies to operate as motor carriers, and with your local Better Business Bureau.

Four large companies you can contact to find out about branches near you are AAACON, 230 West 4lst Street, New York, New York 10037 (212/354-7777); Auto Driveaway Company, 310 South Michigan Avenue, Chicago, Illinois 60604 (312/939-3600); Dependable Car Travel Service, 130 West 42nd Street, New York, New York 10036 (212/947-5230); and Nationwide Auto Transporters, Inc., 2175 Lemoine Avenue, Fort Lee, New Jersey 07024 (201/461-3660).

In and Around Airports

Everything You Need to Know about Air Fares but Didn't Know Enough to Ask

Englishman Freddie Laker's super-cheap air-shuttle service to London has shaken up the airlines on all their routes, and the current air-fare structure, which has remained stable despite drastic changes in prices, seems just on the verge of such a major overhaul that one observer has started envisioning the air-transport system of the future as simply a faster version of today's trains and buses. Until then, however, one principle is bound to remain: In order to pay less to travel, you've got to sacrifice the freedom to make or change your plans at the last minute without penalty; and the penalties for switches go up as the fares get lower.

Travel agents can provide up-to-the-minute details on what's what, but it helps to have at least a basic understanding of how some of the fares work from the minute you start to think vacation.

The Domestics
Of the six basic alternatives to the regular, no-restrictions day-coach fare (of which children aged 2 through 11 pay two-thirds), each has its own particular set of limitations. They may or may not obstruct your travel plans.

Night coach, which saves you about 20 percent on the flights for which it is available, requires that you depart in the evening—usually after about 10 P.M. There's no minimum or maximum length-of-stay requirement and the fare for children 2 through 11 traveling with their parents is discounted by one-third.

Advance-purchase tickets go by various names depending on whom you're talking with, but they generally require that you reserve at least 90 days in advance, put down a nonrefundable $20 deposit within 15 days of that time, and then pay in full forty-five

days before departure. You're guaranteed a departure date, but you're not told the exact flight number until 30 days ahead of time. If you miss the flight, you're accommodated on a standby basis on the next available flight of the airline that wrote your ticket, provided that you show up within 24 hours of your originally scheduled departure. If you or one of your traveling companions gets sick, or if someone in your family gets sick so that you can't leave home, you can, by furnishing the airline with a doctor's certificate, extend the limit of the ticket, enabling you to leave as soon as possible. If you cancel altogether, you can get your money back, less the deposit, at any ticket office. There is no discount for children.

No frills, available only from certain airlines on certain routes, offers up to a 35-percent reduction on regular coach fare. You sit in a special part of the plane and do without meals, liquor, stereo; you may bring your own food but no liquor (an FAA regulation that

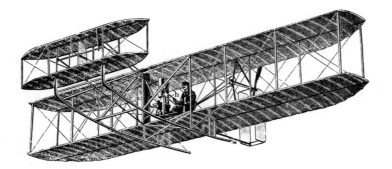

applies no matter where you sit). Also, you must buy tickets seven days in advance and forfeit 10 percent of the purchase price if you cancel. The adult fare is discounted two-thirds for children 2 through 11 traveling with at least one full-fare passenger.

Daylight excursion tickets, like advance-purchase tickets, go by many names, but the rules are similar: you must stay at least 7 days but no longer than 45; leave Monday morning through Friday noon or Saturday noon through Sunday noon; and make a round trip. Savings are up to 25 percent, depending on when you travel. Children pay about half the normal economy-coach fare.

Tour-basing fares, very low and available on a variety of routes, may work out best for you if you need land arrangements at your destination—either a rental car, hotel accommodations, meals, whatever. The catch is that you've got to buy a ground package (the cost of which may or may not be lower than what you'd pay on your own) to qualify. However, the savings are so great on the air fare itself that you can generally come out ahead even with the relatively deluxe accommodations in the packages. No children's discount is available; they pay standard children's fare (two-thirds of normal coach economy fare).

Leisure Class, a new species of standby ticket, can end by giving you a free flight. Offered in various forms on some routes by Eastern, Delta, and National Airlines, it works this way: You buy the special ticket, which costs the same as coach and which you can reserve. If you've chosen to fly Eastern and are among the 5 percent of Leisure Class ticketholders for whom there is no room, the money you paid is returned *and* you're allowed to fly the same route on Eastern or any other airline at another time. (Delta and National, who also put more restrictions on when and where you can fly Leisure Class, allow you to fly free only on their own next flights.)

Since Leisure Class passengers are seated in the order their reservations came in, the later you've reserved, the better your chance of not being seated—and getting a free ride.

The Charters
You will encounter five basic kinds of charter flights:

The old-style *affinity charter*. It used to be the only kind you could get, and it was (and still is) available only to members who have belonged for at least six months to a group whose raison d'être is not travel. However, you can sign up right until departure date. A few of the larger clubs that run many charters include the Government Employees Recreational Association, Box 422, Great Neck, New York 11022 (212/229-2163); the Matterhorn Sports Club, 3 West 57th Street, New York, New York 10019 (212/486-0500); and the United European-American Club, 12229 Ventura Boulevard, Studio City, California 91604 (213/980-1440).

The ABCs. The newest kind of charters, these are also the most flexible. For North American and Caribbean destinations, there is no minimum stay and full payment is required only 30 days before departure. ABC operators are allowed to substitute a percentage of their passenger list up until departure, so you may be able to get a sizable refund if you have to cancel (though it depends on the operator).

The TGCs. Somewhat less flexible, the regulations for this type of charter require full payment 65 days before departure and a minimum stay at North American or Caribbean destinations of 7 days. Since the TGC regulations allow operators to accept cancellations of up to 15 percent of their passenger lists up to departure time, you may be able to get out of your booking without an appreciable financial loss (though, again, how much you lose will depend on the policy of the operator). However, the cost of any empty seats may be prorated among

the remaining passengers, so that your fare can go up at the last minute; there may also be ground arrangements packaged with your transportation on this type of charter.

The OTCs (One-Stop Tour Charters). These charters require that you stay at least 4 days (at North American and Caribbean destinations); buy land arrangements worth about $15 a day; and pay in full 15 to 20 days before departure (30 to 35 if you're Caribbean-bound). You can cancel 30 days before Caribbean departures, 15 days before North American departures, and still get part of or even all your money back, depending on the policy of the operator.

The ITCs. (Inclusive Tour Charters). With this three-stop tour charter whether you must pay in advance is up to the individual tour operator; the price of the whole package will include air fare, transfers, and accommodations at each of three stops (which must be at least 50 miles apart); you'll spend at least one night at each stop and at least 7 days on the whole trip. Policies on cancellations and tour refunds are up to the individual operator.

First-Class Charters. Pay $100 over and above your charter fare and one operator, Nationwide Leisure, will fly you first-class. So far, you can cross only the Atlantic that way, but the programs have been quite a success and if the extra leg room and relative comfort of a first-class cabin in the madhouse of a charter flight appeal to you, ask your travel agent about expansions of the program to the route you want to travel.

How to Decide Which Fare Is Best
The Civil Aeronautics Board, which accepts and rejects fares proposed by the airlines, advises that you first get the agent selling you the ticket to quote the price of the lowest individual discount ticket to your destination. Then ask how you can qualify and what restrictions there are.

Do you need to reserve in advance? Buy land arrangements? Travel round-trip? Can you stop over? Is there any duration-of-stay requirement? Are there any times when you can't travel? How long is the ticket valid? What about cancellation? Can you get all your money back if you need to change your plans at the last minute? Is this fare most advantageous if you are traveling with children? Find out, too, what happens if fare restrictions can't be met.

Then ask about alternative fares for which you might qualify were you able to change your plans to depart or return at a different time, day, or month; alter the length of your stay; or travel by a different route.

"Consumer Facts on Air Fares," a

pamphlet available from the CAB, lists the particulars about these questions and sketches the fare structure for both individual and charter travel. It will help you get the most for your money. To order a copy, write the Publications Services Division of the CAB, Washington, D.C. 20428.

How to Find Out about Charter Flights

There are three good sources for getting information on charter flights. *Travel Smart* (about $19 a year from Communications House, 40 Beechdale Road, Dobbs Ferry, New York 10522) has a monthly listing of flights leaving four months in advance. *Good Deals* (subscriptions $6; single copies $1.50; bimonthly, from 1116 Summer Street, Stamford, Connecticut 06905) lists individual flights and includes a few relevant travel articles about places to go that get heavy charter service. The annual *Charter Flight Directory* put out by the Travel Information Bureau, P. O. Box 105, Kings Park, New York 11754 ($3.95) is also a good source.

What to Watch Out for When You Fly Charter

Buy your charter trip only from a reputable and well-established travel agent; make certain that the agent knows you want to buy the charter only from a similarly established charter operator.

Read the small print in the charter agreement carefully before you sign. Note procedures and penalties for cancellations. The tour operator may specify the kind of plane, the carrier, the departure times and dates, airports, ground arrangements. If any single element is important to you, make sure it's written, and watch out for such terms as "or similar" that let the operator make substitutions.

Get the name, address, and telephone number of the charter operator—at the originating city *and* in the city from which you are to return.

If you're dissatisfied, complain promptly—to the tour operator, with a carbon copy to your travel agent and any other parties involved. Keep a copy for yourself. Write down specifics—names, dates, times, circumstances. The more pertinent documentation you have, the better. If you aren't satisfied, complain to the Federal Trade Commission, 150 Causeway Street, Boston, Massachusetts 02114, and, if air fares are involved, to the Office of the Consumer Advocate, Civil Aeronautics Board, Washington, D.C. 20428. If New York firms are involved, you can also contact the State Attorney General, 1 World Trade Center, New York, New York 10047.

What Happens If You Can't Make the Charter Flight You're Booked for?

Although a lot depends on the regulations of the people who organized the charters, certain generalizations can be made governing instances when you can't make your charter.

If, suddenly, you can't leave when you planned, the first thing to do is to talk to your travel agent. It may be possible to resell your charter ticket (leaving you out nothing more than an assignment fee) and to book you onto another charter. If not, you may be better off traveling one-way on an economy-class ticket and returning with your charter group.

If you can't return as planned because of sickness or a death in your family or "unforeseeable and unavoidable delays in ground transportation or connecting air transportation," the so-called Emergency Circumstances Clause in the CAB charter regulations may come to the rescue: it allows you to stand by for *other* charters run by the same air carrier. In periods of high-volume travel, you may not have to wait very long. The Emergency Circumstances Clause applies no matter what kind of charter you're on.

All about Trip Cancellation Insurance

Missed-flight insurance, as trip-cancellation insurance is also called, is available at airports—and you might think first about buying it there. Actually, you should get it as soon as your liability begins—at the time you buy your tickets.

It costs from $7.50 for a $500 policy on up to $3 or $5 per $100 for as much coverage as you need for nonrefundable portions of package tours.

Be sure to shop around. Some policies pay off if your traveling companion becomes ill or suffers a death in the family; some cover only your own sickness or a death in your own family.

Other Kinds of Insurance Sold at Airports

Then there's the true story about the college student whose father took out a $60,000 flight-insurance policy before he left on a business trip. The plane crashed, the father was killed, and the son spent the next two months vagabonding the United States with his girl friend, buying steak-and-champagne dinners for hitchhikers and other strangers.

Interesting in passing, and also for making the point that if you have enough life insurance already, there's little point in buying more. (Paying for an airline ticket with any of several credit cards automatically buys you additional coverage anyway.)

However, some airport life-and-accident policies—the credit-card policies included—will provide for some health care. And if you'll be incurring out-of-the-ordinary risks on your vacation or if your own policy has limits about how much you can collect for treatments away from home, then these policies can be to the point. Usually, the medical part of the benefits is about 10 percent of the payoff for your death, with no deductible, so that such minor expenses as X-rays are fully covered. Costs in 1977 were just under $20 for 10 days of protection.

Extra Protection for Your Luggage

First it should be said that only a small percentage of the luggage handled annually by the airlines ever goes astray. When it happens to you, however, that fact isn't going to make you feel any better. Especially if your luggage is lost only temporarily—and that "temporarily" is the week for which you had scrimped and saved in order to wine and dine yourself in dressed-up style at some fancy hotel. True, carriers are bound to compensate you for some of the minor expenses you incur. They'll buy you a tie and shaving gear and a toothbrush and shampoo and maybe even some curlers. But they won't shell out for the dressy outfits that are essential to having a good time on a dress-up vacation. And that is precisely the kind of clothing that costs far more at the resort than you would ever pay at home. And no insurance company will pay such prices either.

The message: Make sure that your suitcases are locked up and securely labeled with your name and home address; it isn't a bad idea either, when you hand them over, to watch the agent as he tags your suitcases to make sure that he gets the right tags for the right airport for your luggage.

As for lost or damaged baggage, $750 is the total amount of the airline's liability on domestic flights and flights to the U.S. Caribbean ($20 per kilo on flights to other parts of the Caribbean). This is almost always enough, since the total value of the contents of your suitcases is based on their depreciated value, not on what it would cost you to replace them. This is true despite the fact that you're bound to be carrying the clothes that you most like to wear, not the ones that have been hanging around in your closet unworn for six months.

At any rate, your homeowner's or tenant's policy will usually cover any losses over and above that. The only exception are policies written in the New York City area, where thefts of unscheduled personal property off the premises and from unattended vehicles are not covered. Since only cameras, typewriters, and jewelry are normally covered on separate schedules, such a theft could well include all the contents of your luggage. Now, it is possible to pay extra (about $20 annually on a $10,000 policy) to get continuous coverage against such thefts, but if you don't travel much, it probably isn't worthwhile.

This is one instance when the special insurance that you can buy at airports can be really useful. You might also consider it if you have no homeowner's or tenant's policy.

Two types of airport baggage-insurance policies are generally available:

The first is the kind you buy at the airport insurance counter. It can be purchased to cover from $300 to $1,000 losses or thefts ($25 deductible). Since it's available for periods of one to 180 days, you can get it for the entire trip—or just to protect yourself against the carrier's carelessness. Ten days' coverage would cost you about $7.50 for $300 protection, $11.50 for $500 protection, $18 for $800 protection, $22 for $1,000 protection. A single day's coverage would run you about 10c per $100. However, if that's as much as you're interested in, you can buy additional coverage directly from the agent who checks your bags (provided that you're traveling on the same carrier all the way to your destination; understandably, most carriers will take responsibility only for the bags they handle themselves). All you have to do is ask.

If you are going on a tour, even an OTC on which a charter operator will be handling luggage transfers, make sure that you know who's responsible for luggage losses before you leave, as this can often be a ticklish area and settlements can be delayed while the airline blames the tour operator and the tour operator blames the carrier.

Also, ask about exclusions: some carriers will handle canvas luggage only at the passenger's own risk, which means that if it's destroyed, no amends are made to you. A special baggage-insurance policy would be a godsend at this time, too—the insurer could squabble and you could collect.

When you do fly charter, make sure you know the carrier's baggage loss-or-damage policy and protect yourself accordingly. And whatever you do, never check valuable (or invaluable) papers—or jewelry.

What's the Best Seat in the Plane?

No matter how you look at it, no single seat comes out as being better than any other seat. Safety? Which people would make it through a crash would depend partly on what hit the ground first, partly on the location of fires that might cause explosions or clouds of suffocating smoke. Comfort? If the plane is one that has had the seats next to the exits removed, the seats behind the emergency doors will allow for the most leg room. (However, occasionally those seats don't recline.) Window seats and seats farthest from the lavatories are the quietest; aisle seats give you more room to stretch and more freedom to get up and walk around. As for whether you'll get your meal or your drink earlier by sitting near the galley—it depends on the whims of the crew that day. At any rate, the seat that you liked on your last flight might not be there on the next even if the type of plane is the same. Interior arrangements can be varied in any number of ways, and an airline company that flies a 747 with four hundred seats in coach on a busy day might fly another 747 with only three hundred the next. It's a matter of scheduling. Occasionally, an airline will make available charts that tell you the seating on its flights—but only occasionally. Nevertheless, it's worth your while to ask.

Airline Food

The carriers aren't obliged to serve you anything to eat or drink. Despite appearances, and tastes, though, food is one of the areas in which airlines compete the hardest. Large custom-catering businesses prepare some of the food at airport kitchens; frozen-food purveyors supply the rest—not

just vegetables and desserts as in the old days but entrées as well. A coowner of Mack Brothers, Ltd., a Goshen, New York, frozen-food vendor, boasts that his firm provides "the finest Salisbury steak in the world" to several carriers. The steaks are identical; each airline gets its own special sauce. Airline executives periodically taste-test the products they're serving and then follow up by sending scouts around to find out what doesn't get eaten by the passengers.

If you find that you habitually loathe airplane food, consider ordering a special meal. Most airlines serve an assortment designed for religious and medical diets—fish meals, kosher meals, meals that conform to Hindu and Moslem dietary laws, low-calorie meals, low-cholesterol meals, and so on. There's no extra charge. Some airlines will take your order right up to flight time; to assure yourself of getting one, however, make arrangements when you phone in your reservation.

Bumping

If you're bumped from a flight, the airlines may blame it on their computer. But like so many other computer errors, this one was probably generated by human beings.

In order to cover themselves against cancellations and no-shows—the travelers who reserve and then don't appear, sometimes because they've booked seats for a dozen other flights "to keep their options open"—airlines overbook as a matter of everyday procedure.

Usually, that practice is to no one's detriment. However, when there aren't enough cancellations, somebody has to go. First will be the standby travelers (servicemen or airline personnel), then the people who got on the flight without a reservation, then the last people to get their tickets validated.

There is pressure on the airlines to cut down on their bumping and chances are that it won't happen to you. But it's wise to protect yourself, anyway, simply because it's so easy: make it a policy to reserve early, to pick up your tickets when and where you said you would, and to call if you can't. Also, if it is ever necessary to cancel any segment of a multilegged flight, make sure that the reservations for the remaining flights are not cancelled at the same time. In the event that you are bumped, the airline has two hours to get you onto another flight, according to Civil Aeronautics Board regulations. If the airline can't, you're entitled to a penalty payment equal to the cost of your ticket—$25 minimum, $200 maximum. You should collect it then and there.

Some Help for Traveling Hassle-Free

Firsthand Reports and Great Pieces of Advice

The monthly newsletter *Travel Smart* is full of hints for hassle-free travel. It contains information about baggage allowances; air-fare-structure changes; money-saving gimmicks for transportation and other matters around the globe; plus listings of homes available for exchange; many, many charter flights; major tour operators; and tales of readers who have had mishaps: a man who paid for a Nile cruise and got a bus trip along the river's banks; a group of consumers who went to New Orleans to see the Super Bowl, ended up having to watch it on TV, and were refunded *just $10,* the price of the tickets that were not provided; a newlywed couple who sued an airline for $25,000 over a honeymoon ruined because of a lost suitcase in which birth-control pills had been stored.

In addition, the publication offers subscribers discounts on accommodations, car rentals (up to 20 percent), and rentals of tape-recorded books from a new organization called Books on Tape. If you do much traveling, *Travel Smart*'s $19-a-year annual subscription cost will be worthwhile; even if you don't, it's fun to read. Communications House, 40 Beechdale Road, Dobbs Ferry, New York 10522; $19 annually.

Some Things to Remember about Exchanging Money

Foreign currency bought in the United States almost always costs more than if purchased in the country of origin; the price is usually higher to begin with, and there are special premiums, sometimes up to 10 percent, on those prepackaged change envelopes. You can change your dollars at the airport when you arrive at your destination and—almost always—get a better rate.

Don't shop or pay hotel bills with travelers' checks. You can save from 2 to 5 percent by changing your checks at the bank.

Don't buy more money than you'll need: changing it back again will cost you a lot more than you'd expect—sometimes up to 20 percent.

Before you leave, convert your coins to bills. Coins have little value, when they have any at all, outside their own countries.

Travelers' Checks

If you don't know much about banking, the way the travelers'-check industry makes money may come as a surprise: these profits are made not on the one percent service charge but on the use of your money between the time you pay for the checks and the time you cash them in. The interest from various tax-free bonds and government and corporate securities in which the approximately $2 billion outstanding in the industry at any given time is invested yields an enormous return, which, when you think about it, is reason enough that you should get your money's worth in service when your checks are lost or stolen.

When that happens, some of the companies cashing in on this bonanza are more helpful than others. And that, along with the initial cost of the checks, is what distinguishes the travelers' check companies from each other. The next time you leave on a trip, you may be persuaded to shop around before you buy. Read on.

American Express checks sell for one percent of their face value. You can

get replacements during business hours at any American Express office; on weekends or holidays up to $100 from the nearest Holiday Inn (in the United States; to find it call toll-free 800/221-7282) or Avis Rent-A-Car office (outside the United States).

Bank of America, which also charges one percent of face value for its checks, provides then-and-there refunds of up to $500 during business hours; the rest after the head office's OK. A listing of the twenty-eight thousand agents that Bank of America has in 154 countries is available when you get your checks or call 415/622-4615.

Barclays Bank checks are free at the bank's branches and at certain savings and loan associations. Refunds of up to $250—plus expenses incurred in the course of trying to get your money back—can be had from any of the five thousand Barclays branch banks or eight thousand additional cooperating banks, all of which are listed in a booklet you get when you buy your checks.

Up to $5,000 worth of *First National City Bank* checks cost a maximum $2 during the annual May sale, one percent of face value the rest of the year. You can get a portion of your money back right away at the nearest refund point, whose location you can learn by calling 800/243-6000 or in a booklet, which also contains outside-the-U.S. refund stations—some thirty-five thousand in all, in 180 countries.

Perera Express checks, which you can get by mail (29 Broadway, New York, New York 10006) or from Perera agents or offices, are free in the United States; the on-the-spot limit for a refund is up to one-half with the balance forthcoming after the New York office's OK, promised for no later than one week. Perera also has a booklet listing refund points.

Thomas Cook checks can be purchased at no charge from any of the 840 Cook offices around the world and from some banks; they are also free to people signed up for Thomas Cook tours. Twenty thousand banks, whose names you have to get locally (ask banks, hotels, consulates or embassies, travel agents), are authorized to give refunds up to $250 right away, the rest within 24 hours.

How You Can Lose Your Checks and Never Notice

It happens more and more often that wilier-than-usual thieves, helping themselves discreetly to the contents of hotel rooms, will abscond with only selected checks—and their stubs—so that unless you keep records of those cashed and periodically riffle through to make sure that all the uncashed ones are still there, you might not even notice a loss or, if you do, not until several days have passed. Don't, therefore, leave checks lying around your hotel room. By the same token, don't leave them in a locked suitcase or glove compartment. If possible, put them in a hotel safe. Otherwise, carry them with you. For men, the safest place is the inside jacket pocket; for women, the very bottom of a handbag.

Taking Your Pet

In order to take a pet into most foreign countries and many states, you must have its immunization papers, a health certificate that your vet has signed, and, for a dog, proof of a recent rabies vaccination. Check with the airline, your travel agent, a local ASPCA, or a state agriculture or health department before you go, however. Depending on how you travel, certain rules will prevail.

By air. Since each airplane can handle only so many animals, you should make arrangements well in ad-

vance for the pet, and, for simplicity's sake, try to travel by the most direct route possible. A large or out-of-the-ordinary animal will have to go in the baggage compartment; smaller pets are usually permitted in the cabin. Either way, the animal will have to stay in a carrying case. On domestic flights, you'll pay around $15; on a foreign trip,

one percent of the first-class fare per kilo of weight of the pet carrier with the animal in it.

On the train. No animals.

By bus. No animals.

By car. No rules here, but you should take your pet on a test ride first if he's not used to riding in cars and then check with the vet if he seems nervous or nauseated. Never park him in a closed vehicle in the sun. If you must leave your pet in the car, park in the shade and lower *all* the windows at least two inches.

For fifty cents, you can get a helpful booklet, "Touring With Towser," an annual directory that lists some four thousand hotels and motels that welcome pets; there are also helpful hints. Write the Gaines Dog Research Center, P. O. Box 1007, Kankakee, Illinois 60901.

Some Ideas for Staying Healthy While You're Away from Home

About 20 years ago, a young girl nearly died of an allergic reaction to an emergency antitoxin sensitivity test. It wasn't an isolated instance: in an emergency, it's difficult for doctors to get the sort of detailed medical history on a patient that would alert them to special problems that are not visible but that would affect their treatments—problems such as an allergy or diabetes, a pacemaker, use of anticoagulants, or the like. Medic Alert, founded by the young girl's physician–father, was formed to protect people against just such eventualities. The foundation's million members all wear necklaces or bracelets engraved with pertinent information about their health, carry a special card in their wallets, and have access to emergency hot lines and a computerized medical information file. The lifetime membership fee for the service, about $7, can be paid to Medic Alert, P. O. Box 1009, Turlock, California 95380.

IAMAT (the International Association for Medical Assistance to Travelers) has medical centers in nearly 70 countries; there, English-speaking local doctors, most of whom have had some training in an English-speaking country and charge standard fees for various types of visits, are on duty at all times. All of them are listed in a booklet that you can get when you join, along with a chart that tells you what shots you need to go where. For details, write the IAMAT at 350 Fifth Avenue, Suite 5620, New York, New York 10001.

How to Stay Comfortable on Long Flights

Be wary of overdrinking: both altitude and liquor reduce the oxygen content of your blood, the effect being to double the effective potency of what you drink. And don't overeat: food takes longer to digest at higher altitudes.

One airline—SAS—has come up with some in-the-air exercises to keep the blood flowing through your legs and keep down the swelling in your feet. To get a copy, write the airline at 138-02 Queens Boulevard, Jamaica, New York 11435.

Film Safe?

Running photographic film through airport X-ray inspection machines is "sort of like driving an automobile without insurance; you just never know when your number is up," concluded technical consultant John Rupkalvis at the end of a year-long study of the subject. "If anything stood out," he continued, "it was how unpredictable the possibility of fog is. . . . If you carry a hundred rolls of film, your chances are that seventeen will be fogged at least enough to lower their quality. . . .It may not happen at all, or your film could get zapped the first time through."

Now, if you're just an Instamatic toter, the damage would probably not be enough to bother you. But if you're a discriminating amateur, it may spell disaster. Particularly on color film, when the X-rays can affect each layer of the emulsion differently and thus throw the color balance out of whack, you can get an overall veil of fog. If you're lucky, it will be even. More often than not, however, some parts will be more fogged than others because of the film magazine, spool and camera parts, and such.

One reliable way of protecting your films is to buy film-shielding pouches. They look like air-sickness bags except that they're laminated with lead. You can get them in photo stores or from SIMA Products, 7574 North Lincoln, Skokie, Illinois 60076. If you don't use pouches, try for hand inspection. FAA regulations permit hand inspection of photographic materials, but some agents will do it only when they feel like it—even then, machine operators have been known to chuck the film through the machine afterward, absentmindedly.

Ralph Nader on the Travel Scene

Defending the interest of consumers, informing them of rights about baggage, fares, delays, and cancellations, is what the Aviation Consumer Action Project is all about. For further information, write ACAP, P. O. Box 19029, Washington, D.C. 20036.

Customs Customs

To find out what you can bring back from abroad in the way of common agricultural items—and why—write the U.S. Department of Agriculture in Washington, D.C. 20250, for a copy of "Travelers' Tips." An example: items stuffed with straw are out, but straw hats are OK.

One Checklist for Leaving Home

To avoid making it obvious to thieves that you're away, to cut costs, and to protect your possessions:

Stop deliveries of milk, mail, newspaper, laundry.

Arrange to have lawns mowed, snow cleared.

Put electric on-and-off timers, set to imitate normal lighting patterns in your house, in strategic places.

Check insurance for expiration dates and for coverage against theft.

Lock windows and doors, upstairs and down, in the basement and in the garage.

Store valuables.

Have a neighbor look in on the place; provide a key for emergencies, and, if possible, leave an itinerary.

Arrange for plant care. (Placed out of direct sunlight and swathed in a dry cleaner's plastic bag after a good watering, most plants can last two weeks.)

Disconnect TVs, radios, dishwashers, toasters, and stereos to avoid lightning damage in the event of an electrical storm.

Turn hot-water heater down to 140 degrees (lowered any further, it may collect sludge); set refrigerator at lowest setting, and set furnace thermostat at 55 to 58 degrees. Draw drapes to cut down further on heat loss.

Help for the Handicapped

"Access Travel: A Guide to the Accessibility of Airport Terminals" for the blind, the deaf, the aged, and the handicapped covers 118 airport terminals in the United States, Canada, Europe, and Australia, listing 71 accessibility features such as access ramps, lowered telephones, vending machines with raised lettering. To get a copy, write the Airport Operators Council International, 1700 K Street NW, Washington, D.C. 20006.

Further details on travel for the handicapped are available from Moss Rehabilitation Hospital, 12th Street and Tabor Road, Philadelphia, Pennsylvania 19141 (215/329-5715). The National Park Service publishes "The National Park Service Guide for the Handicapped," listing facilities in the parks (80 pages, from the Superintendent of Documents, Government Printing Office, Washington, D.C. 20402; 95c).

Many organizations sponsor tours for the handicapped: Handy-Cap Horizons, 3250 East Loretta Drive, Indianapolis, Indiana 46227; Evergreen Travel Service, 19492 44th Avenue West, Lynnwood, Washington 98036; the Wheelchair Traveler, P. O. Box 169, Woodland Hills, California 91364; and Tours for the Deaf, Embassy Travel, 247 South County Road, Palm Beach, Florida 33480.

An Assessment of the Travel Guides

Books about the Whole United States

Treating the United States in one volume in enough detail to be able to call the book a travel guide is a tricky task: even a treatment of historic America in one volume means that a lot gets left out. However, there are two all-U.S. books (aimed, it would seem from the writing, primarily at a European market) that succeed rather well, by dint of compressed copy and very small type.

Pan Am's USA Guide: Everything You Need to Know about 50 Great

States—And Guam, Puerto Rico, and the Virgin Islands (McGraw-Hill, 1221 Avenue of the Americas, New York, New York 10020; $5.95). This book discusses each state in an overview, tells about some of the important sites both state-wide and in a heading called "Major Cities to Visit," and discusses things to see and do in those areas. There's a good selection of destinations.

Fodor's USA (Fodor's Modern Guides, 750 Third Avenue, New York, New York 10017; $12.95) manages

to come fairly close to its announced intention of providing you with everything you need to know about traveling in the United States—and it should, in almost a thousand pages. What's astonishing about the volume, despite the length, is the sheer quantity of material covered: in one chapter on "distinctively American vacations," which discusses the most astonishing of the national park service properties, there's enough copy about each that you have an idea of whether or not you want to go. These include the American Indian and the most important sites connected with the history of the Indians; sites connected with cowboys and pioneers, dude ranches and vacation farms; wilderness vacations of all types; reconstructed villages and ghost towns; religious settlements; outstanding museums—and on, and on. To plan a vacation around any one of these, you'd have to do some writing for further information, and some other planning. But the ideas are there. Same goes for planning vacations around destinations, write-ups of which fill up most of the rest of the book. Conclusion: great for reference, at home, but if you do much traveling, you'll need some kind of regional guide.

MiniVacations USA, by Karen Cure (Follett Publishing, 1010 West Washington, Chicago 60610; $6.95), is by no means comprehensive, but while it isn't so great for what the title suggests, it does provide a good deal of information and a respectable selection of destinations within weekending dis-

tance of quite a few major American cities. The subject-by-subject listing of easy backpacking, biking, canoeing trips, and of special festivals and places to go houseboating includes enough suggestions for places to go and things to do within driving distance of where you live that you'll get your money's worth. As the main entries are written more or less like magazine articles, it's also somewhat more fun to read than comprehensive tomes.

Note: Houghton Mifflin Publishers is coming out with a new one-volume U.S. guide toward the end of 1978. It promises to combine some of the strong points of *MiniVacations USA*—that is, some in-depth information—with some of the strengths of *Fodor's USA*—the vast quantity of information. Look into it.

The Multi-Volume U.S. Travel Guides

If you do much traveling around your area, one of these—or a state travel guide—is well-nigh essential if you're to know about the interesting things to see and do in the areas you'll be passing through. As it happens, there are quite a few of these guides—so far, none is perfect, but each has its strengths.

The *AAA TourBooks* (free to members of the Canadian Automobile Association and the American Automobile Association) are quite straightforward. They start each section on each state or province with a few paragraphs of history, geographical description, and information about the economy and so on, then proceed to talk about sights to see in town-by-town listings that are com-

prehensive and are fairly descriptive as far as giving you background goes. A second section of each volume tells you about places to stay and/or eat that are approved by the AAA or CAA. You can expect a certain standard of cleanliness and a certain predictable assortment of facilities. They'll be nice comfortable places, though not always necessarily fancy. The information contained in these listings and the quality of the background information provided are the strengths of the *Tour-Books*.

Same goes for the listings in the *Mobil Travel Guide* (Rand McNally, c/o Box A, Bloomfield, New Jersey 07003; $3.95 per volume). You can be fairly sure that the motels discussed will be clean and comfortable, and that the restaurants will have a certain finished quality: an article in the New York *Times* a while back discussed the fact that good eating—food cooked with attention to the range of qualities that good food can have—is only one of the factors investigated by the Mobil Field Representatives. To find good food on the road, you're best to inquire locally or look into the local guidebooks. There is a great deal of information about places to see and things to do, plus some addresses to which you can write for further information. This is very much the sort of book that you look through when you know where you're going and want to plan the journey: for ideas and good reading, you want another book.

Among the best of the regional travel guides are the *Fodor's USA Series*—New England, New York/New Jersey, Mid-Atlantic, The South, Mid-West, Southwest, and Far West (Fodor's Modern Guides, 750 Third Avenue, New York, New York 10017; $4.95 each). In addition to some solid information on places to stay, there are lists of seasonal events, parklands, hot springs, campsites, museums and galleries, historic sites, nightclubs, summer sports, gardens, music, and so on for each state (by subject). The essays that deal with the states as a whole are sometimes historical, sometimes sprightly and engaging and so nice to read that you want to get up and go. Each is written by a different writer and what you get depends on who he or she was. Some of the sections on places in the Mid-West are very good. As for the restaurant recommendations, there are town-by-town lists, and, for the bigger cities "editor's choices"—"the places *we* would choose if we were visiting the city." Again, it's hard to tell what the criteria are (food or atmosphere), but the recommendations are promising.

Some Books about States

Here is a sampling of some of the

books that deal with individual states or specific areas within the states.

Alaska

A beautiful collection of photos, *Alaska: A Sunset Pictorial* leaves no doubt in your mind as to why you ought to head up as soon as you get the chance (Sunset Books, Lane Publishing, Menlo Park, California 94025; $5.95).

Arizona

For basics, the *Sunset Travel Guide to Arizona* (Lane Publishing, Menlo Park, California 94025; $2.95) is a good bet. Along with maps and photos are descriptions of desert sites, Indian museums, and just about anything else you might want to see. Thomas B. Lesure's *All About Arizona* (Harian Publications, Greenlawn, New York 11740; $3.95) is quite detailed and tells you how things really are out there. It's intended for would-be residents as well as vacationers.

California

Dealing specifically with northern California, the *Sunset Guide to Northern California* (Lane Publishing, Menlo Park, California 94025; $2.95) is as ex-

cellent as all the other West Coast books that Lane publishes. For particulars about places to take your kids, see Elizabeth Pomoda's *Places to Go with Children in Northern California* (Chronicle Books, 870 Market Street, San Francisco 94102; $2.95).

For books about San Francisco, see first *San Francisco: A Sunset Pictorial* (Lane Publishing, Menlo Park, California 94025; $5.95). More than a coffee-table book, it gives photos and essays as a way of telling you about the city. A more detailed description of individual neighborhoods with suggestions for walking tours can be found in Curt Gentry's *The Dolphin Guide to San Francisco and the Bay Area* (Doubleday, 245 Park Avenue, New York, New York 10017; $1.95). If you're hungry: *Best Restaurants: San Francisco and Northern California* (101 Productions, 834 Mission, San Francisco, California 94110; $2.95).

For material on southern California, the *Sunset Travel Guide to Southern California* (Lane Publishing, Menlo Park, California 94025; $2.95) is about the best. Basil C. Wood's *The What, When and Where Guide to Southern California* (Doubleday, 245 Park Avenue, New York, New York 10017; $2.95) gives directions to everything from the TV studios and art galleries to the Rose Bowl.

"Where Can We Go This Weekend?" by George Lowe (J.P. Tarcher, 9110 Sunset Boulevard, Los Angeles 90069; $3.95), gives information about little adventures you can fit into a weekend and a calendar of events.

The Los Angeles restaurant guide is the one by Lois Dwan, the restaurant editor for the L.A. *Times* ($3.95, also from Tarcher). *Bargain Hunting in Los Angeles*, by Barbara Partridge, tells how to buy almost anything for half the price ($3.95; Tarcher).

If you are going to be exploring the coast, look for Mike Hayden's *Exploring the North Coast* (Chronicle Books, 870 Market Street, San Francisco, California 94102; $4.95); it tells about backpacking, having clam bakes, and finding abalone. This book gives a truly beautiful description of the coast from the Golden Gate to the Oregon border. *Discovering the California Coast* (Lane Publishing, Menlo Park, California 94025; $14.95) has glorious photos and much helpful information about the area. Ruth Jackson's *Combing the Coast: San Francisco through Big Sur* (Chronicle Books, 870 Market Street, San Francisco, California 94102; $3.95) will help you discover the back roads. *Gold Rush Country* (Lane Publishing, Menlo Park, California 94025; $2.95) is a wonderful book, full of pictures about the mining history of California. *Back Roads of California: A Sunset Pictorial* (Lane Publishing, Menlo Park, California 94025; $5.95) offers the traveler trips that are "off the beaten track," along with many helpful maps and sketches.

Colorado

Illustrated with many beautiful color photographs, David Lavender's *Colorado* (Doubleday, 245 Park Avenue, New York, New York 10017; $24.95) is not simply a travel book but a personal account of the glories of the author's native state—its waterways, mountains, wildlife—everything that makes Colorado so breathtaking.

Connecticut

The State of Connecticut contains some of the most historic houses in the nation; Randolph Mason's *Historic Houses of Connecticut Open to the Public* (Pequot Press, Old Chester Road, Chester, Connecticut 06412; $2.95) gives you a picture of each, its story, and the story of the people who lived, worked, or studied in it.

If you have children, bring along Richard Flaste's *Guide to Children's Entertainment* (Quadrangle Books, 10 East 53rd Street, New York, New York 10022; $5.95). This is far and away one of the best traveling-with-the-kids books on the market. Flaste has obviously been—with his youngsters—to all the spots he discusses. As a matter of fact, this is one of the best guides to the area whether or not you're entertaining offspring.

Delaware

For a comprehensive, critical guide to Delaware and southeastern Pennsylvania, *The "Go . . . Don't Go" Guide to Delaware and Nearby Pennsylvania*

($4.95) is terrific, critical, well-written, well-illustrated. What more could you want? If a site is of interest only if you're passionate about the subject, the authors tell you; if it's a bore, they'll tell you that, too. There should be more like this around. It's hard to locate; write Longwood Gardens, Kennett Square, Pennsylvania, to find out if you can order it through the gift shop there.

Florida

Norman Ford's *Florida* (Harian Publications, Greenlawn, New York 11740;

$3.95) gives a community-by-community rundown on atmosphere, things to do and see, and, because it's also aimed at would-be residents, em-

ployment opportunities. It's detailed and helpful, as are all Norman Ford's works.

Eating out in Miami: see the *Guide to the Restaurants of Greater Miami* (Brooke House, 9543 Cozycroft Avenue, Chatsworth, California 91311; $4.95).

Georgia

Brown's Guide to Georgia is a bi-monthly magazine devoted to traveling and living in the state. There are articles about canoeing, hiking; restaurant reviews; up-to-date listings of local fairs and festivals. It's well-designed, well-written, and reflects a very sophisticated culture indeed—not at all what you'd expect out of a state that sometimes gets billed as redneck or reactionary (Alfred Brown Publishing Company, 3765 Main Street, Suite 202, College Park, Georgia 30337; $1.00).

Hawaii

Robert S. Kane's *Hawaii: A to Z* (Doubleday, 245 Park Avenue, New York, New York 10017; $2.95) is straightforward and comprehensive; there's information about the lay of the land, things to see and do, places to stay and eat. However, there are no photos. Somewhat livelier, and easier to make your way through (though it hasn't got the information about where to stay and eat that Kane's book has) is *Hawaii: A Guide to All the Islands* (Lane

Publishing, Menlo Park, California 94025; $2.95); there is just a ton of information about sights and attractions, history, background, drives, and such. Robert Wenkam's *Hawaii* (Rand McNally, Box 7600, Chicago 60680; $6.95) is full of breathtaking photographs.

Louisiana

Carolyn Kolb's *New Orleans* (Doubleday, 245 Park Avenue, New York, New York 10017; $3.95) talks about food, jazz, Mardi Gras, the French Quarter, and more.

Massachusetts

Polly Burroughs' *Nantucket: A Guide With Tours* (Pequot Press, Old Chester, Connecticut 06412; $3.50) is helpful, as is *The Family Guide to Cape Cod* by Bernice Chesler and Evelyn Kaye (Barre Publishing, Barre, Massachusetts 01005; $6.95).

Books on Boston: *Boston: the Official Bicentennial Guidebook* (E. P. Dutton, 201 Park Avenue, New York, New York 10003; $1.50) is extremely thorough for sights and attractions and reams of background information—some quirky and interesting facts included—about the city. Jeremiah Murphy's *Boston* (Marlborough House; $2.95) paints the city as seen by a newspaperman who has worked there for fifteen years. *The TWA Getaway Guide: Boston*, by John Wilcock (Frommer Publications, 70 Fifth Avenue, New York, New York 10011; $1.00) is another good source. *All About the Boston Harbor Islands* by Emily and David Kales tells in photos and maps about the islands and recreational opportunities close to the city (Herman Publishing, 45 Newbury Street, Boston, Massachusetts 02116; $4.50).

New Hampshire

Evan Hill's *The Primary State* (Countryman Press, Taftsville, Vermont 05073; $6.95) talks about historical landmarks and places of interest.

New Jersey

Richard Flaste's *Guide to Children's Entertainment* (Quadrangle, 10 East 53rd Street, New York, New York 10022; $5.95) will give you ideas about places to have a great time even if you don't have kids along.

New York

Ted Kosoy's *A Budget Guide to New York and New England* (St. Martin's Press, 175 Fifth Avenue, New York, New York 10010; $3.95) contains information on things to see and do; the slant is for non-U.S. citizens. However, there are better books. For general information, atmosphere, and just about everything else you'd ever want in a travel guide, you can't beat Kate Simon's *New York: Places and Pleasures* (Harper and Row, 10 East 53rd Street, New York, New York 10022;

$4.95). It's great even though somewhat old. *New York: A Guide to the Metropolis*, by Gerard R. Wolfe, outlines some fine walking tours (New York University Press, 21 West Fourth Street, New York, New York 10003; $7.95).

The *New York Walk Book* (Doubleday, 245 Park Avenue, New York, New York 10017; $5.95) tells you all the places in the state where you can walk and hike.

Oregon

For a complete discussion of the state, get the *Sunset Travel Guide to Oregon* (Lane Publishing, Menlo Park, California 94025; $2.95). Lots of photos and maps and where-to-go material.

The Portland Guide Book, by Linda Lampman and Julie Sterling (Writing Works, 7438 S.E. 40th Street, Mercer Island Washington 98040; $3.95) is small but complete. For dining out information on the city and the entire area, see Rubenstein's *Best Restaurants: Pacific Northwest* (101 Productions, 834 Mission Street, San Francisco, California 94110; $2.95).

Pennsylvania

The *"Go . . . Don't Go" Guide to Delaware and Nearby Pennsylvania* is great. See the Delaware listing.

Bicentennial City: Walking Tours of Historic Philadelphia (Pyne Press, Princeton, New Jersey 08540; $4.95) tells you about visiting Philadelphia's historic sites.

Texas

Best Restaurants: Texas (101 Productions, 834 Mission Street, San Francisco, California 94110; $2.95) is a good restaurant guide.

Vermont

Everything from wildlife and crafts to inns is what you find in *The Big Green Book: A Four Season Guide to Vermont*, by Madeleine Kunin and Marilyn Stout (Barre Publishing, Barre, Massachusetts 01005; $6.95). One of the best state guides around.

Wonderful Woodstock, by Peter Jennison (Countryman Press, Taftsville, Vermont 05073; $2.00), tells you about this prosperous old town.

Washington

For what to see and what to avoid, check out Jim Faber's *An Irreverent Guide to Washington State* (Doubleday, 245 Park Avenue, New York, New York; $3.95). *The Seattle Guide Book* (Writing Works, 7438 S.E. 40th Street, Mercer Island, Washington 98040; $3.95) lists landmarks, museums, restaurants—as does *The Spokane Guide Book*, by Barry Anderson ($3.95, also from Writing Works).

Washington, D.C.

The Washington Post Guide to

Washington (McGraw-Hill, 1221 Avenue of the Americas, New York, New York, 10020; $3.95) tells you about political Washington from a tourist's point of view. *The Official Bicentennial Guidebook* (Washingtonian Books, Washington, D.C.; $3.00) is comprehensive and compact—a small paperback full of detail.

Going Places with Children in Washington, edited by Elizabeth Post Mirel ($3.00) and *Dining Out in Washington* ($2.00) by Charles Turgeon and Phyllis C. Richman are also useful; they're available from Washingtonian Books.

A *Guide to the Architecture of Washington, D.C.* (McGraw-Hill, 1221 Avenue of the Americas, New York, New York, 10020; $5.95) tells you about lesser-known houses as well as famous monuments.

The Most Complete State Guides

Back in the 1930s, the Federal Writers Project of the WPA had gifted writers and researchers compiling the ultimate state travel guides—huge, thick, five-by-seven books crammed with facts about various towns in each state. Hastings House (10 East 40th, New York, New York 10016) has reissued a good many of them. There's nothing better.

Books to Help You Decide Where to Go in the Caribbean and What to Do When You Get There

Basically there are three: Fodor's *Caribbean, Bahamas and Bermuda* (Fodor's Modern Guides, 750 Third Avenue, New York, New York 10017; $9.95); Fielding's *Guide to the Caribbean Plus the Bahamas* (Fielding Publications, 105 Madison Avenue, New York, New York 10016; $10.95); and the *Caribbean (including Bahamas-Bermuda) Vacation Travel Guide* (Simon and Schuster, 630 Fifth Avenue, New York, New York 10020; $3.95). Which book you should get depends on what you're looking for.

The *Caribbean Vacation Travel Guide*, which is free to members of the Exxon Travel Club, through the Club, and is distributed on a limited basis through bookstores, is quite straightforward and is written with a certain amount of authority. The individual sections dealing with each island are concise. If you're interested in beaches, or the lodging situation, or shopping, or special events, or gambling, you've only to look for that heading in the section on the island you're interested in learning about. You don't have to wade through pages and pages of consumer notes or history to find what you're looking for, although quite a good deal of the more important matters in those areas is covered as well. The lodging information is given in easy-to-read charts amplified by a couple of lines of "other information" in which there are succinct statements about what's special about each place. For instance: "Charming inn near the volcano" or "Informal simple rooms, some with private bath."

Fielding's *Guide* deals with all of the Caribbean islands (as does the Exxon volume) and there are some chapter divisions—shopping, and so on. But a good deal of what might interest you has to be hunted up (though the index is of some help, it's not the world's most comprehensive). The only objection that could be mustered about Fielding's *Guides* is the relentless consumerism of authors Jeanne and Harry E. Harman, III, who run on and on and on about who was rude to whom or whose package didn't arrive: some of it is to the point, but it has a sort of clubby groupy feel that you may not like.

If you want to learn lots and lots about the history and customs and background of these islands—which are, after all, foreign countries—the book you want is Fodor's *Guide*. While a careful reading sometimes turns up some inconsistencies between the essay write-ups on the individual islands and the specific information on sports, sightseeing, hotels, and such, all in all this is the best guide for the money—the only one that conveys a feeling of the richness and of the cultures that are, after all, just off the United State's southern shore. There is less emphasis on your right to get what you pay for than on what you see, what it means, what there is to appreciate, and how you can best go about having a great time.

A Guide to Canada

It's a big country, and there's lots to see and do. Yet, astonishingly, there's only one travel guide widely available in the United States—except, that is, for the AAA/CAA Tour Books—Robert Kane's *Canada A to Z* (from Doubleday, 245 Park Avenue, New York, New York 10016; $3.95).

It has its strengths; it's well written and there's lots of information. On the other hand, it's sometimes hard to piece together a picture of the various towns because shopping information, hotel information, restaurants, sights, and such are lumped together within each chapter: you'll find information about Winnipeg, for example, in three or four different places in the Manitoba section. Nevertheless, it *is* really the only one, and if you're going and can't get an AAA book, this is worth looking into.

A Source Book for Outdoor Vacations: Backpacking, Climbing, Dog Packing, Horse Packing, Off-Road Touring, River Touring, Winter Bivouacking, Snowshoeing, Ski Touring, Dog Sledding, Diving, Off-Shore Sailing, and More

The *Explorers, Ltd. Source Book*, edited by Alwyn T. Perrin (Harper & Row, 10 East 53rd Street, New York, New York 10022; $7.95) is full of information about just about any sport you would care to name. Not only is there material about equipment, but—and this is more helpful if you're looking to plan a vacation—there's plenty of detail about organizations that can send you free information, about books in each field, about tours and special events and seminars and such dealing with each subject. The writers are all veteran outdoorspeople, and it shows: the assessments of the books and the magazines are the sort of critical once-overs that only someone who really knows a subject can turn out. And you benefit.

Addresses of the various publishers are given so that you can send away for the books you decide you want to buy (if you can't find them in your bookstore).

If you're interested in the outdoor life, this might well turn out to be one of the most valuable reference works on your bookshelves. If all you want is some help finding local guidebooks and local sources of information for planning a far-away outdoor vacation—say, hiking in Mexico or mountain climbing in Oregon—don't fail to look up the *Source Book* at your local library.

Places to Stay Put and Get Away from it All

Inns, Dude Ranches, Farm Vacations

The Oldest Hotel in the United States

Francis Koppeis, innkeeper at the Wayside Inn in Sudbury, Massachusetts, says it's his place. Chuck La Farge, of the Beekman Arms in Rhinebeck, New York, says it's his. The two of them can kid around for hours over the argument.

The truth of the matter will not out, however, until Rhinebeck's town historian decides whether the present Beekman Arms is indeed the inn that was built in Rhinebeck in 1701.

Both are fun to visit.

"As ancient is this hostelry/As any in the land may be," according to Henry Wadsworth Longfellow, whose "Landlord's Tale" section of the *Tales of a Wayside Inn* told of Paul Revere's midnight ride. The Wayside Inn is just a stone's throw from Boston, Cambridge, Concord—all tremendously historic. In honor of Ezekiel Howe, its first owner and leader of the Sudbury soldiers who fought at Concord, today's Sudbury Minutemen use the inn as assembly point for their reenactment, every year on April 19, of the locally famous Sudbury-to-Concord march. That the Wayside Inn also happens to be the home of the so-called Coow-Woow, a cold rum-and-lime libation that some people call the country's first mixed drink, is just one of a long list of attractions that also include a restored stable, a grist mill that supplies flour to the inn's bakery, the Martha and Mary Chapel (the archetypal New England church; there's usually some sort of wedding going on), and

the Redstone Schoolhouse, in which "Mary Had a Little Lamb" was written. All this, plus restaurant and lounges; exhibit rooms where you can see how travelers of bygone days fared; and 10 guest chambers. The inn owes its present state of immaculate repair to a grant from the Ford Foundation in 1955 after a fire devastated much of the original structure. The menu in the restaurant—which is all you may get to sample of the Wayside Inn's hospitality if you don't reserve a room well in advance—lists chicken pie, scrod, beef ribs, Yorkshire pudding, an orangey duckling, and desserts beyond belief. For details: Wayside Inn, South Sudbury, Massachusetts 01776 (617/443-8846).

The history of the Beekman Arms, in the Hudson River Valley, includes visits from George Washington (who kept a lookout for his couriers from one of the upstairs windows), Lafayette, Schuyler, Arnold, Hamilton, Horace Greeley, and William Jennings Bryan (who orated from his second-story window). The hustle and bustle of the eating rooms make this a very gay place; the low-ceilinged tap room, especially, is probably as lively as it was in the days when Franklin Delano Roosevelt, whose family manse is just down the road in Hyde Park, would wind up his campaigns here. There are antiques everywhere—old weapons hung from beams, grandfather clocks and pewter scattered around the public rooms, washstand pitchers and bowls in the guest rooms. For dinner, expect beef and chops, lobster casserole, shrimp.

More information: Beekman Arms, Rhinebeck, New York 12572 (914/876-7077).

The Oldest Inn on the National Pike

Every inn likes to crow about its claim to fame, and at the Century Inn in Scenery Hill, Pennsylvania, in the southwestern part of the state, the vaunt is of the length of its presence on what is now US-40.

Built in 1794, the inn has hosted General Lafayette (May 26, 1825) and Andrew Jackson (twice; once as he traveled to his inauguration). Inside there are plenty of fireplaces, stone walls, cast iron, paneling, and antiques—a Chippendale highboy brought from another Pennsylvania town by Conestoga and the original flag of the 1794 western Pennsylvania Whiskey Rebellion.

On the menu: stuffed pork chops, turkey raised down the road, desserts concocted by local ladies. A really charming out-of-the-way place.

More information: Century Inn, Scenery Hill, Pennsylvania 15360 (412/945-6600).

Quintessential New England Inns

As New England fomented revolution two hundred years ago, so in this age of chain motels it has provided a fertile ground for a boom in one-of-a-kind country innkeeping. The old buildings to house the hostelries are there in abundance, as is an enormous population of weekend travelers hungry for the antique style and personal service that the innkeepers provide. Each inn looks different, of course; but more important are the variations in styles that contribute to away-from-home experiences which may resemble a visit to a hotel, a stay at a house party, or anything in between.

Take the Red Lion Inn. This clapboard-front place, its veranda amply stocked with wicker rocking chairs meant for sitting and watching the action on Main Street, would seem like a resort hotel around the turn of the century but for the modern garb of your fellow visitors and the up-to-date ambience in its three restaurants (a low-ceilinged pub affair; a garden cafe under the spreading boughs of an ancient oak; and a prim formal restaurant of the linen and silver place-setting variety). There are lobbies full of antique chairs and settees, a wonderful old-fashioned elevator enclosed in curlicued grillwork; and a hundred bedchambers done up in four-posters, canopy beds, and gingham curtains of the type sold by mail by Jane Fitzpatrick, who with her husband, state Senator Jack Fitzpatrick, owns the inn. In the summer, the place is crowded with visitors to Tanglewood, summer home of the Boston Symphony Orchestra, and the whole place seems comfortably affluent. (Information: Red Lion Inn, Stockbridge, Massachusetts 01262; 413/298-5545)

As far as ambience goes, the Red Lion is about as far as you can get from a place like Stafford's-in-the-Field in Chocorua, New Hampshire 03817 (603/323-7766), where the atmosphere is very much like that of a house party or a potluck supper where you've gone to sample strangers. You do your own things during the day—go antiquing, cross-country skiing, or walking in the woods—then gather around the porch or, in the winter, the fire for snacks and drinks (you bring your own) before a meal around one big table that is presided over by the innkeeper. It can all be exceedingly pleasant if you get on with your fellow guests and didn't have a romantic dinner à deux in the back of your mind. Only the rooms—complete with antiques, quilts, chintz, homey-looking wallpaper like you'd find in some country cousin's house—allow for much privacy. But if you're in the mood for convivial good times, there's nothing like this big Victorian house with its surrounding fields and forests and mountains.

On the Stafford's side of the spectrum, you'll find Blueberry Hill (mainly for cross-country skiing, meals around a big elegant table, and feet-up-on-the-squashy-sofa public rooms) in Goshen, Vermont 05733 (802/247-6735); and the Inn on the Common, in picture-postcard Craftsbury Common, Vermont 05827 (802/586-9619). On the hotel side, there's the Old Tavern in Grafton, Vermont 05146 (802/843-2375): rescued from decrepitude along with the rest of this off-the-beaten-path white-clapboard town-in-the-forest, this inn is all elegant antiques—English Queen Anne chairs, chest-on-chests, tester beds, and oriental rugs. And there's also the Lyme Inn in Lyme, New Hampshire 03768 (603/795-2222). It's super-quaint with its chaise lounges, wallpapers, and needlepoint-covered brick doorstops. Knickknacks on the tabletops and walls give the place a homey feel.

Barbara Fritchie Slept Here, and Patrick Henry, Edgar Allan Poe, and Walt Whitman

Well, almost. At the Dearborn Inn—which is one of those large, comfortable, well-constructed hostelries that went up on the fringes of college and prep school campuses in the thirties—five historic American homes have been reproduced and turned into lodging places.

Inside, concessions have been made to convenience, but the entrance halls, stairs, sitting rooms—and the exteriors—are identical to the homes they are modeled after.

For more information, write the Inn in Dearborn, Michigan 48123.

Around Disney's World

The Magic Kingdom's surroundings have their own phantasmagoric lodging places, but if the prospect of more Disneyfied smiles at the end of the day

scares you off, consider the weird, wild Chalet Suzanne, the concoction of an eccentric lady named Bertha Hinshaw who collected and collected and collected, adding a bit here and there every step of the way to her country inn.

As a result, you've got your choice of Swiss chalets, Bavarian towers, Chinese pagodas, rooms with hidden balconies and tiny staircases, Oriental seraglios, Gothic chambers—and food that is just that improbable: broiled grapefruit studded with a single chicken liver, Romaine soup (the same stuff which, canned, sells at Fortnum and Mason, and Fauchon), glazed herbed chicken, mint ice. For information, write the Chalet Suzanne in Lake Wales, Florida 33853 (813/676-1477).

Inns of Jamaica

The Jamaica Tourist Board has made a big deal about these small, interesting hostelries set up in old plantation manses and other interesting structures. For details, write the board at 2 Dag Hammarskjold Plaza, New York, New York 10017.

The Inn Books

With the proliferation of country inns and other one-of-a-kind hostelries from one coast to the other, writers of guidebooks have been kept mightily busy churning out their evaluations.

Country Inns and Back Roads
by Norman Simpson

The Berkshire Traveller, as Simpson and his publishing company are known, has been at it for over ten years, so this book is the grand-daddy of the breed. Among Simpson's 150 U.S. and Canadian inns, some are large resorts like the Ojai Valley Inn in Ojai, California; there's a hotel in New York City, the Algonquin; and a host of small places that you probably would not find on your own. They are a diverse lot. One thing they do have in common, though, is membership in an association of innkeepers whose inns are listed in the book. While Simpson does make an annual cross-country inn tour to assess the quality of those he lists and those he is considering, a good inn won't be listed unless the innkeeper joins the association—an arrangement for which Simpson has been criticized. Because some inns don't (or can't) make a place in their budgets for this membership, there are some perfectly fine inns that are not in Simpson's book. Nevertheless, it's still *the* most comprehensive and up-to-date publication dealing with the whole country—and it is one of the most attractive, thanks to the handsome typography and consistently evocative scratch-board drawings by Janice Lindstrom, Jane McWhorter, and Linda Winchester. The chatty style often tells you more about Norman Simpson's experiences with the innkeepers than what the place actually looks like, but the most recent editions have suffered from this less than their predecessors. The Berkshire Traveller Press, Stockbridge, Massachusetts 01262; $4.95.

Lovers' Guide to America
by Ian Keown

This compendium of over a hundred "romantic hideaways, inns, hotels, and resorts" is still the best-written coast-to-coast listing of hostelries with a difference. True, a few of the smaller places—the ones, as the author notes, that survived on love rather than on cash flow—have gone out of business since the book was published in 1974. Kilvarock, in Litchfield, Connecticut, has burned down. But most were doing a booming business long before unusual hostelries became the rage, and they still are functioning and promise to keep on flourishing for some time to come.

Unlike Simpson's book, whose criteria for an "inn" often seem as vague as the raison d'être of the phrase "and back roads" in his title, the *Lovers' Guide* makes it clear why the lodging places were included. They're "nice places . . . *not* for people who'd rather see a floor show than the moonlight . . . who want heart-shaped bathtubs in bathrooms that look like grottoes." They're "inns and hotels that have something special going for them . . . antiquity . . . location . . . charm . . . luxury . . . remoteness . . . or a combination of several of these features . . . places where you can escape neon, piped music, plastic, television . . . conventions, and swarms of children . . . more or less." It's a nice book. Collier Books, 866 Third Avenue, New York, New York 10022; $3.95.

The Inn Book: A Field Guide to Inns & Good Food in New York, New Jersey, Eastern Pennsylvania, Delaware, and Western Connecticut
by Kathleen Neuer

Of the regional inn guides, this is one of the really good ones. To Kathleen Neuer, the term *inn* is "a do-all term for many different modes of getting off the beaten track." She offers farms and castles, estates, grist mills, canalside taverns, a dinner circa 1935, a few aging belles of hotels, and restaurants. "As for restaurant, it comes from the French *restaurer* and means 'to restore.' So it should." So much for her criteria. The quality of her writing—and her sense for good food—is suggested in the following passage from a Q-and-A section that begins the book.

"Is there really any decent food outside New York City?" she asks. And then:

"Yes . . . on occasion food that's the equal of any to be found in the world. There's no better eating . . . than a properly made crab cake, all crunch on the outside, lusciousness within, made with fresh lump crab and no filler. Sausage such as I didn't know existed, smoked in a little smokehouse out back, awaits in Berks County, Pennsylvania. In a lovely inn where the food had been described to me as 'tearoomy,' I ate a shocking lemon tart I can still taste in the roof of my mind. At a bar, an old-fashioned chocolate cake, dark, dense, and devilishly good. On a farm, just-ripened home-made vanilla ice cream served with a mess of fresh raspberries—all you could eat."

She tells you what's good and what isn't at the places she rates, which include restaurants as well as lodging places.

"In real life, even in capitals of gastronomy," she cautions, "every visit isn't going to be the great experience and every course isn't going to measure up. Think of it like splurging on tickets to a play before it opens, or April weather in Paris. A gamble. But worth it." Random House, 201 East 50th, New York, New York 10022; $4.95.

New Revised Guide to the Recommended Country Inns of New England

by Suzy Chapin and Elizabeth Squier

No V.S. Pritchett these ladies,
"The beds are so comfortable and the towels plentiful," they'll gush.
Or:-
"Wicker, wicker, everywhere, some antique, some just wicker, and all just wonderful."

Phrases like these, which might make a strong point in conversation, come off in print as saccharine; and while there are plenty of details of the sort that a male chauvinist would expect women to notice—all about the towels and the decorating—the descriptions make it hard to figure out the mood of the place. The comments about food are more superficial than in the other inn books; indeed, the food is given fairly short shrift.

However, a listing of some 120 inns throughout Connecticut, Rhode Island, Massachusetts, Vermont, New Hampshire and Maine can't be all bad: this just happens to give the area its most extensive coverage. The Pequot Press, Chester, Connecticut 06412; $4.95.

Country Inns of Maryland, Virginia, and West Virginia

by Lewis Perdue

Reading this book, you can't help but wish that good writers in other parts of the country would pick up and go exploring; use their good judgment about food, lodging, and atmosphere; and provide general commentary that is more than a collection of details. Perdue visited some 108 inns, some of which served meals and took overnight guests, some of which only served meals, and some of which took lodgers but didn't serve meals. In his write-ups, he comments not only on the quality of the decor, but also on the quality of the food. If it was exceptional, he says so; if adequate but boring, he says that

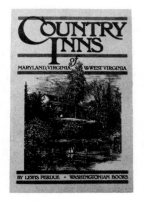

too. He also names the haunted inns, the most historic inns (the Maryland Inn, Annapolis, Maryland; the Red Fox Inn, Middleburg, Virginia); the friendliest inns (Jim Bollinger's Oak Supper Club, Pipestem, West Virginia, and the Strawberry Inn in New Market, Maryland); the best bargain (Leesburg, Virginia's, Laurel Brigade Inn); the most unusual (Gristmill Square, Warm Springs, Virginia); the most romantic (Milton Inn, Sparks, Maryland); the most homey (Sky Chalet, Mount Jackson, Virginia); the most relaxing (Graves Mountain Lodge, Syria, Virginia). He found the best lodging at the Alexander-Withrow House in Lexington, Virginia, and the best food at the Foxhead Inn in Manakin-Sabot, at the Channel Bass Inn in Chincoteague, at L'Auberge Chez François in Great Falls (all three in Virginia), and at Maude's in Owing's Mills, Maryland. The best place to spend a two-week vacation? Mountain Creek Lodge, Pipestem, West Virginia. Washingtonian Books, 1828 L Street, N.W., Washington, D.C. 20036; $4.95.

Country Inns of the Far West

by Jacqueline Killeen, Charles Miller, Rachel Bard, Peter and Neva Vogel

This book covers hostelries in the California mission country, the California wine country, the mining country of California and Nevada, the north coast of California, plus Oregon, Washington, and British Columbia. You get some good descriptions of the inns, the personalities of the innkeepers, and the areas; the line drawings are really nice. 101 Productions, 834 Mission Street, San Francisco, California 94103; $3.95.

Historic Country Inns of California

by Jim Crain

Sixty-five inns along the north coast, in the wine country, the Bay area, the central coast, the gold country, the Sierra, and the southland are presented, and while some are restaurants only, this book is still your best bet for suggestions on interesting places to stay in California. The photographs are not quite as nice as the line drawings in Country Inns of the Far West, but they are better for illustrating what you're getting into. Chronicle Books, 870 Market Street, San Francisco, California 94102; $4.95.

Lovers' Guide to the Caribbean and Mexico

by Ian Keown

Like his first, Keown's second Lovers' Guide also singles out hostelries that eschew piped-in music, tour groups, bus groups, cruise groups, conventions, and provide instead plenty of atmosphere, interesting furniture, at-

tention to detail, views, and privacy. The Caribbean is full of such establishments. Nonetheless, this new guide is not quite the much-needed boon that the first one was. Fielding's Guide to the Caribbean and the Bahamas and Fodor's Caribbean both cover substantially the same resorts; while they also talk about the high-rises and the plastic places, it's always clear from the text which is which. Quite apart from the fact that the constant talk of repairing to one's room, et cetera (with the emphasis on the et cetera) gets to be tiresome after a while, you just don't get as much in Keown. However, if you're going to the Caribbean mostly to stay put in an interesting place with a nice beach or similarly pleasant surroundings—and you're not particularly interested in knowing much more about your destination than what's contained in thumbnail sketches—then this book, half the price of the complete guides, is probably your best bet. Collier Books, 866 Third Avenue, New York, New York 10022; $4.50.

So You'd Like to Keep an Inn?

Mike and Marion Shonstrom, a couple of recent arrivals on the scene, share their experiences, and, with fellow innkeepers from the area, discuss health codes, fire safety, electric regulations, zoning, financial planning, buying, staffing, and promoting an inn—all as part of workshops for would-be innkeepers held, occasionally, at the Shonstrom's place, the Churchill House, in Brandon, Vermont. Encounter sessions, which are also part of the programs, deal with subjects like "Can I do it?" and help participants get acquainted with the impact that running an inn can have on a family's lifestyle. For details, write Mike and Marion Shonstrom at Churchill House, RFD #3, Brandon, Vermont 05733.

Inn Tours by Bike

Inns in New England are so close together that you don't necessarily have to go from one to the other by car. You can, for instance, go by bike.

John Freidin, director of an organization called Vermont Bicycle Touring will help you plot an inn-hopping vacation to suit your tastes and your biking abilities—or he'll sign you up for VBT tours, in which you pedal for anywhere from two to twenty-four days at a stretch with other families, couples, singles, of roughly your own skill level. Since you get maps, you can go at your own speed, stopping at antique shops or historical sites as you please, and join the group only for evening get-togethers which are all the more companionable for the experiences you've shared during the day.

On one of the trips there's a five-mile downhill that ends at a covered bridge. Afterwards, one pedaler quipped: "The only thing lacking was the "Gloria" from Mozart's *Coronation Mass*." On another you stop at the elegant Old Tavern in Grafton, Vermont; the hotel, like the town itself, has been restored to the immaculate condition in which you might have found it back in 1801, and when you go to sleep at night, you'll do it in elaborately carved Victorian beds or pencil-post fourposters with finely-wrought lace testers. You'll visit the Adams Inn, whose main house, underneath soaring pines, has a player piano and a huge stone fireplace; pedal along roads that take you past apple orchards, lakes, wild strawberry fields, and through countless towns whose white clapboard dwellings and tall elms make them look like something out of Norman Rockwell paintings.

VBT will rent you a good ten-speed bike if you don't have your own. If you want to learn how to fix your wheels, you can sign up for one of the organization's unique bicycle repair clinics at which—four hours a day, for four days—you'll be taught everything you're always wishing you knew about derailleurs, brakes, gears, frames. For details on tours, clinics, or trip-planning services, write VBT at R. D. 2, Bristol, Vermont 05443.

Down-on-the-Farm and Home-on-the-Range Vacations

You may get to lug buckets of sap to the sugar shack at maple-syrup time; lie in a hayloft; fish in a farm pond with the grass bugs pricking at your ankles; look at stars that in the city are blotted out by lights; swing on a rope slung from the rafters in a barn; slog through mud fields where the smell of manure overpowers the fragrance of the wet earth; wake up to the sounds of crickets and frogs; or sit down around a big round table at the sort of thresherman's feast that one of your female forebears probably slaved over every day of her life for her menfolk.

There are hundreds of farms and ranches across the United States and Canada that offer just this sort of memorable experience. The arrangement provides the farmers and ranchers with some extra income to offset the pinch of a bad season in cattle and corn; the city folk go away with some exhilarating experiences under their belts.

To find out where these farms and ranches are:

Country Vacations U.S.A., edited by Pat Dickerman, lists more than five hundred farms, ranches, lodges, inns, housekeeping cottages, and so on, where you can get a taste of the rural life. The book costs $3.95 and can be ordered from Farm and Ranch Vacations, Inc., 36 East 57th Street, New York, New York 10022 (add 50c for postage and handling).

The Special Reports Division of the Office of Communication, Room 460A in the U.S. Department of Agriculture in Washington, D.C. 20250, will supply you with a list of state agricultural and travel information agencies that can put you in touch with guest ranches and farms in their state.

For information about Canadian farm vacations, contact the various provincial travel information offices.

When a Dude Ranch Is Not a Dude Ranch

Dude ranches always have horses, but that's about all they have in common. As in New England, where "inn" can mean a whole batch of different things, so also in the West, a "dude ranch" is not a dude ranch is not a dude ranch. There are basically two kinds: actual operating ranches where you can work if you want, and those that are more like resorts and that feature horseback riding and Western ambience in a big way.

At ranches where you can work, you may split wood, pump water, ride along on a cattle drive, or help with the branding. Accommodations are usually fairly spartan and amenities few. One rancher calls his business "crossing dudes with mother cows." Many members of the Dude Ranchers' Association (South Laramie Via Tie Siding, Wyoming 82084) provide this sort of experience. Among them: the Elkhorn Ranch, Sasabe Star Route, Tucson, Arizona 85726; and the Hunewill Circle H Ranch, Bridgeport, Mono County, California 93517. At the Lazy K Bar Ranch in Big Timber, Montana 59011, guests can join in dude rodeos as well.

The main difference between the dude ranches of the nonworking type (which are to the West what inns and other unusual hostelries are to the East) is that the average length of stay is somewhat longer; the ambience of a ranch derives to a great extent from the camaraderie that develops when people stay for a week or two or three—long enough, in other words, for everybody to get to feeling easy with one another.

All of which goes to show that before you even set out for a ranch your host should have a pretty clear idea of what you want; and *you* should have an equally clear idea of what you're going to get. If you want a swimming pool or saunas or golf or birds to watch or trout to fish for or cattle drives or chores to wear yourself out with, then make sure they're available before you reserve.

Here are sources for lists of dude ranches:

Country Vacations U.S.A. (see above) lists various kinds of ranches and usually specifies which is which. If you're interested in the other kind of "dude ranch"—one that is more like a resort—see *Country Inns and Back Roads* (see page 26). The following organizations can also supply lists: the Arizona Office of Tourism, 1645 West Jefferson, Room 428, Phoenix 85007; the Colorado Dude and Guest Ranch Association, Box 6440 Cherry Creek Station, Denver 80206; the Nebraska Division of Tourism, Box 94666 State Capitol, Lincoln 68509; the New Mexico Department of Development, 113 Washington Avenue, Santa Fe 87501; the New York Department of Commerce, 99 Washington Avenue, Albany 12245; the Travel Information Section of the Oregon State Highway Division, Salem 97310; and the Wyoming State Travel Commission, 2320 Capitol Avenue, Cheyenne 82002.

Hotels

There's a Small Hotel

Mammoth lodging places that stay full

with conventions and tour groups can be annoying: the story about the executive who spent ninety minutes checking in, ten minutes waiting for the elevator to get to his room (which wasn't ready when he arrived)—well, it's simply not all that far from the everyday truth.

Wise hoteliers have not ignored the potential of a market made up of just such businessmen, and so it is that smallish hotels, where people can enjoy giving and getting personal service, have started popping up in cities that didn't have them five years ago; small hotels that have been there all along have been polishing up—if only their image—to cash in.

Herewith, a sampling from some major cities.

Chicago. At the Whitehall, you can have the concierge buy your theater tickets and unpack your bags; the management makes note of your preferences for a certain brand of Scotch, a bedboard, a typewriter in your room—and keeps them on file from one visit to another. Information; 105 East Delaware Place, Chicago, Illinois 60611 (312/944-6300).

The Tremont at 100 East Chestnut (312/751-1900) has a tiny lobby full of antiques that looks more like someone's living room; the restaurant is Cricket's, managed by the people who own New York City's 21 Club.

Kansas City. The Raphael Hotel. This is where newspaper and network executives stayed during the Republican National Convention in 1976. For details, write the hotel at 325 Ward Parkway, Kansas City, Missouri 64112 (816/756-3800).

Los Angeles. A faltering older hotel that has recently been spruced up, the Beverly Rodeo, in Beverly Hills, has phones in the bathrooms, fancy penthouse apartments and suites, and service fine enough to compete with some very good larger places in the area. Particulars: 360 North Rodeo Drive, Beverly Hills, California 90210 (213/273-0300).

Minneapolis. L'Hôtel Sofitel. A brand-new establishment, with a French-speaking hotel manager and bidets in the bathrooms. More information: 5601 West 78th Street, Minneapolis, Minnesota 55435 (612/835-1900).

Philadelphia. The Latham Hotel, 17th and Walnut, Philadelphia, Pennsylvania 19103 (215/LO 3-7474).

San Francisco. The city that has three five-star hotels listed in the Mobil Travel Guide also boasts several fine small hotels: the Raphael, 386 Geary Street at Mason, San Francisco, California 94102 (415/986-2000); the Huntingdon at 1075 California Street, at the top of Nob Hill, San Francisco, California 94108 (415/474-5400); and the

Miyako, a Japanese hotel where, in addition to traditional western-style rooms, you can get mats-on-the-floor take-off-your-shoes Japanese rooms, complete with Japanese baths (1625 Post Street at Laguna, San Francisco, California 94115; 415/922-3200).

New Orleans: A City of Small Hotels

If you're a fanatic about where you lodge, you can go crazy in New Orleans, which is full of small, almost French establishments that for the most part don't look just like every other hotel you've ever seen. Among them, in the French Quarter:

The Hôtel Maison de Ville, 727 Toulouse Street, New Orleans, Louisiana 70130 (504/561-585 It has wrought-iron balconies, an elegant shiny brass nameplate, and a magnificently carved door. The main structure was built in the early eighteenth century for an apothecary who, legend has it, invented the cocktail. Inside: pure French-Spanish New Orleans, and antiques that may include, depending on which room you have, a silk-draped Chippendale bed. A continental breakfast, with fresh-squeezed orange juice and wonderful coffee, is served every morning.

The Saint Louis, 720 Rue Bienville, New Orleans, Louisiana 70130 (504/581-7300). The man who built this hotel pulled out all the stops, even going so far as to have its exterior specially treated to make it look as if the structure had been put up two centuries ago. In the rooms, the pale canteloupe-colored linens match the exterior, and there are terrycloth bathrobes; color TVs; electric shoe polishers; bidets; and scores of other nice touches. French president Valéry Giscard d'Estaing has stayed there, as have Dick Van Dyke, George Segal, and John Denver.

Out of the Vieux Carré, there's the Pontchartrain (2031 St. Charles Avenue, New Orleans, Louisiana 70140; 504/524-0581), whose Caribbean room serves an exquisite trout véronique. And the Lamothe House, in a restored mansion, at 621 Esplanade Avenue, New Orleans, Louisiana 70116 (504/947-1161), is filled with antiques: Victorian chandeliers and ottomans, a Biedermeyer settee and mahogany bookcases in the lobby; white marble Gothic fireplaces; half-tester double beds and fourposters in the guest rooms; and, in the old garden, banana, sweet olive, pear, and fig trees, maidenhair ferns, and a fish pond.

The Most Spectacular Hotel in the World

Walking through the splendid new

Beverly wing of the Beverly Wilshire Hotel is like walking through Hollywood sets for the cultures of the world, or through the pages of a decorating magazine. Each floor is done up differently: one is avant-garde, with Thonet chrome and black rawhide chairs, molded white enamel lamps, sofas covered in kid, graphics by Vasarely. Another is Spanish, and the headboards are upholstered in painted calf leather, the armchairs in hand-embroidered fabric made especially for the hotel. Yet another is Mexican—birds and flowers and other folkloric motifs swirl down the adobe hallways. Still another is devoted to California design, the walls of the corridor covered with sky-blue vinyl and lit by white sconces and lanterns, the rooms a garden of Boussac fabrics. Then there are the Italian, French, and Champagne floors (the last devoted to the beverage), and the suites, each one different from every other, decorated according to the tastes and ideas of the people to whom they're dedicated: Yves St. Laurent, Jimmy Stewart, Irene Dunne, Christian Dior, Marc Bohan, Omar Sharif, Andrés Segovia. Every bathroom is marble; every towel is Fieldcrest's finest. There are thousands of yards of exquisite eight-eenth-century paisleys, floral chintzes. Presidents, kings and queens, princes and princesses, actors and actresses, heirs and heiresses, and stars of all stripes come to stay here—not only because of the quality of the design, but also because of the service, which was a big reason for the five stars the hotel received in the 1977 Mobil Travel Guide. The welcome mat has been out for Queen Margrethe of Denmark; Carl Gustav XVI of Sweden; King Hussein; Betty Ford; the Emperor of Japan; the King of Tonga, whose four hundred pounds necessitated reinforcements in his mattress; Madame Nhu; Mark Spitz; Jacques Cousteau; Barbara Hutton; Sidney Poitier; David Rockefeller; Art Buchwald; and Rex Harrison. Rooms in a hotel that houses such celebrities don't come cheap—$50 to $90 a day; suites go for $115 to $400 a day; apartments cost $2,500 to $8,000 a month. If you want to reserve, contact the hotel at 9500 Wilshire Boulevard, Beverly Hills, California 90212 (213/275-4282).

A Texan's Dream of Xanadu

The Celestial Suite atop the Astroworld Hotel in Houston rents for upwards of $2,500 a day and stays rented, usually by corporate types, for most of the year. There are thirteen reasons for its popularity, starting with the mini-dome bar, a parlor carpeted in AstroTurf marked off with a baseball diamond.

There's a Lane of Lanterns and a

Foyer of Fountains, also carpeted in AstroTurf and lined by plastic trees.

And more:

The Crusader Room: ashtrays made of swords, a color TV under a canopy, an outsize bed, a Roman bath that holds a hundred gallons, and a shower big enough for an orgy.

The Lillian Russell Room: a brass bed, and tiny flowers hand painted onto the chamber pot—inside and out.

The Marble Library: velvet chairs, stained glass, and more marble than books.

The Sadie Thompson Room: mosquito netting and a tropical ceiling fan create an effect that would look just like a Disney version of a South Pacific bamboo hut if it weren't for the mirror hung over the bed.

The Tarzan Room: lined with leopard hides and some unusual orange-and-gold zebra skins.

For more information about the hotel, write Box 1555, Houston, Texas 77001 (713/748-3221).

Resort Hotels

The First Resorts

Those big palaces that look like white clapboard skyscrapers turned on their sides and have ceilings that seem miles away from the floors—they're a vanishing breed. The cost of heating them has been prohibitive for a long time and is getting more so all the time; the cost of letting them go through the winter unused, however, is almost as high.

Nevertheless, a few are still open for business—some making a go of it on the strength of their summer traffic, some opening in the winter, and some just limping along.

Herewith, an assortment of some of the older, grander ones.

Alabama. The Grand Hotel, Point Clear. This is the third building on the site; the first was the first resort hotel in the South. Lots of Deep South ambience: massive oaks shading the sugary beach, the golf course, and the soft gray timber-and-brick hotel building. For information: Point Clear 36564.

Arkansas. The Crescent Hotel, Eureka Springs 72632 (501/253-9766). Built in 1886, this massive white establishment is among the handsomest buildings in a town that is full of beautiful structures—gingerbready houses in shingles and clapboard, arranged along twisting streets that

climb an Ozark hillside.

California. The Hotel del Coronado, Coronado 92118. With 575 rooms, this mass of turrets and balconies built on an island off the San Diego coast in the gay 1880s has housed more celebrities than you could care to name, including the Duke of Windsor (who, legend has it, met Wallis Simpson here), Benjamin Harrison, Richard Nixon, and so many presidents in between that it has been designated a California Historical Landmark and is listed in the National Register of Historic Places. Billy Wilder set his movie *Some Like It Hot* here.

In the Crown Room, the high, arched ceiling is made of naturally finished sugar pine fitted together with wooden pegs. There's a magnificent big outdoor swimming pool (and another pool, for men only, indoors), plus facilities for massages, steam baths, and saunas. A really impressive new addition, a tower whose rooms have floor-to-ceiling windows, stands on the edge of the broad long beach.

Florida. The Belleview Biltmore, Clearwater 33517 (813/442-6171). This huge old building, whose nearly four hundred rooms make it the biggest wooden resort structure in the state, has counted the Duke of Windsor and the first baseball commissioner among its guests. The sixth hole of the East Course (one of three golf courses) and the walled Olympic-sized swimming pool are among its outstanding features.

The Gasparilla Inn and Cottages, Boca Grande 33921 (813/964-2201). J.P. Morgan, Henry Cabot Lodge, and a few Vanderbilts have spent vacations in the wicker rocking chairs scattered around its hospitable public rooms. Other features: golf, tennis, Gulf swimming—and no room keys.

Maine. The Atlantic House Hotel, Scarborough Beach 04074 (207/883-4381). You can play golf on a nearby course or walk out to the sandy beach at this Mansard-roofed establishment on Prout's Neck.

The Colony Hotel, Box 511, Kennebunkport 04046 (207/967-3331). One of Maine's largest summer resorts, the sprawling Colony, which has a motor inn and guest houses in addition to the big old main lodge, is fairly informal, and right on the water.

Narragansett-by-the-Sea, Kennebunk Beach 04045 (207/967-4741). This ninety-room structure of weathered shingles sits right on one of Maine's few good beaches.

Michigan. The Grand Hotel, Mackinac Island 49757 (906/847-3331). There are no cars on the island occupied by this grand old resort—only bikes and horse-drawn vehicles—which is one reason that the old-time atmosphere is more authentic here

than at many other equally handsome establishments. The Straits of Mackinac, which you can see from most of the island, make the hotel fairly remote, yet it's generally busy. The pillared veranda is so long that you couldn't recognize your mate if he or she were standing at the other end of it. There are beaches, a snaky-looking swimming pool, and facilities for tennis, shuffleboard, badminton, baseball, and biking.

New Hampshire. The Balsams, Dixville Notch 03576 (603/255-3400, 617/227-8288, or 212/563-4383). Fifteen thousand acres surround this ancient hotel, which is set against a forested slope of northern New Hampshire. Activities at the venerable hotel include golf, tennis, swimming in the lake or an Olympic-sized pool, rowing, canoeing, volleyball and badminton, shuffleboard, horseshoes, croquet, hiking on trails or old logging roads, and, in winter, skiing.

Mount Washington Hotel, Bretton Woods 03575 (603/278-1000). This hotel had begun to deteriorate somewhat after the famous treaty of Bretton Woods was signed here, but it has recently been spruced up and now the resort is among the good ones. Tennis, golf, riding stables, hiking trails, swimming pools, and pleasant rooms attract a good convention business.

Mountain View House, Whitefield 03598 (603/837-2511). It is not surprising to learn that this establishment has been owned by the same family for nearly five generations: the place is immaculately kept, as it would be by a family who called it home. The atmosphere here is pleasantly decorous—somewhat formal (or stuffy, depending on your tastes and point of view). Activities include golf, tennis, swimming, and a playground and recreation program for children.

Spalding Inn Club, Whitefield 03598 (603/837-2572). Though this is officially a club—repeat guests get priority—you don't have to be a member to get a room. Like the Mountain View House, the Spalding Inn Club is on the decorous side, well maintained, and beautifully set in the White Mountains. There are sixty-one holes of golf in the immediate area, as well as facilities for lawn bowling, swimming, and fishing.

Wentworth-by-the-Sea, Route 1B, Portsmouth 03854 (603/436-3100). Changing all the time since its establishment in 1873, Wentworth-by-the-Sea seems even bigger than its 450 rooms because of the expansiveness of its grounds, the wide-open sky of the brief stretch of New Hampshire shoreline on which it sits, and the massiveness of the white clapboard building itself. There's a long porch amply stocked with rocking chairs, plus an eighteen-hole golf course, a swimming pool, and tennis courts.

New Jersey. The Chalfonte Hotel, Cape May 08204 (609/884-8934). Gingerbread, an amazing concoction of lacework in wood, decorates the columns, arches, balconies, and walls of this building. The effect is as rococo as that of the 281 other buildings in this town, most of which are on the National Register of Historic Places. The hotel's rooms are old-fashioned; not all have private baths.

New York. Mohonk Mountain House, Mohonk Lake, New Paltz 12561 (914/255-1000). This eighth-of-a-mile-long establishment on 75,000 acres has never been restored, though it was built in 1870. But then, it never had to be, because the family that has owned it for the past century has maintained it well. And so it is that here you will find antique delights that in many other places were sacrificed in the name of progress—things like enormous closets, bathtubs twice the size of modern ones, and a vast, polished-pine dining room still unswathed in carpet and cloth. On the grounds there is a lake (which can be seen from many of the rooms) with appropriate facilities for enjoying it—boats and, in winter, skate rentals. There is also a network of trails, begun when a Victorian lady, thinking she was lost in the woods, threw back her head and hollered until she was found by a rescue party from the hotel—just two hundred yards away.

The Smiley family, the hotel's owners, are Quakers, so smoking is not permitted, and drinking is allowed only before dinner or in your room—but that makes for a sort of peaceful ambience you don't find everywhere. Christmas is a special family time, and the Fourth of July here is a guaranteed goosebump raiser.

Washington. The Lake Quinault Lodge, Lake Quinault 98575 (206/288-2571). The lodge was built in the 1920s and has not changed much since then (though the wooden floors have mellowed and the huge trees surrounding the shingled structure have grown). It is situated on a lake in Washington's forest.

Some Great Resorts and Some Near-Greats

These are the places that have everything—golf, tennis, masseuses, swimming pools, hairdressers, super-efficient room service, kitchens that would make it in New York, and more: reputation and tradition.

The Pleasure Dome that Singer Built

Addison Mizner designed the Boca Raton Hotel and Club, Boca Raton, Florida, in collaboration with the Singer sewing machine heir Paris

Singer in the twenties; it opened in 1926 to a glittering house full of stars and celebrities, whose signatures are displayed in a guest book kept under glass in the lobby. The original hundred rooms built, cloister-style, to embrace gardens of exotic tropical plants have grown to nearly seven hundred in the course of a half-century, but the baroque opulence of the place has not diminished a whit. The columns of the dining room are gold-leafed; the public rooms are full of ancient Central American artifacts and Spanish credenzas and such that date back practically to Inquisition days; and the gardens have become, if anything, even more elaborate, as have the facilities. Today there are tennis courts, four golf courses, the same mile of incredible beach, a marina, and three swimming pools, two of them Olympic-sized. The rooms are grand—both the posh ones in the oldest section and the modern ones in the newest area, a high-rise with views—and the rates are scaled to match: about $80 to $165 per person, three meals included, from December through April and June through September, slightly lower the rest of the year. For details: Boca Raton Hotel and Club, Boca Raton, Florida 33432 (800/327-0101).

Italian Renaissance, Colorado Style

"Permanent and perfect" were the qualities Charles Tutt and Spencer Penrose had in mind when they built The Broadmoor in Colorado Springs, Colorado, in 1918. Craftsmen were imported from Europe to decorate, by hand, the walls, ceilings, and floors of the public rooms. The dining rooms have handmade carpeting, and art objects from around the world decorate lobbies and salons. In the rustic tavern, all knotty pine and red-cushioned booths, there are lithographs by Toulouse-Lautrec. From the windows of the nine-stories-up Penrose Room there are panoramic views—of Cheyenne Lake to the west, and, beyond that, the front range of the Rockies; and, to the east, the residential area of the Broadmoor grounds and the city of Colorado Springs. Perhaps the most splendid features of all, however, are the sports facilities: three golf courses (designed, respectively, by Robert Trent Jones, Donald Ross, and the Arnold Palmer organization); tennis courts in numbers that seem to increase every year; three swimming pools; and facilities for squash, handball, riding, skeet- and trapshooting, downhill skiing, and ice skating. The huge ice rink has become a favorite training ground for curlers, speed skaters, hockey players, and some of the best U.S. and Canadian figure skaters, Peggy Fleming among them. Even if you don't take any lessons

yourself, you can watch the skaters spinning, arching, and swooping across that great frozen expanse. Occasionally there are ice shows, hockey games, and various other competitions. The astonishing thing about the Broadmoor is that all the sports facilities are of the same high quality as the ice rink, and that, in late winter and early spring, you can often enjoy several sports on the same day—ski, for example, on the same day you play 18 holes of golf and a couple of games of tennis in the clear-as-a-bell mountain air. The rates, May through October, are about $40 per person. For information and reservations, write The Broadmoor, Colorado Springs 80901 (303/634-7711).

California Elegance

Robert Louis Stevenson, who courted his wife and was married on the California coast, called the terrain "the finest meeting place of land and water in existence," and it is: rocks strewn at random, waves crashing white and mighty over them, birds wheeling across the wide skies—it is splendid on sunny days, mysterious when the fog rolls in and the cries of the birds come from heaven knows where. A resort less magnificent than the Del Monte Lodge, in the middle of it all in Pebble Beach, would be a tragedy.

The eighteenth fairway of the Pebble Beach course, one of the resort's facilities, gives the best view of surf and shore, but there are others at almost every turn. When you're not looking at that "finest meeting place," you're surrounded by forest—the 5,328-acre Del Monte Forest, a private estate that holds dozens and dozens of the sort of mansions that will convince you that the rich are truly very different: they have privacy because they have the wherewithal to install hedges high enough to hide their houses, hedges that enhance the landscape and are nice to look at even when you wish you could see what lay behind.

Most of the rooms in the lodge (built just before the First World War as an annex to the hotel where Alice Roosevelt Longworth honeymooned and which President McKinley used as his summer White House) are vast—closets, balconies, windows, beds, and such are all huge—and decorated like something out of an interior design magazine. They are a worthy match for the food, all of it elegant continental fare.

Golf—on the Pebble Beach Golf Links and the Robert Trent Jones-designed Spyglass Hill Course—was the sport that made the Del Monte Lodge famous, but you don't have to know how to swing a club in order to enjoy the place. In addition to the shopping in nearby Carmel and the sightseeing in Monterey and along the celebrated Seventeen-Mile Drive, there are tennis, swimming in pools and at a beach, horseback riding through the forest, sailing, and skeet- and trap-shooting. The rates are about $50 a day per person, double occupancy, MAP. For details: Del Monte Lodge, Box 627, Pebble Beach, California 93953 (408/624-3811).

Shining Tradition

Staying at the Greenbrier, in White Sulphur Springs, West Virginia, is like stepping back forty years to a day when people really lived as they did in Fred Astaire-Ginger Rogers movies. You wouldn't think of not dressing for dinner, at least if you're supping in the main dining room; and dancing after dinner is just what one does. The rooms in the hotel itself, even those that haven't been redone in the last few years, have a certain boudoir elegance and snugness to them, like somebody's best guest room. The "cottages," a short walk away from the hotel, are like Fifth Avenue apartments.

Everything else about the hotel, from the lobbies and the endless string of public rooms to the shops and the golf clubs, is equally fancy without being ostentatious—and, more important, equally comfortable. These qualities—elegance and comfort—are among the Greenbrier's distinctive features; another, its immensity, makes the comfort and easy atmosphere all the more remarkable. Not only are there three fastidiously manicured golf courses (over which, until a few years ago, Sam Snead presided), but also nearly two dozen tennis courts, (15 of which are indoors, accompanied by a spectators' gallery and machines for videotape replay and ball delivery), platform tennis courts, indoor and outdoor swimming pools, saunas, mineral and steam baths, whirlpools, and on and on.

The setting of this white palace is truly spectacular. The thirty miles of hiking trails and two hundred miles of riding trails (grooms meet you in the riding circle next to the formal gardens) meander and climb through the surrounding woodlands—acres and acres and acres, some belonging to the resort itself, the rest part of the surrounding Monongahela National Forest. The nearest town is White Sulphur Springs, whose population is all of three thousand; most of the townspeople work for the Greenbrier in some capacity, and whole families have traditionally worked for the hotel. Sometimes you get the feeling that they're welcoming you to their home—and in a sense they are. Rates for doubles are about $55 to $65 per person, American Plan. For information: The Greenbrier, White Sulphur Springs, West Virginia 24986; (304/536-1110).

And Some More of the Same

The Homestead, in Hot Springs, Virginia, is another one of those old resorts that got their start in the days when society women sought cures and husbands at springs and which survived the onslaught of the twentieth century by providing conventioneers with the services that socialites expected and got in days gone by. There are some seven hundred rooms now, yet each night when guests are at dinner, maids make their rounds, emptying ashtrays, replacing bathroom towels, turning down beds. The Great Hall, a classic lobby full of pillars, chandeliers, and baronial fireplaces, sees daily afternoon teas, complete with music by a string ensemble. Gentlemen wear jackets and ties in the dining rooms, women their best gowns; everyone stuffs himself, genteelly, then resolves to work it off later by making use of the sports facilities, which do justice to the service in other areas. There are three golf courses, one with the oldest tee in the United States (ca. 1892). And you can play tennis (on any one of 15 courts—take your pick of surfaces) or tenpin or lawn bowl; shoot trap or skeet; swim; fish; ride; or, in winter, go skiing or ice skating. The balneological facilities are among the most complete on this side of the Atlantic. All the original facilities are still here—a hot mineral pool for men, 40 feet in diameter (ca. 1761), another for women, 50 feet across (ca. 1836), and a separate small one, installed (or so legend says) for Mrs. Robert E. Lee and rigged with a chair on a platform which can be lowered by windlass into the bath. The water, of roughly the same composition as that in Schlangenbad, Germany, and famous for its wonderful effects on the skin, is nearly as clear as the air above it. And there are plenty of recent additions: cabinet baths, whirlpools, saunas, and equipment for hydrotherapy, diathermy, and infrared and sunlamp treatments. Every treatment is administered as scientifically and thoughtfully as it would be in Europe, where spas are a lot more than resorts with bigger-than-usual health clubs. Important people have been coming to the Homestead for years. William Howard Taft, Woodrow Wilson, Warren Harding, Calvin Coolidge, and Lyndon Johnson visited while in office, as did vice-presidents Nixon, Agnew, Ford, and Rockefeller. When you visit this red-brick bastion of the good life, you'll soon see why. Rates are about $110 for two, American Plan. For information: The Homestead, Hot Springs, Virginia 22445 (703/839-5500).

Hawaiian Splendor

The Mauna Kea Beach Hotel, in Kamuela, Hawaii, on the Island of Hawaii, the Big Island, is by far the most fantastic work to date of Laurance Rockefeller, who has used his millions to create palatial resorts in the most sumptuous settings. To a setting that once resembled the deserts of Nevada or Utah, he added hundreds of palm trees; grass; and irrigation systems that handle millions of gallons to keep the grass green; more than half a million plants of some two hundred varieties, imported from neighboring islands; tennis courts set in a garden; a championship golf course designed by Robert Trent Jones with Pacific views from every green; and an impressive, swooping, balconied building as white as the sands of the crescent of beach it overlooks, filled with art and artifacts from Asia and the Pacific: carved canoe decorations, ancient ceremonial bowls and other food implements, tapas, masks, tikis, and so many other objects that the long lobbies and corridors are something of a museum. Perhaps the most spectacular piece is a seventh-century pink granite Indian Buddha placed dramatically at the top of a stairway in the North Garden.

So that you would never make the mistake of forgetting that you are in Hawaii, and not the Caribbean, the menus in the various restaurants incorporate island fruits, vegetables, and fish in a way that reflects the varied Pacific-Asian-European heritage of the archipelago. The guest rooms are furnished in rattan.

And to keep you entertained: a palm-edged swimming pool; charter boats for fishing excursions (marlin, mahimahi, tuna, bonito, opakapaka—the chefs will cook your catch); hunting from November through January on the 227,000-acre Parker Ranch, which surrounds the resort; riding; and snorkeling and scuba diving in waters with one-hundred-foot visibility.

Rates range from about $60 to $75 per person, Modified American Plan, depending on whether your room faces the mountains or the ocean. For details: Mauna Kea Beach Hotel, Kamuela, Hawaii 96743 (808/882-7222).

A Little Desert Opulence

Frank Lloyd Wright's ideas about what a great resort should be were the inspiration for the Arizona Biltmore, in Phoenix, a Gatsby-esque empire in the desert with ceilings in the dining room, the lounge, and the lobby of pure gold leaf; and grounds of nearly twelve hundred acres—most of it either irrigated and gardened, manicured beyond belief into a golf course, or left natural and run through with trails on which you can go for horseback rides on the horses of the hotel's stables. There are tennis courts and a swimming pool, of course—along with just about anything else you could ask for in the way of recreational facilities. The kitchen is good enough to bring diners from all over the surrounding valley. And there are afternoon teas in that splendid lobby. Rates: from about $40 to about $75 per night depending on the season and the room, European plan. For information, write the resort at P. O. Box 2290, Phoenix, Arizona 85002 (602/955-6600).

And a Desert Encore
The Wigwam, in Litchfield Park, Arizona, on the outskirts of Phoenix, got its start in 1918 when Goodyear Rubber, as part of the war effort, went into the cotton business. The company moved some executives to a ranch in Arizona, and, for their entertainment, put up an establishment called the Organization House, which eventually became the core of the Wigwam, the name by which it is known today to the hundreds of devotees who go there year after year to escape rain or winter.

Most of the rooms are in low adobe buildings with views of gardens (eucalyptus, palms, bougainvillea) or golf courses (two Robert Trent Jones layouts, good ones, and a third that is split into two nine-holers). Golf is the big deal, but you can also play tennis, go riding or swimming or biking. Everything is terribly genteel, fastidiously maintained. Rates run about $60 to $90 per person, American plan, in February and March; about $50 to $75 in October through January and in April and May. The resort is closed May through September. For more information, contact the resort in Litchfield Park, Phoenix, Arizona 85340 (602/935-3811).

The Chain Where the Good Life Is the Watchword

Laurance Rockefeller's Rockresorts are magnificently conceived and operated resorts in magnificent settings. They're modern but not sterile, built with unusual care to detail, furnished like country places out of House and Garden, always the last word in elegance, but never stiff.

The locations: the Cerromar Beach Hotel and the Dorado Beach Hotel, both in Dorado Beach, Puerto Rico; the Jackson Lake Lodge, in Grand Teton National Park, Wyoming; Caneel Bay Plantation, in St. John, U.S. Virgin Islands; Little Dix Bay, on Virgin Gorda, British Virgin Islands; the Woodstock Inn, in Woodstock, Vermont; and the Mauna Kea Beach Hotel, on Hawaii's Big Island, in the Kamuela area.

For particulars: Rockresorts, 30 Rockefeller Plaza, New York, New York 10020 (212/765-5950).

Skinny Tripping

Naturism is not exactly sweeping the United States and Canada—but the movement has been around for going on half a century, and it seems it is here to stay—not just among the young. "Nudists . . . more than any other group of people, realize that humans are born smooth and turn wrinkled; are skinny, fat, short and tall in equal measure; suffer disease and accident and are repaired as well as possible by doctors; and come in two varieties, male and female." So explains "Dare to Go Bare," a booklet distributed free by the American Sunbathing Association, the association of nudist groups in the United States and Canada, which is based, as coincidence would have it, in Orlando, Florida (at 810 North Mills Avenue, Orlando, Florida 32803). Actually, ASA members think of themselves as family groups, and the dozens and dozens of nudist parks around the country are mainly family oriented. There are facilities for children, playgrounds, recreational programs, even separate buildings and a junior association group with a convention, officers, and leadership development programs. Just like the Jaycees.

So that everything stays more or less in that spirit, ASA clubs screen members, welcoming families and single women and encouraging single men "to extend a friendly invitation to a single gal, or female relative, to join him in contacting a club." Once you're in, you have access to the facilities of other clubs in the United States and Canada and around the world; you get a list of ASA clubs and their resort facilities, access to ASA film developing services, and a subscription to The Bulletin, the official ASA journal—a tabloid-sized paper full of notes about people, letters to the editor, discussions about nudist beaches, and club news (Polar Bare

swim by the new Portland, Oregon, club; firewood-cutting work parties; a "Nude Year's Eve" party; and such). The photos: a nudist in the snow hands on hips next to his camper van; a couple of kids at an Indiana pond; a head-and-bare-shoulders shot of the ASA president. "If God had intended us to go around nude, He would have made us that way," reads the Bulletin's version of "All the news that's fit to print"; the weather forecast, stationed nearby, reads "Sun all over. Complete exposure." The ASA also sells Dare to go Bare T-shirts, terry towels ("This is Nudist Country"), and an ASA Park Guide ($3.25 for nonmembers, $2.75 for members).

The ASA is not the only organization that takes an interest in the nudist life. There are two magazines, which the ASA has ceased to endorse (The Natural Life . . . the Family Nudist Magazine, $10 annually, 1134 Haverhill Road, West Palm Beach, Florida 33409; and Nude Life Magazine, also $10, from Box 296, Indian Springs, Nevada 89018).

Then there are two tour operators (V.I.B.—Vacations in the Buff—at 244 East 46th Street, New York, New York 10017; and Skinny Dip Tours at 30 East 42nd Street, New York, New York 10017) that specialize in cruises and beach trips in the buff to the Caribbean, Hawaii, and such.

And, of course, there is a book: Nude Resorts and Beaches, $1.25 from the Popular Library, 600 Third Avenue, New York, New York 10016.

Rockefeller Rent-a-Villa

The former first lady of Arkansas, Jeannette Rockefeller, has over fifty apartments on the French side of the island of St. Martin that rent for about $75 to $450 a week ($250 to $1,600 a month) during the off-season, twice that during the season. That includes half-day maid service six times a week. Getting a cook costs you $15 a day extra. The way into town for supplies may take you over rutted roads, through jungles of tamarind trees, mangos, palms, past snatches of views of tropical lakes. Once there, you're in France—or so you feel. The signs are in French, there are patisseries, wonderful sausage shops, and in the markets the patrons tote string bags. The food is also French: fresh vegetables, fish just out of the sea, wonderful cheeses, pâtés, meats, poultry. Home again? To the beach—the kind of soft-sand beaches you go to the Caribbean to find. For details, write J. Rockefeller, St. Martin Rentals, Lot 3 Terres Basses, Marigot, St. Martin, French West Indies—or P. O. Box 660475, Miami Springs, Florida 33166.

A House away from Home in the Caribbean

If you get a big house, and get another family to go along with the deal, renting a Caribbean villa for your vacation can be economical—quite apart from the other advantages, which include more privacy and more space than in a hotel and the chance to get to know the islands from a resident's point of view. Caribbean Home Rentals (5600 North Dixie, Suite 1704, West Palm Beach, Florida 33407) has about a thousand villas on twenty-seven islands—Antigua, Barbados, the British Virgins, the Grenadines, Anguilla, Antigua, and on and on. Rental fees run from $250 to $2,400 per week in winter, $150 to about $1,600 in summer; some are incredibly fancy, with maids, butlers, housekeepers, laundresses, gardeners, watchmen, saunas, antique furnishings; some are simple apartments. And there are all sorts of houses in between.

In Plymouth, Montserrat: John Wilson (Box 122), Jacqueline (Box 221), Montserrat Estates (Box 221), and Neville Bradshaw Agencies (Box 270).

In St. Barts: Sibarth Gustavia, St. Barthelemy, French West Indies.

In Guadeloupe: `Gite de France, Gosier, Guadeloupe, French West Indies.

In St. Lucia: Rent-a-Home (Box 337) and Happy Homes (Box 12)—both in Castries, St. Lucia, British West Indies.

In Trinidad or Tobago: the Tobago Cottage Owners Association or the Tobago Estates Agency (Box 160), both in Scarborough, on Tobago, West Indies.

In Jamaica: the Jamaica Association of Villas and Apartments, 200 Park Avenue, New York, New York 10017.

Tourism, Indian Style

In an effort toward making jobs and money for members of their tribes, Indian leaders have gone into the tourism business in a big way. You can always see the dances, but in some areas you can also stay in Indian-owned resorts where the decor and sometimes the food reflect the first American culture. If nothing else, there's a gift shop where Indian crafts are sold.

One resort, Kah-Nee-Ta, is particularly noteworthy. Owned by the Confederated Tribes of the Warm Springs Reservation in Warm Springs, Oregon 97261 (503/533-1112), and occupying some 627,916 acres 115 miles from Portland, the land is all canyons and caves, bluffs and mesas; the main lodge a posh modern concrete-and-paneling affair, multi-leveled with a ceiling in the main lobby whose supports look almost like those on the inside of a teepee. You can stay in the main lodge, where the rooms' main distinctions are the interesting almost Marimekko-like bedspreads; take a cottage or a campsite; or camp in one of the teepees that punctuate the skyline not far from the lodge. Whichever you choose, you have access to a spectacular swimming pool filled by mineral hot springs; Roman mineral baths and spas; an 18-hole golf course; and a dining room in which specialties include wild game hens baked in clay, buffalo steak and venison, brook trout, Columbia River salmon. In season there are occasional salmon bakes and other Indian festivities.

Here are some other resorts:

The Mescalero Apaches' luxurious Inn of the Mountain Gods in Mescalero, New Mexico 88340 (505/257-5141). It's about three and a half miles from Ruidoso and thus a good place to stay for a day at those famous horse races; and the new Sierra Blanca ski resort, which the tribe also owns.

The Utes' Bottle Hollow Resort, P. O. Box 124, Fort Duchesne, Utah 84026 (801/722-2431). On Bottle Hollow Lake, surrounded by hunting-and-fishing big-sky country, the resort also has a beautiful modern swimming pool, and puts you within a short drive of Dinosaur National Monument and the spectacular Flaming Gorge National Recreation Area.

Florence Creek Lodge in Desolation Canyon—not far away but accessible only by rafting the rapids of the Green River—is operated by the same tribe; the fact that Butch Cassidy hid out in the same canyon ought to give you an idea of just how remote it is. For information about either resort, address your letter care of the Bottle Hollow Resort.

The Western Cherokees' Tsa-La-Gi Inn in Tahlequah, Oklahoma, is less distinctive but also very comfortable, modern, and convenient to a host of attractions in the area concerned with the history of this very interesting tribe. For more information write Box 119, Tahlequah, Oklahoma 74464 (918/456-0511).

Then there are a host of smaller establishments: Hon-Dah—low key and pleasant, especially the cabins, which are a little away from the road—is located in northern Arizona's White Mountains at the Fort Apache Indian Reservation (Box 597, McNary, Arizona 85930; 602/336-4311). Pino Nuche Pu-ra-sa ("Gathering Place of the People of the Pine River Valley") Motel and Southern Ute Tourist Center, in Ignacio, Colorado, is in the southwestern part of the state, close to Mesa Verde National Park, the Aztec National Monument, Chimney Rock, and the Durango-to-Silverton narrow gauge railway. In May, the Tourist Center is the site of the very social Bear Dance; in July, of the Sun Dance: and in September, the Southern Ute Fair, a harvest festival. El Camino Motel (Box 482, Cherokee, North Carolina 28719; 704/497-3600) and the slightly fancier Boundary Tree Lodge (Box 464, Cherokee, North Carolina 28719; 704/497-2155) are both on the Cherokee Indian Reservation—and both are good places to lodge when you go to see *Unto These Hills*, the famous outdoor drama; Oconaluftee Indian Village, a re-created Cherokee village of two hundred years ago; and the Great Smoky Mountains National Park.

For a more complete listing of recreational facilities owned and operated by American Indians, you can write the American Indian Travel Commission, 10403 West Colfax Avenue, Westland Bank Building, Suite 550, Lakewood, Colorado 80215.

On the Beach at the Club Meds

Contrary to what you may have thought, it's married couples, families of one generation or two or three, and senior citizens who make up the bulk of the guests at the Club Meds around the world.

The singles are there in quantity, it's true—but Club Meds are not only for singles. There are a couple of reasons that they've gotten that reputation: singles *do* have a great time because the activities bring strangers together without the usual meat-market folderol; singles and the other truly beautiful people who tend to gravitate toward equally beautiful beaches that are Club Med specialties get watched, remembered, and then talked about back home; and the way the whole Club Med set-up leaves everyone feeling liberated colors the memories.

You feel liberated because you never have to dress up if you don't want to; you don't have to tip, or make reservations for this or that, or do anything in particular. To buy a drink, you pay with beads you wear as bracelets or necklaces, which along with bikinis and Tahitian sarongs called pareos (and a watch, of which more later) are the Club Med uniform.

There is a lot of togetherness. If you go down by yourself, you're paired up with a roommate. When you eat dinner, you sit down at long tables for eight or ten. You sign up for activities that are enjoyed in groups: scuba diving schools; sailing clinics; tennis; French language labs. You need the watch so that you arrive on time—if you don't, the G. O. (*gentil organisateur*, Club-Med talk for staff member) starts the show without you. The huge activities offerings, along with the free-and-easy ambience, are two of the primary reasons for taking a Club Med vacation. However, if you want to get off by yourself, you can do that, too. For lunch, you can grab a yogurt and some fruit from the huge buffet tables and wander away. The beaches offer plenty of privacy if you walk far enough.

To vacation at any of the more than seventy-five Club Meds around the world, you first need to join the club; dues ($10 the first year, $6 annually thereafter; no membership fee for children under 12) will entitle you to visit clubs on the other side of the globe as well as those close to home, which include one in Martinique, Buccaneer's Creek, whose tip-of-the-island location gives it the best beaches on the island; the Caravelle, a onetime luxury resort on Guadeloupe which has a sort of Grand Hotel main building and balconied new wings; Fort Royal, a cottage colony also on Guadeloupe, whose tots-only Mini Club draws young marrieds and single parents of both sexes; Hanalei Plantation on the Hawaiian island of Kauai, where there's some surfing and deep-sea fishing and golf in addition to the more traditional Club Med sports; and a new one on Paradise Island in the Bahamas, tennis-oriented and (unlike those in other areas) geared mainly to North Americans. For the future: a second Bahamian Club, on Eleuthera, and a ski-oriented Club Med in Colorado.

For a listing of what's available and how much it all costs, contact the club at 516 Fifth Avenue, New York, New York 10036, or in Los Angeles at 530 West 6th Street, Los Angeles, California 90014.

More on Resorts

Covering resorts is difficult, simply because they come in so many varieties and because there are so many. It's not surprising that no single publication has done a first-rate comprehensive job. However, there are three good places to look.

The March and April 1978 issues of *Better Homes and Gardens*. As in a similar May 1975 roundup, the criteria are clearly spelled out—no resorts in national parks, no dude ranches, no resorts that emphasize one sport to the exclusion of others (i.e., only "full service" resorts)—as is the method of selection: resorts recommended by scouts from all parts of the country were visited by the editors, given a thorough scrutiny and a written evaluation, which was subsequently compared to those of other editors (and the personal prejudices of each taken into account) before the final selection was made. The main activities at each resort are shown by symbols; explanations of the symbols spell out very precisely what is meant. For instance, a resort doesn't get a tennis court symbol if it has only a couple of courts with sagging nets and cracked concrete. The listings are regionalized, so that the subscribers of each part of the country get a listing of resorts in their own area—East, Midwest, West. To get a copy, write the magazine at 1716 Locust Street, Des Moines, Iowa 50336, and specify which area you're interested in knowing about.

Very Special Resorts (the Berkshire Traveller Press, Stockbridge, Massachusetts 01262; $3.50). This sampler is more extensive, taking in as it does a few resorts in Canada and Hawaii—but it is also older. If you'd rather have your information in book form, get it; otherwise, stick with *BH&G*.

Lovers' Guide to America, by Ian Keown (Collier Books, New York; $3.95). Keown is writing about hotels and inns as well as resorts, so the resorts listings are somewhat less than comprehensive. Those that he does include are mainly old and rather formal and often expensive establishments—but they're all very fine places, the sort of hostelries that make a point of keeping standards up no matter what. Unless there's some drastic turn of events in the world, this book will be a good guide to resorts for a long time to come. However, he is dealing in the expensive resorts, so if you're on a budget, you had better look into the *BH&G* or *VSR* listings.

Spas: Fat Farms, Beauty Resorts, Watering Spots Plain and Fancy

You go to a spa to get pampered, to recuperate from the ravages of hectic times, to replace ill health, unwanted pounds, or, at the very least, tired blood with a fitness and an energy that will make you feel great enough to tackle ten times the chores that wore you out in the first place.

When you do go home feeling fine, do you call it a miracle? Perhaps. But each spa has its own carefully thought out and tested regimen for shaping you up; the spas, which stay in business on the strength of their successes, would be the first to tell you that it's their *method* that got the results. However, there are a lot of different spas working "miracles" on ordinary people, and each one has its own particular way of going about it. Some are places where you sip mineral waters, or dunk in them. Some are really health clubs—but health clubs with facilities for overnight guests. Some are places where the diets are the key—low-calorie diets, vegetarian diets, even fasts. And then some, too, are a combination of the above. There are some unbelievably fancy spas around—and some very unpretentious ones, too. There is, in fact, a spa to fit every health philosophy and every pocketbook. If you don't believe that, read on.

The Oh So Social and Super Chic

It's not the methods that set these spas apart, but their price tags (an all-inclusive $900 to $1200 per week) and their clientele (the famous and the rich). The service is never short of superb, with several staff members per guest; the food is low-calorie, but low-calorie gourmet and so far from ordinary low-calorie food that you would scarcely recognize it as such. You can be sure that you get what you pay for.

Maine Chance, nestling into Camelback Mountain in Phoenix, Arizona 85018 (602/947-6365), is one of the oldest. The 105-acre successor to Elizabeth Arden's first beauty spot in Maine (hence the name), this one is an elegant place—all marble and travertine, crystal, French antiques and Arden pinks, the walls hung with Chagalls and O'Keeffes; the acres and acres of grounds manicured to a fare-thee-well, green tapestries embroidered with rose gardens, palms, citrus, cactus. At any given time there will be about forty women on hand enjoying the palace and the treatments:

steam cabinets or saunas or wax treatments, massages, facials, hair and nail care sessions, makeup classes, and thrice-daily exercise. Each guest's schedule comes on a filled-in appointment card that is delivered, along with grapefruit and coffee (or, at the most, an egg and whole grain toast) on that morning's breakfast tray. Getting up to eat and other such mundane activities, including making decisions, are just not part of the Maine Chance routine. With exquisite meals exquisitely served on tables set with English bone china and monogrammed linens, Maine Chance is, as they say, a sort of beautifully staffed private home—"a lady's refuge in an unladylike world" in the words of one delighted guest.

Stanley Marcus reputedly called The Greenhouse, in Arlington, Texas 76011 (817/640-4000) his hothouse for wilted ladies. And a hothouse it is: huge and totally glass-enclosed, humidified and air-cooled and so close to being hermetically sealed that before the outdoor pool was added, some guests (Princess Grace of Monaco among them) would go for walks on the nearby highway or parking lot just to get some real air. This is not to say that the environment is anything short of being as delightful as the name suggests, or as thoroughly elegant as you would expect of an establishment operated in conjunction with the Neiman-Marcus store, or as extravagantly feminine as would attract (again and again) the finest flowers of southern society. As this is Texas, The Greenhouse is also a bastion of southern manners. Not only do all the cosmeticians, exercise supervisors, and other beauty professionals talk with accents that would make Vivian Leigh's Scarlett O'Hara sound like a Bostonian, but they've all got that special southern politeness that makes you feel so very welcome. The Greenhouse consequently collects its share of celebrities: socialites, stars, wives of senators, wives of ambassadors. No less than Lyndon Baines Johnson called Lady Bird's week here one of his best investments ever: she lost weight, changed her hair, and learned (as makeup ladies occasionally will tell their classes, by way of encouraging the timid to experiment) that she had eyes.

While The Greenhouse ministers to women, the Golden Door, in Escondido, California 92025 (714/744-5777) takes men for about eight weeks out of every year, and couples for a month. The exercise at this establishment, which looks something like a Japanese inn with its weathered wood trim and its gardens and courtyards, are tougher and more vigorous than at some other beauty spots; there is somewhat more emphasis on fitness as an end and

beauty as a concomitant rather than the other way around; and the after exercise life is somewhat more informal.

Then there's La Costa, a very large resort with tennis, golf, riding, shopping, the works—as well as a place for men and women to diet, exercise, and otherwise get healthy. You can enjoy the facilities even if you're not following the spa regimen to the letter, and the facilities are something else: there are Swiss showers with 17 different hot and cold jets; saunas, steam rooms; whirlpool baths; Roman baths; exercise rooms with bikes, rollers, slant boards, stretching equipment. The menus in the dining rooms list the calorie counts of each item. Masseuses, hairdressers, and manicurists who have been there for years can tell you tales of the celebrities they've pummeled and groomed—and that's one reason that a lot of well-off not-so-famous people go to visit. As you might expect, everybody dresses to the nines for dinner. As for overall R&R and weight loss, you've got to discipline yourself since no one is insisting on early curfews and no one keeps the cakes and cookies that are offered to other diners off your table. But if you go with some determination, shaping up is possible—and also amusing. Where else, after all, could you get the latest talk about this star's face-lifting scars, that magnate's girdle, this senator's girl friend, that starlet's raw language. The spa is located about a half hour's drive from San Diego in Carlsbad, California 92008 (714/438-9111).

And, as a sort of La Costa East, there's the Spa at Palm-Aire, in Pompano Beach, Florida 33060 (305/972-3300). Both sexes are admitted, but there are separate facilities (which include strap-on weights, exercise tables, stationary bicycles, and such). The program incorporates exercise on the ground, with and without the gadgets, with underwater exercise, plus underwater massage, open-air massage, herbal wraps, hot and cold soaks, whirlpools, Turkish baths—and a no-liquor, no-coffee, no-smoking 600-calorie-a-day diet. Sally Struthers, Leslie Caron, Harry Reasoner, O.J. Simpson, and Billie Jean King have all done the program.

Focusing on Food
Obesity, says Dr. Rune Schuylander, manager of the Berkshire Health Manor in Copake, New York, is not healthy.

So what else is new?

Certainly not the ways of getting rid of it, which are as old as the hills around the rambling old manor house where Dr. Schuylander's guests undergo supervised water fasting and low-calorie dieting. (How does fasting

feel? Terrific, when you step on the scale and see it registering two pounds less than it did the day before—and that's not unusual for just slightly overweight people; hunger departs after the first day.)

Schuylander's place is not the only weight-loss retreat in the world. There are others: Shangri-La, in Bonita Springs, Florida 33923—10 miles from the beach, with nude sunbathing around the pool; Esser's Health Ranch, 4005 Lucerne Avenue, Lake Worth, Florida 33460; Orange Grove Health Ranch, Box 316, Route 4, Arcadia, Florida 33821; the New Age Health Farm of Neversink, New York 12765, only a couple of hours from New York and run by a Salzburg lady and her husband, with a lacto-vegetarian diet the specialty; and the Pawling Health Manor, near Hyde Park, New York (Box 401, 12538). Most allow for low-calorie or vegetarian dieting instead of fasts; and all of them ease you off fasts gradually with some form of light diet. Activities, however, are minimal. Bring a book.

And more fasting spots. Dr. Acers' Vita-Dell Spa features the early-to-bed, early-to-rise life (13-495 Palm Drive, Desert Hot Springs, California 92240). New Image, the first such facility in Canada, offers a week of fasting, mainly for weight reduction (1867 Yonge Street, Suite 600, Toronto MAS 1Y5). The Bay 'n Gulf Health Resort, three hundred yards from the Gulf at Redington Shores, Florida, offers fasts plus fresh-fruit-and-vegetable, nuts-and-seeds diets (18207 Gulf Boulevard, 33708).

Taking the Waters
Going somewhere just to sip is a sort of old-fashioned European custom, and since the spas that make the news in the United States have much more to do with health clubs, it is easy to believe that American spas are completely different from the European ones. However, that's not necessarily so.

The truth of the matter is that in the old days, the belles of balls of the East, the South, and even the West would travel to places like Saratoga to be seen and admired, and, incidentally, to sip—and many of the resorts where they did it are still around.

Hot Springs National Park, set in an Arkansas valley with 47 thermal springs that have been known since before DeSoto, started out as a U.S. Reservation, so designated by the U.S. Congress of 1832. It is a spa in the Marienbad style, with five mountains in the park, all luxuriously forested with oak, hickory, shortleaf pine, and ribboned through with trails for hiking and driving. In addition, there's Bathhouse Row, where you can drink the water out of the springs or bathe in it. Around seventy physicians prescribe special thermal treatments, and you can get massages, take steam cabinet treatments, and so on: the services are remarkably low priced because of the presence of the National Park Service, which regulates everything, including the treatments given by the hotels in the city of Hot Springs, which surrounds the park. You can get more information from the Chamber of Commerce, Convention Auditorium, Convention Boulevard and Malvern Avenue, Hot Springs, Arkansas 71901 (501/623-5541). Also in the area: fishing on man-made lakes, boat trips, petting zoos, outdoor dramas, and so on.

In the same tradition is Saratoga Springs, where the springs themselves are protected and developed as part of the Saratoga Spa State Park, Saratoga Springs, New York 12866; the town itself is a very refined place because of the Saratoga Performing Arts Center (home of the New York City Ballet and the Philadelphia Orchestra in the summer) and two horse-racing tracks. Socialite horse owners turn August into one of the closest approximations of the elegant social life of the Gilded Age.

There are baths and mineral waters at the Greenbrier, in White Sulphur Springs, West Virginia, and at the Homestead, in Hot Springs, Virginia. West Virginia has another set of baths and springs in the pleasant little town of Berkeley Springs; the baths are very plain and businesslike, and also quite inexpensive. For details you can write the town's Chamber of Commerce (zip 25411). Then there's the Hot Wells Health Resort in Boyce, Louisiana 71401.

More Spas

Secrets from the Super Spas, by Emily Wilkens (Grosset & Dunlap, New York; $7.95) lists all the spas of all sorts—weight reduction spas, watering spas, beautiful people spas—in the United States, Canada, and the rest of the world.

Go on a Cruise

The boat's the thing that will make or break the trip—plus your ports of call. For cruising in the Caribbean there are several how-to guides. Basically, however, the best information you're going to find anywhere is in Fielding's *Guide to the Caribbean and the Bahamas* (Fielding Publications, 105 Madison Avenue, New York, New York 10016; $10.95). The author team, Jeanne and Harry E. Harman, III, discusses ports of embarkations, the whole cruise outlook, which carrier to choose, which cruise to choose, yachting in the Caribbean, decks, making reservations, socializing, dressing, officers, tipping, and so on. The ship-by-ship assessment of which boats you'll find going is critical. You end up knowing what's good and what's bad about each ship—and, in case you've never been cruising before, you should know that a cruise ship is not a cruise ship is not a cruise ship. Couple the Harmans' talk with the information you can get from a good travel agent, and you should have a good time.

Tennis Resorts, Camps, Clinics

You can take a tennis holiday at just about any motel with some courts—and if you want to play all day and can take your own partner, that may be your best bet, since the chances are that there won't be lines of others waiting to take over the court.

But for the particular ambience of the tennis life, and for plenty of good instruction, you're best off with a tennis camp, a tennis clinic, or a resort that specializes in tennis.

(What's the difference? *Tennis camps* are intensive instructional programs usually set up at colleges, private schools, or summer camps; you lodge in their dormitories. *Tennis clinics* are weekend or week-long packages offered by hotels or resorts with good tennis facilities; you'll also find golf courses, swimming pools, saunas, and plenty of other amenities. *Tennis resorts* are resorts that have chosen tennis as their raison d'être.)

Some of the best tennis vacation spots include Margaret Court's Racquet Club Ranch in Tucson, Arizona (3935 North Country Club Road, zip 85716); the T-Bar-M Tennis Ranch in New Braunfels, Texas, in LBJ's Hill Country (Box 469, zip 78130); and John Gardiner's Tennis Ranches in Scottsdale, Arizona (57000 East McDonald Drive, zip 85252) and Carmel Valley, California (Box 155, zip 93924). Also, most larger resorts have extensive tennis facilities. The Greenbrier, in White Sulphur Springs, West Virginia, for instance, has a huge array of outdoor courts and a large indoor facility as well, as do many of the big resorts in the Catskills—particularly the Concord Hotel in Kiamesha Lake, New York. For details, write the resorts in White Sulphur Springs 24986, and Kiamesha Lake 12571.

For a more extensive list of tennis camps and resorts and large resorts with tennis facilities worth making a trip to enjoy, see *The Tennis Catalogue* by Moira Duggan (Macmillan, 866 Third Avenue, New York, New York 10022; $7.95).

More tennis for travelers. A $35-per-year membership in an organization called Travelers' Tennis automatically gets you temporary membership in more than two hundred private and public tennis clubs and organizations. When you visit, you pay exactly what a local club member would pay to use tennis courts or any other club facility; any guest you bring must pay the regular guest fees.

With a membership in Travelers' Tennis, you're sent a directory of participating clubs that lists each club's facilities as well as rates for court use and lessons and the names of key personnel. The directory is issued twice a year.

You're also provided with quarterly updates and a newsletter, *Tennis Times,* which contains articles about tennis, traveling, health, and about hotels and restaurants in the area of the club that happens to be featured in that issue's lead article. For more information, write Travelers' Tennis, Penthouse Level, New Market Mall, Painesville, Ohio 44077 (216/352-0791).

American Plan (AP), Modified American Plan (MAP), European Plan (EP)

Once and for all, just what do the terms mean?

AP, or American Plan, rates include three meals a day. Rates are usually quoted per day per person, based on double occupancy (two people occupying a room); if you stay in a room by yourself, you'll pay more than half a couple.

MAP, or Modified American Plan, rates include two meals a day. Again, rates are usually quoted per person per day.

EP refers to the European Plan, on which rates do not include meals.

A Comfortable Outdoors

Ski Resorts without Snow

It used to be that a gondola ride up the mountainside and lunch on top were the only reasons to even set foot anywhere near a ski resort once the snow had melted. And that's still true at some of the smaller places.

However, as the cost of operating a ski resort climbs and it gets increasingly impractical to own property that brings in money only during the winter months, more and more ski resort operators are installing extra facilities to attract guests during summer as well. The basics, after all, are already there. There are great lodges with facilities designed for the often hedonistic skiing set. There are interesting shops and galleries that interest the nonskiers, and plenty of good restaurants. And above all, there's that clean mountain air.

Even at resorts that have been doing this for a long time—places like Sun Valley, Aspen, and Vail—where the recreational offerings of all different types seem to be endless, the rates are lower during the summer than they are in winter, and they are certainly lower than at those resorts that do the bulk of their business during summer.

Sun Valley, Idaho, the first great American ski resort, was also one of the first to go to year-round operation; that happened in 1938, with the addition of riding, fly-fishing, golf, swimming, trap- and skeet-shooting, and croquet. Now there's also a center for the arts and humanities, which includes photography, ceramics, theater, and dance. The Sun Valley Lodge, a rugged-looking four-storied brown building trimmed in blue and built in 1936, and its contemporary, the pseudo-Tyrolean Sun Valley Inn, used to provide the only dining and entertainment opportunities in the area. They have been joined by dozens of others, some at a new nearby condominium development called Elkhorn, some in the once placid but now booming town of Ketchum, a favorite hideout of Ernest Hemingway and his fourth wife Mary and now home to Hemingway's fish-and-game commissioner son, Jack, and one of his three daughters. In addition, there are opportunities for dozens of other games and sports: archery; backpacking and day hiking; biking; bowling; bridge; fly fishing; float tripping; golf (on two eighteen-hole courses); horseback riding; horseshoe playing; ice skating; kayaking; sailing; swimming; tennis (with videotape replay and ball machines); trap- and skeet-shooting; volleyball. Plus hayrides, hydrotherapy pools, saunas, masseuses. Rentals, lessons, guides are available for whatever you want, if you want them. For information, write the resort in Sun Valley, Idaho 83353.

Not all the resorts are equally well endowed. Sun Valley is, after all, Sun Valley, and even if you don't immediately sense the immensity of the Sawtooth Range, of which Mount Baldy is a part, the terrain is magnificent.

But ski resorts being ski resorts, and the Rockies being the Rockies, the mountain air is equally energizing in other areas; and the landscape is equally impressive; and the opportunities for kayaking and rafting and fishing—and above all, hiking—are comparable.

At *Aspen, Colorado*, for example, there are nearly fifty tennis courts and two golf courses (one with nine holes, one with eighteen), arts and crafts classes and fairs, health centers, an ice rink, and a major summer music and cultural festival that brings artists and musicians by the dozen from all over the continent. There are also lessons in climbing; soaring; gliding; flying; and yoga. The Aspen Chamber of Commerce, 328 East Hyman Avenue, Aspen, Colorado 81611 can send details.

The China Peak, California, area offers a wilderness school (P.O. Box 236, Lakeshore, California 93634).

Jackson Hole, Wyoming, is also exceptionally lively. It has its own music festival—not so big and therefore a little more intimate than the one in Aspen—as well as art galleries, musicals and melodramas (somewhat touristy, but good fun nonetheless), and a first-rate rock climbing school. There are about a dozen tennis courts in the area, as well as an eighteen-hole Robert Trent Jones-designed golf course. For details, contact the Jackson Hole Ski Corp., Teton Village, Wyoming 83025.

Vail, Colorado, has fifty tennis courts in various locations, two eighteen-hole golf courses, and arts workshops in addition to the usual mountain activities. The summer rates are, in most spots, exactly half what they are in winter. For information: Vail Associates, Box 7, Vail, Colorado 81657.

Keystone and *Steamboat Springs* both have extensive tennis-clinic facilities. The lodge at Keystone, which is a fairly small place with some ghost towns just down the road, is one of the finest new facilities in the Rockies; at Steamboat, you can end the day relaxing in the hot springs for which the town was named. For more information, contact Steamboat Village Resort, P.O. Box 1178, Steamboat Springs, Colorado 80477; or Keystone at Box 38, Keystone, Colorado 80435.

Stowe, Vermont, has some of the East's most extensive summer facilities. There is considerable hiking on the surrounding national forest land—you can, for example, climb Mt. Mansfield or trek along the Long Trail, which runs from the Massachusetts to the Canadian border through Vermont. There is also plenty of riding, at an English manor house of an inn called Edson Hill (where there are also some very charming lodgings); fishing for pickerel, perch, bass, trout in mountain streams; summer theaters, arts and crafts shows; auctions; fireworks; scenic driving tours, a classic car rally; golf on two eighteen-hole courses; tennis on any number of courts (some public, some open only to the guests of the various lodges). Visits to the Trapp Family Lodge, of *Sound of Music* fame, are also fun, especially in the afternoon when you can take tea and scrumptious buttery cakes in a big comfortable room with a view of the mountains that drew the Trapp family to Stowe in the first place. For details, write the Stowe Area Association, Box 1230, Stowe, Vermont 05672.

Bretton Woods, New Hampshire, also has an active summer program—as well it should since the town has been a summer favorite for many years more than it has been a ski destination. The Mount Washington Hotel, the reason for its summer fame, is surrounded by the White Mountains

National Forest; its Presidential Range has some of the highest mountains and the best hiking trails in the East. Many of these trails are above the timberline and offer those peak-behind-peak views that never cease to make you catch your breath in amazement. There are trout in the Amonoosuc River, which flows through the hotel property, plus a fine eighteen-hole golf course, plus twelve outdoor clay courts and a program of tennis clinics, *plus* riding and swimming, *plus* all the regular attractions of the area—summer theater, interesting shops, an arts festival, and the funky, scenic cog railway to the top of Mount Washington. For more information, write the Mount Washington Hotel, in Bretton Woods, New Hampshire 03575.

The *Mad River Valley, in Vermont,* benefits from the presence of the posh Sugarbush Inn, a country club sort of lodging place that has some big comfortable rooms, a good restaurant, and a well-balanced activities program that includes special doings for children and special packages for tennis, golf, soaring, and so on. But even if you stay in one of the budget hostelries that make the valley a good-value spot the year round, there is plenty to do: hiking on the Long Trail or in the Green Mountain National Forest, for example; or riding at Applewood Farms, or swimming in any of a number of pools; or fishing in the Mad River for rainbow, brook, and brown trout. There are arts festivals, a jazz festival; paddle tennis, squash, and volleyball courts; softball diamonds; and rivers and rentals for canoeing and kayaking. Ballooning, too. The Sugarbush Valley Ski Area, Warren, Vermont 05674, can send details.

Some other good bets in the East: *Mount Snow, Vermont* 05356: for sailing, canoeing, kayaking, golf on an eighteen-hole course, tennis and concerts at the Marlboro Music Festival; and *Stratton, Vermont* 05155: for swimming, fishing, an arts festival and a bluegrass festival, canoeing and kayaking, golf on an eighteen-hole course and instruction at a special training center where greens, tees, and sand traps simulate all sorts of tricky shots you might encounter elsewhere, tennis clinics, and a special wilderness skills training program.

More Mountain Summer Programs

The spring issue of *Ski* magazine usually gives a good rundown of what's planned for the summer at the biggest mountain resorts; the emphasis is on places for active people, but active people who like their comforts.

Ruth Rudner's *Off and Walking*—of which half is given over to some of the most readable and relevant how-to-hike

information you'll find anywhere—provides where-to-hike particulars, and, of the seven treks covered in this "Hiker's Guide to American Places," four are near ski resort towns: There are hikes in the Uncompahgre National Forest, near Telluride, Colorado; in Yosemite National Park, California, home of the Badger Pass Ski Area; in the Tetons around Jackson Hole, Wyoming; and in the White Mountains of New Hampshire, where, in winter, skiing is a way of life.

More than most other hiking writers, Ruth Rudner pays attention to your comforts; before writing the book she spent most of her hiking life wandering from Alpine hut to Alpine hut, where she was always bedded down in relative comfort and fed bountifully. In *Off and Walking,* she outlines similar hut-to-hut hikes in Yosemite and the White Mountains, so, though you're out overnight, you've got a roof over your head and you're not carrying pounds and pounds of food and gear. Writeups of the other hikes include details on the civilized amenities in the area and information on the trail guides for the area, their prices, and the addresses of their publishers — so that if you want to day-hike instead of backpack you don't have to wait until you get to the area to read up on its hiking possibilities. You can get her book

from Holt, Rinehart and Winston, 383 Madison Avenue, New York, New York 10017; $4.95.

State Park Vacations

Among the best bargains in resorts are the lodges and cabins you find at the various U.S. state park systems. None of them are what you'd call rock-bottom cheap: rates are rarely below $15 for two. But they're seldom outrageously high and rate the status of bargains simply because you get such good value for your money.

Your room, for instance. It may be motel-modern and boring, or it may be pine-paneled or log-cabin rustic. However, because the parks are there mainly to serve John Q. Public and families who aren't interested in really roughing it, the basic amenities—decent beds, tubs and showers and a sink in the room—are always there. In addition, there is generally a restaurant on the premises; the food (heavy on the steaks, fried chicken, and blue-plate specials) will at least be plentiful, sometimes even good.

But the best part of these resorts is the giant assortment of other facilities, and it's here that state park resorts become not just a cheap vacation but a very good vacation at any price.

How many private resorts—of any type—are surrounded by acres and acres of woods, let alone woods crisscrossed by hiking trails? *And* how many have access to lakes where the fishing is good enough to keep even inveterate anglers happy? State park resorts have all this plus golf courses, tennis courts, swimming pools, *and* guided nature walks, games, square dances, bridge parties, quilting bees, trail rides on horseback, and all the other activities that have the more developed state parks booked up for weekends and summer vacation weeks for months in advance.

Because the park rangers are obliged to entertain not just their lodge guests but also lots of campers and day visitors as well, it's almost a fact of life that the variety of activities to be found is at least as large as what you would find at a far more expensive summer resort.

Only here in the state parks there's a democratic, never-dress-up kind of atmosphere. You meet people from all walks of life. You're not cloistered with the same types you meet at home. You don't feel as if you've dropped into some strange country club.

The places are overrun with families during the summer, which means that if you have children, they're bound to make friends. If you want to escape with your mate, the two of you, you had better try somewhere else—unless it's winter, in which case the resorts are usually more peaceful than a country inn.

Herewith, a rundown of what you find in some of the states:

Arkansas. One star is the Queen Wilhelmina Inn atop Rich Mountain near Mena. A $1.3-million structure modeled after an 1890s resort hotel named in honor of the queen of the Netherlands, it opened in the fall of 1975. (The original hotel closed down after just three years, for reasons that are still unknown, and was left to slowly fall apart.)

On the 64-acre property that surrounds the present wood-and-native-stone structure, there are hiking trails, including a section of the 200-mile-long Ouachita Trail; naturalist programs that investigate the profusion of fruit trees, medicinal plants, flowers, mosses, ferns; a petting zoo; a miniature sightseeing train; a miniature golf course—and the 55-mile Talimena Scenic Drive. For information and reservations, contact Marshall Thomson, Superintendent, Queen Wilhelmina State Park, Rich Mountain, Mena, Arkansas 71953 (501/394-2863). For information about other Arkansas state park facilities, contact the Department of Parks and Tourism, 159 State Capitol, Little Rock 72201 (501/371-1511).

Georgia. Stephen C. Foster State Park, which sits on an island of solid ground in Okefenokee Swamp, the "land of the trembling earth," has cabins. Surrounded by swamp, more or less, where many of the insects and animals are nocturnal, you hear night noises such as you would never imagine—a din of crickets, frogs, and more. There are many other interesting state park lodges in Georgia; for details about them, contact the Department of Natural Resources, Parks and Recreation Division, Trinity–Washington Building, 270 Washington Street, S.W., Atlanta, Georgia 30334.

Indiana. The list of half a dozen state park inns includes one that is modern and on a mountaintop with a view of the Ohio River (Clifty Falls, which is one of the best state parks in the state for hiking) and five others that are relatively rustic. At Turkey Run State Park, whose lodge was built in 1916, you can ride, go horseback riding, biking, hiking, fishing, play tennis, or join one of the ranger programs. A few other parks, among them 1,864-acre Lincoln State Park near Lincoln City and Abe Lincoln's boyhood home, have cabins. For detailed information, contact the Department of Natural Resources, Parks Division, 616 State Office Building, Indianapolis 46204.

Kentucky. The facilities are really outstanding here, not just because of the lodges, which are modern and sometimes even architecturally striking, but also because of the imaginative activities available—critter races, watermelon hunts, and so on. Most, like Lake Cumberland State Resort Park, are on huge man-made lakes. Lake Cumberland State Resort Park offers miniature golf; rentals of bikes, houseboats, ski boats, pontoon boats, fishing boats; a nine-hole golf course; a riding stable; playgrounds; shuffleboard courts; two swimming pools; tennis courts at the disposal of guests of the modern lodge and the cottages, some of which are rustic, some of which are modern. Kentucky Dam Village State Resort Park—just down the road from Kenlake State Resort Park (also on 160,300-acre Kentucky Lake) and Lake Barkley State Resort Park (on 57,920-acre Lake Barkley, another man-made lake, which adjoins Kentucky Lake)—has an eighteen-hole golf course, an enormous boat dock, six kinds of cottages and a lodge, hiking trails, playgrounds, a pool, a beach, and tennis courts. Rental equipment is available for just about every sport the park offers. The operators who man the Kentucky State Resort Park reservations desks, which you can telephone by dialing toll-free, can provide details and further information; to get the toll-free number for your area, call WATS information. Or write the Department of Public Information, Frankfort 40601.

Maryland. At thousand-acre Elk Neck State Park, 12 miles south of Elkton, Maryland, you can go crabbing or sit on the beach. Details from the superintendent, Elkton 21921; for information about cabins in parks in other parts of the state, write the Department of Natural Resources, Tawes State Office Building, Annapolis 21401.

New Jersey. The cabins at High Point State Park, one of the few parks in the state to offer such facilities, are not very fancy, but the experience of having your own place in the middle of

a 12,686-acre preserve with wonderful views makes it easy to do without luxuries. Details from the park superintendent, Sussex 07461.

New York. Several of the state parks have cabins, but the most extensive facilities by far are at the Allegany State Park, where there are some 65,000 acres of hiking trails, scenic drives, and facilities for boating, fishing, picnicking, tennis, snowmobiling, cross-country skiing, and so on. For further details, write the Allegany State Park Commission, Salamanca 14779.

Ohio. The excellent state park system here offers some 486 cabins and lodges. Punderson State Park's lodge is a Tudor manor house; Salt Fork Lake State Park's lodge is about five times the size, with 148 rooms, all quite modern. The lodge at Shawnee State Park is right on the edge of the woods; those at Burr Oak State Park and Hueston Woods overlook lakes. For further information, contact the Department of Natural Resources, Division of Parks and Recreation, Fountain Square, Columbus 43224.

Oklahoma. A very fine state park system. Of the fifteen preserves with cabins, seven also have lodges, some of them truly magnificent. Both the Fountainhead Lodge at 102,500-acre Fountainhead State Park, and the Texoma Lodge at 93,080-acre Texoma State Park have every facility you could imagine: golf, tennis, table games, bridge, chess, checkers, backgammon, swimming, fishing, waterskiing, pedal boating, sailing, canoeing, pontooning, riding, biking, movies, music, drama, theater. Even air strips. The Fountainhead looks on the outside like the inside of Frank Lloyd Wright's Guggenheim Museum, only divided in half—that is, long stark horizontal sweeps of balconies. The style is such that you'd visit even if it weren't for the rates, which are under $30 for doubles. For details on this resort and the others, write the Department of Tourism and Recreation, 504 Will Rogers Building, Oklahoma City 73105.

South Carolina. The Santee State Park has handsome octagonal cabins on stilts above the Santee-Cooper Reservoir, which is great for fishing; if you're lucky you'll catch a stringer full of white bass before breakfast. Barnwell, Cheraw, Edisto Beach, Givhans Ferry, Hickory Knob, Hunting Island, Myrtle Beach, Oconee, Pleasant Ridge, Poinsett, and Table Rock also have cabins. For details on this very good state park resort system, write the Department of Parks, Recreation, and Tourism, Box 113, Columbia 29201.

Tennessee. The cabins at 4,000-acre Norris Dam State Park—woodsy and right on the 129-mile-long man-made lake—are representative: rustic and comfortable. Paris Landing State Park in Buchanan, on Kentucky Lake, is equally delightful. But the quality here is not consistent: Pickwick State Park's lodge is not so well managed, and attracts, on occasion, a somewhat raucous crowd. A complete list of properties can be had from the Department of Conservation's Division of Parks, 2611 West End Avenue, Nashville 37203.

Texas. The prices on nightly cabin rentals—a mere $10—make the state's park system stand out. For a list, write the Parks and Wildlife Department, the John H. Reagan Building, Austin 78701.

West Virginia. Another state whose park system is first-rate. You'll find everything from modern resorts to streamside cabins where your only light comes from gas lanterns, the cooking facilities consist of a wood-stoked stove, and the water is from a nearby well. Pipestem, relatively new and another one of those places that has everything, is the fanciest. For details, contact the West Virginia Department of Natural Resources, Division of Parks and Recreation, State Capitol, Charleston 25305.

And more. The park systems of Florida, Louisiana, Massachusetts, Missouri, Nebraska, Pennsylvania, and Virginia also have cabins or cottages, lodges, motels. The state travel offices can send particulars.

National Park Lodges

There are lodges in many of the national parks. Often, they are far grander than those on the state preserves, but some of them are merely utilitarian. Activity programs are, mostly, less determinedly cheerful than at state parks, and, for the most part, they are more educational in tone. The surroundings? They'll outclass the fanciest private resort.

On the *Blue Ridge Parkway*, the Peaks of Otter Lodge (Box 489, Bedford, Virginia 24523) is newish, great for its views.

Bryce Canyon National Park has the Bryce Canyon Lodge (Box 400, Cedar City, Utah 84720).

In *Glacier National Park*, there are three big old hostelries, all like sets for a Nelson Eddy musical. The Many Glacier Hotel, on Swift Current Lake, has perhaps the most scenic location. For details: Box 4340, Tucson, Arizona 85717 in the winter; East Glacier, Montana 59434 mid-May through mid-September.

The *Grand Canyon* is what you see from the rooms with a view at the Grand Canyon Lodge (Grand Canyon, Arizona 86023).

In *Lassen Volcanic National Park*, there's Childs Meadows, edged on three sides by grasslands and forests (Mill Creek, California 96061).

Mesa Verde National Park, whose red stone cliffs were home to some early American Indians, has the Far View Lodge, aptly named and decorated in a modern southwestern motif.

At *Oregon Caves National Monument*, you can lodge at the Oregon Caves Chateau and Cottages (Oregon Caves National Monument, Oregon 97523).

Yellowstone National Park. Of the several lodging places in the park, the most outstanding is the Old Faithful Inn, which is all wood paneling, lofty ceilings, and rustic charm. For information, write the Yellowstone Park Company, Yellowstone National Park, Wyoming 82190.

Yosemite National Park also has several lodging places; the stone-and-timber Ahwahnee, one of those magnificent old-fashioned places that was "rustic" when built, is the most luxurious. For details: the Yosemite Park and Curry Company, Yosemite National Park, California 95389.

Reserve well ahead at all of these.

Canadian National Parks
In Canada, the most accessible parts of the national parks have always been treated as recreation areas, the "backsides" left for wilderness activities. Almost all of the old established parks have lodges.

However, there are a couple that are really outstanding.

In *Banff National Park*, there are two: the Banff Springs Hotel, a 550-room chateau of a hotel that is a Canadian institution and a complete resort with restaurants, health clubs, tennis courts, and so on; and the Chateau Lake Louise, the lake right at the base of the knoll on which it's set with the Victoria Glacier on its back.

Waterton Lakes National Park, the Canadian side of the United States' Glacier National Park, has the 1928 Prince of Wales Hotel, 82 rooms with fine views.

Jasper National Park has Jasper Park Lodge, built in 1953 after a fire destroyed the original 1920s structure. Smaller than the palaces in Banff, this new lodge is low-slung and almost understated despite its exciting setting between the mountains and a mirror of a lake. There are facilities for golf, tennis, and all manner of other activities.

For more information about the Canadian parks, write the Canadian Government Office of Tourism, 150 Kent Street, Ottawa, Ontario KIA OH6.

The Story of a Very Grand Hotel
The common sense of it is that a hotel as famous as Canada's Banff Springs could not possibly have come through all those long years without seeing a good deal of toil, trouble, and the parade of humanity that lends itself to the kind of historical treatises that are fun to read even when you're ordinarily not crazy about historical treatises. And so it is that *Banff Springs: The Story of a Hotel*, by Bart Robinson, is quite an engaging little book. You'll enjoy it if you've been in the area. Summerthought, Ltd., Box 1420, Banff, Alberta TOL OCO; $5.95.

Getting Really Away From It All

Some hotels stay in business because they're right in the middle of things and convenient to everything. And then there are those that traffic in isolation—the feeling that there's no one for miles and miles and miles around.

Here are a few of them.

A Hawaiian Hunting Lodge

Fourteen thousand acres of cattle range, mountains, and tropical rain forests, 750 feet above the wave-pounded coastline of the quiet isle of Molokai: it's enough to turn you into a hunter if you aren't one already. The place: the Puu-O-Hoku Ranch, Molokai, Hawaii 96748.

Andrew Carnegie Never Had It So Good

Greyfield, a three-story plantation manse on Cumberland Island, Georgia, has been in the same family ever since 1901, when Thomas Carnegie (Andrew's brother) built it and started filling it with impedimenta—silver candlesticks, scrapbooks, and knick-knacks. Paying guests have been enjoying all of it, as well as the silence of an island 70 percent of which is owned by the National Park Service, since 1966.

Meals are made up of island gleanings (oysters, mullet, shrimp, lamb); the bar is a mix-it-yourself affair. There are no facilities for tennis or golf—just the simple pleasures of island life. Information: Drawer B, Fernandina Beach, Florida 32034.

Alaska on $5 a Night

The West of vastnesses that amazed the continent's earliest explorers has long since vanished—except in 586,400-square-mile Alaska.

Alaska has ten rivers at least 300 miles long; the Yukon alone stretched 1,979 miles from its source in Canada to the Bering Sea. And there are three million lakes of 20 acres or more surrounded only by wilderness.

As it happens, quite a few of the Alaskan waters course through the Tongass and Chugach National Forests (which make up part of the 88,000 square miles of government preserve in the state), and it's on these riverbanks and shorelines that you find certain National Forest cabins whose rental price recently went up—from a wallet-busting $2 a night.

There are, in all, some 150 cabins, some of them A-frames made of cedar or boards, some of them log structures. One has a separate bathhouse and a hot mineral-spring bath. One, the Shelikof on West Krozof Island, is located on a beautiful ocean beach. The Forest Service supplies a listing that provides honest details not only about the condition of the cabin, but also about the activities available in the area. Examples:

"Excellent rainbow trout fishing with fish occasionally reaching 26 inches in length. Fair deer hunting."

"Bear sometimes a problem."

"Good runs of coho and sockeye salmon most years. Some deer hunting in the fall. Bear sometimes a problem."

"Stream fishing for steelhead in early spring. System supports good runs of pink, sockeye, and coho salmon. Deer relatively scarce, but bear plentiful enough to be a problem at times."

You may, in other words, want to bring a gun; the Forest Service advises a rifle of 30-06 caliber or larger for protection. If that really gives you the creeps, the Alaskan forest won't be your cup of tea.

If wilderness is what you want, though, you can't find a paradise farther away from it all. Civilization may be twenty-five to fifty miles away. Streams beg to be fished. The forests and bird life will be like nothing you've ever seen before. On the beaches you can look for wildflowers and collect edible greens like wild celery, yarrow, bluebells, bunchberry leaves, rice root, or chocolate lily roots. You can pick salmonberries in late June and early July; blueberries starting in mid-July; cranberries starting in August; and nangoonberries beginning in September.

You've got to boat or fly in; the Forest Service can help you arrange a charter and can issue reservations, which you should get six months in advance. The address: P. O. Box 757, Sitka, Alaska 99835.

Play Pioneer, but Close to Home

West Virginia's Kumbrabow State Forest (named for the Kumps, the Bradys, and the Bowers, three families instrumental in purchasing the land for the state) has five amazing log cabins where the stoves take wood and gas lanterns provide the illumination. You've got to go out to the well to get

your water. If you arrive at night, you may have to wait till morning to get your bearings. Outside, you'll find a waterfall, a stocked trout stream, and miles and miles of trails through rugged highland forests. For information, write the superintendent in Huttonsville, West Virginia 26273 (304/335-2219).

Hike-in Hotels in Glacier National Park

Jim and Louis Hill of the Great Northern Railway built them around the time of the First World War—Sperry and Granite Park, two rugged-looking stone lodges, one jutting out on a lava outcrop opposite a panorama that takes in the McDonald Valley, Logan Pass, the Garden Wall, the Livingston Range, and a few Canadian peaks; the other in an alpine area of peaks, waterfalls, and more vistas. Since only the restrooms (in a separate building) and the kitchens have been modernized, both lodges are very much as they were when built: at Sperry, you see after dark by the light of a kerosene lantern, and at Granite Park by candlelight; at both places you dine by lantern light and, if you wash in your room, you do it with cold water. The various trails to each lodge generally require about four hours of walking; once you arrive you're well situated for day-hiking in the area.

Both establishments are open only in July and August, and the rates for overnight guests are in the neighborhood of $25 per person. For reservations and information, contact Belton Chalets, Inc., Box 188, West Glacier, Montana 59936 (406/888-5511 from 8 A.M. to 8 P.M. mid-June through September).

The Lodge in the Canyon

It's new, but don't let that scare you.

With only thirty rooms, the Mountain Creek Lodge, which sits at the bottom of the Bluestone River gorge in the shadow of the equally new, and much busier, Pipestem Resort in Pipestem State Park near Hinton, West Virginia, is intimate and cozy. It's close enough to the river so that the splashing and rushing of the waters will sing you to sleep; you're surrounded by the same sort of hardwood forests that make up most of this corner of West Virginia (four-thousand-acre Pipestem being surrounded, in turn, by a twenty-five-thousand-acre game-management area); and you can get there only by aerial tramway.

Information: Pipestem State Resort Park, Pipestem, West Virginia 25979 (304/466-1800).

Stomping at the Salt Lick

The Elk Summit Road gets narrower and narrower as it moves away from Lolo, Idaho, finally ending at the Muleshoe Wilderness Camp. The end of the road also marks one gateway to the 250-square-mile Selway-Bitterroot Wilderness, the largest classified wilderness in the United States.

"A year of exploration," says the government description, "would still leave many parts unseen." Two weeks at the Muleshoe Wilderness Camp would give you only a taste, but this taste might do you for a lifetime. Hoodoo Creek runs through the center of the camp, and you can ride and hike to nearby lakes—or go swimming or kayaking or fishing. There is not a person in sight other than fellow occupants and an occasional ranger stopping by to check in—only deer, moose, and elk gathering at the salt lick on the grounds.

For information about cabins, write Box 83, Harrison, Idaho 83833 (208/689-3422 or 208/689-3315).

Here, They'll Even Cook Your Snook

Florida in the good old days. A big screened-in porch. Awnings. A sign: "Lounge." You expect to see Hemingway coming down the steps.

The Rod and Gun Club in Everglades City, Florida, built in 1922 on the foundations of that town's first house, is one of those away-from-it-all places that seem to have claimed a permanent right to call itself "undiscovered" even though its fame has spread to all sorts of high places. In a town of just five hundred, the fishing has to be good to keep people coming back, and it is: not just for trout and redfish but also for canny, fighting snook. Club guides take their celebrity cargoes to the Ten Thousand Islands, the Shark River, and Cape Sable. You can go, too.

And because Everglades City is also the gateway to the Everglades National Park, you can also tour the swamp in sightseeing boats and look for herons, egrets, cormorants, anhingas, ibis, and bald eagles.

For details and reservations, write the club in Everglades City, Florida 33929 (813/695-2101).

Retreats: When the World Is Too Much with You

Pascal opposed what he called diversions. They distracted men from the true purpose of living, which, in his Jansenist world, was the pursuit of the understanding of God.

If you're in agreement, and want to do some serious soul-searching, consider a retreat.

Retreat houses and renewal centers have been around for years, but until recently they were only for the clergy, world renouncers, and other zealots. Now, however, doctors, lawyers, artists, housewives, and executives can attend. Usually there's no obligation to minister to your soul in the company of other group members; you are generally free to make of your stay what you will, though some guidelines may be given and certain dietary practices observed. Most retreats are in lovely places and are set up to provide peace and tranquillity with a minimum of hassles and headaches. Here is a sampling of what you can find:

Buddhist. The Insight Meditation Society, Pleasant Street, Barre, Massachusetts 01005 (617/355-4378). Celibacy and vegetarianism are practiced.

Eclectic. The Arica Institute, 24 West 57th Street, New York, New York 10019. Elements of Zen, Sufism, yoga, and other eastern cults.

The Esalen Institute, Big Sur, California 93920; also 1793 Union Street, San Francisco, California 94123. Open en-

counters for couples, et cetera.

Jewish Mystic. The World of Kabbalah, 27 East 20th Street, New York, New York 10003 (212/866-3795). Believers say that Kabbalistic texts are a code, the unlocking of which brings you into personal communion with God. Music, chanting, and dance are ways of breaking the code.

Quaker. Powell House, R.D. 1, Box 101, Old Chatham, New York 12136. Meditation, silent meetings, and various thoughtful weekend and weeklong programs, in a rambling old white house.

Roman Catholic. Mount Augustine Apostolic Center, 144 Campus Road, Staten Island, New York 10301. Retreat programs for spiritual renewal, studies in eastern mysticism and faith healing at a Roman Catholic monastery whose courtyard has a very soothing view of the harbor.

Mount Saviour Benedictine Monastery, Pine City, New York 14871. Hooded monks, private retreats.

Sufi. Abode of the Message, Box 396, Lebanon, New York 12125. "Letting go, staying centered" is the idea behind this Islamic mysticism. Activities include prayer, mediation, and classes in the various Sufistic practices—including the whirling dervish dances.

Tibetan Buddhist. Karme-Choling, Tibetan Buddhist Meditation Center, Star Route, Barnet, Vermont 05821. Nonascetic Buddhism (you can smoke, drink, eat meat), plus much meditation, solitary retreats in huts scattered through the woods, and workshops on meditation and Buddhist teachings. Dormitory lodgings.

Similar centers are Karma Dzong (Salina Star Route, Boulder, Colorado 80302) and the Tibetan Nyingmapa Meditation Center (2425 Hillside Avenue, Berkeley, California 94704).

Yoga. Amanda Ashram, fifty miles outside New York City. For information, write the Yoga Society of New York, Inc., 100 West 72nd Street, New York, New York 10023.

Satchidananda Ashram, Yogaville East, P. O. Box 108, Pomfret Center, Connecticut 06259. At this rather elegant, marble-floored manse-turned-religious center, the day begins at 5 A.M. and is devoted to the practice of Integral Yoga, which includes mediation, breathing exercises, chanting, lacto-vegetarian meals, celebacy, and discussion.

Zen. Dai Bosatsu Zendo, Star Route, Livingston Manor, New York 12758. Students meditate, work in the fields, keep house; guests can join.

Zen Mountain Center, Tassajara Hot Springs, California. The Tassajara (whose Bread Book has long been celebrated for the wonderful assortment of bread recipes it presents) was

once a resort popular for its myriad hot springs; it was bought in 1966 by the Zen Center in San Francisco. You can take a cure, soak in the sulfurated Giant Plunge, go walking in the woods—or learn about Buddhism, and, in particular, about Soto Zen. Meals are vegetarian. For details about the Zen centers and zendo in other parts of the country, write the San Francisco Zen Center, 300 Page Street, San Francisco, California 94102; the California Bosatsukai Flower Sangha, 5632 Green Oak Drive, Los Angeles, California 90028; or the Zen Studies Society, 223 East 67th Street, New York, New York 10021.

Travel in the New Age

There are two books you should know about. The first is *The Spiritual Community Guide* ($3.50), which describes the many and various philosophies (Alan Watts, Master Subramuniya, Lama Govinda, Werner Erhard, Kahuna Ka'Ona, Swami Satchidananda, Tim Leary) that are making waves in what the editors call the "New Age" (which has to do with the planetarization of consciousness); it also lists some three thousand yoga and meditation centers, Ashrams, natural-food stores and restaurants, bookstores, and the like; and about a hundred major spiritual groups some of which have variations on retreat centers. The other book is *A Pilgrim's Guide to Planet Earth* ($5.95). In the book are some thoughts on travel—what to take, shots and documents, transportation, money, work,, where to stay, health, food, travel and the psyche, the woman traveler, walking. There is a listing, region by region, throughout the world, of gurus, hospitals, spiritual centers, books, celebrations, things to see, along with brief overviews of the areas from a New Age point of view. You get the information in the briefest bits—but there are many bits. The Spiritual Community, P.O. Box 1080, San Rafael, California 94902.

More Vacations for the Thinking Person

Ukiah, California, in the high pasture and timber lands in the coastal mountains between the Redwood Valley and Cape Mendocino, has been the home of the Mann family ever since the San Francisco earthquake of 1906; today, the Mann ranch, all 3,500 acres of it, is still the family home, and is the site of seminars that focus on aspects of anthropology, the fine arts, medicine, mythology, philosophy, psychology, and religious studies. In 1977, the seminars' leaders included Rene Dubos, Bruno Bettelheim, and Rollo May. There is time, during the three or four days you're there, to visit with them—and to walk, swim, and enjoy the impressive Mann House, its massive fireplaces, beams, high ceilings. The cost of the seminars and meals runs about $100 to $250, slightly more if you opt to stay at the ranch. For more information, contact the Mann Ranch Seminars, P. O. Box 570, Ukiah, California 95482 (707/462-3514).

World's Largest Thatched-Roof Resort

So the Fernandez Bay Club, on lovely, verdant Cat Island in the Bahamas, calls itself. How big do you have to be to be the world's largest in this field? Not very big: ten double rooms and one cottage are what you find here. It's also fairly inexpensive. For details: Fernandez Bay Club, Cat Island, Bahamas.

Out of the Way in the Caribbean

Not all of the islands have been built up to the hilt with high-rise hotels and glossy stores for the cruise-passenger trade. There are still quite a few islands where you can really get away from it all—just pad down to the beach, barefoot, and snooze and read and listen to the gentle sound of the ocean lapping at sands so soft that they feel like bath powder underfoot.

St. John, in the U.S. Virgin Islands, is one of them. Three quarters of its fourteen-thousand-acre interior is part of the Virgin Islands National Park. There are mountains, and jungles growing over the ruins of old forts and plantation houses in an area that saw one of the most spectacular slave revolts of the eighteenth century; you get to see the sights via jeep trail or hiking trail. The Reef Bay Trail takes you two and a half miles through a forest, past petroglyphs left over from the days when the Arawaks and the Carib Indians lived here and, finally, down to the beach where you can cool off with a swim. Caneel Bay Plantation, expensive and owned by Rockresorts, is about the biggest place to stay; write Box 4930 in St. John for details. For more information about the park, write the Superintendent at Box 806, St. Thomas 00801. The U.S. Virgin Islands Tourist Office can tell you more about St. John; write to 10 Rockefeller Plaza, New York, New York 10020.

Mustique, where Princess Margaret sunned herself and, some say, trysted with a young Briton, is three square miles of coconut plantations, citrus groves, deserted strands—L'Ansecoy, Lagoon, Macaroni, Obsidian, and Pasture beaches. The island is privately owned by one Colin Tennant, who was the force behind the Cotton House

Hotel, which is the only place to stay on the island. But since Tennant furnished it with old steamer trunks, beautiful antiques, and quirky pieces he bought here and there at home and during his travels, it's quite a place. For details, write the resort at Mustique, St. Vincent, West Indies.

Palm Island, which, like Mustique, lies in the Grenadines, is the realization of one man's dream; the palms, some three thousand of them, are there because John Caldwell, an uprooted Texan, chartering passengers in the area, planted them over the years whenever he took his charges ashore for picnics and such. There is one place to stay, the Palm Island Club; it's quiet—with low-slung bungalows walled in stone and foot-wide vertical louvers—and it's as unpretentious a place as you'd expect of a man who occasionally will tell people that he's lived for a long time on twelve hundred dollars a year. For more information, write the Palm Island Club in St. Vincent, Grenadines, West Indies.

Petit St. Vincent Island, across the waters from Palm Island, is another resort that is an island; 113 acres are there for the use of just under fifty guests who live in big bungalows scattered around the beaches, the bluffs, the hills. The bungalows have patios, sundecks, big beds, some stone walls, hardwood ceilings, wicker and rattan furniture, tile floors, khuskhus rugs. It's an informal sort of place, but daily rates of about $80 to $125 per couple have a tendency to make it not blue-jeans-informal but white-shorts-informal—soigné, in other words. For more information, write Petit St. Vincent Resort, St. Vincent, West Indies.

Vieques, off the coast of Puerto Rico, is three to five miles wide and twenty-one miles long. It's small, very informal and low-key, but it has been made livelier by the presence of a U.S. military reservation that has generated a handful of prosperous little bars. La Casa del Frances, in a French plantation home, is one of the nicest places to stay; there are also quite a few very tiny guest houses and a couple of housekeeping cottages. Good snorkeling and scuba diving off the coast. For details, write the Puerto Rico Tourism Company, 1290 Avenue of the Americas, New York, New York 10019.

Bequia, in the Grenadines—seven miles square and nine miles (and an hour and a half by boat) from St. Vincent—has mountains, uncrowded powdery white beaches, an unreliable water supply, and a small boat-building industry that occasionally has islanders making merry until dawn for a boat christening. It is just one of the relics of the whaling business, which grew up because of the relatively shallow waters offshore, where whales

came to feed and New England salts came hoping to get rich quick as a result. There's also the Whaleboner Bar, whose bar used to be the jawbone of a humpbacked whale and the rest of whose decor came from similar sources. Princess Margaret Beach is lovely. For details, write the Eastern Caribbean Tourist Association, 220 East 42nd Street, New York, New York 10017.

The British Virgin Islands are capitalizing on the natural splendor—still unspoiled—of the sixty islands, only fifteen of which are settled. There's lots of cruising and boating in the area, some of the most spectacular skin- and scuba-diving around, wonderful beaches in such quantity that you can snatch one to yourself—either near where you're staying or by having a local boatman ferry you to another Virgin—and small, personality-plus hostelries, some of which are expensive and ultraluxurious and some of which are unpretentious and quirky. For more information, write the B.V.I. Tourist Board, c/o J. S. Fones, 515 Madison Avenue, New York, New York 10022.

Camping in the Caribbean

Barefoot all the way, you cook food from the markets and the fish stands, stay out in the soft Caribbean air about as much as you can—and never dress up. Caribbean camping sites—understandably—are very popular, so make your arrangements well in advance.

At Strawberry Fields, between Ocho Rios and Port Antonio, on the northern coast of beach-happy Jamaica, you sleep out in one-room thatched-roof cottages or in tents on platforms. For details, contact the Caribbean Campgrounds, 54 West 56th Street, New York, New York 10019.

At Cinnamon Bay, St. John, Virgin Islands, you can get tents or concrete cottages with screened-in porches with the beach only about 150 yards away. At Maho Bay, within the Virgin Islands National Park, not far from Caneel Bay, boardwalks lead up from a white sand beach to your quarters—canvas cottages. For details, write the Cinnamon Bay Campground at P. O. Box 120, Cruz Bay, St. John, U.S. Virgin Islands; and Maho Bay Camps at 17 East 73rd Street, New York, New York 10021.

Less extensive facilities can be found in the French West Indies on the Basse-Terre section of Guadeloupe at the French National Park and on Martinique at Marin, at Macabou, and at Anse-à-l'Ane. The French West Indies Tourist Board at 610 Fifth Avenue, New York, New York 10020, can send more information.

Trips into History

Who Got Here First?

Archaeological Finds

They Are What They Threw Away, or What You Learn When You Go on a Dig
Archaeological excavation. The object of the game—sifting through another civilization's trash—is not all that romantic when you think about it. Nor is the activity itself. On a dig you spend a lot of time bent over, scraping dirt a few inches at a time, sifting through the soil for the tiniest pottery chip, the shortest bit of animal hair. You may be sleeping in tents, bathing (if you're lucky) in a fresh flowing stream; the people on one U.S. dig had nothing but a horse trough and described the feeling of a plunge into its tepid water at the end of each day as "luscious."

However, there's something compelling about digging, and if you're patient, have stamina, and are not bothered by the spartan living conditions, you can really get hooked: at the very least you have the satisfaction of knowing that you've contributed to scientific research and the feeling of good fellowship that comes from sharing, for one or two or three weeks, a single goal and a demanding life style. As your skills improve, so do the rewards.

What does all this cost? Transportation to the dig—which may be remote and therefore costly to get to—and sometimes room and board as well. You can either volunteer—in which case you'll spend most of your time digging, fetching, and carrying—or you can enroll in a field school where, in addition to the above, you'll also get instruction in correct archaeological techniques and a chance to perfect the skills you're taught.

Notable among the good field schools are the Arkansas Archaeological Survey Training Program (five- to six-day basic or advanced workshops in laboratory techniques, archaeological photography, excavation, site survey, mapping—all while you help excavate) and Northwestern University's Adult Archaeological Field School in Kampsville, Illinois, about 60 miles north of St. Louis in one of the oldest and most important archaeological sites in the Midwest: the one-

week dig programs teach you, among other things, excavation techniques. The cost at the Arkansas program is $11 ($6 for membership in the Arkansas Archaeological Society and $5 for the program, not including room and board. Camping sites are provided nearby, free, as are facilities for showers and hot dinners, for which you pay extra). The Kampsville program costs about $100 and up, including room and full board, materials, and instruction.

For further information: the Annual Training Program and Society Dig, Coordinating Office, Arkansas Archaeological Survey, University Museum of Arkansas, Fayetteville, Arkansas 72701; and the Northwestern Archaeological Program, 2000 Sheridan Road, Evanston, Illinois 60201.

Then there's Earthwatch—a Boston-based program in which participants' fees—anywhere from $500 to $900, depending on the program—support expeditions going to Virginia, Ireland, New Mexican Indian ruins, Majorca, and so on. Details about current programs are available from Earthwatch at 10 Juniper Road, Belmont, Massachusetts 02178.

For a complete list of field schools in the United States, write the Society for American Anthropology, American Anthropological Association, 1703 New Hampshire Avenue N.W., Washington, D.C. 20009. For a list of digs around the world that accept volunteers (and those that sponsor field schools) contact the Archaeological Institute of America, 260 West Broadway, New York, New York 10013. The list costs about $3, plus 50¢ postage.

Digging Deeper: Some Further Reading for Amateur Archaeologists
The magazine *Archaeology*. A subscription is included in membership in the Archaeological Institute of America, which costs $25 a year. Starting in the spring there are monthly sections devoted to opportunities for field work and sites where you can go to watch. The rest of the magazine deals with current research and the latest finds.
The Beginner's Guide to Archaeology, by Louis Brennan (Dell, New

York; $2.25). In addition to the general information about the discipline, there are lists of each state's archaeological societies and sites.

America's Ancient Treasures, by Franklin Folsom. If the history of ancient peoples of the Americas is not an interest of yours already, it may well become one when you leaf through this book.

Take this, for starters: "More and more reports, if they are accurate, suggest that man has been in this hemisphere much longer than archaeologists have thought possible. Dates for artifacts found at Old Crow Flat in the Yukon indicate that men lived there 20,000 years ago. . . . An archaeologist working near Cobleskill, New York, believes artifacts he has excavated were made 70,000 years ago. Others are convinced that man lived in the Mohave desert 100,000 or more years ago. In 1973, a still older date was offered for stone tools excavated near Puebla, Mexico. Very reputable geologists say that these artifacts may be 250,000 years old. Archaeologists may find that date impossible, but they have also not discovered any flaw in the scientific methods used by the geologists. And the geologists themselves admit the date is exceedingly puzzling. If Mexico has material of such extreme age, there may be similar material in the United States and Canada. If this proves to be so, there will be something very new for archaeologically minded visitors to look for in museums and sites. . . . When did people first settle in America?"

One of the good things about this book is that in putting forth the pieces in the puzzle—region by region, state by state, and town by town—Folsom does not just rattle off dates and name strange lost tribes. Each section of the book deals with a region, and at the beginning of each section he explains briefly what archaeology in the region is all about and tells a little of the history that archaeological excavations there have brought to light. Scattered throughout his descriptive lists of sites are photographs of diggers at work, drawings of archaeological finds, good captions to explain both, and short articles detailing the significance of objects frequently found in that area: fluted points, for example, or baskets, acorns, dwarf mammoths, tipi rings. He also discusses other archaeological matters. For example there is the Union Pacific site where in 1960 a railroad man struck upon a huge mammoth that subsequent excavations proved to have been killed by hunters hurling rocks from the top of the bank of the creek where it was drinking. The author describes carbon-14 dating and how it works, tree-ring dating, and stratigraphy ("When people live in the same place a long time, the rubbish they throw away piles up. The oldest garbage is at the bottom of the pile. The newest at the top").

Use this book to plot a whole archaeological trip, or contact archaeological sites listed at the book's end to find out about joining digs in your own area. Or get the book just to read it: this is one directory that transcends the genre. Rand McNally and Co., Box 7600, Chicago, Illinois 60680; $2.95.

Where the Explorers Explored, and What It's Like There Today

The Museum That Tells the Story

Perhaps more vividly than any other spot on the continent, the Hillendale Museum in Mendenhall, Pennsylvania, tells the story of the opening up of North America, and the growth of European knowledge of the area, starting with the days when it was common knowledge that if you sailed too far westward, you'd fall off the edge of the world. However, the Hillendale Museum is not actually a museum in the usual sense of the word; there are no collections of ancient and irreplaceable objects. Instead, the labyrinthine corridors that make up the museum are lined with abstract globes and dioramas that show how mountains, bad weather, and rocky coasts acted as barriers to exploration and how rivers, used as roads, determined what got discovered when.

Sections of globe, each representing a different time and stage in the exploration of our continent, are turned with the west at the top, so that when you look at them, North America lies ahead of you just as it did to the explorers. Parts of the world that were unknown during the era in question are entirely blacked out; as more and more of the continent is discovered, more and more parts are filled in. A narrative on a cassette player that you carry around with you tells the dramatic stories behind all the discoveries, many of which were no more than accidents of the search for something

else. Coronado, who went to find the seven cities of Cibola, instead found the Great Plains and what is now Kansas. In all, he traveled some six thousand miles. At almost the same time, de Soto went north to South Carolina, Georgia, Mississippi, Alabama, and western Arkansas. At one time, he was just four hundred miles from Coronado's party in Kansas. Often these early explorers were on horseback, but just as often they were on foot, with Indians carrying their loads. There are tales of inhuman treatment of the Indians that would curdle your blood. By the end of the taped tour, which lasts long enough and is detailed enough that very young children don't enjoy it (and those who have not yet started sixth grade are not admitted), you have quite a feeling for the discovery of the continent, you have gotten to know a few explorers, and you have shuddered at some of the stories. It's quite a place.

For reservations, which are generally necessary, write the Hillendale Museum, Hillendale & Hickory Hill Roads, P. O. Box 129, Mendenhall, Pennsylvania 19357.

The Vikings in America

The New World for the first of the Old World's expatriates was the craggy coast of Labrador and the high meadows above its rocky headlands, close to the easternmost landfall of North America. The point at which they settled is hardly more developed today than it was when they first landed—so when you visit you will probably feel, as they must have, that you have truly come to the edge of the world.

Such places are never cheap or easy to get to. In this case, you've got to drive all the way through Newfoundland to the end of the isolated Great Northern Peninsula, along a dirt road that is dusty when it's dry and a swamp when it rains; the farther you travel, the lighter the traffic and the scarcer the gas stations.

What you find when you get there is an archaeological excavation, L'Anse aux Meadows, which in 1964 proved beyond a doubt that between A.D. 850 and A.D. 1050 Norsemen settled there and lived a civilized life. Guides can tell you about it; there's also a fascinating booklet, "Historic Newfoundland" (available from the Newfoundland Department of Tourism, Confederation Building, St. John's, Newfoundland), that should whip up your enthusiasm.

However, you do the drive not only for the history, but also for the whole edge-of-the-world experience, the frontierness of it all. There are views that are grand beyond belief: the coast is jagged, with coves and bays, only occasionally smoothed out by a tiny crescent of a sand beach. Icebergs drift by well into the summer. The

fishing villages and fisherfolk are as rugged as the landscape. The Department of Tourism (address above) can send you details about travel in the area, and about the fishing, which is very good.

Other remnants of Vikings in America have been found in places that seem rather strange until you remember that the Vikings were very adventuring people.

Alexandria, Minnesota. Even though the authenticity of the marked-up boulder known as the Kensington Runestone has never been entirely verified, the townspeople have made a big thing of its 1898 discovery (it was found next to the roots of a tree on Olof Ohman's farm). A 28-foot statue of a Viking stands at the foot of Main Street in this fishing and resort center. They've also built a museum to house the rock, which has, in its day, been exhibited at the Smithsonian and at the New York World's Fair of 1965. The inscriptions, translated, read:

EIGHT GOTHS AND TWENTY-TWO NORWEGIANS ON EXPLORATION JOURNEY FROM VINLAND OVER THE WEST. WE HAD CAMP BY TWO SKERRIES ONE DAY'S JOURNEY NORTH FROM THIS STONE. WE WERE AND FISHED ONE DAY. AFTER WE CAME HOME (FOUND) TEN RED WITH BLOOD AND DEAD. AVE MARIA, SAVE FROM EVIL and HAVE TEN OF OUR PARTY BY THE SEA TO LOOK AFTER OUR SHIPS FOURTEEN DAYS' JOURNEY FROM THIS ISLAND YEAR 1362.

Alexandria calls itself the Bass Capital of the World because of the local fishing. The Chamber of Commerce (Alexandria, Minnesota 56308) can send particulars about the Vikings and about local outdoor life.

Oklahoma. In this state, there are two runestones, each dated some three and a half centuries before the Alexandria stone. One, now at the end of a small trail at the Clem Hamilton Heavener Runestone State Park in Heavener, is twelve feet high, ten feet wide, and sixteen inches thick—carved with eight runes cut ¼ to ¾ of an inch deep, and bearing the date November 11, 1012; the stone, which was first sighted in the 1830s by an Indian hunting party and known for over a hundred years as "the Indian Rock" was somehow lost for a while. Mrs. Gloria Farley, who remembered seeing it as a child, found it again in 1951 and set about trying to authenticate it. The other runestone is in the Kerr Museum in nearby Poteau, Oklahoma. Discovered in 1967 by a couple of young boys, it came in two pieces—one piece bearing seven perfect runes, the other found in November, two months later, bearing the missing eighth rune. The stone was dated November 11, 1017. The Oklahoma Tourism and Recreation Department, 500 Will Rogers Building, Oklahoma City, Oklahoma 73105, can send you more information about both towns.

Maine. Small, but there nonetheless—on a boulder near Fort Popham—is a semicircular granite fortification on the shores of the Kennebec River, Maine, near Popham Beach State Park. The Boothbay Harbor Region Chamber of Commerce, Box 365, Route 27, Boothbay Harbor, Maine 04538, and the Bath Area Chamber of Commerce, 45 Front Street, Bath, Maine 04530, can provide details about other things to see and do in the area.

Leif Ericson landed here. Or so the people in tiny, peaceful Jensen Beach, Florida, say. One of the last quiet spots on the state's Atlantic coast, Jensen Beach annually stages a pageant in which the explorer's North American landing of 1002 is reenacted, to the accompaniment of special Scandinavian Leikarring dances, boat races, and a big picnic.

For more information about the feast and about the area, contact the Jensen Beach Chamber of Commerce, 51 Commercial Street, Jensen Beach, Florida 33457.

Coronado in America
Near the point at which Coronado entered what is now the United States, you can stand on a peak at the end of a foot trail and look over the territory that Coronado saw much more intimately nearly five hundred years ago, in 1536. Exhibits along this desert trail tell some of the story of the expedition that took this thirty-year-old man from the Arizona–Mexican border northward across the Gila Salt River and into what is now New Mexico, close to Gallup, more than two-thirds of the way to Colorado's border, then across New Mexico and the Texas and Oklahoma panhandles, and then almost halfway across Kansas to the Missouri line. First he was looking for the Seven Cities of Cibola, where the streets were supposed to be lined with goldsmiths' shops and houses of many stories, and the doorways were supposed to be studded with emeralds and turquoise. Later he was led on by the tales of an Indian called the Turk, who told them of an unbelievably rich land to the East.

When he got here, all he saw were towns of straw houses, probably those of the Wichita Indians.

Coronado killed the Turk. It had all been, he learned, a Pueblo Indian plot hatched in the hopes that the Spaniards would die of starvation.

Then, disillusioned, impoverished, and injured in a fall from his horse, Coronado returned to Mexico City in midsummer of 1542, about two and a half years after the beginning of the trip.

You can picnic on the spot, see the exhibits, and walk the trail to Coronado Peak. For more information, write the Coronado National Memorial, Star Route, Hereford, Arizona 85615.

The Coronado Trail. U.S. Route 666, which parallels the Arizona–New Mexico border from Douglas at the Mexican border to I-40 near Gallup, New Mexico, is an interesting road to drive if only because of the fact that Coronado went there before you. But the most scenically marvelous section—mesa and desert country—takes you the 117 twisty miles (about three and a half hours driving time) between Springerville and Clifton, through the town of Alpine, through forests of aspens and conifer that make for spectacular gold-and-green autumns, and along the Mogollon Rim (an escarpment that angles across the Arizona high country for nearly 200 miles). There are several Forest Service campgrounds along the Trail and on side roads that make good spur trips and that will get you even farther than the relatively untrafficked U.S. 666 from the twentieth century, and make it even easier to imagine how it must have been for Coronado and his men.

For specific information on the area, write the Supervisor of the Apache National Forest, Springerville, Arizona 85938.

Hernando De Soto Was Here
May 30, 1539. Don Hernando de Soto stepped out on the beach near what is now the De Soto National Memorial, in what is now Bradenton, Florida, and with his six hundred conquistadores began an expedition into the interior of North America—the first European expedition on record. He spent four years in the wilderness, traveled four thousand miles, lost half his crew, and staked Spain's claims on lands beyond the Mississippi. Interestingly enough, he was at one time only about four hundred miles from where Coronado and his men were learning that the Indian they knew as the Turk had duped them.

At the National Memorial there are exhibits of Spanish armor and Spanish weapons; there's a movie that explains the expedition and its hardships, and you can learn about colonial Spanish life in a living history area where there are demonstrations of cooking, crossbow shooting, and blacksmithing.

For details, contact the De Soto National Memorial, Box 1377, Bradenton, Florida 33505.

A reenactment of the landing is staged once a year, in March, by the town fathers. The "Conquistadores," in elaborate costume, splash ashore from their boats. Cannons boom, the crowds go mad, and a week of merrymaking begins, during which bearded conquistadores "capture" shopping centers and retirement villages; merchants put on sidewalk sales; vendors hawk Spanish edibles; and there are square dances and boat races and bike races and a dance, an art show, beard-growing contests, flamenco dancing, and a treasure hunt. In some places the salespeople and waitresses dress up like pirates. For a schedule and information about places to stay, write the Manatee County Chamber of Commerce, P. O. Box 321, Bradenton, Florida 33506. Festival information: De Soto Celebration, Inc., 809 - 14th Street, West, Bradenton, Florida 33505.

Ponce de Leon's House
The oldest continually inhabited residence in the Western Hemisphere, Casa Blanca, in Old San Juan, Puerto Rico, is the ancestral home of the explorer's family. It's furnished as the house of any well-to-do citizen might have been in the sixteenth and seventeenth centuries. Guides show you around and point out items of interest, including some of the famous man's books. For information on the island and on other things to see and do in Old San Juan—spectacular churches, forts, and the city walls—contact the Puerto Rico Tourism Company, 1290 Avenue of the Americas, New York, New York 10019.

Spotting Sir Francis Drake
How it got there, nobody knows, but a weathered, rudely worked tablet, bearing an inscription by Sir Francis Drake, the English explorer, was found in 1936 on San Quentin Point inside San Francisco Bay. You can see it, and learn about the explorer's voyages, at the Bancroft Library at the University of California at Berkeley. (There are also some interesting museums, waterfront restaurants, graffiti, crafts shows, and astonishing student life to enjoy and observe; campus tours leave the Student Union at the foot of Telegraph Avenue every weekday.) In the museum where the Drake artifact is displayed, there are some other interesting objects, some interesting stories—though no explanation as to how the plaque got to San Quentin.

> BEE IT KNOWNE UNTO ALL MEN BY THESE PRESENTS IVNE. 17. 1579. BY THE GRACE OF GOD AND IN THE NAME OF HERR MAIESTY QVEEN ELIZABETH OF ENGLAND AND HERR SVCESSORS FOREVER I TAKE POSSESSION OF THIS KINGDOME WHOSE KING AND PEOPLE FREELY RESIGNE THEIR RIGHT AND TITLE IN THE WHOLE LAND VNTO HERR MAIESTIES KEEPEING NOW NAMED BY ME AN TO BEE KNOWNE VNTO ALL MEN AS NOVA ALBION
> G FRANCIS DRAKE

Drake's landfall. Drake's actual landing place was a foggy cliff-edged triangle of land up the coast from San Francisco about fifty miles at what is now Point Reyes National Seashore, and even though there has been no unquestioned evidence as to his exact landing place in the area, no one believes that he landed elsewhere, let alone at San Quentin. Point Reyes (which borders the San Andreas Fault and is, geologically, related to points several hundred miles down the coast) has changed little since the buccaneer-explorer disturbed the thousand-year-old civilization of the Miwok Indians in 1579 when he stopped to repair his vessel, the *Golden Hinde*. Most historians, including those of the Drake Navigators Guild, say that he landed and built his fort off the shore of the Drake's Bay section of the seashore. The beach is protected from wind by massive shining white clay cliffs, which might well have reminded Drake's homesick men of their own home country and given them cause for naming their discovery as they did—Nova Albion.

You can swim underneath the cliffs, or picnic, fish, and beachcomb in the area. The seashore is a fascinating place for other reasons, however: the changeable weather and the variety of bird life that inhabits the marshlands (the estero at Limantour is one of the few on the Pacific never to have been dammed or in other ways altered by man). There are also the sea lions that you can see offshore near Point Reyes Promontory. During spring and fall migrations, there may be hundreds of them sunning themselves on the rocks of the coves below a special overlook set up to provide good viewing. Inland, you can hike and camp along hilly wooded trails.

For further information, contact Point Reyes National Seashore, Point Reyes, California 94956. *The Visitor's Guide to the Point Reyes National Seashore*, by Alice F. Dalbey (Chatham Press, Riverside, Connecticut; $1.95) provides still further details about the seashore—enough that you will soon be ready to pack your bags.

Drake's ship. A replica of the *Golden Hinde*, recently sailed over from England, is open for guided tours. You can learn about some of Drake's doings at Pier 39 on the San Francisco waterfront at Fisherman's Wharf.

Cabrillo's California
Today, San Diego is one of the most delightful places around. But can you imagine that enormous dome of sky and those mystic foggy days without another soul around to even share it with?

That's what it must have been like for the Portuguese explorer Juan Rodriguez Cabrillo when he went west, for he was the first European to set foot on what is now California. It was 1542.

The landing is commemorated at the Cabrillo National Monument on Point Loma, where he landed. There is a statue and a Visitor Center that explains the state of exploration of the continent at that time.

Some other sights of particular interest include the view from the tower of the lighthouse—which takes in ocean, islands, and the foothills and mountains inland—the gray whales' migration between mid-December and mid-February; and the tidepools along the shore, which are some of the best in Southern California.

Once a year, in September, there's a reenactment of the landing.

For further information, write the Superintendent at Box 6175, San Diego, California 92106.

Marquette and Joliet
The two explorers who traveled throughout the Midwest are remembered at the Chicago Portage National Historic Site (c/o Cook County Forest Preserve, Cummings Square, River Forest, Illinois 60305). It's located on the site of the portage that led from the Great Lakes to the Mississippi River.

In the Wake of Henry Hudson and the Half Moon
The banks of the river named after the Dutch explorer have probably changed as drastically as any other place on the continent. However, riding along on the Hudson River Day Line boats, which leave Manhattan during the summer for trips to Poughkeepsie, will give you something of the feeling that Hudson must have felt. There are still the soaring Palisades and the rocky highlands. The farther you go from the city, the easier the imagining gets. For information about when the trips go, contact the New York City Convention and Visitors Bureau, 90 East 42nd Street, New York, New York 10017.

The First Great American Expedition
It was just after the Louisiana Purchase, in the early nineteenth century, that Meriwether Lewis (1774–1809), William Clark (1770–1839), and 330 others set out from St. Louis under orders from President Thomas Jefferson "to find the most direct and practicable water communication across the continent."

It was the first time Americans had gone exploring in their own continent.

Because the expedition was thoroughly documented as to the trees, fish, animals, and topography encountered; and because much of the rest of the country was known at the time, their route is known precisely and can be followed even today. Historical markers commemorate their visits, so in addition to seeing the scenery they saw, you can also learn a good deal about the men, and the Indian woman Sacajawea, on the trip.

In Idaho, you can follow the Lewis and Clark Highway, U.S. 12. On its way to Missoula, Montana, 229 miles away, it crosses the state, starting at Lewiston, curling along the banks of the Lochsa River (sometimes nearby, sometimes at stream's edge, with mountains on either side). This fine paved road always parallels, and in some cases actually touches, the explorers' true route. It cuts through some wild territory: For the 101 miles between Lolo pass on the Montana border and Kooskia, on the Nez Perce Indian Reservation, about halfway to the Washington border, there's only one settlement, Lowell, and it's only a hamlet.

The real Lewis and Clark Trail was actually what is now the Lolo Trail, an ancient pathway that was being used by Indians when Lewis and Clark, the first white men to see Idaho, spent nine days on it in 1805. Now a Forest Service Road, it makes for rugged driving, and there are no facilities of any kind; the road is navigable only from mid-July, after the snow banks have melted, until early September, before the first snow of the year has fallen. But along the way there are magnificent top-of-the-world views over the Selway-Bitterroot wild country—all canyons, forests, and mountains. There are also cairns left by Indians of long ago. One of them marks the way to treeless Post Office Knob, a onetime fire lookout which offers another splendid view, and others mark the explorers' campsites. The Powell Ranger Station, where you can get a map and up-to-date information about road conditions, is on the site of the campsite of September 15, 1805. There, because they found no game, the explorers shot a horse for food. For more information, contact the Clearwater National Forest, Route 3, Orofino, Idaho 83544.

Sacajawea's birthplace was in Salmon, off Route 28. The location of the Lemhi Indian Village of the expedition's guide is marked by a boulder.

In Montana there are a number of sites related to the explorers and their famous guide.

Camp Fortunate, where the Indian woman (who had been kidnapped from her tribe at an early age) was reunited with her brother, and where she persuaded his fellow tribesmen to give the explorers some more horses for their journey, is in Armstead, off Route 91.

A Lewis and Clark expedition campsite for the night of August 1, 1804, is marked near La Hood, off Route 30.

A Sacajawea memorial is in a small park across the road from the Sacajawea Hotel in Three Forks. There are some pretty fir trees and an inscribed boulder. Nearby, at the Missouri Headwaters State Monument, is the site of the Indian's kidnapping.

In North Dakota you can see a statue of Sacajawea in the State Capitol at Bismarck.

Fort Mandan, in Washburn, was Lewis and Clark's winter quarters. There they prepared for their trip into the unexplored west; and there they met Sacajawea, then about sixteen years old and pregnant by Toussaint Charbonneau. In the spring, after the child was born, the group (including Sacajawea and the baby) departed.

In Oregon you will see some of the most important of all the sites connected with Lewis and Clark's expedition; most of them are mapped out in a "Lewis and Clark Trail" brochure you can get from the Travel Information Section of the Oregon State Highway Division, State Highway Building, Salem 97310.

The Fort Clatsop National Memorial in Astoria, Oregon, is a truly significant spot. A slide program, "The Voyage of Discovery," tells you the story of the expedition, and there are exhibits (equipment used by the explorers) and demonstrations (firing of flintlocks, hollowing out of log canoes). The main thing, however, is the replica of the fort itself—fifty feet square and made of logs after William Clark's original design. The size is particularly impressive in view of the fact that thirty-five men spent a winter here. For details, contact Route 3, Box 604-FC, Astoria 97103.

The salt cairn where Lewis and Clark boiled sea water to get salt for the group's trip back to St. Louis has been reconstructed in Seaside, Oregon, on Lewis and Clark Way.

At Cannon Beach, a plaque marks the site of the beaching of a 105-foot-long whale. The story goes that Lewis and Clark, wintering at Fort Clatsop, nearby, had been told about a whale driven ashore; Clark noted in his diary that "The Indian woman . . . observed that she had traveled a long ways to See the great waters, and that now that the monstrous fish was also to be seen, She thought it very hard that She could not be permitted to See either (She had not yet been to the Ocian.)" The beach is seven miles long; you can swim, surf-fish, or comb the sands for Japanese fishing floats and other jetsam that washes up regularly, especially after storms. The Oregon Coast Association, P. O. Box 670, Newport, Oregon 97365, can send you more information about the coast.

Mount Sacajawea, near Enterprise, towering over the Eagle Cap Wilderness of the Wallowa-Whitman National Forest, was named for the Indian woman. You can find out more about hiking and exploring in the forest by writing the Supervisor in the Federal Office Building, Baker 97814.

A mural in the state capitol building depicts Sacajawea watching the explorers get ready to portage Celilo Falls; outside the building, she is shown in sculpture, on foot, pointing the way for Lewis and Clark.

In South Dakota, there is another monument to Sacajawea in Dakota Memorial Park in Mobridge. The story behind the concrete memorial put up in 1929, in the words of the chief clerk at that town's Fort Manuel: "This evening the wife of Charbonneau, a Snake Squaw, died of a putrid fever . . . aged about 25 years." (However, there are other tales that place Sacajawea's grave at Fort Washakie, Wyoming, where, on the Wind River Reservation, there is a more elaborate monument, on which her time of death is placed at about 75 years later.)

In Washington, there is also a Lewis and Clark Highway: Route 14, between Clarkston and Ilwaco, from the Idaho border to the Pacific Ocean, along the Columbia River and the Snake.

Sacajawea State Park, in Pasco, is on the site of a Lewis and Clark campground. In this 284-acre preserve, you can fish, swim, and picnic. Indian artifacts are exhibited in the interpretive center. Information: Chamber of Commerce, Box 550, Pasco 99301.

Lewis and Clark Campsite State Park, in Chinook, commemorates another campsite, this one with an ocean view. You can fish, swim, camp, picnic.

Fort Canby State Park, near Ilwaco, is where the explorers finally saw the Pacific.

Lewis and Clark Trail State Park, in Dayton, has a grove of trees that sheltered the explorers at yet another campsite. It's near the scenic Kendall Skyline Drive in the Umatilla National Forest and the spectacular Palouse River Canyon and Falls, where the Palouse River, bound for its confluence with the Snake, has cut a deep canyon through the wheat-lands of the area and hurtles over a 198-foot cliff.

Where to find out more. When addresses are not specified, write the state tourist offices of the areas that interest you: the Idaho Division of Tourism and Industrial Development, Capitol Building, Boise 83720; the Montana Department of Highways, Helena 59601; the North Dakota Travel Division, Capitol Grounds, Bismarck 58505; the Oregon State Highway Division, State Highway Building, Salem 97310; the South Dakota Tourism Department, Pierre 57501; the Washington Department of Commerce and Economic De-velopment, General Administration Building, Olympia 98504.

The Man Who Made the Frontier Famous

Daniel Boone was fighting the French and Indian war when he met John Findley, who told him of a land to the west, in Kentucky, where the buffalo were so plentiful you had to avoid being trampled; where turkeys swarmed the woods by the flock; where the land was so fruitful that animals grew fat on the fruit and nuts that fell from the trees.

Boone's father had been one of those early Americans who kept moving westward to get more elbow room, and he bequeathed that restless spirit to Daniel. So it was no wonder that Findley's tales caught Boone's imagination and not surprising that he spent more than half his lifetime in the quest—even when the search meant invading Indian hunting grounds, risking his life, hacking his way foot by foot through thick eastern forests and mountains that had seen almost no white men.

Boone was born in Berks County, Pennsylvania in 1734. He spent most of his childhood in North Carolina, married there, and died, poor, in Missouri. But he made his mark on Kentucky, for it was this territory that he opened up on his expedition through the Cumberland Gap and later on when he helped cut out the Wilderness Road (which was, for most pioneers, the first step in the long way west). Historic sites commemorating Boone's presence are, consequently, all over Kentucky today, and a Boone odyssey can be fun, for these sites are in the best parts of the state: in the rolling farm country, where barns, old roads, and fence rows overgrown with honeysuckle make for a sort of friendly, frayed-around-the-edges landscape—the kind you'd expect to have disappeared under the onslaught of the twentieth century; and in the mountains, which are wild and forested and sparsely settled by rugged mountain types who talk with a twang and are among the friendliest people to be found anywhere.

Boone's first fort. One of the most important sites in Boone's Kentucky is Harrodsburg, in the middle of the state not far from Lexington's Bluegrass. Surveyed just before the Revolution and settled in 1774, this town of seven thousand was the first white settlement in Kentucky, and as is full of historic sites as you'd expect. At Old Fort Harrod State Park, one of the places you won't want to miss, the log stockade and cabins that the settlers constructed—as shelter and as protection against the Indians, who were not at all happy about having their hunting grounds invaded—have been rebuilt, furnished, and staffed with costumed guides, so that you can get a pretty fair idea of what life was like back in Boone's day. The explorer's letters are on display at the park's entrance, in a Georgian-style mansion built in the 1820s, when the settlement had matured.

"The Legend of Daniel Boone," a goose bumpy musical drama presented under the stars in an amphitheater where crickets nearly drown out some of the lines, tells more of the tale—as does an old cemetery whose mossy headstones mark the graves of the earliest pioneers.

Harrodsburg is, in addition, the home of Shakertown, the immaculate reconstruction of the religious settlement that flourished here for about a century beginning in 1805; the Beaumont Inn, one of those Kentucky hostelries where gorging on fried chicken, country ham, corn pudding, and other such rich southern specialties is the order of the day; and the Inn at Pleasant Hill, the Shaker settlement's restaurant and hostelry,

which offers meals prepared according to original recipes and rooms furnished, Shaker-style, with trundle beds and wall pegs (for hanging up the extra chairs). For more information: Old Fort Harrod State Park, Harrodsburg, Kentucky 40330, or the Harrodsburg Chamber of Commerce.

The Cumberland Gap. To appreciate the importance of this stream-cut notch in the Appalachians, you have to realize how much an additional thousand feet of altitude would have meant to those pioneers who were attempting to transport all their earthly goods—on foot, by horseback, and in wagons—across mountains steep enough to make today's backpackers huff and puff. The Gap took on even greater significance when, in 1775, it became the starting point for the Wilderness Road, a pathway axed through the woods by Daniel Boone and some thirty others on the orders of Judge Richard Henderson, who wanted to establish a new colony, Transylvania, in the Bluegrass of central Kentucky. As soon as Indian attacks were reduced, travel became increasingly heavier, and by the end of the Revolution some twelve thousand settlers—seeking land and opportunity away from heavily settled Virginia—had traveled the Wilderness Road. When, in 1792, Kentucky entered the Union, its population was 100,000; it was twice that by 1800. Most of those people had come by way of the Wilderness Road and the Cumberland Gap—and the settlers streaming in from the eastern seaboard kept on using the Wilderness Road and the Gap until the early 1800s, when more direct routes through the mountains were finally opened up. All this is told at the Visitor Center at the Cumberland Gap National Historical Park, whose twenty thousand acres sprawl into Kentucky, Virginia, and Tennessee.

Inside the park, you can visit a restoration of an old pioneer settlement or go for a hike on trails where the landscape seems little changed since Boone first appeared on the scene. Some are inside the park. One other that follows the old Wilderness Road ends at the site of an old iron furnace on the outskirts of what is now Cumberland Gap, Tennessee, a placid small town that borders the park. For details, contact the park superintendent at Box 840, Middlesboro, Kentucky 40965.

Boone's woods. In Boone's day, the "wilderness" extended far beyond the bounds of the 635,000-acre Daniel Boone National Forest; there were no roads as there are here, and the trees in the forest grew tall and strong without benefit of the management techniques used today. Yet the area still gives you an idea of what Boone must have found

when he explored the area: there are still wild turkey, deer, ruffed grouse, gray squirrels, fox, duck, quail, rabbits, mink, and raccoon; acre upon acre of trees; wild rivers whose white waters crash over boulders and wooded banks; and placid flat-water streams that look remote and mystical in early-morning fogs. You can canoe, fish, hunt, hike, swim, or camp—or, because there are roads through these woods now—just get in your car and take in the sights that so enthralled the famous frontiersman. For information about specific activities, contact the Forest Supervisor, Daniel Boone National Forest, 100 Vaught Road, Winchester, Kentucky 40391.

How Boone described the Kentucky he saw. "Eden . . . a great forest on which stood myriads of trees, some gay with blossoms, others rich with fruits. . . .

"Trees ten feet in diameter and one hundred fifty feet tall, huge forests of oak, hickory, chestnut, walnut, and poplar, home to unlimited game.

"We began to hunt . . . and found everywhere abundance of wild beasts of all sorts through this vast forest. The buffalo were more frequent than I have seen in the settlements . . . we practiced hunting with great success."

Boone's Flintlock and His Jacket. They're on display, along with the bark of a birch in which he carved his name and the inscription "Killed a Bar," at the Filson Club, 118 West Breckinridge Street, Louisville, Kentucky—a privately supported historical society in an old Georgian building where you'll also see Indian artifacts, relics of other pioneers, and a collection of firearms. For more information about Louisville—an interesting place to visit for many reasons—contact the Visitors Bureau in Founders Square, Louisville 40202.

Where Daniel Boone lives on. Daniel Boone IV, a blacksmith, descended from the famous frontiersman, makes his home in Burnsville, a town of about fifteen hundred in the northwestern part of North Carolina near the Tennessee border. For a living, he designs decorative ironwork and repairs farm and household utensils for the hill people who come into town from their out-of-the-way farms and mountain cabins. He was the one who wrought the handsome gates outside the Daniel Boone Native Gardens, six acres of North Carolina flowers and shrubs in the town of Boone, which is not far from Burnsville.

A celebration in his honor. The Daniel Boone Festival is held in Barbourville, Kentucky, not far from the massive impoundment of the Cumberland River, every year in mid-October.

People of this town of thirty-six hundred turn out to square dance, blast muskets, and saw away, mountain-style, on their fiddles. Men grow beards and wear coonskin caps (even though Boone himself favored a broad-brimmed hat). Women cook up special southern feasts.

For details contact the Chamber of Commerce, Barbourville 40906.

More Booneiana. At Pilot Knob, near Winchester, Kentucky, a marker commemorates the spot from which Boone first viewed "the beautiful level of Kentucky."

In Frankfort, Kentucky, you'll find Boone's grave and that of his wife Rebecca, at the Frankfort Cemetery, on East Main Street.

In Boone, North Carolina, another outdoor drama is presented, this one written by Kermit Hunter about the pioneers' move west. For information write "Horn in the West," Box 295,

Boone, North Carolina 28607. Request information also about other sites in this beautiful mountainous region. Winchester, Kentucky, a residential town just east of Lexington, is the site of a reconstruction of Boone's second settlement in Kentucky, the one at the other end of the Wilderness Road. Costumed craft workers installed in log block houses and log cabins demonstrate the making of candles, brooms, kegs, pottery, soap, dolls, and other pioneer playthings and necessities; you can buy the output nearby. Some of the other cabins contain original pioneer furniture. For details write Fort Boonesborough State Park, Route 5, Richmond, Kentucky 40475.

Another Kentucky Explorer

Actually, it was Dr. Thomas Walker who led the first expedition through the

Cumberland Gap. He named the Cumberland River and was the first English colonist to systematically explore Kentucky and record what he found. You'll encounter his name again and again as you travel through the region.

Who was he? Born in 1715, a surgeon by profession, he lived in Virginia. Castle Hill, near Charlottesville, was his home—and a very elegant home at that, with lovely moldings and polished floors. The boxwood around the house is among the tallest in the world. For information about this and other interesting houses to be seen around Charlottesville, contact the Charlottesville and Albemarle County Chamber of Commerce, Box 1564, Charlottesville, Virginia 22902.

How We Peopled the Continent: Settlements and Immigration

The Spanish: The United States' First Permanent Settlement

In few other lands was the Spanish reputation for cruelty more justified than on the northeast coast of Florida around St. Augustine. The region's governor, Don Pedro Menendez de Aviles, under orders to destroy a nearby French Huguenot settlement, slaughtered some three hundred men, women, and children; the nearby River of Dolphins was subsequently called Matanzas, Spanish for "slaughters."

But this colony—whose founding in 1565 makes it the oldest permanent settlement in the United States—stayed under the Spanish Crown until 1821. Although there was almost constant friction during that time, quite a genteel civilization grew up.

Much of that civilization, almost as serene as it was in those less populated times, is up for viewing in today's St. Augustine, a town of about fifteen thousand. The story of the Spanish settlement is told at the local visitor center—a good spot to begin your St. Augustine stay—and at an outdoor musical drama called *Cross and Sword*, Florida's official state play.

The Castillo de San Marcos, which protected St. Augustine over the years, has been restored to much the same condition in which you would have

found it in the late seventeenth century, when it was constructed. Most of the blocks of which it was built—made of coquina, a sort of cement formed naturally by tiny clams called donax—survived numerous sackings, burnings, raids, and wars. You can see how strong coquina is when you watch the rangers from the National Park Service, the agency responsible for maintaining the Castillo, give their daily cannon-firing demonstration. When that cannon blasts, you know it.

When you've had your glimpse into those good old days, you can walk across the soft grass, cross a road, and, at a restoration/re-creation of Spanish Colonial St. Augustine, see how the civilians lived. The houses are whitewashed, plain but comfortable nonetheless. In one, there is only a single chair—and it was for the men, not the women. Then there are some craftspeople—a silversmith, who turns out silver spoons using crucibles and hammers and all manner of intriguing equipment; a harnessmaker; a saddler; a potter—and a cigarmaker, a wizened old fellow who can roll those smokes almost faster than you can blink. He is a great talker—provided, that is, you speak to him in Spanish. Then there's the weaver, who collects fur from her friends' dogs, cats, pigs, and ponies, then washes it and spins it into yarn that she subsequently weaves into cloth. She'll show you samples, and if

she's weaving or spinning when you arrive, she's happy to let you have a try. Indeed, of all the restoration complexes you are likely to encounter, this is among the best, not just because of the considerable variety of crafts demonstrated, but also because of the craftspeople's knowledgeability and friendliness.

Outside the restored area, there are a number of other historic sites to see—among them the ancient dwelling that is St. Augustine's oldest house, with its wonderfully fragrant garden, and the surprise-upon-surprise Lightner Museum—installed in the halls, ballrooms, baths, and chambers of one of Henry Morrison Flagler's grand but long-dead railroad hotels. The St. Augustine Alligator Farm is among the tourist attractions you will *not* want to skip. It's amusing if for no other reason than that alligators are strange and fascinating creatures, and here they're shown off en masse, along with an ungainly ostrich.

The beaches here are long and wide, and when you drive out of town a short distance, they're uncrowded as well. As for the town, it's a relatively peaceful place, compared with some of Florida's bigger tourist cities, and its age gives it a patina that not many other beach resorts in the state can match.

For more information write the St. Augustine Chamber of Commerce, 10

Castillo Drive, St. Augustine, Florida 32084.

A French Connection

It was in 1564 that French Huguenots led by René de Laudonniere established their settlement on the St. Johns River in northeast Florida. It lasted less than two years—partially because the French did not learn to plant and cultivate their own crops but relied instead on the Indians to do the work. The Indians didn't appreciate the responsibility one bit—and made life miserable for the French with their complaints. However, the major reason for the failure of the settlement was the arrival of Don Pedro Menendez de Aviles, a religious zealot who, under orders from the Spanish king, executed several hundred French Protestants, and that, more or less, was the end of that. Now, though, the fort that the French built before the Spaniard's arrival (triangular, with walls made of dirt and wood, enclosing houses thatched with palms) has been re-created by the National Park Service as part of the Fort Caroline National Memorial. The setting on the river makes for a pleasant visit. The history, certainly, is sobering. For details on a visit to the area write to the Fort Caroline National Memorial, c/o the Castillo de San Marcos National Monument, 1 Castillo Drive, St. Augustine, Florida 32084; the St. Augustine Chamber of Commerce, 10 Castillo Drive, St. Augustine, Florida 32084; and the Jacksonville Area Chamber of Commerce, Drawer 329, Jacksonville, Florida 32201.

A First for the French

The first European settlement on the Atlantic Coast north of Florida was at what is now the St. Croix National Monument, in the middle of the St. Croix River, near Calais, Maine. Samuel de Champlain—who was the first governor of French Canada—settled on Dochet's Island in the winter of 1604. You can see the island from the high point of Route 127 five and a half miles from St. Andrews, New Brunswick, which is across the river from Calais. The next winter, Champlain settled—unhappily—on the island of St. Croix, after which the river was subsequently named. The island's sandy soil wouldn't support a garden, fresh water had to be brought from the mainland after the spring dried up, and as winter set in and the river froze, the settlers couldn't get across to their wood lots, their gardens, or their water supplies. Thirty-five of the seventy settlers died of scurvy. Today when you visit the island—you need your own boat to get there—you can see the depressions that marked the graves of the half who succumbed. "Winter in

this country," wrote Champlain, "lasts six months."

For details about the monument write the Superintendent, c/o Acadia National Park, Box 338, Bar Harbor, Maine 04609.

Play it Again, Sam

Having failed at St. Croix and before that at Fort Caroline, the French, in the person of Samuel de Champlain, tried again to establish a settlement in the New World in 1605.

This one was at Port Royal, and this one took hold, so that by 1632 new settlers were arriving from France by the boatload. Champlain set up L'Ordre de Bon Temps, a social club whose members spent their days preparing ever more extravagant feasts for each other. That good times, the aim of the club if we're to believe the name, were had by all cannot be doubted, as the club is still in existence today. To qualify for membership, you need only stay three days in Nova Scotia, the province in which Port Royal, the first permanent settlement north of the Gulf of Mexico, is located. To join, you simply register at entry-exit points with any of the province's travel information offices.

The story of the Port Royal settlement, and of the province as a whole and the constant battle between the French and the English for control, is told at the Fort Anne National Historic Park at Annapolis Royal, the first provincial capital. On display are relics, mostly French, from that earliest seventeenth century civilization; English objects from the eighteenth century; and Acadian exhibits that tell the unhappy tale of the persecution of that particular group of farmers. Not far away, Champlain's settlement has been re-created as Port Royal National Historic Park. The banquet rooms where the good times were enjoyed is open for tours, as are the chapel, bakery, kitchen, blacksmith studio, artisans' workshops, and the room in which Indians traded furs with the French. The guides can tell you all manner of amusing stories about those fascinating times. For further information contact the Nova Scotia Department of Tourism, Hollis Building, Halifax, Nova Scotia B3J 2R5.

Quebec—That Wonderful Walled City

Founded in 1608 by Samuel Champlain, fresh from his good times at Port

Royal, the city of Quebec missed being the oldest settlement in North America by a couple of years. Jamestown and St. Augustine, among others, preceded it.

But it's one of those amusing accidents of history, a grace note on the theme of city development, that Quebec, more than any of the others, grew up like a city of the continent of its founders. Each century's new buildings sprouted around the structures of the preceding centuries, never displacing the old but instead co-existing with it. Consequently Quebec gives you the feeling of being in a very old city far more strongly than some other communities that are actually older.

Wherever you go there is something old, and interesting, to see—and one of the nice things about the city is that you don't always have to go out of your way to get to them. Buildings with history that would put them, in other towns, at the top of the tourist's must-see list are commonplace in Quebec.

Many of the older buildings—which were originally palaces and government buildings—are being restored and reconstructed as part of an elaborate program aimed at turning La Place Royale in the Lower Town (the part of Quebec at the base of the promontory that made the city's location so strategic throughout history) into a vital neighborhood that is part museum, part Ghirardelli Square, with shops and eateries installed in the ancient buildings.

And there are plenty of other things to see. To find out more, write the Direction Générale du Tourisme, Cité Parlementaire, Quebec City, Quebec GIR 2B2.

The English

England Loses a Colony

That the Roanoke Colony, the first English settlement in Virginia, disappeared without a trace was one of the strange accidents of history.

Governor John White, who had gone back to England to stock up on provisions, wasn't able to return to Virginia as soon as he had planned: England was in imminent danger of invasion by the Spanish Armada. He kept a stiff upper lip about it, because he really had no choice; the Queen, after all, was the Queen, and Virginia was her colony. But when he finally did touch the Virginia shores again, three years after his departure, he found the houses of his settlement taken down, a fortlike palisade set up, and the letters CROATOAN carved on a post at its entrance—indicating that the settlers would be found on Croatan Island (most of today's Ocracoke and part of Hatteras Island) or among the friendly

Croatoan Indians farther inland. However, a string of storms and other mishaps forced White to return to England without searching for the members of the Roanoke Colony (among them Virginia Dare, White's granddaughter, and the first English child born in the New World), and they were lost forever. Jamestown subsequently became England's first entry into the race to claim North America by squatter's rights.

In the visitor center at the reconstructed Fort Raleigh, a National Historic Site, the story is told through artifacts found in a 1947–48 archaeological excavation; you hear the tale somewhat more romantically in an outdoor drama by Paul Green, *The Lost Colony*, shown in the Waterside Theater at the National Historic Site.

The setting—across Roanoke Sound from Kill Devil Hills, Kitty Hawk, and Cape Hatteras' seemingly endless beaches and immense dunes—would make a visit pleasant even if there had been no colony at all to think back on. The natives—motel desk clerks, local business people, and especially the commercial fishermen—still speak with a vague English accent, and, on occasion, use phrases like "I'm much obleeged ter ye fer actin' in such a claphat manner," meaning "Thanks for hurrying."

For information about Hatteras and Fort Raleigh write the Superintendent at Box 457, Manteo, North Carolina 27954; the Dare County Tourist Bureau, Manteo, North Carolina 27954; and the Outer Banks Chamber of Commerce, Box 202, Kitty Hawk, North Carolina 27949.

For information about the drama write Box 68, Manteo, North Carolina 27954.

"We let fall our Grapnel neere the shore, & sounded with a trumpet a Call, & afterwardes many familiar English tunes of Songs, and called to them friendly; but we had no answere."

—Governor John White,
upon arriving at Roanoke Island, 1590

The Queen's First Success

"The fifteenth of June we had built and finished our Fort, which was triangle-wise, having three Bulwarkes, at every corner, like a halfe moone, and foure or five pieces of artillerie mounted in them."

So wrote George Percy in 1607, on whose diaries, along with those of Captain John Smith, the 1954 reconstruction of the original fort was based. Jamestown Festival Park, twenty-five acres of state-sponsored exhibits, includes more than the fort: there are

replicas of the *Susan Constant*, the *Godspeed*, and the *Discovery* (the three ships in which the colonists crossed the Atlantic) moored at a point about a mile away from the original mooring place (long washed away by tides and storms); an information center; historical exhibits; the remains of an old Indian trail to Williamsburg; and reconstructions of Chief Powhatan's Lodge. The most striking aspect of the fort itself is its authenticity: not only in the wattle-and-daub construction of the ten buildings inside the pine-palisaded fort, and in the costumes of the guides, but in the dirt walkways, even the tobacco, a seventeenth-century strain of which is grown there. The ships, too, are authentic-looking: they are amazingly tiny. How could a group of people keep from jumping down each other's throats when forced into such close quarters?

The real Jamestown. Nothing remains of the actual settlement except the fences, foundations, hedgerows, property ditches, and streets which have been excavated at the Jamestown section of the Colonial National Historical Park, under the auspices of the National Park Service and the Association for the Preservation of Virginia Antiquities. At the Historic Park, which adjoins the Festival Park, you'll see the first landing site and the New Towne, into which Jamestown expanded about thirteen years after its founding, and, perhaps most impressive of all, the Glasshouse, where craftspeople make glass as it would have been done at the time. A five-mile drive takes you through the park, much of which is still wonderfully thickly forested.

When the people of Jamestown protested what they took to be England's high-handed way of ruling, they created such havoc that the Crown took away Jamestown's status as capital. As a result, the settlement dwindled away into a ghost town and stayed in that condition until the twentieth century, when heritage seekers finally rediscovered it. Today the whole historic triangle is fascinating—Williamsburg, to which the Virginia capital was moved; Yorktown, site of the famous Revolutionary War battle; and Jamestown. Together they provide a capsule history of England in the New World. For information about planning a visit, write Box 210, Yorktown, Virginia 23490.

Setting the Scene for the First Thanksgiving at Plymouth

The men and women who stepped from the *Mayflower* onto Plymouth Rock on Cape Cod to found Plimouth Plantation were as industrious and capable as John Smith's men and women were unskilled and undisciplined. Yet so great were the hardships of that first winter—not just the cold, but the lack of food and proper clothing—that these God-fearing people came near to dying as well.

The poignant story of that winter—and of the colony's eventual success—is told in a reconstruction of the original Plimouth Plantation two miles south of Plymouth proper. A plain wood stockade surrounds the simple peak-roofed wooden houses. There are far fewer trees here than in lush Virginia, and you can well imagine how cold these clapboard structures must have been—so unprotected, so close to the shore and the frigid blasts of the ocean's winter winds.

Plymouth proper is full of interesting historic sites, not the least of which is the storied rock itself—an unprepossessing-looking boulder just like any other but for its cloistered surroundings. At the Greek Revival-style Pilgrim Hall Museum, built in 1824, you can see some of the Pilgrims' own furniture, bric-a-brac, and other pieces of decorative art. For the rest, there is only one house in Plymouth today which is known to have been occupied by some of the original Pilgrims—John Howland, his wife Elizabeth, and their son Jabez lived for a time in the Howland House at 33 Sandwich Street. You can imagine how the two elderly Pilgrims must have sat close to the great brick fireplace to the right of the entryway in the main room. The *newest* item in the house is the eighteenth-century trapunto Bride's Quilt; there are dozens of older pieces, including seventeenth-century furniture and a seventeenth-century Masonic document.

In all, there are some nine historic sites in Plymouth; combination tickets are available. For information about what to see, write the Plymouth Area Chamber of Commerce, 65 Main Street, Plymouth 02360.

The Massachusetts Department of Commerce & Development (Division of Tourism, 100 Cambridge Street, Boston 02202) publishes a 101-mile driving tour, "Presidents and Pilgrims," which takes you to Plymouth, plus JFK's birthplace, the Museum of the American China Trade, the Adams National Historic Site (home of generations of Adamses), and some other interesting coast towns just south of Boston.

Where the Immigrants Landed

Ellis Island, off the shore of New York City, was the first place in America that thousands upon thousands of steerage passengers ever saw.

What was it like?

Allowed to decay for many years, most of the buildings are in bad shape. It's hard to tell what they were once like.

However, you can begin to imagine when you make the tour with guides from the National Park Service, which maintains Ellis Island as a part of the Statue of Liberty National Monument. You can catch boats for Ellis Island next to those for the Statue of Liberty (which occupies another island in New York Harbor).

Soon after you step out of the boat from the mainland, you're herded into the buildings through a snaky set of corridors—without much explanation. You climb a set of stairs into a huge tiled hall where benches are arranged, schoolroom fashion. The guide then puts a cassette into his tape player, and turns up the volume. The room sounds as if it's full of the tired, the poor, the huddled masses—and they sound frantic.

Subsequently, the setup is explained. The hall was the first room the immigrants entered. Opposite the doorway at the top of the stairs, across the room, sat a panel of observers. The sick and the crippled always had trouble with the climb up the staircase. Their infirmities would be detected, and they'd be shipped home. A variety of other tables, manned with immigration officers and doctors, awaited the immigrants, few of whom could speak English, and made for an altogether bewildering experience.

Today walls of the corridors are full of scaling paint and peeling plaster; the buildings look almost as if the occupants packed up and left in a hurry. There are a few big old desks and some kitchen equipment but not much else to see. Yet a tour of Ellis Island is something you don't want to miss.

For further information about getting there, contact the Superintendent at 26 Wall Street, New York, New York 10005.

"Remember, please, that you and I are descended from immigrants and revolutionists."
  —Franklin D. Roosevelt,
     to D.A.R. members and others
     visiting Hyde Park

America's Biggest Pin-up Girl

The symbol of the nation, unveiled on October 28, 1886, has some impressive vital statistics.

She's 35 feet around the waist, weighs 225,000 pounds; is 305 feet tall. Her hand is 16 feet, 5 inches long; her index finger is 8 feet long. Her head is 10 feet across, her mouth 3 feet wide. Two hundred thousand pounds of copper—enough to make a hundred piles of pennies, each one the height of the Empire State Building—went into making her.

Why can't tourists go up into the right arm? Because the balcony around the torch holds only twelve people; there would be lines—and complaints—ad nauseum. The only way up is a narrow 45-foot-high ladder.

The Statue of Liberty is maintained by the National Park Service. For information about the monument, write the Superintendent at 26 Wall Street, New York, New York 10005.

Gold! and Other Natural Resources. How They Changed History and Where You Can See the Evidence

How They Settled Skagway

When you think that on August 14, 1896, three men working Rabbit Creek in what is now the Klondike discovered gold between some flaky slabs of rock "like cheese in a sandwich," and that a boat sailing from this same area carried a score of prospectors and hundreds of thousands of dollars worth of gold into San Francisco—it won't be tough to imagine the wild and woolly times of the area's first settlements.

The Skagway Story, by Howard Clifford, relates some of the more fantastic stories—the story about the gold discovery itself, about the ship arriving in Seattle with its "ton of gold," the lawlessness and the unpopular Soapy Smith, the hard times and courage of Captain William Moore, prospector, riverboat captain, packer, and trader, who believed in the mineral wealth of the Yukon before it was ever discovered, and who traveled a rough 700 miles to get the message about the discovery to Juneau, where it could be transmitted to Ottawa and the Canadian government, which had requested the information. Amazingly, the tales of the enormous wealth were met with indifference for a while. *The Skagway Story* tells of the hotel, the women, the entertainers, the mailmen, the storekeepers, the claim-jumpers. It is full of stories—and pictures, which are fascinating. If you're going to the area, you ought to get it and look it over before you go. Alaska Northwest Publishing Company, Box 4-EEE, Anchorage, Alaska 99509; $4.95

Boom Towns, Ghost Towns, What They Were Like and Where to Find Them

"Every land on earth, every period of time, has known its deserted villages, but only the Western United States has propagated them in wholesale quantities. Sired by hope and suckled on honest labor, they were cities that flourished for a day, and faded, and were forgotten . . . .

"Into remote lands, that for untold centuries had known only sage-brush and jack rabbits, suddenly would be flooding a tidal wave of seething humanity—prospectors, mining engineers, surveyors, opportunists, longline skinners, faro dealers, tradesmen, painted women of the night, bullwhackers, saloonkeepers, assayists, Chinese, Indians, Cousin Jacks, Yankees, Chileans, Mexicans—a roaring deluge drawn from every mining camp between Sonora and British Columbia and all bound for the same destination—the same Poor Man's Paradise! Jostling, shoving, boasting, quarreling, cursing, exhibiting ore samples and assay certificates, buying and selling 'mines' without ever laying eyes on the property, fighting to purchase flour at $75 a sack and bacon at $3 a pound—fighting for a chance to pay a dollar a night for a pair of dirty blankets and space on the ground to roll them. That was your mining stampede—a typically Western extravaganza, repeated over and over again, for a period of more than sixty years."

Nell Murbarger, who made these comments in *Ghosts of the Glory Trail*, has more to say, all of it lively and engrossing. She talks about the people she met when, drawn to ghost towns like fat people to a refrigerator, she prowled the hills of the Great Basin states—Nevada, Utah—looking for boom towns that went bust. "That it has been my privilege to salvage a few crumbs of that . . . rich history is one of the great satisfactions of my life," she writes. It's a privilege to read what she has to say, too. Desert Printers, Palm Desert, California 92260; $7.00.

Gold Rush Country

The towns and villages that the California argonauts left behind them clung to life for a long time—by the fingernails. Recently, Californians have been getting nostalgic about this epochmaking backyard of theirs, and in much the same way that eastern sightseers beeline to New England come the weekend, Californians seek out their gold country. Fancy restaurants and interesting eateries flourish, along with boutiques, antique shops, country inns, and such. There's enough to see and do to fill a book—several, in fact, have been filled.

One of the best, though, is Sunset's *Gold Rush Country*. Each of the three chapters devoted to the Southern Mines, the Central Mother Lode, and the Northern Mines centers around one town in which you can find accommodations. You're then brought up to date on museums and historic sites, old cemeteries, ghost towns, and the like in the area. This is one of Lane Publishing's most popular efforts, and it's now in its fourth edition—so what you find is reasonably up-to-date. However, if you go into an area specifically to visit one attraction, it's always a good idea to call ahead to make sure of its opening and closing hours and to verify the fact that what

Intimate glimpses into the past and present of 275 Western Ghosttowns by NELL MURBARGER

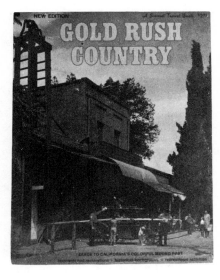

you're going to see is still there. If you can't get a copy in your bookstore, write Lane Publishing, Menlo Park, California 94025; $2.95.

Some More Good Ghost-Town Yarns

The prospect of getting rich quick never failed to rouse men's passions. Their hopes or their fortunes soaring, they'd celebrate; and since they'd usually celebrate with whiskey, the celebration would usually end with a fight. Fights might lead to feuds, feuds to murders.

Writers have not been able to leave the subject alone, and there are dozens of books—some guides, some histories. Here are a few:

Mining Camps and Ghost Towns, by Frank Love (Westernlore Publishers, Box 41073, Los Angeles, California 90041; $7.95). This is a history of min-

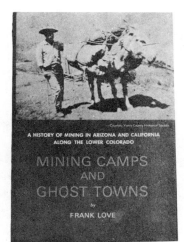

ing in Arizona and California.

Ghost Towns and Mining Camps of New Mexico, by James E. and Barbara H. Sherman, is an 8½ x 11 paperback, full of fascinating photographs of the towns and their citizens in the good old days and snapshots of today's towns. There are also reproductions of clippings and advertisements from the old newspapers such as "UNDERTAKING! A.T. GRITT & CO. (Successors to W. J. Olinger.) Experienced Embalmers. A Complete Stock of Coffins, Caskets, Etc. Leave orders with CERRILOS SUPPLY CO. Thos. P. Gable Mg'r." or "THE CERRILOS HOUSE? RE-OPENED. The Old Man at Home July st, ready for Business. I ask my old customers to call and give me another trial. I will try and do the square thing by all . . . " or "DICK MATHEWS, Has now opened out in his new building in Cerrilos, with a fine stock of Milwaukee Beer, Golden Wedding Old Bourbon and Rye Whiskies, And Pure Blackberry Brandy, The attention of the public is called to the superiority of this stock. . . " The pictures and clips make this one of the livelier of the genre. University of Oklahoma Press, 1005 Asp Avenue, Norman, Oklahoma 73069; $5.95.

Old War Games: 1776, 1812, 1863

Where It All Began

Boston has never been a tear-it-down town, and for that reason, if for no other, most of the historic sites connected with the Revolution are still standing—along with dozens of others that are not particularly historic, merely old.

The Freedom Trail, a 1½-mile-long walking tour marked with signs and mapped out on brochures that are available at visitors' centers on the Boston Common, takes you through some of the handsomest of the town's old red-brick neighborhoods to nearly two dozen structures that you've probably been reading about in one way or other ever since you were a kid—Faneuil Hall, the Cradle of Liberty where Boston hotheads met to argue their grievances; the site of the Boston Massacre, where British troops fired on one of the angry mobs that seemed to be their lot; the Old South Meeting House, the site of the meeting that preceded the Boston Tea Party; Paul Revere's House and the Old North Church, from whose windows two lanterns signaled the arrival of British troops. And that's only the beginning of what there is in Boston.

For details write the Greater Boston

Convention & Tourist Bureau, 900 Boylston Street, Boston, Massachusetts 02115. The office also sells the *Official Bicentennial Guidebook* ($1.50 plus 50c for postage and handling). Though published in 1975, the book contains excellent sightseeing information—for staying on the beaten path or for straying from it.

A Replay of History's Most Savage Tea Party

"Boston Harbor a teapot tonight!" whooped the Indians—who were, according to John Adams a little later, "no ordinary Mohawks—depend on it."

History knows the truth of it, and you'll know how it felt to throw tea overboard when you visit the Boston Tea Party Ship and Museum on Congress Street Bridge on Fort Point Channel in Boston, where, in addition to exhibits and artifacts that explain the whys and the wherefores of that party, you can take your turn at throwing a tea chest overboard.

The best way to get there is on foot, as the Indians did, from Old South Meeting House. Follow the Tea Party Path—Milk Street, Post Office Square, then Congress Street. For Boston information, write the Greater Boston Convention & Tourist Bureau, 900 Boylston Street, Boston 02115.

Paul Revere's Best Bell

"The sweetest bell we ever made," Paul Revere inscribed on the bell of King's Chapel, Boston—the oldest Anglican Church in New England and, as of 1785, the first Unitarian Church in America. The bell tolls every Sunday at 11 A.M. and at noon on Wednesdays.

The church, built in the mid-eighteenth century, is a handsome structure inside. The pews are enclosed, originally to keep drafts off the parishioners. In the churchyard is the grave of the woman after whom Nathaniel Hawthorne modeled Hester Prynne, heroine of the *Scarlet Letter*.

"The happy, the peaceful, the elegant, the hospitable, and polite city of Philadelphia . . ."

—John Adams

Philadelphia, 1776

They call it the nation's most historic square mile, and perhaps it is: the Declaration of Independence was adopted there; the Continental Congress met there, as did the Constitutional Convention of 1787. The city was also the nation's capital from 1790 to 1800.

But Philadelphia is fascinating to visit for another reason: a $2 billion refurbishment program has left Congress Hall, the Old City Hall, Independence Hall, and Carpenters'

Hall—and the neighborhood around them—in pristine shape. There's a new mall area near Independence Hall, and the Liberty Bell is displayed in a handsome new pavilion there. Philadelphia isn't the city it was when Washington, Jefferson, and Franklin confabulated along its avenues. But the cobblestone streets, the pedimented doorways, and white-corniced windows of the red-brick buildings make you feel as close to the past as you ever will in such a metropolis.

Independence Hall, especially, is good for goose bumps: if a building can be said to have charisma, this one does, and you're bound to be moved at the sight of those dark wooden tables in the first-floor Assembly Room where the Declaration of Independence was signed. You can see the inkwell in which the pens were dipped to sign it and the chair from which Washington presided during the signing of the U.S. Constitution. The Liberty Bell will affect you as well: you can even run your fingers along the crack.

For details about the park, write the Superintendent at 313 Walnut Street, Philadelphia 19106; for information about the many other fascinating things to see and do, write the Convention and Tourist Bureau, 1525 John F. Kennedy Boulevard, Philadelphia 19102.

Betsy Ross Stitched the Flag Here

Washington, Robert Morris, and some other august members of a secret committee from the Continental Congress visited the Philadelphia seamstress and upholsterer in her home at 239 Arch Street some time in 1776 or 1777; asked her to sketch designs for a flag featuring six-pointed stars; were persuaded to take five-pointers (which are easier to cut); and accepted the design for the banner that was subsequently unfurled at the Battle of Cooch's Bridge, the war's only Delaware skirmish—or so goes the story that Ross' grandson, William Canby, re-

peated in 1870. There's not much documentation, and the truth of the matter is still open to question. But the house is interesting to visit anyway for the assorted Betsy Ross memorabilia displayed there. Ross's grave is in the garden.

For details about the many other Philadelphia historic sites, contact the Convention and Tourist Bureau, 1525 John F. Kennedy Boulevard, Philadelphia 19102.

Benedict Arnold's March to Quebec

Following his 194-mile route through Maine, you take in some of the area's most magnificent scenery. Starting at Fort Popham, on the coast near Boothbay Harbor, you travel along the Kennebec River through Augusta, Fort Halifax in Winslow (probably the oldest blockhouse in the United States), Skowhegan, Solon, and northwards, through the Maine woods and mountains. The trip is especially scenic in the fall, which is when Arnold did it in 1775. His route is marked along the way with plaques that tell the story of the march. For maps, write the Maine State Development Office, State House, Augusta 04333.

The Lair of the Swamp Fox

To visit Snow's Island, the landfall from which General Francis Marion struck at the British and the Tories, follow U.S. 378 nine miles east of Kingsburg, South Carolina, turn right at the historical marker, and proceed five miles south on a dirt road to the Pee Dee River. You can cross to the island, opposite, only if you have a boat. In fact, you many not even be able to get as far as the river bank, since the dirt road is often flooded. Snow's Island is almost as inaccessible today as it was during the eighteenth century.

To find out more about the area as a whole, contact the South Carolina Department of Parks, Recreation, and Tourism, Box 133, Edgar A. Brown Building, Columbia 29201.

Washington's Worst Winter

Valley Forge.

It's just a name in a history book, or, when you visit the area, it's a park made up of some exceptionally lovely tip-tilted fields and some woods full of flowering trees that turn the place into a pink-and-white fairyland in the spring.

Faced by such scenes, you'll find it hard to imagine the suffering that Washington's eleven thousand men endured here during the winter of 1777-78. But a special tape tour, which you can rent at the information desk in the park, will fill you in on the tale, with excerpts from the soldiers' letters and diaries.

Already demoralized by defeats at Brandywine, Paoli, and Germantown, they were also hungry, badly clothed, scarcely trained. Until they snatched wood from the surrounding farms and built huts, there was no shelter—nor were there any hospitals. Even when the huts were completed, there was not much comfort: they were rude, smoky, crowded. Twelve men were packed into each tiny hut. No new clothing arrived. The snow, the voice on the tape tells you, was red with the blood of these early Americans' footprints. There was not much food, but lots of disease: smallpox, typhus, typhoid, pneumonia. Men froze to death.

All in all, not a happy story—but then no tale concerned with war ever is.

There are many other fascinating historical sites in the area to which this Valley Forge tour need be only a footnote: there are gardens, picnic grounds, tiny shopping villages, crafts marketplaces. For information about the area, contact the Montgomery County Convention and Visitors Bureau, Court House, Norristown, Pennsylvania 19404.

How They Fought in the Revolution

Every year, on weekends between April and November, a group of fourteen hundred men from all parts of the eastern United States get together to play soldier, Revolutionary War style, at encampments staged by the Brigade of the American Revolution, of which they're all members.

The authenticity of these get-togethers is positively staggering: the Billopp's Corps, a unit from Staten Island that is one of 104 that belong to the Brigade, wears not red but green, because the Crown questioned the allegiance of these Loyalists; members of the American Morgan Rifle Corps, who were sharpshooters and scouts, wear flat-brimmed hats instead of tricorns—to keep the sun from their eyes. When the units get ready to shoot, they go through fourteen steps, the very steps that the soldiers of the Revolution learned from Friedrich Wilhelm von Steuben, who called himself a baron (though he wasn't) but who, as a Prussian, was most effective at turning the ragtag group of men that Washington brought to Valley Forge into a fighting army that could meet the British on equal terms. At these encampments, even the fighting is authentic: cannons boom as loudly as they did during the Revolution; lines of soldiers creep forward; volleys are fired in unison, which was the custom of the day; and drummers and fifers beat the pace and the direction of the movements. There are casualties: men fall to the ground and writhe in agony. At the end, a white flag is waved, and a conference between British and American officers determines the victor.

It's all very amusing to watch, and

tells better than any static exhibit anywhere the story of warfare during the American Revolution.

Visiting these encampments is interesting for other reasons. The men who belong to the brigade do it because history fascinates them: all the outfits and movements have been carefully researched, and when you engage them in conversation you can learn some pretty interesting things about the period. Quite a few members bring the whole family, so around the grounds you encounter mobcapped wives stitching quilts or doll clothes or darning socks in the manner of eighteenth-century ladies; or youngsters writing lessons with quill pens or playing with antique toys such as the cup and ball. You can also see cooking done over open fires with strange utensils the uses of which will be explained to you.

For a schedule of where the Brigade of the American Revolution will be at any given time, contact the adjutant, Robert C. Showalter, at 32 Douglas Road, Delmer, Delaware 12054.

For more information about appearances of the First Maryland Regiment, which does much the same thing, contact the Maryland Department of Economic and Community Development, Tourism Division, 1748 Forest Drive, Annapolis, Maryland 21401.

The End That Was a Beginning

At Yorktown, Cornwallis was caught between the French naval forces at sea and the American forces under Washington on land. Besieged for eight days, the English general requested terms. That was 1781.

Today, the battlefield, part of the Colonial National Historical Park, is crossed by roads leading to the various encampment areas; markers and displays along the way help you visualize the action, which is well explained at the outset at the Visitor Center.

For details write the park superintendent in Yorktown, Virginia 23490.

"The Distinctions between Virginians, Pennsylvanians, New Yorkers, and New Englanders are no more. I am not a Virginian, but an American."
—Patrick Henry,
opening statement of
the First Continental
Congress

What Happened Where in 1776

There are a handful of books and booklets that do a very thorough job of covering the subject.

"Guide to Historic Places of the

American Revolution," published by the Department of the Interior and available for about $2 from the Superintendent of Documents, U.S. Government Printing Office, Washington, D.C. 20402. A state-by-state description, with a bibliography, a chronology, and photos.

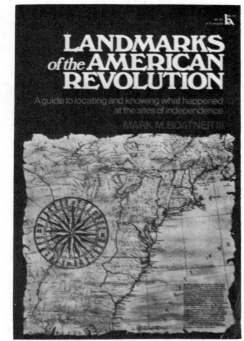

Landmarks of the American Revolution: A Guide to Locating And Knowing What Happened at the Sites of Independence, by Mark M. Boatner III. This impressive tome is meant for the scholar as well as the dilettante: each entry in the state-by-state, town-by-town listing tells the whole story of what happened in the area concerned —there's often more information than you could get at the actual site (for local authorities aren't always up on their Revolutionary War history), so the book makes a good traveling companion. Hawthorne Books, 260 Madison Avenue, New York, New York 10016; $6.95.

Where Francis Scott Key Saw (by the Dawn's Early Light) That the Flag Was Still There

Strategically located on Whetstone Point in the Patapsco River, Fort McHenry—which was ornamented by that famous huge flag stitched by local seamstress Mary Young Pickersgill— was important because it protected Baltimore from attack. The British, fresh from the burning of Washington and the conquering of Napoleon, were itching to get Baltimore, too.

For twenty-five hours they bombarded the fort. The bombs, as Francis Scott Key, a visiting lawyer, wrote, were bursting in air. It was quite something to behold, and even the National Park Service, which now maintains the fort, doesn't try to put on anything to show you what it was like.

Today Fort McHenry is, in fact, a rather peaceful spot, despite its location at the end of a busy highway on either side of which you see all the fixtures of a busy heavy-freight harbor: the fort sits alone in the middle of grassy lawns on a windswept point, and its earthworks give you fine views over the river and the dozens and dozens of boats of all sizes and shapes which always seem to be floating around on it.

Also in Baltimore—which is quite a good town for 1812 history and sightseeing in general: the manuscript, in Key's own hand, of the national anthem (at the modern, fascinating Baltimore Historical Society museum); the Flag House, a tiny but charming place on the fringes of an urban neighborhood that used to be the home of Mary Pickersgill; and the U.S. Frigate *Constellation*, the U.S. Navy's first commissioned ship and the world's oldest ship continuously afloat, interesting for the look she gives into shipboard life of the nineteenth century. For details about things to see and do in Baltimore, and places to eat, contact the Visitor Information Center, 102-104 St. Paul Street, Baltimore 21202.

The Civil War

The Bloodiest Battle in North America

It's Gettysburg. Between July 1 and 3, 1863, 51,000 men were wounded, lost, or gave what Lincoln later called in dedicating the cemetery in which they were buried, "the last full measure of devotion." During the fifty minutes of Pickett's Charge alone, ten thousand of the fifteen thousand involved in the assault became casualties—and that was only one day's slaughter. The Confederate ambulance wagons made a file seventeen miles long as they left Gettysburg.

Except for the monuments and the grave sites, the Gettysburg battlefield looks much as it did in 1863. The fences are there, and the rocks, and the fields and the knobby hills, and even the cannons. But the ground will never again be just any old ground, and you can't help but realize that as you make the tour mapped out on a brochure distributed by the National Park Service, which maintains this National Military Park in southeastern Pennsylvania. At various locations on the battlefield, rangers lead walks and give talks about

what it was like—what the men thought, what the nurses thought, what happened to the civilians. Despite the various wax museums and gift shops that serve to bring you back to the realities of the twentieth century, Gettysburg is a moving experience indeed. For details about the battlefield, write the Superintendent at Gettysburg 17325. To find out more about the town, write the Gettysburg Travel Council, Inc., 35 North Carlisle Street, Gettysburg 17325.

"Vicksburg is the key. . . .The War can never be brought to a close until that key is in our pocket."
—Abraham Lincoln

Vicksburg

The War, as southerners persist in calling the hostilities of the early 1860s, still looms large in the South, and nowhere more than in Vicksburg, Mississippi, a pleasant middle-sized Mississippi River town of hills, green parklands, and fine old mansions nuzzled by boxwood, magnolias, camellias, and a profusion of other plantings which make the town, in the spring, a frothy pink paradise. It is hard to imagine that it has not always been this way, hard to imagine the events of the Civil War, when a hard-pressed U. S. Grant, his military reputation on the line and the fortunes of the Union at stake, laid siege to the community—pounding it with mortar and cannon fire for forty-seven days and nights; sending civilians into hiding in caves dug in the soft soil; driving the Confederate soldiers, who started out on a diet of salt pork and cornmeal, to consume mule meat and ground peas.

The Vicksburg National Military Park and Cemetery—thirteen hundred acres of trees and greenswards—surrounds the town, and it's there you can learn the story of the battle, which is an interesting one and fairly easy to visualize even if you're not usually good at such things. A sixteen-mile drive, mapped out in National Park Service brochures, is well marked with plaques and explanatory signs, and by the time you leave the fields you will certainly understand how the success at Vicksburg cut the South in two and virtually assured a northern victory.

Also to see in Vicksburg: old houses, open to tours, with shrapnel and bits of cannonballs embedded in their walls, or beautiful antebellum antiques.

A Great Civil War Museum

In Vicksburg, Mississippi, look at the Old Court House Museum, a National Historic Landmark. When you realize that the imposing Greek Revival building was constructed with slave labor, that it has thirty columns and one of the oldest clocks still in use in the United States, that it was built with mortar made with sugar for added strength—it's fairly hard to believe that in 1946 there was talk of demolition. However, one Eva Whitaker Davis wrote a radio program and a weekly newspaper column, kept one room of the building open to visitors, and otherwise knocked herself out to keep the building standing, and so it is what you see today. Items in the collection it contains—one of the biggest group-

ings of Civil War memorabilia in the South—were given by friends all over the region and purchased by the Warren County Historical Society, which had been formed to save the building.

What you see: old photographs, one of the largest glass-negative collections extant, of famous steamboats. Wedding gowns and christening dresses dating from 1846. A Vicksburg newspaper from the siege days—printed on wallpaper. A knitted sash that belonged to George Washington and that was subsequently worn by Jefferson Davis. General Grant's chair. A Confederate flag of the Vicksburg Artillery: "Victory or Death," it reads. And countless other fascinating items.

For more information contact the Warren County Tourist Promotion Commission, P. O. Box 709, Vicksburg, Mississippi 39180.

"Events have succeeded one another with disastrous rapidity. One brief month ago we were apparently at the point of success. Lee was in Pennsylvania, threatening Harrisburgh, and even Philadelphia. Vicksburgh seemed to laugh all Grant's efforts to scorn.... Now the picture is just as somber as it was bright then. Lee failed at Gettysburgh.... Vicksburgh . . . capitulated, surrendering thirty-five thousand men and forty-five thousand arms. It seems incredible that human power could effect such a change in so brief a space.... The Confederacy totters to its destruction."

—General Josiah Gorgas,
Confederate Chief of Ordnance,
in his journal

How They Ran the Blockade
Painted the color of the early morning fog, the blockade runners—some two thousand of them between 1861 and 1865—would slip through into the Confederate harbor protected by Fort Fisher, near Wilmington, North Carolina. They would bring silks, brandies, rifles, wool, and ammunition to the South, then head back to Nassau, Mexico, Cuba, or Bermuda, laden with cotton.

Relics of the three hundred or so that didn't make it through the blockade, dredged up from the harbor, are on display at the Blockade Runner Museum, one mile north of Carolina Beach, North Carolina. The project of a retired Wilmington textile executive who had spent his childhood listening to the blockade runners reminisce, the Blockade Runner Museum contains a forty-foot diorama of Fort Fisher which, with changing lights, smoke, and a taped narration, gives you the story of the bombardment to which the Fort finally succumbed: Union troops fired some fifty thousand shells to the

South's three thousand five hundred.

The real Fort Fisher, a State Historic Site about five miles south of the Blockade Runner Museum, is open for tours. You can also visit any number of wonderful gardens, including those at Orton Plantation, in Wilmington, or just enjoy the sands of Carolina Beach. For information about the area, contact the Wilmington Chamber of Commerce, P. O. Drawer 330, Wilmington 28401.

A Club for the Civil War
The Round Table brings together students of Lincoln, the Civil War, and the Reconstruction once a month for dinner meetings at which some special Civil War-era scholar gives a talk. For a four-day period (Thursday through Sunday) each May, there are battlefield tours with special speakers, banquets, and good guides. Dues are $10 annually, but you don't have to be a member to join the activities. For further information contact Arnold Gates at the Lincoln Herald, 289 New Hyde Park Road, Garden City, New York 11530.

More about the Civil War
The U.S. Government Printing Office makes its contribution to the wealth of information published on the subject. Most of the pamphlets are inexpensive and deal with various national historic sites, battlefields, and so on. Examples: "Andersonville: the Story of a Civil War Prison Camp," "Antietam National Battlefield Site," and "John Brown's Raid."

To find out what's available, write for the Civil War bibliography. The Government Printing Office's address is Washington, D.C. 20402.

The Largest All-Masonry Fortification in the Western World

Garden Key, one of seven in the Dry Tortugas islands, seventy miles west of Key West, seems a strange place to put a fortification like this one, but the location was strategic, and so work proceeded—for nearly thirty years. The fort was abandoned before it was finished, but not before it had seen some action: Union troops occupied it during the Civil War and Samuel Mudd was imprisoned here for setting John Wilkes Booth's broken leg.

The islands today are spectacular—isolated, almost barren, except for the variety of animal and bird life, including frigate birds and terns, who nest on nearby Bush Key from May to September. For more information about the islands write the Superintendent of Fort Jefferson National Monument, c/o Everglades National Park, Box 279, Homestead, Florida 33030; there you can also get information about getting

to the islands, accessible only by charter boat or plane.

The War (and Peace) Machine: The Pentagon Is Just Another Office Building

America's defense machinery has evolved from that ragtag lot who followed George Washington to Valley Forge into a well-oiled piece of bureaucratic machinery. Tours of the Pentagon, which have been available ever since the Bicentennial, show you just how well oiled it is—like any other office, this has its strengths and its weaknesses, except that the Pentagon has more of each simply because it is so big. The Pentagon, a mile around, is the world's largest office building. The Capitol would fit in any one side. There are seventeen and a half miles of hallways, navigated by 23,000 office workers. There are cruise missiles, paintings by Norman Rockwell, Peter Hurd and others, flags of the states and the territories, even a Union Jack—but it is still an office building, and for that reason if for no other, the Pentagon offers an interesting glimpse of the government. If you'd like to learn more, you can write to the Pentagon Tour Director's Office, Room 3C-1054, The Pentagon, Washington, D.C. 20310, or phone 202/695-1776.

Ideas: Religious and Utopian Settlements

People have been looking for a "better way" since the beginning of time, and Americans are no exception.

Religious and philosophically based utopias sprouted all over the place in the nineteenth century. Some were founded by U.S. citizens, some by immigrants, who, persecuted in their homelands, tried to find their answers in the new nation.

Sometimes they did, but sometimes they didn't and the settlement failed. All of them left marks on their neighborhoods—tales of old-timers, historical markers, or whole restorations of the former villages. The concepts to which these footnotes of history will introduce you are invariably interesting, or at least quaint; most of them are in out-of-the-way places that are fine for unwinding.

An Experiment That Worked

Life in the Amana Colonies in Iowa's Iowa River Valley is not what it used to be: unity of Church and State, communal ownership of the means of production, communal eating facilities, and sharing of all goods and gains—practices instituted by the founders, a Lutheran splinter group called the Community of True Inspiration—were abolished in the 1930s during a drastic reorganization that separated church from state and handed out ownership of the community's property as stock. Nevertheless, the Amana Church Society continues as the religious foundation of the present-day Amanas, and in the seven adjoining villages that make up the Amana Colonies there is still a good deal more feeling of true community—of being one's brother's keeper—than in most other parts of North America.

The story of the Amanas is beautifully told at the Horse Barn Farm Museum in South Amana, where Henry Moore is adding his scale models of the Amanas towns to the display of antique farm implements; at the Amana Heim Museum in the town of Homestead, which was purchased by the commune because of its railroad; and at Heritage House in Amana. At Heritage House, there are exhibits on the making of calico and soap, pottery, ice-cutting, bookbinding, basketry, woodworking, winemaking, and gardening—all traditional Amana industries. There are also exhibits of handwork, antique toys, and heirlooms of Amana families. There are exhibits in an old Amana doctor's washhouse and woodshed, and in the Amana Village Schoolhouse. All seven towns boast interesting shops where the woolens, baked goods, meats and sausages, and other Amana products are sold; there are quaint and personable restaurants; and you can tour the Amana Refrigeration plant, where they make microwave ovens, refrigerators, freezers, air conditioners, dehumidifiers, and even trash compacters—all the modern labor-saving devices you would not expect to find associated with the colony. For more information about the town, contact the Amana Colonies Travel Council, Amana, Iowa 52203.

Utopia on the Wabash

New Harmony, Indiana, in the southern part of the state close to the confluence of the Wabash and Ohio Rivers, is another one of those sleepy small towns with a past. Built in 1814 by the German followers of one Father George Rapp, it was for many years an industrial center on the frontier: the Harmonists, who lived in snug brick and clapboard houses, shipped whiskey, beer, food, and other goods. After eleven years, the Rappites sold the entire settlement, lock stock and barrel, to Robert Owen, a Welsh industrialist who believed that education was the key to all earthly happiness, and who, therefore, established America's first kindergarten, trade school, free coeducational public school system, free library, and women's club. But the people of Owen's New Harmony were intellectuals, not workers, and the settlement floundered. Owen went back to England. But some of the settlers stayed on and left descendants. In the 1940s, Mrs. Jane Owens, the wife of one of them, began using her father's legacy to good use to restore the buildings in her husband's hometown, and today when you visit you'll find quite a few open to tours, with guides to explain what went on. The ideas behind the settlement are high-flown—they may or may not interest you. But the town itself, right on the Wabash River, is really charming, and museums like the Workingman's Institute, upstairs from the public library, have curious exhibits like an eight-legged calf first shown at a turn-of-the-century county fair. There are some gift shops along Main Street, two really fine restaurants, and one of the nicest modern hostelries anywhere, the New Harmony Inn. For more information, write the New Harmony Visitor Center, Church Street, New Harmony, Indiana 47631.

Why the Mormons Went to Salt Lake City

"Ascending the upper Mississippi in the autumn, when the waters were low, I was compelled to travel by land past the region of the Rapids. . . . My eye wearied to see everywhere sordid vagabonds, and idle settlers, a country marred, without being improved, by their careless hands. I was descending the last hillside upon my journey when a landscape in delightful contrast broke upon my view. Half encircled by a bend of the river, a beautiful city lay glittering in the fresh morning sun; its bright, new dwellings, set in cool green gardens, ranging up around a stately dome-shaped hill, which was covered by a noble marble edifice, whose high tapering spire was radiant with white and gold. The city appeared to cover several miles; and beyond it, in the background, there rolled off a fair country, chequered by the careful lines of fruitful industry. The unmistakable marks of industry, enterprise, and educated wealth everywhere made the scene one of singular and most striking beauty."

—Colonel Thomas Kane,
U.S. Army, upon
seeing Nauvoo, Illinois

Nauvoo, the town that so impressed Colonel Kane, was at one time larger than Chicago; it was as grand a place as he surmised. Yet by the next year, the Mormons, whose settlement it was, were gone. They left in a hurry—some dishes were found on tables with the food uneaten—under pressure from jealous fellow settlers, disappointed get-rich-quick types who made the Mormons their scapegoats and who had murdered Joseph Smith, the religion's founder and leader, in Carthage, Missouri, on the other side of the river.

Most of the houses of nineteenth-century Nauvoo were made of wood—wood brought down from the Mormons' own forests in Wisconsin—and they deteriorated with time. But the brick buildings have survived, and most are restored and open to visitors as testimony to some very ingenious men and women—John Browning, the gunmaker, for one—and to the power of a religion. Nauvoo is worth visiting for the peace of the town itself; there are only a couple of Mom-and-Pop motels and a quaint, country-inn sort of hotel that still has baths down the hall. This is rural America at its best.

For information and help in planning a visit, contact the Nauvoo Visitors Center, P. O. Box 215, Nauvoo, Illinois 62354.

The Shakers

An outgrowth of the Quaker religion, the Shaker sect was one of the most extensive, most enduring, and most important of the communal movements that began in the late eighteenth century and flourished with the unfolding of the nineteenth. One of the beliefs of Mother Ann, who brought the English sect to America, was that religion should not be separated from the secular concerns of human life. "Trifles make perfection, but perfection is not trifle," was one of the Shaker mottoes. When you think about it, you can understand how so much effort and ingenuity came to be brought to bear on the objects of daily life—objects that are today, because of their design and workmanship, among the most highly priced antiques on the market. But bringing religion into daily life was only a part of the Shaker creed. Shakers believed in the Bible as the source of all religious teaching, in confession of sins, in life after death, in God as a feminine *and* masculine personality, and in a rigid code of conduct that involved faith, hope, honesty, continence, conscience, simplicity, meekness, humility, patience, thankfulness, prudence, and charity.

There were scores of interesting footnotes to the Shaker beliefs that make visits to the various Shaker museums and restoration villages around the United States as intellectually interesting as they are visually stimulating. Each Shaker village interpreted the Shaker doctrines in subtly different ways, and after you've seen a couple you'll be able to detect a few of those differences.

The major Shaker museums and historic sites in the United States today are at Pleasant Hill, near Harrodsburg, Kentucky; at Old Chatham, New York; and in Hancock, Massachusetts.

Shakertown at Pleasant Hill, the finest Shaker site in the South, has some twenty-seven original buildings, some of which have been fixed up to show how the Shakers lived, some to house overnight guests. Shaker-style food is served at the Trustees' House Restaurant on the grounds. For details, contact the community at Harrodsburg, Kentucky 40330.

The Hancock Shaker Community in Hancock, Massachusetts, five miles west of Pittsfield in the Berkshires, is the best place in the East to see Shaker architecture. Among the seventeen buildings is the famous Round Barn, a magnificent trilevel structure designed for efficiency and so beautiful that you can't help but think of buildings by Frank Lloyd Wright and Le Corbusier for comparisons. The other buildings are maintained and furnished just as if the Shakers were about to return. The atmosphere is peaceful and very serene, and the community's thousand acres serve to separate it from the sometimes-bustling Berkshire traffic. For details, write the community at P. O. Box 898, Pittsfield, Massachusetts 01201.

The Shaker Museum in Old Chatham, New York, is the biggest and oldest of all the museums devoted to the Shakers. Thirty-six galleries house eighteen thousand objects—furniture, inventions, costumes, crafts, complete shops and rooms. A complete blacksmith's shop displays two triphammers, one of which was rescued from the junkmen just as they were about to cart it away from the mother community at Mount Lebanon, New York, in the 1940s. A blue storage bench from Canterbury, New Hampshire, built in 1792, still boasts its original coat of paint. There are rug-making rooms, a broom-making shop, a dressmaking shop, and a mill room. Shaker chairs are everywhere. And this is just the beginning. For information write to the Museum in Old Chatham, New York 12136.

Smaller, but interesting, are Shakertown at South Union, Kentucky 42283, fifteen miles west of Bowling Green, and the Shaker Museum Structure that is one of five buildings at the Fruitlands Museum, in Harvard, Massachusetts 01451.

Where to Buy Shaker Antiques

Furniture and artifacts made by members of this religious sect are prized on the antiques market now. If you know who the good dealers are, you won't get taken for a ride. Here are a few you can rely on:

Connecticut. Ed Clerk Antiques, Bethlehem 06751.

Maine. David and Nan Gurley, Appleton (mailing address: Star Route, Liberty, Maine 04949); Avis Howells Antiques, 21 Pearl Street, Belfast 04915.

Shaker round barn, Hancock, Massachusetts.

Massachusetts. Antiques at the Sign of the Bluebird, 69 Hartwell Avenue, Littleton 01460.

New York. Greenwillow Farm, Ltd., Box 226, Chatham 12037.

Ohio. Path of the Patriots, 412 Brydon Road, Kettering 45419.

Virginia. Hazel Hayes, Second Street, Waterford 22190.

Fine Reproductions

The fact that the Metropolitan Museum of Art sells products made by the North Family Joiners in its gift shop should give you some idea of the quality of work you will see in this cabinetmaking shop set up in an old mill building in Housatonic, Massachusetts. There are Shaker lap desks, pegboards, cupboards, mirrors (whose 12 x 18 dimensions were established by a Millennial Law that decreed "A looking glass larger than this ought never to be purchased by a Believer").

Why the name "North Family"? The North Family at the Mount Lebanon Shaker Community was the novitiate family: nonmembers lived there, adhering to Shaker practices on a trial basis, while the community at the same time evaluated the aspirant. "We felt," says cabinetmaker Charles Caffall, who *is* the North Family Joiners, "that the name would express the appreciation we feel for Shaker work, though we do not live the strict Shaker life." Also in the mill building are a producer of hand puppets, a silk-screen studio, and a school that offers workshops in dance and drama. For further information, contact the North Family Joiners, Box 567, Housatonic, Massachusetts 01236.

Another good source of Shaker artifacts, in the Midwest: the Guild of Shaker Crafts, Inc., 401 West Savidge Street, Spring Lake, Michigan 49456.

Learn Shaker Cabinetmaking

What you make, you may keep—or throw away if you feel you've really botched it. The program offered by the North Family Joiners lasts a year, costs $1,750 to cover materials, and will leave you with a mastery of the techniques of hand tools and power machinery; and a thorough knowledge of the construction, design, and finishing of pieces; of turning on the lathe; of repair and restoration; and of running a shop of your own. For more information, contact the North Family Joiners, Box 567, Housatonic, Massachusetts 01236.

A Shaker Banquet

Travelers that the Shakers invited to dinner may not have cared for the austere style of the furnishings, but they all brought back glowing reports of the food: though pledged to restrain their animal appetites where members of the opposite sex were concerned, the Shakers pulled out all stops at the dinner table and in the kitchen. They relished eating, and they ate amply and well, expending the same care on their cuisine that they did on furniture and tools.

To see what the cooking and the kitchens were like, the best place to go is the Hancock Shaker Village. Once a year, for a week in August, the museum stages World's Peoples Dinners, which are open to the public, as are cooking demonstrations that go along with the feasts.

Next best: the Trustees' House at Shakertown at Pleasant Hill. Some of the dishes on the menu are cooked according to Shaker recipes; the Thanksgiving spread is extravagant.

A Shaker Slumber

To get upstairs, you climb an amazing spiral staircase—one of two in the Trustees' House, where most overnight accommodations are located. The rooms themselves, furnished with simple trundle beds, Shaker rockers, and extra chairs hung on pegs on the walls, are remarkable—worth a detour. Write the Inn at Pleasant Hill, Route 4, Harrodsburg, Kentucky 40330.

The Last Shakers

There are only twelve, in two communities—one, population four, in East Canterbury, New Hampshire; the other, with a population of eight, at Sabbathday Lake, near Poland Springs, Maine. Both are prosperous, comfortable, homey places; there is a refreshing tranquillity to Shaker settlements. Both also have museums—which in themselves are interesting enough to make a visit to the settlements worthwhile. For details, write the museums at Poland Springs, Maine 04274 and at East Canterbury, New Hampshire 03224.

A Comprehensive List

Current interest in the Shakers has resulted in a spate of books, catalogues, pamphlets, booklets, and papers about the sect. The Guild of Shaker Crafts (401 West Savidge Street, Spring Lake, Michigan 49456) offers a good selection of what's on the market, including *Hands to Work: Shaker Folk Art and Industries* ($8.95), *Religion in Wood: A Book of Shaker Furniture* ($7.95), *The Perfect Life: The Shakers in America* ($7.95). The Guild also publishes a very interesting quarterly newspaper that carries items about Shaker antiques, articles by and about the Shakers who are still alive, and news about Shaker museums and artifacts. A subscription is $4 a year from the Guild.

See also *A Guide to Shaker Museums and Libraries* ($1 from the Guild of Shaker Crafts). It lists large museums with good collections of Shaker objects as well as museums devoted solely to the Shakers.

The Huguenots

New Paltz, New York—the center of a green and varied land in the Hudson River Valley—was home to a dozen of these exiles starting in the late seventeenth century. The Street of Huguenots, where most built their houses (now owned and maintained by the Huguenot Historical Society), has been called "America's Oldest Street." Whether the epithet is true or not, the little road is remarkably peaceful and the smallish stone houses are in perfect repair, almost as if they had been built yesterday. There are many other things to see in the area, and dozens of interesting resorts, including the Mohonk Mountain House and Lake Minnewaska Mountain Houses. For more information, write the Ulster County Publicity Committee, County Office Building, Kingston, New York 12401.

The Moravians

Old Salem, in Winston-Salem, North Carolina, was established by this group from Pennsylvania in 1753. A restoration of the original village includes buildings displaying fire engines, decorative arts, and household items. There are also a bakery, craft shops, restored homes, and the oldest tobacco shop in the country. Details can be had from the Convention and Visitors Bureau of the Greater Winston-Salem Chamber of Commerce, Box 1408, Winston-Salem, North Carolina 27102.

Two and a half acres of restored and reconstructed log cabins and houses—about twenty of them—depict the daily life of this simple and strong people, who lived in the Tuscarawas Valley at Schoenbrunn Village, near New Philadelphia, Ohio, from 1772–1782. Since the cabins are furnished almost entirely with reproductions, you can touch almost everything; craftspeople are on hand to demonstrate pottery and other handwork. The gardens have been planted with red corn, calico corn, sweet corn, squash, pumpkins, turnips, and herbs. Schoenbrunn is quiet, away from it all. For details, write the Schoenbrunn Village State Memorial, Box 129, New Philadelphia, Ohio 44663.

A German Commune

In the early part of the nineteenth century, a comfortable community was developed in Zoar, Ohio, midway between Canton and New Philadelphia, Ohio. Life here was *gemütlich*. Houses were brick, painted in bright colors. The garden, laid out in a geometric pattern to symbolize the New Jerusalem, was lush. Communal ownership here was only a matter of expediency, not philosophy.

The Zoar Society prospered for many years, but in 1853 its original leader, whose strong personality had held the whole project together, died. Then followed years of decline, culminating in the society's dissolution in 1898.

For details, write the Ohio Historical Society, Ohio Historical Center, Columbus, Ohio 43211.

The Spartan Life in Pennsylvania

Some three hundred people belonging to three different orders—a celibate brotherhood, a celibate sisterhood, and an order of married "householders"— lived in the medieval-style buildings of the Ephrata Cloister, near Lancaster, Pennsylvania. Following the demanding precepts of one Conrad Beissel, they slept on beds that were little more than narrow benches with wooden pillows (the floor is more comfortable); and they walked in hallways that were strait and narrow to remind them of the path of righteousness, and through

doorways that were so low they had to stoop to get through (to teach humility). The philosophy behind the symbolism is fairly interesting, as you'll see when you get the brochure from the Ephrata Cloister, P. O. Box 155, Ephrata, Pennsylvania 17522. Christmas is an especially nice time to visit; in summer, a special musical drama written by Beissel is presented.

A British Flop

The idea behind the 1880 settlement of Rugby, Tennessee ("a typical damn British undertaking," quipped one former settler, "on a typical damn British scale") was to provide a comfortable life for the younger sons of British gentry—who stood to go through life penniless because the law of primogeniture deprived them of an inheritance while custom denied them the right to earn a living. The British, consequently, thought the settlement was a pretty good idea. They brought carpenters to build houses, as well as other necessary artisans.

But most of the carpenters ended up carving out cricket fields and parks and bridle paths. Hard work was not one of the strengths of these settlers, and to compound their difficulties a typhoid epidemic struck about two years after their arrival, throwing the settlement

into an early decline.

Seventeen of the original buildings can still be seen, and most are open to the public. The Christ Church (Episcopal), which is still used for worship, has a beautiful original rosewood reed organ, made in London in 1849; the alms plates were carved by the same man who carved one of Queen Victoria's thrones. For more information about this placid little town, contact the Rugby Restoration Association, Box 8, Rugby, Tennessee 37733.

Heavens on Earth

by Mark Holloway

This history of utopian communities in America between 1680 and 1880 is a good book to consult after you've seen one: it's interesting to learn how the others compared, philosophically and practically—and it's always good to have such information under your belt when you visit another restoration. Holloway discusses not just the Shakers and the Harmonists, but also the Fourieristic phalanxes and the Oneida community. There's enough human interest that it doesn't get tedious. Dover Books, 180 Varick Street, New York, New York 10014; $2.00.

The Presidents

One sure way to put your town on the map is to get it into the Guinness Book of World Records. Failing that, arrange to have one of the locals elected president. Business will boom at even the tiniest service station as tourists and Sunday sightseers flocking to the town use up their gas circling the president's block. Soon the gas station will get a slick new building. Real-estate values will zoom. Nearby resorts will prosper. The president's house, or his boyhood home, or both, may become a National Historic Landmark (if not a National Historic Site). You're guaranteed a steady tourist business for years to come. If you think that the sudden fame of Carter Country is a fluke, think back on the sites associated with other presidents.

Those Illustrious Adamses

The family that gave the United States

its second and sixth presidents lived in the same eighteenth-century house from the time John Adams bought it, in 1787, until it was given to the United States in 1946. A handsome Georgian clapboard structure, it's full of polished eighteenth-century side chairs, highboys, oriental rugs. Mrs. John Adams started the garden. For details, write the Superintendent of the Adams National Historic Site at 135 Adams Street in Quincy, Massachusetts 02169.

James Buchanan Had a Bathroom

When you think of the crude plumbing of the day, it is remarkable that Wheatland, the home of the bachelor fifteenth president, had a bathroom: the tin tub is encased in polished wood, and above it, there is a shower. However, it is not for its bathroom

alone that this red-brick Federal-style house is considered one of the finest restorations in the country. The furniture, the design, and the setting are all magnificent.

The James Buchanan Foundation for the Preservation of Wheatland, 1120 Marietta Avenue (Route 23) in Lancaster, Pennsylvania 17603, can send you further information about visiting the house and about the surrounding Pennsylvania Dutch country.

Silent Cal

From the looks of it, at least, his origins were simple. Calvin Coolidge was born in Plymouth Notch, Vermont, not far from Woodstock, and he grew up in Plymouth Notch. In 1923, he also took the oath of office there, from his father, a notary public, just after the death of Warren G. Harding. If you can imagine how Norman Rockwell would paint a poor but comfortable dwelling, you have some idea of how Coolidge lived all those years. Nothing fancy: small rooms with low ceilings and plain furniture were his lot—in direct contrast to the open feeling you get out in the rolling pasturelands that make up this part of Vermont. Plymouth Notch itself is mostly how it was when Coolidge lived there—a little street full of white clapboard houses and blackeyed susans growing next to the old pine-paneled church that Coolidge attended. The Plymouth Cheese Company, where Vermont cheddar is manufactured according to the old ways, is also still there. The only changes, in fact, are that the barn that used to house the horses of visitors stopping at the tavern across the street has been turned into a display area for vehicles and tools; and, down the hill, a Calvin Coolidge Memorial Center has been built as part of the Coolidge Centennial. It houses special exhibits about the former president and his term and his times. For details, contact the Memorial Center at Woodstock, Vermont 05091.

What's Cooking in Carter Country

For a long time, Plains, Georgia, was a little nothing of a town. One-half-mile across, it had no laundry, no hotel, no doctor, not even a restaurant to speak of. It didn't rate mention on a road map.

But that was before one of its favorite sons, Jimmy Carter (or Mr. Jimmy as he's called thereabouts when he's not called just plain Jimmy) left town for the White House.

When that happened, the owner of the Amoco gas station was suddenly a celebrity, as were the jack-of-several-trades who owns both the world's largest worm farm and a dusty old antique, junk, and souvenir store at the end of the town's main (and only) street, and an eighty-eight-year-old sometime-clerk at said antique store: they are brother, cousin, and uncle of Jimmy Carter.

The following sites also became famous: the mayor's house, the Baptist Church, a peanut patch, the Lions Club swimming pool, a ranch house, a high school, a hospital, a schoolteacher's house, a cemetery, and a Methodist Church. The fact that Jimmy Carter has something to do with each of these spots, in one obscure way or another, is enough to bring Sunday drivers by the thousands every day of the week—and twice that number on weekends. The crowds, in turn, have meant camper-trailer jams at the intersection; a six-man police force instead of a hired watchman; an Avis outlet; a public restroom; a visitor center; a parking lot; and sightseeing

tours—not one but several—that take in all of the abovementioned points of interest and then some. And last, but certainly not the least visible, are the souvenir T-shirts. The town's new popularity has warranted the reopening of the boarded-up stores that share the main street with the antique shop.

Schlock notwithstanding, the tours and the Plains Cartermania give you a reason to visit where before there was no attraction beyond the super-rural out-of-the-way red-clay-and-peanut-fields countryside. Once you arrive in that corner of Georgia, you see what was there all along—some really fine small towns, one full of magnificent antebellum mansions, another with a restoration village that is a sort of Sturbridge of the South—authentic right down to the red-dirt sidewalks.

Some good places to write to find out more include the Westville restoration, Box 1850, Lumpkin, Georgia 31815; the Eufaula Chamber of Commerce, Box 347, Eufaula, Alabama 36027; the Historic Chattahoochee Commission, P. O. Box 33, Eufaula, Alabama 36027; the Historic Columbus Foundation, P. O. Box 5312, Columbus, Georgia 31906.

Eisenhower's Kansas

Abilene, Kansas, whose population is just over sixty-five hundred, according to a recent accounting, has two main claims to fame—the first as a roistering cow town and cattle shipping center during the 1860s, its second as the boyhood home of Dwight David Eisenhower.

Eisenhower, of course, figured in history for many years before his presidency, so instead of just a presidential library, there is a whole Eisenhower Center. Of its four buildings, one is the famous library stocked with Ike papers. It is huge and of interest primarily to scholars. The Center also includes the chapel in which the former President is buried, and a museum.

One particularly spectacular item on display there is a desk set encrusted with Persian turquoise with a peacock rising out of its base. It is one of the several objets d'art presented to Eisenhower by the Shah of Iran. When you think that one lady spent half an hour gazing at this incredible object alone, and that there are dozens of other such diamond-and-ruby-set gifts of state, not to mention Ike's olive-drab Army Cadillac and the Chippendale chairs and Sheraton table used at planning sessions for the Normandy invasion, you have some idea of the scope of the collections. Personal items from the Eisenhowers' marriage and family life are there, too. Eisenhower's boyhood home, also a part of the center, is a plain old-fashioned block of a dwell-

ing, clapboard on the outside and furnished like many other Midwestern houses: old but not antique beds, bureaus and tables, some rockers, some squashy chairs, plenty of doilies and filmy curtains. Much of it is exactly as Eisenhower's mother kept it until her death in 1946. Even her plants are still alive.

Abilene is right off I-70, a major east-west interstate highway, about sixty miles west of Topeka. While you're there you can also take in Old Abilene Town, which portrays the cattle days with original buildings and replicas, and Lena's Cafe, where Eisenhower used to eat when he was in town. The fried chicken is famous.

For particulars, write the Chamber of Commerce, Box 446, Abilene, Kansas 67410.

On the Eisenhower trail. In Denison, Texas, a town with about twenty-five thousand inhabitants due north of Dallas on the Oklahoma line, there is the Eisenhower Birthplace State Historic Site, at 208 East Day Street; the Travel and Information Division of the Texas Highway Department, Box 5064, Austin, Texas 78763, can send additional information about the town, which is near Lake Texoma. The Eisenhowers' Gettysburg, Pennsylvania, farm (which adjoins the National Military Park) has been given to the government with the proviso that Mrs. Eisenhower can live there as long as she likes; therefore, it is not yet open to the public.

Is There a Ford in Your Past?

The Robert Morris Inn, in Oxford, Maryland, right on the banks of the Tred Avon River, boasts that Susan Ford, the daughter of the thirty-eighth president, ate there. That was in 1975. Since then, the inn has done a good deal of brightening up. But the big clapboard structure and its handsome annex were great to begin with (some of the rooms overlook the tiny main-and-only street, some of them the river—and these fill up at night with lovely moist air off the river that is wonderful for sleeping). To find out more about the inn, write the innkeepers in Oxford, Maryland 21654.

Grant's Galena

Galena, Illinois, a town with four thousand inhabitants, banked against the hillside in the most northwestern corner of the state, used to be a cultural and commercial center of the Midwest. However, the tales you hear when you visit today are stories of its years of decline, for it was about 1860, close to the time that the town was beginning to fade out of the Midwestern mercantile picture, that U. S. Grant came to Galena, fresh from a celebrated string of failures at farming, auctioneering, and account collecting. His future looked decidedly less than bright.

He worked in his father's leather-goods store for a year, then went off to fight in the Civil War. When he came home in 1865, a victorious general, thirty-six white-robed ladies waved American flags and threw bouquets as he proceeded down the main street under a banner inscribed "Hail to the Chief who in Triumph Advances." During the welcoming ceremonies, the grateful townspeople presented him with a $16,000 house, completely furnished, on Bouthillier Street.

Grant used the house on and off for twenty years, and after his death in 1885 it stayed in the family. His son gave it to the city; ownership devolved on the state, and the state restored it, using the original plans. Much of the ornate Victorian furniture and objets d'art you see when you go through it were Grant's.

Also in Galena are the modest brick house that Grant rented when he first arrived in Galena; some ten museums; and about three dozen antique shops. Every year in mid-May, the townspeople put on a Civil War Cantonment. They reenact a battle, give a cavalry exhibition, and compete in artillery, bowie knife, and tomahawk contests. Private homes are open for tours twice a year, usually in June and September. There are also special festivities for Christmas—caroling, free hot chocolate in the shops, and candlelight open houses at the mansions. For more information contact the Chamber of Commerce, 221 South Main Street, Galena, Illinois 61036.

More spots on the Grant trail. The powers that be of Kane, Pennsylvania (called the "icebox of Pennsylvania" because of its plateau setting in the vast Allegheny National Forest) once arrested Grant for fishing without a license. For information about scenic drives, camping, hiking, and boating in the forest, contact the superintendent at forest headquarters, P. O. Box 847, Warren, Pennsylvania 16365. There is also the General Grant National Memorial, at Riverside Drive and 122nd Street in New York City, the object of the old riddle "Who's Buried in Grant's Tomb?" For information about the shrine, contact the National Park Service, 26 Wall Street, New York 10005.

Herbert Hoover's Quiet Quaker Home

Orphaned in the 1880s, Herbert Hoover went to live with his uncle in a plain frame house in Newberg, Oregon. Now restored and open for tours, it contains some original furnishings, including, as you'll be told, the furniture in the bedroom that the future president had to himself. In the garden is the pear tree that Hoover used to climb. Hoover attended the Friends Pacific Academy in Newberg, a Quaker school of which his uncle was superintendent and that later became Fox College. When you visit Newberg, you can tour the campus.

The Chamber of Commerce (520 East First Street, 97132) can send details about the town and the historic sites; the Oregon State Highway Division, Highway Building, Salem 97310, can send particulars about the area, which is also well described in the book *Sunset Travel Guide to Oregon* (Lane Publishing, Menlo Park, California 94025; $2.95).

Old Hickory's Hermitage

"I feel much alarmed at the prospect of seeing General Jackson President. He is one of the most unfit men I know for such a place."

—Thomas Jefferson

If you had visited the home of the United States' seventh president, Andrew Jackson, when he built it in Nashville, Tennessee, in the 1800s, and then revisited it again today, you would probably notice only a couple of changes. The house is furnished entirely with original pieces (the only national shrine that can make that claim) and the exteriors have been little changed. But the trees that were barely taller than a man when Jackson lived there have grown into a cathedral-like forest; the grass has grown soft in its age. The view down the lawns makes it a joy even to stand outside and queue for your turn in the house (as you may well have to do because this is such a popular place). Once inside you'll see all manner of Jacksoniana—the bed in which the president died, a dining room table at which nine presidents have eaten, all Jackson's shaving paraphernalia, and so on. What is perhaps most striking, though, is the way all the memorabilia fits together to give you the impression that you are in a living person's home. Nothing is decorated—but the Hermitage is a very homey, lived-in place; more than most historic houses you'll see, it shows off a life rather than a collection of furniture. Perhaps that's why it was one of Franklin Delano Roosevelt's favorites.

A film shown on the premises tells Jackson's story and that of his marriage, which was interesting because he had been married to his wife for two years before they both found out that her divorce from her previous husband had not been official. In those days, the very idea of cohabitation even under those most innocent of circumstances was so scandalous that there was plenty of grist for the slanderers' mills during the election of 1828. Rachel, depressed by the sordidness, died before he got to the White House.

For further information about Nashville, write the Nashville Area Chamber of Commerce, 161 Fourth Avenue North, Nashville, Tennessee 37219.

More Jacksoniana: North and South Carolina both claim his birthplace; he was born in the frontier region known as the Waxhaws along the border. However, there is a state historic park commemorating his birth with a museum full of Jackson items and a campground, fourteen miles south of Rock Hill.

Some Jeffersoniana

"All my wishes end where I hope my days will end . . . at Monticello."

—Thomas Jefferson

To visit Monticello is to look into one of the most intriguing minds ever to leave its mark on U.S. history. Thomas Jefferson, who planned and built both Monticello and the University of Virginia, started work on Monticello at age twenty-six and continued designing and redesigning for the next thirty years. Work on Monticello, in fact, outlasted his wife, who died after six children and ten years of marriage.

The house is beautiful, and the inventions and labor-saving devices for which Jefferson has become so famous are as incredible as they're made out to be. The seven-day clock in the entrance hall, for instance, is ingeniously rigged to run by the weight of cannon balls; the work table and chaise lounge, the novel quartet stand, the revolving door with shelves, the bed that was also a room divider. And then there are the manicured lawns and gardens outside.

But these are just the beginning. Dig a little deeper and you start getting to know the man himself—prodigiously energetic, endlessly inventive, disciplined beyond belief but at the same time, in the words of John Quincy Adams, a man of "strong prejudices and irritated passions." Jefferson died, as he had hoped, at Monticello—on the fiftieth anniversary of the signing of the Declaration of Independence—and he is buried there.

There are, in addition to the two Jefferson sites, many other things to see and do in the rolling Albemarle Country in the center of Virginia (not far from the ultra-scenic Skyline Drive). For the details, contact the Charlottesville and Albemarle County Chamber of Commerce, Box 1564, Charlottesville 22902.

Lincoln's Successor Started out as a Tailor

Taught to read and write by his wife, Andrew Johnson never spent a day in school; he had been apprenticed to a tailor when he was twelve. Though he ran away—subsequently working at jobs that eventually got him into politics—he was always proud of his skills, and as governor of Tennessee presented the governor of neighboring Kentucky with a suit. The tailoring tools he used, his shop, his brick home, and his grave are what you see at the Andrew Johnson National Historic Site, at Greeneville, Tennessee 37743, where he spent most of his life.

LBJ Country

Perhaps no other president can be so strongly identified with a single spot as LBJ and that in-between place—part high plains and cedar-dotted plateaus, part softer, more humid lands speckled with wildflowers, in season—known as the Texas Hill Country.

Johnson's family had been there for years, and Johnson was tied to his homeland more strongly than most other Americans. Four generations of his family had lived on the land and are buried in the Johnson family cemetery —his sister, his parents, his grandparents, his great-grandmother—not to mention the aunts, uncles, cousins, and family friends.

The cemetery, which was a constant presence throughout his life, is just one part of the Lyndon B. Johnson National Historic Site, which, from his retirement, LBJ helped create.

Near the cemetery is his birthplace with a reconstruction of the two-bedroom farmhouse with a kitchen presided over by one of those old-fashioned cast-iron stoves. You can also visit the LBJ Ranch House, a long, rambling white house, where LBJ lived in retirement; the one-room Junction School, whose teacher, Miss Kate Deadrich, was persuaded to take on four-year-old Lyndon in 1912 (and where he reportedly said, "Someday I'm going to be president"). Across the Pedernales River, in Lyndon B. Johnson State Park, there's swimming, tennis, easy hiking, picnicking.

Also part of the LBJ National Historic Site are properties on the west side of Johnson City: the house where Johnson lived from the age of five until he left for college, and a complex of log-and-stone buildings that preserve the wild, lonely frontier Texas of his grandfather (a cattleman) and his grandmother, who once hid underneath the house to escape a Comanche raiding party. There are a couple of barns and stone buildings and a log house; horse-drawn freight wagons will transport you from one to the other.

In the area there are also about a dozen dude ranches—both working ranches and resorts. Nine A.M. cowboy breakfasts (eggs, bacon, grits, scalding coffee strong enough to stand your hair on end, cooked over the open fire) are the order of the day. It's a great way to spend a vacation: the sun shines most of the time, and the air is so clear you can see even the most distant trees etched against the sky as if they were next to you.

The Travel and Information Division of the Texas Highway Department, Austin, Texas 78701, can send you material about area dude ranches as well as a brochure called "Hill Country Trail," which takes you to local points of interest. For further information, write the Lyndon B. Johnson National Historic Site, P. O. Box 329, Johnson City, Texas 78636.

Lincoln Lands

The backwoods of Kentucky, Illinois, and Indiana were the stomping ground of this most revered, much written about president. Not only does there seem to be documentation about the very chairs he sat in at this time or that during his career, but there is a nearly equal interest in the lives of his parents and his siblings.

The Lincoln Heritage Trail Foundation has mapped out a 2,200-mile driving trip to connect most of the Lincoln sites. State and even county roads, all marked with distinctive Lincoln medallions, lead you along. The tour is nice because it gets you off beaten tracks and into the still-rural part of the country, of which Lincoln could still say, "To this place, and the kindness of these people, I owe everything." To get a copy of the map, contact the Lincoln Heritage Trail Foundation, 702 Bloomington Road, Champaign, Illinois 61820.

The Really Important Sites

There are four: the Lincoln Birthplace National Historic Site, near Hodgenville, Kentucky; the Lincoln Boyhood National Memorial, in southern Indiana near Lincoln City; the whole of Springfield, Illinois; and New Salem, about 18 miles northwest of Springfield.

At the Lincoln Birthplace, on the site of the Sinking Springs Farm that Thomas Lincoln bought in December of 1808 for $200 in cash, the mud-chinked one-room log cabin has been given a home inside a fancy marble-and-granite temple affair, which is incongruous but does keep the mud from melting away. Outside is the sinking spring after which the farm was named and what's left of the Boundary Oak; until it died in 1976, it was one of those vast, gnarled, ancient plants that never fail to make you catch your breath in awe. In the visitor center where Thomas Lincoln's Bible is displayed, there's an excellent audiovisual program that will fill you in on Lincoln's life and set the tone for your visit to the cabin and to other Lincoln sites in the area.

The Lincoln Boyhood National Memorial, near Lincoln City, Indiana, has a museum and a memorial to Nancy Hanks Lincoln, who is buried here. A short walk away, at a living historical farm, costumed interpreters clean muskets, plow the fields, clean house, make quilts, do the laundry, and cook meals in the manner of Lincoln's era.

Springfield, Illinois—especially if you visit after you've already learned about Lincoln—is quite an eerie place: you expect to see the president come around almost any corner. On a walking tour, you can see Lincoln's modest clapboard dwelling place—the only house he ever owned—and the house in which he courted and wed Mary Todd. You'll also want to visit the train depot from which Lincoln departed for Washington; the Lincoln family pew at the First Presbyterian Church; the building in which Lincoln practiced his law; his grave; and, in the Springfield Marine Bank, an original ledger of Lincoln's bank account.

New Salem lasted as a town for only about ten years; what's there now, though entirely reconstruction, is nonetheless interesting, for it was in buildings similar to these that Lincoln lay awake nights throwing pine shavings on the fire to get more light to read by; where, clerking for Denton Offutt, he walked six miles to straighten out an overcharge; where he served as postmaster, worked as a rail-splitter, mill hand, surveyor, farm hand; where he voted for the first time; where he first ran for office; and where he met Ann Rutledge. In the fall, there's a crafts festival, and in December, special festivities for Christmas.

For information about the Birthplace, write the Superintendent at Route 1, Hodgenville 42748, and the Kentucky Department of Public Information, Capitol Annex, Frankfort 40601. For information about the Boyhood Memorial, write the Superintendent in Lincoln City, Indiana 47552. The Springfield Convention and Tourism Commission, 500 East Capitol Avenue, Springfield, Illinois 62701, can tell you more about that town's Lincolniana.

Footnotes

The Washington County Historical Society and the Springfield Chamber of Commerce in Springfield, Kentucky

40069, publish an interesting booklet that pinpoints sites connected with Lincoln's parents and grandparents—Nancy Hanks's home at the time of her marriage, a Thomas Lincoln home, the grave of Captain Abraham Lincoln (the president's grandfather), the home of the woman who sewed Nancy Hanks's wedding dress. Farmington, six miles outside Louisville on U.S. 31E, has a handsome house, designed after one of Thomas Jefferson's plans, where Lincoln stayed with his friend Joshua Speed during a particularly trying period during his courtship of Mary Todd. Illinois's Lincoln Trail Homestead State Park, about eight miles south of Decatur, includes the site of the first Illinois home of Thomas and Sarah Bush Lincoln. As for the site of the Lincoln Trail State Park, about two miles south of Marshall, Illinois—the Lincolns passed through here in 1830 on their way from Indiana to Macon County. The Lincoln Log Cabin Historic Site, south of Charleston, Illinois, houses the last home of the president's father and stepmother. The Metamora Courthouse State Memorial, near Metamora, Illinois, has one of two remaining structures on the rugged Eighth Judicial Circuit, which Lincoln rode: attorneys of that day served such a thinly scattered population that they had to ride the circuit to make a living. The courthouse displayed at the Postville Courthouse State Memorial, near Lincoln, Illinois, is a reproduction—the original is at Greenfield Village in Dearborn, Michigan. Lincoln was also the only town named with Lincoln's knowledge and consent; he helped organize and incorporate it and christened it with watermelon juice. The town's Chamber of Commerce, 600½ Broadway, Lincoln 62656, distributes a brochure mapped with the Lincoln Circuit. Clayville Rural Life Center, near Springfield, ten miles south of New Salem, used to be an inn, and Lincoln was a frequent visitor; crafts demonstrations and crafts fairs are the order of the day now.

The Chicago Historical Society, North Clark Street and North Avenue, in Chicago, has a whole section devoted to Lincoln's life. On display in this large, modern museum are his slippers and his spectacles, the bed in which he died, his pocket file, beaded moccasins, and other personal items—as well as a letter in which he says, "Nothing new here, except my marriage, which to me is a matter of profound wonder." For more information about the town, you can write the Chicago Convention and Tourism Bureau, 332 South Michigan Avenue, Chicago 60603. And there's the house in which Lincoln died, in Washington, D.C., at 516 10th Street. The small Petersen townhouse, which belonged to a German immigrant tailor, is fur-

nished as it was when Lincoln was carried across the street from Ford's Theatre, whose basement houses an important collection of Lincolniana that includes the suit he wore to the play that horrible night. For information about both sites, contact the National Capital Parks-Central, 1100 Ohio Drive, S.W., Washington, D.C. 20242.

An Incident at the Courthouse
"The trial was proceeding poorly for Melissa Goings, charged with murdering her husband. Her attorney, Abraham Lincoln, called for a recess to confer with his client and he led her from the courtroom.

"When court reconvened and Mrs. Goings could not be found, Lincoln was accused of advising her to flee, a charge he vehemently denied. He explained, however, that the defendant had asked him where she could get a drink of water, and he had pointed out that Tennessee had darn good water!

"She was never again seen in Illinois."
—from the Metamora Courthouse records

The Assassination
Some sites: the southern Maryland farm home of Dr. Samuel Mudd, who treated John Wilkes Booth, can be seen by following Route 5 south, turning left on Route 382 just south of Waldorf, then following route 232 for about half a mile to the house (privately owned). The physician's grave is at St. Mary's Church, Bryantown, a tiny town at the intersection of Routes 5 and 232. For information about the other things to see and do in the area (beaches, historical museums, fishing), write the Tri-County Council for Southern Maryland, Waldorf, Maryland 20601.

The Lincoln Memorial
It's in Washington, D.C., of course. And where, you ask, did the government get the marble used in the Memorial? Near Aspen, Colorado. There's a scenic drive to the quarries, which you'll want to include on your Lincoln itinerary. For details about the area, contact the Aspen Chamber of Commerce, Box GG, Aspen, Colorado 81611.

A Book on the Subject
Maurine Whorton Redway and Dorothy Kendall Bracken followed the president's footsteps from Kentucky through Indiana and Illinois and to Washington and tell the story of what they saw and learned in Marks of Lincoln on Our Land (from Hastings House Publishers, 10 East 40th Street, New York, New York 10016; $3.75). There are some good stories about Lincoln lounging around the elegant bedroom in the White House in his stocking feet, or chasing insects with

his worn bedroom slippers—plus quotes, lots of pictures, and a good bibliography. Though published in 1957, it's still remarkably up-to-date, so you can use it as a guide through Lincoln country as well as an armchair travelogue.

Monroe's "Cabin-Castle"

Highlands, which James Monroe built near Charlottesville to be near his friend Thomas Jefferson, was small and simple, more snug than grand—which was surprising considering the expensive high-flung tastes of his wife and daughters. For details about the house write Ash Lawn (the name it was given under subsequent owners) in Charlottesville, Virginia 22901, or the Charlottesville and Albemarle County Chamber of Commerce, Box 1564, Charlottesville 22902.

The office in which Monroe practiced law from 1786 to 1789 is at 908 Charles Street in the placid little town of Fredericksburg, Virginia, about an hour south of Washington. It is set up as a museum and displays the elegant Empire-style furniture he bought as Ambassador to France and used in the White House during his term (1817–25). The law office is one of the sites on a walking tour that takes you along the tree-lined streets to the houses of George Washington's mother and sister, an antique apothecary shop, and an amazing just-for-show replica of a Virginia village store of the 1800s. For information contact the Fredericksburg Visitor Center at 706 Caroline Street, Fredericksburg 22401.

Nixon's Nemesis

The famous Watergate office/apartment complex is at the intersection of New Hampshire and Virginia Avenues. In the Watergate Mall—part of the center—there are all manner of intriguing shops and boutiques where you can buy everything from ladies' clothes to hand-crafted wares. For area tourism information, write the Washington Area Convention and Visitors Bureau, 1129—20th Street N.W., Washington, D.C. 20036.

The Polks' Places

James K. Polk, who served as the eleventh president, from 1845 to 1849, was not one of the presidents whose presence in a town for a few weeks was boasted about for years hence.

However, when you visit his birthplace in Pineville, North Carolina, just south of Charlotte and not far from Andrew Jackson's birthplace, you will learn some surprising things about the man. When he took office, he had four goals. "One," he said, "a reduction of the tariff; another the independent treasury; a third, the settlement of the Oregon boundary question; and lastly, the acquisition of California." This president that nobody talks about did just what he said he would do. In addition, he began and ended a war—the Mexican War—that added Texas to the United States. During his administration, three states were admitted, Oregon was organized as a territory, Utah was settled, California's government was organized, immigration was increased.

For more information about the birthplace, contact the Office of Archives and History of the Department of Art, Culture, and History, Raleigh, North Carolina 27611. The Chamber of Commerce at Box 1867 in Charlotte 28233, can send you information on other area attractions, the most important of which is Carowinds, a big, slick family entertainment complex based upon the history of the Carolinas. Carowinds has one of the most unusual of the U.S.'s rollercoasters—a hair-raiser that goes backward as well as forward and upside down.

Polk's ancestral home, built by the president's father, is in Columbia, Tennessee, a town of about twenty thousand inhabitants due south of Nashville.

FDR's Homes

There were three—his birthplace and home on the rolling plateaus overlooking the Hudson River in Hyde Park, New York; Campobello Island, in New Brunswick, where he summered from his boyhood until he was stricken with polio there at the age of thirty-nine; and Warm Springs, Georgia, where he stayed regularly at the "Little White House" and swam in a pool that seemed to improve his condition.

All of them are historical parks under one jurisdiction or another; all are preserved as they were when the Roosevelts enjoyed them.

Considering the family's patrician background, you might expect to find quite elaborate displays of antiques and objets d'art. Not so. The Roosevelts were not so much collectors as they were savers. The Hyde Park house, which is the most elaborate of the three, is full of pieces brought from here and there by members of the family. As Eleanor Roosevelt once said, "Many people in looking at the house will think the furniture old-fashioned, and they will be right, for it was good furniture when it was built and fortunately none of the people who lived in the house ever had the desire to change it because of some whim or passing taste." The red shingle-style cottage on Campobello

Home of FDR at Hyde Park, New York.

Island reflects the same sort of philosophy about furniture. It's full of wicker pieces that, as Mrs. Roosevelt predicted, are right back in style. "If one keeps things long enough," she said, "taste usually changes and returns to them." The Warm Springs house is similarly comfortable, and, since it's in Carter Country, you can observe the different life-styles of these two very different people. For more information about the Roosevelt homes and their areas, write the following: The Roosevelt Campobello International Park Commission, Campobello Island, New Brunswick, and the Tourist Information Office of New Brunswick, P. O. Box 12345, Fredericton, New Brunswick E3B 5C3. The Home of Franklin D. Roosevelt National Historic Site, Hyde Park, New York 12538, and (for information about the area) Hudson River Valley Association, 105 Ferris Lane, Poughkeepsie, New York 12603. Roosevelt's Little White House and Museum, Warm Springs, Georgia 31830, and the Georgia Bureau of Industry and Trade, Sixth Floor, Trinity-Washington Building, P. O. Box 38097, Atlanta, Georgia 30334.

Teddy Roosevelt

You get a good overview of the life of the twenty-sixth president at the Theodore Roosevelt Birthplace National Historic Site, a reconstruction of the house in which he was born on the original site at 28 East 20th Street in New York City. You'll see quite an ordinary, comfortable upper-middle-class home of the period; the ceilings are high, the furniture is shiny and curlicued, and the windows are opulently curtained. In the nursery upstairs, along with the Roosevelt crib you see the stairs that Teedie, as his family called him, climbed to get out onto the porch where his father had built him a gym: the gym was an effort to help the child get over the asthma he suffered. There are also two museum areas, one in which the exhibits depict his private and public life, the other dedicated to his outdoor pursuits and his work for conservation. Many sketches and photographs of his famous African safari of 1910 are on display.

That the frail young boy who spent his early life in this house grew up to be one of the most dynamic people in

American history is obvious here—as it is at his house in Oyster Bay, New York, a sprawling Victorian house that is chockablock full of the relics of his adventuring life—trophies and Zuni pottery, Philippine arrowheads, paneling (in one room) of Philippine and American woods, a Polar Bear rug given him by Admiral Robert E. Peary. Roosevelt's grave is nearby in Young's Cemetery. For further information about all these Roosevelt sites, contact the National Park Service New York District at 26 Wall Street, New York, New York 10005.

Roosevelt also made his mark on North Dakota, to which he repaired shortly after his wife of three years died giving birth to their first child (on the same day that his mother died). It was in 1883 that he first discovered North Dakota—the pastoral prairie-clovered valley bottoms along the Little Missouri River, the badlands, a haunting maze of canyons, buttes, cones, tablelands, flame-colored hills whipped by wind and water into bizarre shapes. The 70,000-acre Theodore Roosevelt National Memorial Park, established to commemorate the President's conservation efforts throughout the country as well as his activities in North Dakota, is in three units—one near Medora, another about seventy miles north of Waterford City, and, halfway between the two, a third at Roosevelt's Elkhorn Ranch, which is accessible only by a rough dirt road.

To find out more about the park write the Superintendent, Theodore Roosevelt National Memorial Park, Medora 58654. The Gold Seal Company, which has restored the town of Medora, can provide you with further information about that town; the address is Box 198, Medora 58654.

Truman

At the Harry Truman Library and Museum, at U.S. 24 and North Delaware Street in Independence, Missouri, you can see a reproduction of the president's White House office and hear his voice describe the room; see the table on which the U.N. Charter was signed, the piano Truman played, his limousine, and the Japanese surrender document signed aboard the *Missouri* on September 2, 1945. For more information you can write the museum in Independence 64050.

George Washington Slept Here

If any president has had his movements charted more carefully than Lincoln, it's Washington.

It's not that the first president's presence in any single place should make it all that unique. Washington

slept around a good deal, which is to say that his jobs as a surveyor, then as the commander in chief of the army, and later as the head of the government involved considerable traveling. He did so much traveling, and slept and ate and paid visits to so many restaurants and homes and inns and taverns and cities, that you would be hard put to visit them all. But it's interesting, all the same, to note just who is boasting.

South Carolina's state tourism office publishes two George Washington Trail minitours, one for the central part of the state, one that takes you along the coast. As president, Washington really did visit both areas on a good will visit to the state. Both tours take in some very nice country: inland, there are granite and wooden historic markers, old churches and homes, Christmas tree farms, soybean fields, and peach orchards; on the coastal trail, you run into restaurants where you can eat roasted oysters off newspapers and drop the shells through a hole in the center of the table, tidewaters and marshlands, roads surfaced with broken shells. For the maps and other information, contact the South Carolina Department of

Parks, Recreation, and Tourism, Box 71, Room 29, Columbia, South Carolina 29202.

Washington the Surveyor
In 1763, Washington explored the Great Dismal Swamp—a 600-square-mile wilderness even today—and formed the Adventurers for Draining the Great Dismal Swamp. His company dug drainage ditches, but Washington sold out. For details on what you can see and do there, contact the North Carolina Department of Commerce, P. O. Box 25249, Raleigh 27611.

George Washington Slept in More Houses in This County Than in Any Other Place in America
Such, anyway, is the boast of the Montgomery County Convention and Visitors Bureau (One Montgomery Plaza, Suite 207, Norristown, Pennsylvania 19401). True or not, Washington did spend at least one winter here—Montgomery County is the location of Valley Forge. Many of the restaurants in the area date from Washington's time. The food and the ambience have changed since Washington stayed there, but the structures are worth seeing all the same, and the

peaceful rolling countryside, part of it given over to horse farms and part to woodlands, is one of the most delightful places in the Northeast for a weekend getaway.

His Last Appearance in Full Dress Uniform

That, the people from Allegany County, Maryland, will be quick to tell you, happened at Fort Cumberland in Cumberland, Maryland, when he reviewed his troops after the Whiskey Rebellion. The one-room cabin—all that remains today—was also the place where Washington learned his military strategy, about Indian warfare, and about surviving in the wilderness. Wilderness is not what you find there now—the tiny cabin (its roof is now tiled) is in Riverside Park; but this westernmost section of Maryland is wild enough once you get out of town. To find out more, contact the Allegany County Division of Tourism, Baltimore at Greene Street, Cumberland, Maryland 21502.

Washington's Will

Along with Martha's, it's on display at the Fairfax Court House, 4000 Chain Bridge Road, in Fairfax, Virginia.

Washington's Crossing

The celebrated crossing of the Delaware River, after which Washington and his 2,400 troops surprised the Hessians at their Christmas Eve merrymaking and began to turn the tide of the American army's fortunes during the Revolution, is reenacted annually on Christmas Day at Washington Crossing State Park, Washington Crossing, Pennsylvania 18977. Some sixty people participate, at their own expense; as many as thirteen thousand come to watch "Washington" in authentic Durham boats, cross the Delaware River. Bucks County, where the event begins, is a pleasant woodsy New York exurb —decidedly pleasant for afternoon drives. For more information, contact the park or the Bucks County Historical-Tourist Commission, Fallsington, Pennsylvania 19504.

Washington's Mother's House

Along with his sister's handsome eighteenth-century plantation house, the president's mother's house is in Fredericksburg, Virginia. The garden is full of wonderful boxwood; the house itself, full of beautiful objects, is a homey place thanks to the ladies of the Fredericksburg Garden Club, who are always filling it up with amazing flower arrangements. (Example: a centerpiece of green apples.) For more information about Fredericksburg, which is about an hour's drive south of Washington, D.C., contact the Fredericksburg Visitor Center, 706 Caroline Street, Fredericksburg, Virginia 22401.

A George Washington Memorial Parkway

Constructed for the Bicentennial, this road links Mount Vernon, the Custis-Lee Mansion, Alexandria (which contains many fine homes and buildings associated with Washington), and the Lincoln Memorial. It turns along the Potomac. For a map, write the Superintendent, in the Lynn Building, 1111 19th Street North, Arlington, Virginia 22209.

Washington in West Virginia

The State Department of Commerce (State Capitol, Charleston 25305) publishes a George Washington Country Tour—368 miles through the hilly country that Washington explored along the Ohio River.

Washington's Bathtub

In the tiny town of Berkeley Springs, West Virginia, they'll tell you that Washington lolled in a natural stone tub full of the waters of "Ye Fam'd Warm Springs," which are still one of the best reasons, aside from its small-town ambience, to visit the place. That bath was in 1748, when Washington and a party of surveyors were working in northern Virginia for Lord Fairfax; subsequently, Washington gushed so much about the waters that Berkeley Springs was for a time quite *the* place to be. For more information about the remarkably inexpensive soaks you can have there today—in big Roman tubs or special showers—contact the Morgan County Chamber of Commerce in Berkeley Springs 25411.

Eat Like the General

"Give us some of your canvas-back ducks, with a chafing-dish, some hominy, and a bottle of Good Madeira, and we shall not complain." So Washington ordered a meal at Gadsby's Tavern, now restored, in Alexandria, Virginia. Period rooms are open to viewing. Perhaps more to the point, though, is the menu, for which some Colonial dishes have been adapted. For more information write the Tavern at 128 North Royal Street in Alexandria; for more information about the other George Washington sites in the city contact the Chamber of Commerce at 400 South Washington Street, 22314.

Good-bye to His Officers

Washington said farewell to his officers at Fraunces Tavern in New York City. A reconstruction on the site of the original tavern is both a museum, where you can see various bits of Revolutionary War memorabilia, and a restaurant. The Long Room was the scene of the farewell.

After you've looked over the handsome rooms, you can dine. For details, contact the Museum at 54 Pearl Street, New York, New York 10004.

George Washington's Birthday Celebrations

There are dozens, if for no other reason than that there's a school holiday and it's a good time to liven up a long winter.

One of the oldest is the George Washington Celebration in the central Florida community of Eustis, a center of citrus fruit growing that is surrounded by the Ocala National Forest. There are parades, carnivals, water shows, street dancing, and a big fireworks show. For details, contact the Chamber of Commerce at Box 1210, Eustis 32726.

Some More Information

William Howard Taft's house in Cincinnati, Ohio (P. O. Box 19072, 45219) is a National Historic Site, as is Kennedy's birthplace at 83 Beals Street in Brookline, Massachusetts 02146.

How to Find
The Historic Places

History's Social Register

The National Register of Historic Places—yes, there really is one—is available from the Superintendent of Documents, U.S. Government Printing Office, Washington, D.C. 20402; $7.80.

Best Books
for History Hunters

Discover Historic America, by Robert B. Konikow (Rand McNally, Box 7600, Chicago 60680; $4.95), is a good deal for the money. It rounds up literally hundreds of historic sites around the country, then, in an index, classifies them according to subject: American Indians, artists and sculptors, Black History, burial grounds, the Civil War, commerce and industry (cooperage, foods, fur trading, industrial history, ironworks, laundering, lumbering, mills, mining, newspapers, oil, photog-

raphy, rice, sugar, telephones, tobacco, whaling, whiskey and wine), community restorations, education, entertainment and sports (baseball, basketball, the circus, football, jazz, movies, theater, wild west shows), forts and stockades, landmarks, maritime museums, pioneer sites, sunken treasure, musicians, mysteries of history, presidents, plantation houses

and famous homes, American Revolution sites, special collections, transportation sites, women's suffrage.

The book is fairly long, though not long enough to give you too many details about each site. Nonetheless, it's fairly comprehensive.

American Travelers' Treasury: A Guide to the Nation's Heirlooms (William Morrow and Company, 105 Madison Avenue, New York, New York 10016; $5.95) is part of the Americans Discover America series. It lists (as the cover says) "where to find—*in every state*—ghost towns, castles, frontier trading posts, fine arts collections, Indian artifacts, antique cars, architectural gems, ethnic museums, wineries, reconstructed villages, pioneer relics, plantations, American folk art, mission churches, and other unique displays of our national heritage." And it does. However, in the five hundred eighty-eight pages in which it does so, there's hardly anything about each one. There are no pictures, and there is no index. But for concocting tours, it is pretty good.

Also see: *Great American Mansions and their Stories* ($10) and *More Great American Mansions and their Stories* ($11.50), available from Hastings House, 10 East 40th, New York, New York 10016. These books tell you about most of the really important historic and architectural and merely splendid homes around the country and relate

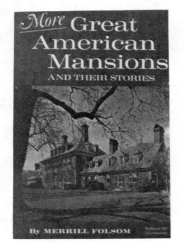

the interesting, sometimes gossipy stories behind them. If you like to visit wonderful houses, these books will tell you where to find them. *America's Historic Houses: The Living Past* (Country Beautiful, Waukesha, Wisconsin 53186; $9.95) does the same thing, only with a different group of houses. Also, this is a larger, coffee-table-sized book. All three, however, have nice pictures.

Women in
American History

There were some headliners among them, it's true, but for the most part women were what *The People's Almanac* called "the footnote characters of history"—people whose contributions were important, but not important enough to make the seventh-grade history texts. *The American Woman's Gazetteer* by Lynn Sherr and Jurate Kazickas gives women, at long last, their due.

The American Woman's Gazetteer is one of those books that, like *The People's Almanac,* you can't put down. The women you read about, in a state-by-state and town-by-town listing of historical sites connected with them, had to overcome prejudice against women outside the home stronger than that in our own era. They struggled against enormous odds. Every page turns up a fascinating story: the well-known tales of Annie Sullivan and Helen Keller at the pump; of a black woman writer who was successful but died poor; of the wife of Napoleon's nephew; of Amelia Earhart's courage; of an orphan who escaped from the East and, masquerading as a man, set out to live the life of a bronco-buster and cattle rancher in the West; of heroines of war, of suffragettes, benefactresses, social reformers, artists, writers, and other women of courage and distinction. Every entry presents you with a brief life, and since they're all told in such an engaging fashion, this is far more than a book to take along with you when you travel. You can stay up all night with it—it's that good. Bantam Books, 666 Fifth Avenue, New York, New York 10019; $7.95.

Arts and Crafts, Music and Dance

Film, Dance, Drama, Etc.

Shakespeare Is a Summer Festival

Every night from June until August, in wooded amphitheaters, high school auditoriums, and reproductions of the Globe Theater around the continent, Shakespeare gets his hour on the stage as part of summer theater festivals devoted to his work. During one recent summer, nearly two dozen of Shakespeare's plays were on view—from the *Merry Wives of Windsor* (four productions) to *Romeo and Juliet, Richard II, Troilus and Cressida, Twelfth Night, The Taming of the Shrew* (three productions each) right on down to *Titus Andronicus* (one production). Here's where you'll find the goings-on:

Anniston, Alabama. In the northern part of the state, halfway between Birmingham and the Georgia line. For schedules, write Box 141, Anniston 36201.

Carmel-by-the-Sea, California. The Forest Theater Guild does one or two plays a year in a pleasant pine-rimmed outdoor theater. Daytimes, you can visit the beaches, the rocky state parks along the coast, the dozens of posh boutiques in this studiedly low-key rich man's village. For details, write Box 1500, Carmel-by-the-Sea 93921.

San Diego, California. Before each performance at this roofed-over Globe theater, built in 1935 for the International Exposition, English country dancers, madrigal singers, jugglers, and the like make merry on the lawns in front of the playhouse. Balboa Park, where it's located, is also home to some remarkable museums and gardens. For schedules, write P. O. Box 2171, San Diego 92112.

Boulder, Colorado. The Colorado Shakespeare Festival, held in this Rocky Mountains university town, does about three plays each season in its open-air theater. For details, write the University Theatre, University of Colorado, Boulder 80302.

Miami Beach, Florida. Here there is Shakespeare-by-the-Sea, for six weeks starting usually in the middle of June. For details, write the Miami Beach Chamber of Commerce, 1688 Meridian Avenue, Miami Beach 33139.

Louisville, Kentucky. The Shake-

speare here is in Central Park—and it's free. For details, write the Visitors Bureau, Founders Square, Louisville 40202.

Monmouth, Maine. The Theater at Monmouth, in a tiny Victorian Hall muralled with bosomy ladies—one of the oldest operating theaters in the country—specializes in classical drama, so in addition to seeing plays by Shakespeare, you might also take in some by Shaw or Molière. Monmouth is about 50 miles from Portland. For details, write the theater at Cumston Hall, in Monmouth 04259.

Madison, New Jersey. Some Shakespeare and some more modern works can be seen nightly (and twice an evening on Saturday). For details, write the Festival in Madison 07940.

Woodbridge, New Jersey. Home of the Garden State's second Bardic festival, the New Jersey Shakespeare Festival of Woodbridge, Woodbridge is, however, the site of only a few performances: the company takes one featured play to high school auditoriums and woodsy county parks around the state. For details, write the Festival at 428 South Park Drive, Woodbridge 07095.

New York, New York. Producer Joe Papp, one of the czars of the New York drama scene, has been promoting low-cost innovative theater in Manhattan for years. His year-round New York Shakespeare Festival's Central Park portion (always imaginative to the last detail, and free) is one of his triumphs, and one of the things New Yorkers consider nicest about their town: lately not all the programs have been works by Shakespeare—in fact, in 1977 the free summer productions were those that winter audiences had paid to see. No matter. Heading for Central Park after work, picnic basket in hand, and lining up to get the free tickets that are distributed about six o'clock; then picnicking on the lawns while jugglers, strolling troubadours, actors reciting poetry, and assorted musical groups entertain is a New York City summer tradition. For the latest schedule, write the New York Convention and Visitors Bureau, 90 East 42nd Street, New York, New York 10017.

Lakewood, Ohio. Audiences in the Cleveland area nearby have had a *Julius Caesar* set in the sixties, a teeny bopper's *Love's Labour's Lost*, and a whole string of other very innovative productions as part of the Great Lakes Shakespeare Festival. In addition to Shakespeare's works you'll also see productions of other classics, which in the past have included works such as John Millington Synge's *Playboy of the Western World* and Augustin Daly's *Under the Gaslight.* For details, write the box office at the Lakewood Civic Auditorium, Franklin at Bunts, Lakewood 44107.

Stratford, Ontario. The biggest and most celebrated of the Shakespeare festivals, the Stratford Festival also offers you some of the best theater anywhere, which in addition to brilliant Shakespeare may include Molière, new Canadian works, chamber music, films, Offenbach, and much more. All told, there are three theaters in this otherwise not too interesting town. For information about tickets and places to stay—both of which you should arrange for well in advance—write the Festival Theater Box Office, Stratford N5A 6V2.

Ashland, Oregon. The Oregon Shakespeare Festival—getting to be a half-century old—is the only place in the world outside Shakespeare-loving Germany where you can regularly see the Bard's work performed without intermission—as it was in the sixteenth century. There are two theaters—an open-air Globe and an indoor stage. For information on tickets and lodgings—for which you should write well in advance—contact the Festival in Ashland 97520.

Odessa, Texas. A red-carpeted Globe Theater and the world's largest jack rabbits are this town's chief claims to fame, along with a good Shakespeare festival, about which you can get details from the box office at 2308 Shakespeare Road, Odessa 79761.

Cedar City, Utah. Zion and Bryce Canyon National Parks nearby make the setting of this festival one of the most spectacular; it's also one of the gayest, with the local ladies donning Elizabethan robes to hawk Tudor tarts, serenade theatergoers, and play puppeteer for Punch and Judy shows. For more information, write the Utah Shakespearean Festival in Cedar City 84720.

Burlington, Vermont. Folk dancers and minstrels entertain on the lawn of the theater, which is just a few minutes' walk from Lake Champlain; the plays are almost always Shakespeare's. For tickets, write the Royall Tyler Theatre at the University of Vermont, which sponsors the festival, in Burlington 05401.

Washington, D.C. The Sylvan Theater, on the grounds of the Washington Monument, is the home of this Shakespeare Summer Festival, which is a sort of city counterpart to the campfire talks at other, more rugged National Park Service areas. For further information, write the festival at 1100 Ohio Drive, S.W., Washington, D.C. 20242.

The Big U.S. Film Festival

In New York City, where it's held every September, critics wear themselves out for the New York Film Festival. There are dozens of big premieres and lots of hoopla. The New York Convention and Visitors Bureau (90 East 42nd Street, New York, New York 10017) can send you a schedule and information about other city goings-on for the duration.

A Pageant Where Real People Pose As Works of Art

And they do it so well—at the Pageant of the Masters, part of the Festival of the Arts at Laguna Beach, California—that even people sitting up front can barely tell that the tableaux they're seeing aren't oversized sculptures. For one pageant, for example, an ancient Scythian comb with elaborate ornamentation was created; for another, Robert Krantz designed "Fantasy of Wings," which depicts a young woman surrounded by soaring pigeons. The actors' costumes are of muslin painted with oils and stiffened so that an ill-timed breeze won't riffle them. As many as 150 performers will be on stage during the course of an evening, which might be made up of twenty or more tableaux. It's such an impressive show that it sells out way ahead of time for the entire six weeks of performances. Generally, however, a few tickets are returned for resale, so it's worth contacting the box office if at the last minute you decide you're interested.

For details, write the Festival of the Arts at 650 Canyon Road, Laguna Beach, California 92651.

The Chautauquas

Visiting the Chautauqua Festival is like going to college for a week or two: there are lectures, classes, all sorts of evening programs, orchestral concerts with a resident orchestra, ballets, jazz programs, opera, pop shows, poetry readings, and more lectures. You can sign up for a week-long jazz workshop, or study potting, needlepoint, philosophy, psychology, education, political science, or just about anything else you could study at a university, and quite a lot more. At Chautauqua, New York, where the first such institution—a training camp for Sunday School teachers—was founded in 1874, you can also swim, sit on the beach, go fishing, play tennis and golf, and sail. Lodgings in quaint old Victorian hotels are as little as $40 a couple a day, all meals included. Guest houses cost still less. Everything else, except special opera and theater presentations, is covered by the daily admission charge, which ranges from $2.50 to $6 or so, depending on the evening program. For more information, write the Chautauqua Institution, Chautauqua, New York 14722.

More Chautauquas: in Boulder, Colorado, all summer long; and in Huron, South Dakota, during July. For details, write the Chambers of Commerce—1001 Canyon Boulevard, Boulder, Colorado 80302; and Huron, South Dakota 57350.

Summer Dance

Business people, house spouses, musicians, writers, and just about everybody else takes a long breather during the summer. Not dancers. Relaxing for any appreciable length of time means trouble. And so, during the summer, the dancers are dancing. Where to see them?

At Jacob's Pillow, in Lee, Massachusetts. Founded by dancer Ted Shawn, Jacob's Pillow has been a

mecca for balletomanes ever since its founding many years ago; this is one of *the* very best dance festivals in the United States. For details on who's dancing when, write Box 287, Lee 01238.

At the American Dance Festival, in New London, Connecticut, there's some more dancing. For details, write the box office in New London 06320.

And some more: at Artpark, in Lewiston, New York (Box 371, Lewiston 14092), in the western part of the state;

at the Chautauqua Institution (Chautauqua, New York 14722); at the New Jersey Shakespeare Festival at Drew University (Madison, New Jersey 07940); at Wolf Trap Farm Park for the Performing Arts (1624 Trap Road, Vienna, Virginia 22180); at the Saratoga Performing Arts Center in Saratoga Springs, New York (Drawer B, Saratoga Springs 12866); and at the Rockland County Dance Festival (Calls Hollow Road, Stony Point, New York 10980).

Jamaica Dance

Folk dance plus modern dance makes up the repertoire of the National Dance Theatre Company in Jamaica, with performances in Kingston in July and August. The Jamaica Tourist Board can send you more information; write 2 Dag Hammarskjold Plaza, New York, New York 10017.

Square Dancing

If you wrote off square dancing back in high school when it was the stock activity for coed gym classes, think again. There are more than 230 national square-dancing associations, and if all the square dancers joined hands, they would form a chain long enough to stretch from California to Maine. All those square dancers must know something.

The fact is that it's fun. Apart from the fact that it makes you feel a hundred miles away from the more inconsequential matters of the fourth quarter of the twentieth century, there's nothing quite like the giddy feeling you get when you swing a partner around and around, or run through the intricate patterns of the dance until you're breathless. And there's nothing quite like the warm feeling of community and group accomplishment that you get after you've run through some squares without a hitch—and if you do flub, nobody's going to be terribly upset. "Square Dancing Is Fun," a brochure put out by one North Carolina square-dance club, might be overstating the case somewhat in lumping *all* square dancers in the category of "good, clean, tolerant and lovable citizens," but it is pretty hard to imagine anger and hostility in a situation where everybody is rosy-cheeked and sweaty with exertion and so keyed up that less inhibited members of the group are letting out whoops and hollers with every other do-si-do.

To start out, all you've got to do is learn some of the dances, and you can do that just about anywhere; most dancers start at local clubs, or at various square-dancing clinics and conventions.

Square-Dancing Conventions

At the National Square Dancing Con-

> "1. The music is to consist of a fiddle, a pipe or tabor, a hurdy gurdy. No chorus is to be sung until the dancing is over.
> 2. No lady is to dance in black stockings, nor to have her elbows bare.
> 3. To prevent spitting, no gentleman will chew tobacco or smoke.
> 4. No whispering to be allowed. If anyone should be found to make insidious remarks about anyone's dancing, he or she shall be put out of the room.
> 5. No gentleman will appear with a cravat that has been worn more than a week or a fortnight.
> 6. Long beards are forbidden, as they would be very disagreeable if a gentleman should happen to put his cheek beside a lady's.
> 7. No gentleman must squeeze his partner's hand, nor look earnestly upon her, and, furthermore, he must not pick up her handkerchief, provided it were to fall. The first denotes he loves her, the second he wishes to kiss her, and the last that she makes a sign for both."
> —Square Dancing Rules of 1876, quoted in *Class Notes*

vention, some forty thousand square-dancing freaks circulate family, recycle, coordinate, pass the ocean, chase right, track two, teacup chain, triple trade, triple scoot and substitute, turn and left through, and generally wear themselves out on the dance floor. They come from all over for the usual squares as well as for clinics in contra dancing, workshops in clogging (a form of Appalachian dance) and in rounds dancing, and lots more. National Conventions will be held in Oklahoma City, Oklahoma (June 22-24, 1978); Milwaukee, Wisconsin (June 28-30, 1979); Memphis, Tennessee (June 26-28, 1980); and Seattle, Washington, in 1981. For details, write the American Square Dance Society, 462 North Robertson Boulevard, Los Angeles, California 90048.

Some Square-Dance Resorts

You go for a week, square dance twice a day, every day—at clinics in the morning and at dances in the evening—and, in between, enjoy the hiking or the swimming or the fishing around the resort property, and the eating in the dining room. Fontana Village, a family resort at Fontana Dam, North Carolina 28733, caters to a mom-and-pop-and-the-kids trade during the summer and to square dancers in the off season, sometimes as many as eight hundred at a time. There are nearly a dozen major square dance get-togethers here every year in spring and fall.

At Kirkwood Lodge, on the shores of Lake of the Ozarks at Osage Beach,

Missouri, square-dance vacations are the order of the day from June through mid-October. There are water sports available in the area, but most people come just for the dancing. The huge hardwood floor of the dance hall sits on top of a cork platform that makes the dancing easier on the legs. Most sessions are for intermediates and experts only, but occasionally there are weeks open to beginners. Write. The address: Osage Beach, Missouri 65065.

Square-dance seminars for beginners are given at least once every summer at Andy's Trout Farms Square Dance Inn and Campground in Dillard, Georgia, in the hilly northern part of the state. There are callers' clinics, clogging weeks, and all manner of special holiday celebrations. For a schedule, write P. O. Box 129, Dillard 30537.

More Square-Dancing Clinics for Learners
There are two national square-dancing magazines in which you can get information about square-dancing schools for beginners and special workshops at resorts in the United States: *American Square Dance* (P. O. Box 788, Sandusky, Ohio 44870) and *Square Dancing* (462 North Robertson Boulevard, Los Angeles 90048). A year's subscription to each is $6; single copies are also available.

World Square-Dance Championships
Bluegrass music and some gospel singing go along with some of the fanciest square dancing on the continent. You watch from the stands at the Civic Center in Asheville, North Carolina, the Appalachian town where the championship is held every year in October, close to the height of the fall color season. For details write Dennis Abe, Box 283, College Park, Maryland 20740.

A Giant National Polka Festival and a Dance Floor as Big as the Dance Deserves

The first National Polka Festival at Hunter Mountain, New York, in the Catskills, was held in August 1977. Daily polka contests were part of the show, but if you've ever had the yen to twirl your way around a polka floor big enough to accommodate this very unsedate frolic of a dance, you probably would have found the real star to be the dance floor. Big enough to accommodate a thousand dancers at once, it was housed in what the festival organizers described as "the largest tent in the United States." Fifteen of the top polka bands played music from Poland, Czechoslovakia, the Ukraine,

and Germany, while nondancers guzzled huge quantities of beer.

For details about future events, write Box 297, zip 12442.

Country Dancing

Morris dancing, reels, rounds, and some other dances you've probably read about in old novels, along with some whose names you might not know, caused quite a stir in their day: the Puritan fathers, you might remember, banned dancing altogether. Yet when you visit a meeting of the Country Dance and Song Society of America and dance your way through the movements, it's hard to imagine the rationale of those dour old men, unless it was to put a damper on all good spirits and to squelch any of those feelings of freedom that come from being light on your feet and swirling in the arms of a dozen different partners.

One of the great things about country dancing in this century is that at all Country Dance and Song Society balls, the dances are taught. The caller takes you slowly through the movements before the music starts. If you get a little confused, nobody minds too much: there are plenty of other people in the same boat, and the real aficionados—the ones who dance twice a month or more and spend their vacations at special dancing camps—keep the groups moving right along.

The Society has dance centers in Auburn, Alabama; Altadena, San Francisco, Isla Vista, San Diego, and Santa Monica, California; Manchester, Connecticut; Washington, D.C.; Atlanta, Georgia; Chicago and St. Charles, Illinois; Richmond and French Lick, Indiana; Berea, Louisville, Hindman, Morehead, and Lexington, Kentucky; Potomac and Baltimore, Maryland; Boston, Massachusetts; Minneapolis, Minnesota; Allendale, New Jersey; Garden City, Rochester, Larchmont, and New York, New York; Brasstown, Charlotte, and Asheville, North Carolina; Media, Philadelphia, and Pittsburgh, Pennsylvania; Knoxville and Rutherford, Tennessee; Brattleboro, Vermont; Charlottesville, Williamsburg, and Wise, Virginia; Seattle, Washington; and Peterstown, West Virginia. You can get the exact addresses from the national headquarters at 55 Christopher Street, New York, New York 10014.

Country-Dancing Camp
In July and August, the Country Dance and Song Society sponsors a country-dancing camp at Buzzards Bay, Massachusetts, at the base of Cape Cod. It's just a short drive from Plymouth Rock, but it's doubtful that

you'd even get the urge to go visit during the week you're at the camp. The dancing and music-making—there are fiddles, concertinas, accordions, tambours, penny-whistles, and guitars playing somewhere almost all the time—will keep you busy enough, and when you're not enjoying the tunes or the dancing, you'll probably feel like going for a swim or just putting your feet up for a rest.

There are great special weeks for families, where country, morris, and sword dances are taught to groups of adults, four- and five-year-olds, and six to twelve-year-olds. Between dances there are crafts programs, juggling lessons, family sings, family dances.

In addition, there are all-dance weeks, all-folk-music weeks, and American dance and music weeks. There's always some dancing, but the emphasis changes. Nearly all the activities are held in open-air pavilions, which keeps you cool and gives you a chance to get plenty of sea air. It's a great sociable way to spend a vacation, and not very expensive either—just about $150 per person, including room, board, and tuition. Write the CDSS (55 Christopher Street, New York, New York 10014) for details. Weeks fill up quickly, so make your plans early.

Jamaica Country Dance
It's quite unlike what they do at the CDSS, but just as interesting. Groups come out of the mountains in the summer to perform at the Independence Festival in August. During the rest of the year, you can go up into the towns themselves for the performances. For more information, contact the Jamaica Tourist Board at 2 Dag Hammarskjold Plaza, New York, New York 10017.

Quick Tunes and Good Times
by Newton F. Tolman

A nifty, folksy little book that tells about this New Englander's experiences with the music that goes with the dances: the custom of the family orchestra, how square dancing almost died out in his small town, and how some young people who came up took an interest in the music and started playing up such a storm at it that they eventually made it to the Newport Music Festival. Tolman also tells you about jigs, planxtys, strathspeys, rants, reels, and hornpipes; about the time the oboe player came to town; and about his own repertoire: Chorus Jig, Cicilian Circle, Rose-Bud, Wake-up Susan, and on and on. Sounds like fun. William L. Bauhan, Publisher, Dublin, New Hampshire 03444; $5.50.

Where to Learn Your Decorative Arts

There are a handful of forums where amateurs can come to take short courses about antique furniture, silver, glassware, and such from the pros.

In the East, you'll find them at Historic Deerfield (Box 321, Deerfield, Massachusetts 01342); at Old Sturbridge Village (Sturbridge, Massachusetts 01566); at the New York State Historical Association (Cooperstown, New York 13326); at Corning's Museum of Glass (Corning Glass Center, Corning, New York 14830); and at the Pennsylvania Farm Museum at Landis Valley (c/o Pennsylvania Historical and Museum Commission, Box 1024, Harrisburg, Pennsylvania 17120).

In the South, contact the Arkansas Arts Center in MacArthur Park (P. O. Box 2137, Little Rock, Arkansas 72203); the Pilgrimage Garden Club (Box 1776, Natchez, Mississippi 39120); the Colonial Williamsburg Foundation (Williamsburg, Virginia 23185).

In the Midwest, you'll find these learning sessions at the Henry Ford Museum and Greenfield Village (Dearborn, Michigan 48121) and at the Minneapolis Institute of Arts, 2400 Third Avenue, Minneapolis, Minnesota 55404.

See Your Favorite old TV Show at a Museum

The library at the Museum of Broadcasting at One East 53rd Street in New York City contains just about any program you might care to see.

Roots? Roots.

Amos and Andy? Amos and Andy.

Arthur Godfrey Time? That too. Plus the Mary Martin musical version of *Peter Pan,* Jackie Kennedy Onassis' walking tour of the White House, the men on the moon.

And radio shows, too: Edward R. Murrow, FDR's fireside chats, the radio debut of Judy Garland.

Consoles are available for your viewing or listening, and you can stay as long as you like (though museum members may take your place after a certain time). It's fascinating, this replay of the life and times of America. For details, write the museum in New York (10022).

The Cemetery as Art Gallery

Some good books to take along with you when you go cemetery-seeing:

Early New England Gravestone Rubbings by Edmund V. Gillon, Jr. Photos and rubbings from the burial grounds around New England, a short discussion of the motifs (death's heads, angels, portraits, willows and urns, and various other symbols and oddities), and information about how to take rubbings. The epitaphs are fun. An example: AS YOU ARE NOW, SO ONCE WAS I: AS I AM NOW, SO YOU MUST BE. SO PREPARE FOR DEATH AND FOLLOW ME. This is not a scholarly work; for complete history and documentation the author refers you to *Gravestones of Early New England* by Harriette M. Forbes (1927). But for most purposes, this book is quite interesting and gives a good idea of the variety of headstones you'll find when you go looking.

Victorian Cemetery Art, also by Edmund V. Gillon, Jr. Listen to what he says: "The Victorian cemetery . . . amounted in many towns to an additional park, for public use. Where we shun our cemeteries, the Victorian family delighted in them and could think of no better place, say, for a family picnic. . . . For one thing, cemeteries were at that time quite new. Early day frontier burial . . . had given way . . . to burial on church property—the famous village churchyard. As villages became cities, crowding began. . . . With the founding of Mount Auburn Cemetery, outside of Cambridge, Massachusetts, in 1831, a new concept appeared—a wooded area . . . specifically set aside

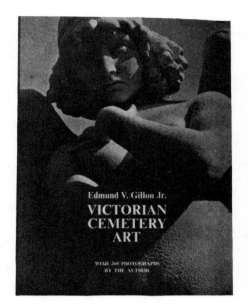

with grassy hills, solitary grottoes, 'enlivened with music from feathered songsters' . . . The large amounts of space in the Victorian cemetery were to revolutionize cemetery art and permit the use of sculpture in a way that the crowded churchyard had never allowed." So begins the book, which is mostly photos that show you in fascinating detail how the Victorians used their cemetery sculpture and symbolism to say a last few words about their dear departed. They should have you looking at those idylls-in-the-country in a new light. Dover Books, 180 Varick Street, New York, New York 10014; $4 each.

Sounds of Music

Some Jazz Festivals

The entire city of Hampton, Virginia, goes berserk over the Annual Hampton Jazz Festival, which runs Friday through Sunday, the last weekend in June (usually), and which turns the Coliseum into a mass of far-out hair and wild outfits. General hysteria reigns. It's hard to get tickets unless you plan ahead, and rooms are booked up about two months before the festival: act accordingly. The box office at the Hampton Coliseum (Box 7809, Hampton 23669) can send ticket information; the Hampton Department of Commerce in City Hall (same zip) can provide general information.

The Monterey Jazz Festival, in Monterey, California, features about three days of top-notch music in September—people like Dizzy Gillespie, Chuck Mangione, John Lewis, the James Cotton Blues Band. Some concerts are themed around an instrument (guitar, flute) or a type of music (Latin, blues). This is a big, shiny affair, so you have to get tickets well in advance. Write Box JAZZ, Monterey 93940, or the Monterey Visitors and Convention Bureau, Box 489 (same zip).

The Big Apple Jazz Festival fills up the spring concert schedule in New York City. The Convention and Visitors Bureau (90 East 42nd Street, New York, New York 10017) can send schedules.

More jazzmania. In Kansas City, Missouri, in April; for details, write the convention bureau in Kansas City (1212 Wyandotte Street, Kansas City 64105).

And, of course, New Orleans, where the Jazz and Heritage Festival makes things hop a little faster a week every year in April. For the details, write Box 2530, New Orleans 70176.

Summer Concerts

It's not long after Memorial Day that the music scene in the cities goes into a slump. Concert calendars shrink. You can't find a recital if you look for one. There's barely a musician in sight. They've all taken off for the mountains, the seashore, the nicest parts of the countryside to hold forth for the hot weather months at summer music festivals. If you follow them, you can count on hearing some good music—old music that doesn't often get played

in the cities, new music that's too wild for the cities, old favorites that city audiences have gotten tired of (sublimities like Beethoven's Ninth) but which take on a new meaning when you hear them under the stars with the crickets protesting the silence between movements. Just about any small resort town will have its weekend chamber music series: some, however, stage more ambitious festivals, and bring lots of big-name performers for night after glittering night of virtuosity. A good assortment follows.

The Big Deals

The Marlboro Music Festival, in Marlboro, Vermont, about ten miles from Brattleboro, features some of the most exciting concertizing on the East Coast. The programs for the weekend performances aren't picked until the preceding Thursday, and what you hear is for the most part determined by what the musicians have been working on that week; the concerts are really almost incidental to the music-making that goes on under the aegis of artistic director Rudolf Serkin. Most of the tickets sell out within a week or two of an early April mailing, but a hundred, all outside, are saved to be sold on the day of the performance at the box office about an hour before curtain time. To get on the mailing list, contact the Marlboro Music Festival at Marlboro, Vermont 05344, or, before early June or after mid-August, at 135 South 18th Street, Philadelphia, Pennsylvania 19103. For information about lodging in the area, write the Chamber of Commerce at 180 Main Street in Brattleboro, Vermont 05301.

The Saratoga Performing Arts Center at Saratoga Springs, New York, is another big deal. A pop season begins and ends a glittering seven weeks of the Philadelphia Orchestra with Eugene Ormandy and George Balanchine's New York City Ballet. Saratoga Springs is an elegant place if ever there was one; the August horse racing season brings the very rich to town in droves, and you can scarcely get a room. Most performances are given in a huge open-ended pavilion; you can buy seats under cover or take a blanket and sit on the velvety lawns. Tickets are available through Ticketron or by mail from the Saratoga Festival Office, Drawer B, Saratoga Springs, New York 12866; to find out about places to stay, write the Chamber of Commerce in Saratoga Springs (same zip). Reserve well in advance.

A similarly extravagant affair can be found at Tanglewood, in Lenox, Massachusetts, during the Berkshire Music Festival. Tanglewood, an old Berkshire Mountains estate, is the summer home of the Boston Symphony Orchestra. Concerts are given mainly on Saturday nights and Sunday afternoons, and there are usually open rehearsals on Saturday mornings. The repertoire is generally proven twentieth-century pieces, major works, old favorites. Midweek there are occasional pop concerts plus chamber and small orchestral concerts given by the students at the Berkshire Music Center on the fringes of the estate. For tickets, call Ticketron or write the Festival ticket office in Lenox, Massachusetts 01240; the Berkshire Hills Conference, 107 South Street in Pittsfield 01201, can send information about country inns and other interesting places to stay in the area.

Wolf Trap Farm Park, in Vienna, Virginia, is the national park for the performing arts, and as such it presents a thorough cross-section of what's going on with American music and what Americans are listening to in the way of music—a huge mix that includes everything from Beverly Sills and Cleo Laine to Aaron Copland (conducting the New York Philharmonic) or Martha Graham, the Preservation Hall Jazz Band or the Metropolitan Opera: it just depends on the season. The setting, on an estate in the green hills outside Washington, D.C., couldn't be more delightful. For more information, contact the Wolf Trap Farm Park Box Office at 1624 Trap Road, Vienna, Virginia 22180.

Blossom Music Center at Cuyahoga Falls, Ohio, a woods-rimmed cedar-shingled shell halfway between Akron and Cleveland, is the summer home of the Cleveland Symphony Orchestra, which presents quite a few of the four to six weekly concerts (the balance being pops—Fred Waring, Chet Atkins, some Scott Joplin, et al). Even the classical concerts are relaxed affairs, though, with aluminum folding chairs set up all over the lawn. Pop concerts have the effect of carpeting the lawns with blue jeans. For details, write the Blossom Music Center Box Office, 1145 West Steels Corners Road, Cuyahoga Falls 44223. For lodgings, write the Cleveland Convention and Visitors Bureau, 511 Terminal Tower, Cleveland 44113.

The Ravinia Festival at Highland Park, Illinois, is where the Chicago Symphony Orchestra does a good deal of its summer concertizing. You can expect quite a few one-composer concerts, at least two concert operas (sung without scenery), and soloists of the stature of Beverly Sills and Alfred Brendel. Mornings and afternoons, there are chamber concerts and recitals in another theater on the grounds, and master classes by the artists in residence are open to the public for audit. In addition, the music season is usually followed by a week of ballet and two or three weeks of theater. For the details of the schedule, write Box 896, Highland Park, Illinois 60035.

Aspen, Colorado, would be an exciting place in the summer for the mountain setting alone. However, it's also the home to one of the big and important American music festivals—an orgy of jazz, choral, operatic, and orchestral goings-on that scarcely lets up for two months. The concerts held on Friday evenings and on Saturday and Sunday afternoons are just the tip of the iceberg, as it were. Many seldom-heard works that require odd combinations of instruments are performed here simply because there are so many musicians on hand; and the repertoire—medieval through the latest contemporary works—is about as interesting as you'll find anywhere. For tickets and schedules, write Box AA in Aspen 81611; for lodgings, write the Aspen Resort Association at Box 1188 (same zip).

In Canada, Festival Canada, in Ottawa, includes chamber operas, three major full-scale opera productions, a chamber music series, an assortment of recitals and concerts, as well as performances of folk songs and dances. For details, write the box office at the National Arts Center in Ottawa K1P 5W1.

Music in the Mountains
The Grand Teton Music Festival in Jackson Hole, Wyoming, takes place at the foot of some of the craggiest mountains in North America. Sometimes the music is accompanied by spoken commentary by artists, or followed by free cookies or watermelon—which lend a pleasant informality. Orchestral performances are usually on Saturday; contemporary music of all types is featured on Thursdays. For details, write Box 20, Teton Village, Wyoming 83025; for lodgings information, write the Chamber of Commerce in Jackson 83001.

At the White Mountains Center for Music and the Arts in Jefferson, New Hampshire, members of the resident Summermusic Orchestra, mostly musicians come up from New York, hold forth in a tent set up on the grounds of the Waumbek Inn, one of those rambling white clapboard structures with a lineup of rocking chairs on a mountain-view veranda. There are open rehearsals and evening concerts on Fridays, Saturdays, and Sundays; occasional small chamber concerts are presented in the middle of the week. For tickets, write the box office at Box 145, Jefferson 03583. The White Mountains Region Association, in Lancaster 03584, can send you details about super-quaint country inns where you can spend the night in the area.

A Musical Garden
The Peter Britt Gardens Music and Arts Festival, in Jacksonville, Oregon, features more or less nightly programs of orchestral music, plus afternoon chamber concerts and recitals—some in crumbling, Bronte-esque gardens that were terraced and landscaped during Gold Rush days by a daguerrotypist who made good, some in the tiny ballroom of a turn-of-the-century hotel in the center of this antique community.

Tickets for chamber concerts should be purchased in advance. Because of the concurrent Oregon Shakespearean Festival at Ashland, about thirty miles away, you should reserve ahead for a room. For all information, write the Peter Britt Gardens Music and Arts Festival, Box 669, Jacksonville 97530.

Music in the Ivy League
In the gently rolling farms-and-woods country of the central Connecticut River Valley, Hanover, New Hampshire, positively buzzes during the summer with the goings-on of the arts festival at Dartmouth College's Hopkins Center. Everything is under one roof: concerts of old and new music, a chamber series by a resident quartet, recitals by guest artists, classic and contemporary drama, pop concerts, films of opera and ballet. The town itself is a comfortable, affluent sort of place. It's full of ivied brick buildings and big old trees, but because of the presence of the college, it's far more sophisticated than its size would warrant.

For specifics on the festival, write

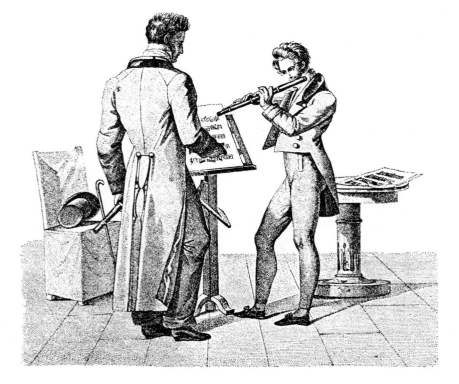

the Hopkins Center at Dartmouth College in Hanover 03755. The Chamber of Commerce (same zip) can send you details about the fine country inns and interesting hotels in the area.

Music in Some Mansions
The Caramoor Festival is held at an estate of Italian Renaissance opulence in Katonah, New York, about an hour's drive from Manhattan. Chamber concerts are presented in the mansion's Spanish courtyard; larger works, including opera and ballet, are given at an outdoor theater surrounded by ninth-century columns. For details, write the box office in Katonah 10536.

Certainly one of the most interesting concerts in the area takes place in Newport, Rhode Island, for just two weeks starting at the end of July. Each of the three daily concerts features the sort of music that was long ago relegated to obscurity by short-sighted critics, and most of the concerts are presented in the gilt-and-marble ballrooms of the palatial Newport mansions, some of which are sort of miniature Versailles. Sometimes there's music by Gershwin and Kern, sometimes a celebration of lesser-known American composers. Sometimes you'll hear the Beethoven or Bach that nobody knows. You won't, however, be bored by the repertoire. Tickets are always available at the door, but you've got to get there at least a half hour before curtain to get good seats. For specific schedules or tickets, write the festival at 50 Washington Square, Newport 02840.

Music in a Country Churchyard
There's a special festival in each part of the state. In Portsmouth, on the coast, the Strawberry Banke Chamber Music Festival takes place on a restoration of the old part of town, down by the water. The clock on its Olde South Meeting House, where concerts are held, may gong nine times in the middle of a piece. Afterward: cookies and cake and punch on the lawn, which is where you may sit if you don't arrive forty minutes before the 8:15 starting time. Late June through August. For details, write the Chamber of Commerce at 10 Vaughan Street Pedestrian Mall, Suite 10, Portsmouth, New Hampshire 03801.

Music in the Vineyards
The Music at the Vineyards festival, in Saratoga, California, about sixty miles south of San Francisco, brings an annual world premiere of a work commissioned especially for the occasion, as well as pieces that call for unusual instrumentation, to a series of three pairs of weekend concerts. Free champagne on the terrace-with-a-view at intermissions. For details, write the box office at Box 97, Saratoga 95070.

Also look into the August Moon Concerts at the Charles Krug Winery in Napa, California (Box 535, Napa 94558).

Back to Bach
Carmel, California, the northern coastal home town of a Shakespeare festival and a blue million of the poshest shops this side of Neiman-Marcus, also hosts some inspired music-making at recitals, daily evening concerts, and matinees during the Carmel Bach Festival; the historic basilica of the Carmel Mission is the scene of some of the special choral and orchestral events. Every year, you'll hear either the Passion According to St. John, the Passion According to St. Matthew, or the B Minor Mass. Be sure to get your ticket in advance, from the box office at Box 575, Carmel 93921. The Carmel Business Association, Box 4444, at the same zip, can send you information about the chic little inns in the area.

At the Rochester, New York, Bach Festival, the words of the cantatas sometimes get lost in the vaulting of the neo-Gothic cathedral where they're sung—as they were meant to be. The soloists are all professional, and the orchestra is made up of members of the Eastman School of Music Faculty and the Rochester Philharmonic. For tickets, write the festival box office at 121 Vassar Street, Rochester 14607.

Bethlehem, Pennsylvania, has a big Bach Festival in May on the campus of Lehigh University. Write the city's Chamber of Commerce at 11 West Market Street (zip 18018) for details.

And in late February, the Florida Symphony Orchestra joins a 140-voice Bach Choir for a two-day festival devoted to Bach (and his contemporaries) at Rollins College in Winter Park, Florida (Box 2733, Winter Park 32789, for details).

More Bach. The Abbey Bach Festival in St. Benedict, Oregon, one weekend at the end of July. The Chamber of Commerce (zip 97373) can send you particulars.

Mostly Mozart
The festival by that name is a major exception to the summer-music-festival-in-the-country rule—and it's the big event of New York City's musical summer. The music, performed by important orchestral and chamber groups and soloists, is mostly by Mozart, but there are exceptions. For details, write the New York Convention and Visitors Bureau, 90 East 42nd Street, New York, New York 10017.

The Vermont Mozart Festival, in Burlington, Vermont, is smaller, but pleasant; some of the concerts are inside, some outside on the wooded University of Vermont campus. For details, write the Lane Series Office,

Waterman Building, University of Vermont, Burlington 05401.

In Puerto Rico
The Casals Festival—which grew up on the island around cellist-and-resident Pablo Casals—has become *the* major cultural affair in the Caribbean; the attendance of artists like Claudio Arrau and Rudolf Serkin, Isaac Stern, and Daniel Barenboim have made it one of the most important musical events in the world. Before the concerts—usually clustered during the first two weeks in June—or afterward, you can do the usual Puerto Rican things—watch the cockfights, visit the Old-World-Spanish sections of San Juan and markets—or just lie around on the beach and soak up the hot sun. For details on the festival, write the Puerto Rico Tourism Development Company at 268 Munoz Rivera Avenue, Hato Rey, Puerto Rico 00919 or in the Sperry Rand Building at 1290 Avenue of the Americas, New York, New York 10019.

Sousa Revisited

The Virginia Beach Music Festival, in Virginia Beach, Virginia, is four long days of band music that climax in a stupendous concert at which fifteen hundred musicians of all shapes and sizes mass on a high school football field to clarion, rousing pieces like "Anchors Aweigh" and the national anthem. All performances are free. For dates and more information, write the Virginia Beach Chamber of Commerce, Box 390, Virginia Beach 23458.

A town of barely three thousand inhabitants, Bottineau, North Dakota, on the Canadian border, isn't what you'd call a lively place (except perhaps during the annual water fowl migration, when hundreds of thousands of Canada geese converge on the nearby J. Clark Salyer National Wildlife Refuge). But it is the home of the celebrated International Peace Garden—and of one of the United States's big band festivals, the International Youth Band Festival. It brings some hundred-odd bands from nearly twenty countries to compete as part of an International Festival of the Arts. For details, contact the Chamber of Commerce in Bottineau 58318. Also, at Moose Jaw, Saskatchewan, an International Band Festival with about five thousand musicians and seventy bands; the Department of Tourism in Regina S4P 3N2, can send more information.

Bands in Gazebos for Concerts on the Green

There's nothing more romantic than sitting out on the soft grass of a New

England town square, watching the stars come out, munching your picnic dinner, and listening to the sometimes schmaltzy, sometimes stirring music of the town band. It's an experience you don't find just anywhere nowadays.

At last look, however, summer evenings saw such concerts happening in the following towns. If you're in the area, ask.

Maine: Bangor, Bar Harbor, Bridgton.

Massachusetts: Ashby, Attleboro, Barnstable, Beverly, Falmouth, Gloucester, Lunenburg, Manchester, Marion, Mattapoisett, Oak Bluffs on Martha's Vineyard, Orange, Petersham, Vineyard Haven (also on Martha's Vineyard), and Wareham.

New Hampshire: Claremont, Concord, Hillsboro, Lancaster, Manchester, Sunapee Harbor.

Rhode Island: Wickford.

Vermont: Burlington, Lyndonville, Montpelier, St. Johnsbury.

A Choral Fest and a Giant Sing-In

At the Cincinnati, Ohio, May Festival—the big deal on the musical calendar of a very civilized city—massed choruses of staggering size and hordes of superstars of the opera world perform ambitious works for orchestra and chorus, cantatas, and operas (sung here concert style) for about a week at the end of May. At a just-for-fun concert with ten-cent beer during intermission, the audience joins in to sing works like Beethoven's Ninth or the Magnificat in D with a full orchestra, under the baton of a well-known conductor. To order tickets—and do it in advance—contact the Cincinnati Musical Festival Association, Music Hall, 1241 Elm Street, Cincinnati 45210. For lodging information, contact the Chamber of Commerce, 4th and Race, Cincinnati 45202.

Gian Carlo Menotti's Festival

The composer founded his first one about twenty years ago in Spoleto, Italy; the first American counterpart took place in 1977 in Charleston, South Carolina, with such a flourish that the local ladies were opening their homes to visitors who couldn't get rooms in the hotels. There are ballet and opera productions, chamber music concerts, and a play. The first time around, the closing concert took place in one of the fine public gardens of the city.

For more information, write the Spoleto Festival U.S.A., P. O. Box 157, Charleston 29402, and the Spoleto Housing Bureau, P. O. Box 975, Charleston 29402.

Summer Opera

The hall in which presentations of the Lake George Opera Festival, in Glens Falls, New York, are held is a high school the rest of the year, and the atmosphere doesn't change just because there's professional grand opera on stage: local ladies sell brownies during the intermission. But everything is in English, the annual selections are invariably interesting, and the quality of the singing you'll hear is quite high. Besides, Lake George—with water so clean you can drink it right out of the lake and acres upon acres of rolling pinewoods and intimate, low-key resorts—is a delight to visit in the summer. For details, write the box office at Box 471, Glens Falls 12801.

The Central City Festival brings opera to Central City, Colorado, the last two weeks in July. Metropolitan Opera singers carry on in the manner to which they are accustomed in a tiny turn-of-the-century opera house at performances that are sandwiched between square dancing exhibitions in front of the town's old blacksmith shop. Write for the schedule and for tickets in advance from the Central City Opera Festival, 910-16th Street, Suite 636, Denver 80202.

The Santa Fe Opera, in Santa Fe, New Mexico, is definitely big-league—not just because of the important singers and the extravagant productions, but also because of the innovativeness in the choice of music. There are familiar works, but there are also a lot of world and American premieres and totally unknown operas done on this mountain-ringed stage. The works alternate in repertory during July and August. For details, write Box 2408, Santa Fe 87501. For lodgings information, write the Chamber of Commerce, La Fonda Hotel, Santa Fe 87501.

Take Your Turn on Stage at the Met

Some people spend years in school working toward a debut, but if you don't mind being onstage without singing, you can hire on as an extra—a so-called supernumerary. You might be a witch, or a monk, or maybe a spear carrier or a spy or a slave, a prostitute, angel, tailor, butcher. And in exchange for standing there, flying, swordfighting, or occasionally letting out a scream or a polite laugh, you'll even be paid—a minimum $4 per act. No singing, though—and no bows at the end.

Prerequisites? You've got to look the part required. Call the assistant stage manager: 212/799-3100.

The Society for the Preservation and Encouragement of Barbershop Quartet Singing in America— on the Loose

"Wait Till the Sun Shines Nellie," "After the Ball," "Rings on Her Fingers," "K-K-Katy," "Shine on Harvest Moon," "By the Light of the Silvery Moon," "Sweet Genevieve," "My Gal Sal," and dozens of other familiar tunes with not-so-familiar names from the gay nineties and similarly gentle times—their harmonies, the kind that can make you choke up if you don't watch out, are what the S.P.E.B.S.Q.S.A. (as the society is called, for short) is all about. You can join if you want—write the International Headquarters at 6315 Third Avenue, Kenosha, Wisconsin 53141, for the name of the chapter nearest you. Or just take in a Convention, where you'll hear more barbershop groups than you ever knew existed sing more old-time favorites than you didn't know you didn't know. If you can imagine a hotel bursting at the seams with barbershop quartet singers, harmonizing together off the cuff more or less all day long and into the night, barely stopping for the formal presentations, then you've got a pretty good idea of what it's like. "Harmony Heaven," somebody called it once.

The Kenosha office can keep you posted on the convention plans.

Folk Songs/Canada

The northern folk tradition thrives at two Canadian folk song festivals. The narrative ballads, sung without accompaniment in modal tones, may sound strange to your ears accustomed to an eight-tone scale and a certain set of harmonies and a certain kind of accompaniment—but once you get used to them, they're something to hear.

Old Timers on Stage

The Miramichi Folksong Festival, held in Newcastle, New Brunswick, is barely known outside the province, despite the fact that it's been going on for twenty years. The reasons for that situation are also the reasons that a visit can be quite a moving experience: organized and run from the kitchen table of one Maisy Mitchell, it's an all-amateur affair, and the performers are usually old people who have been singing songs from the woods and ballads from the old country since the turn of the century. Gray heads and bent backs and gnarled fingers—and bright eyes—are what it's all about those three days at the end of June. An octogenarian on stage just learned to play the fiddle three years ago, but he's been singing the same songs at the festival for twenty years, and the people who have been attending all that time—and there are more than a few—welcome him up there like an old friend. Some of the other singers have gravelly voices that wouldn't pass muster with RCA, but there's passion in the delivery—and that's what music is all about. You can get more information about this institution from the New Brunswick Department of Tourism, P. O. Box 12345 Fredericton, New Brunswick E3B 5C3.

City Folk

Performers at the Toronto Islands Mariposa Folk Festival, held at the end of June every year in Toronto, are mostly professional, and they represent not only the northern tradition but also the music of the Shetland Isles, Trinidad, Scotland, Ireland, the Bahamas, England, and various parts of the United States. In 1977, a group of musicians and craftspeople of English, Scottish, Irish, and French backgrounds came over from Newfoundland to fiddle, sing, dance, tell stories, play the accordian and the harmonica, and demonstrate some of their craft works. That may be repeated. Founded in 1960, the Mariposa Festival is a very big deal and quite a fine place to spend a weekend. For ticket and accommodations information, write the Mariposa Folk Festival, 131 Roehampton Avenue, Toronto M4P 1P9.

And a Medley of Others

In Winnipeg, Manitoba, the Winnipeg Folk Festival (253 Hugo Street South, Winnipeg) in July; in Dartmouth, Nova Scotia, the Maritime Old-Time Fiddling Contest in early July (30 Guysborough Avenue, Dartmouth B2W 1S5) and the Annual Bluegrass & Old Time Music Festival at the end of that month (100 Main Street, Dartmouth B2W 1S5); in Carlisle, Ontario, the Bluegrass Canada annual (Carlisle L0R 1H0) in June; the Canadian National Open Banjo Competition in July, in Durham, Ontario (RR #4, Durham N0G 1R0); the July Kingston, Ontario, Bluegrass Festival (10488 Shields Court, San Diego, California 92124, c/o Gary Lyons) in July; the Annual Southwestern Ontario Fiddle Championship, in June, in Petrolia, Ontario (c/o Mrs. H. Mosienko, Box 733, Petrolia); the Canadian Open Old-Time Fiddler Contest, in August, in Shelburne, Ontario (Box 27, Shelburne L0N 1S0); and the Western Canada Olde Tyme Fiddling Championship in late September and early October, in Swift Current, Saskatchewan (Box 203, Swift Current).

Folk Doings/U.S.A.

Music and arts and crafts and a little bit of square dancing and jamming all night get-togethers come by the score all over the United States. When you go, you can usually take in a small arts and crafts show, watch a dulcimer being made, listen to someone play a finished one, take in some bluegrass picking and some bluegrass fiddling (a very different thing, mind you, from old-time fiddling). The music goes on all night around the campfires. The past three years have seen a burgeoning of new festivals. Some of the bigger, or older, or for some other reason more interesting affairs include the following.

In the South

In Alabama: the various festivals in May, August, and October at Horse Pens 40, a grassy woodsy park near Oneonta, about which you can get details from Warren Musgrove at Route 1, Box 279, Steele 35987; the Southern States Bluegrass Festival in July, in Cullman (c/o Box 698, 35055).

In Florida: the Florida Folk Festival, held at the Stephen Foster Center in White Springs (c/o Box 265, 32096) every September, and, at the beginning of October, the Ochlockonee River Bluegrass & Folk Music Festival in Tallahassee. You can get details from Kilbourn Productions at 816 North Upland Avenue in Metairie 70003.

In Georgia: the Annual Georgia State Bluegrass Festival in Lavonia (105 Lakeview Drive, Chester, South Carolina 29706).

In Kentucky: the Bluegrass Music Festival of the United States, every June in Louisville (2125 Citizens Plaza, Louisville 40202); and, also in June, the Kentucky Folksong Festival in Grayson (Route 2, Box 180, Grayson 41143), and the Mid-America Folk Heritage Week in Lexington (c/o 905 Mason-Headley Drive, Lexington 40504).

In Louisiana: the Louisiana Rebel Bluegrass Country Festival & Memorial Days at Rebel State Park in Marthaville; for details, write c/o P. O. Box 871, Many, Louisiana 71449.

In the Midwest

In Illinois: the Annual Southern Illinois Folk Festival at the Du Quoin State Fairgrounds (c/o Box 303, Du Quoin 62832).

In Indiana: in June, Bill Monroe's Annual Bluegrass Festival, in the hilly southern part of the state in Beanblossom (write Monroe Festival Headquarters at 1206 Bell Grimes Lane in Nashville, Tennessee 37207).

In Kansas: in June, the Annual Haysville Bluegrass Jamboree; the Kansas Bluegrass Association at 2781 Hiram in Wichita 67217 can send details.

In Missouri: in June, in the Missouri mining-town theme park Silver Dollar City (65616), the Mountain Folks Music Festival; in July, the Annual Ozark Mountain Bluegrass Festival in Eminence (Box 118, 65466); and, in September, the Annual Bluegrass Pickin' Time in Dixon (Box 466, 65459).

In Wisconsin: the June–July Summerfest in downtown Milwaukee (write c/o 120 North Harbor Drive, 53202).

In the West

In California: the San Diego State University Folk Festival, every April in San Diego (c/o Folk Arts Records, 3743 Fifth Avenue, San Diego 92103); in May, the Annual Topango Banjo-Fiddle Contest (c/o 5922 Corbin Avenue, Tarzana, 91356) and the Annual Grubstake Days in Yucca Valley (c/o the Chamber of Commerce at 56297 Twentynine Palms Highway in Yucca Valley 92284).

In Oklahoma: in August, Grant's Annual Blue Grass & Old Time Music Festival—the first west of the Mississippi—in the town of Hugo (c/o Route 2, 74743), and, at the Bluegrass Kingdom Park in the town of Cement, the National Banjo Championship & The Finest in Bluegrass Music Festival (c/o 4457 NW Nineteenth Street, Oklahoma City 73107).

In Oregon: every August, the Annual Canyonville Pioneer Days in the town of Canyonville (c/o Box 877, Canyonville 97417).

In Texas: in August, in San Antonio, the Texas Folklife Festival (Box 1226, San Antonio 78294); and, in October, in Gilmer, the Annual East Texas Jamboree (c/o Box 854, 75644)—almost half a century old.

In the East

In Massachusetts: in April, in the Annual New England Folk Festival in Natick (57 Roseland Street, Somerville 02143)—going strong since the Second World War.

In New York: the Annual New York City Bluegrass & Old-Time Country Music Band Contest & Crafts Fair, usually held at South Street Seaport and sponsored by the Bluegrass Club of New York (417 East 89th Street, New York, New York 10028).

In North Carolina: in June, Lester Flatt's Mount Pilot Festival at Bluegrass Park in the town of Pinnacle (Route 1, Box 285, 27043), and, in August, the Annual Mountain Dance and Folk Festival in the Great Smokies, in Asheville, whose Chamber of Commerce (Box 1011, 28802) can send more information.

In Virginia: in August, the Annual National Championship Country Music Contest, at Lake Whipoorwill Park in the Mountains around Warrenton, whose Jaycees (Box 508, 22186) can send details).

The Compleat American Folk Scene
The National Council for the Traditional Arts, Inc., at 1357 Connecticut Avenue, N.W., Suite 1118, in Washington, D.C. 20036, publishes a directory of bluegrass festivals, old-time fiddling, blues events, gospel sings, ethnic gatherings, Indian events, and more—over a thousand in all ($3.25).

Everything You Always Wanted to Know About Bluegrass Between Two Covers
Bluegrass Unlimited magazine has it: articles about big-time stars, regular rundowns of their performing schedules, letters from enthusiasts, ads about ever-more-novel picking helps, directories of the big- and bush-league bluegrass festivals and of nightspots and day spots where you can regularly go to hear bluegrass. For information about subscriptions ($7 annually) or about ordering the annual festival list, write the magazine at Box 111, Broad Run, Virginia 22014.

Some Good Old-Time Fiddling

Pioneers didn't have many kinds of instruments, and the fiddle was one of the few. So its music had to supply what contemporary pieces get from drums, bass, horns, and such—as a result, there's a special whang to it that makes you tap your toes and get ready to dance: there is melody enough to have you singing in the shower, and a beat that just doesn't quit. But probably the best part is the gusto with which fiddlers do their thing. Fiddlers will drive hours to get together with their fellows, then stay up most of the night sawing away in jam sessions. When you think that this is just their everyday behavior, you can imagine what they're like when there's some question of a fiddling festival or a fiddling convention: thousands pilgrim from around the country to join in on a very specific brand of fiddling-convention fun: barbecues, all-you-can-eat breakfasts, street dancing, hoedowns, singalongs, and sometimes even the traditional snake parade of fiddlers and fans to wind it all up. The entire time, the fiddlers who aren't performing on the stages, or watching in the audience, are off in odd corners of the grounds or the local motels and campgrounds, fiddling away, one right after the other, scarcely letting up even to swig some beer or down some homemade pie that someone's spouse is passing around.

One of the biggest—and therefore one of the most spectacular—of the fiddling conventions in the United States is the National Old-Time Fiddlers' Contest, held the third full week in June in Weiser, Idaho, the self-styled "fiddling capital of America", and the home of the Fiddlers' Hall of Fame. This is Hells Canyon country—seventy miles southeast of Boise—so you won't lack for things to do once you get there—that is, when you have had your fill of fiddling. And there are also parades, big buffet dinners, costume contests, and a draft-horse pulling competition. You can get details about ordering tickets—which you should do well in advance—from the Contest Chairman, c/o the Chamber of Commerce in Weiser 83672.

More hot fiddling, and lots of it: In April, in Union Grove, North Carolina, where fiddlers have been coming to compete in the Annual World Championship Old-Time Fiddlers' Convention, since the roaring twenties; in Athens, Texas, whose fiddle-in started in 1932 and has been drawing country-music lovers by the thousands on the last Friday each May ever since; in Barre, Vermont, during the foliage time, in early October, for a regional contest that draws competitors from New York and Canada as well as New England; and at Craftsbury Common, Vermont, in late July; and in Galax, Virginia, in the hilly southwestern part of the state, every August.

For details, write: the Annual World Championship at Box 38, Union Grove, North Carolina 28689; the Texas Tourist Development Agency, Box 12008, Capitol Station, Austin 78711; the Northeast Fiddlers' Association, c/o Wayne Perry, R.F.D. 1, Stowe, Vermont 05672, about both Vermont events; and the Galax-Carroll-Grayson Chamber of Commerce, 405 North Main Street, Galax 24333.

And Some Scottish Fiddling
Alexandria, Virginia, is one of those lovely Georgian walking-distance towns, and it also has a Scottish heritage that just doesn't stop. In addition to some Scottish games and Scottish holiday celebrations, the townspeople keep their heritage alive with music—at a lively National Scottish Fiddling Championship. For details, write the directors at 200 Forest Drive in Falls Church, Virginia 22046.

The Grand Ole Opry

Even if you hate country-and-western music, you ought to see the Opry: this Nashville, Tennessee, radio show—the longest running radio show in America—is an institution, a mecca for millions, a cultural phenomenon, and a toe-tapping good time besides. That it manages to be folksy despite the posh new concert hall it has called home since a recent move from its longtime base in the Ryman Auditorium in downtown Nashville attests to its vitality.

Because the Opry is a radio show, sitting in the audience is not quite like the experience you'd have at a TV broadcast or an ordinary concert: the only thing that keeps most people in their seats at long stretches is the fact that it's a bother to disturb everyone else in the aisle to get out, and that few want to miss the stars, who parade in front of the mike one after another after another in a stream whose only interruptions are for commercials—for Coca Cola, RC, assorted candy bars, and the insurance company that sponsors the event. The performers—people like Tammy Wynette, Loretta Lynn, Webb Pierce, Porter Waggoner, Minnie Pearl, Hank Snow, Jim Ed Brown, and a slew of others whose names are household words to millions of longtime Opry listeners—mostly look like glitzy versions of cowboys and showgirls—the women in low-cut gowns or fluffy little-girl dresses and the men in rhinestoned leisure suits. They're all very professional showpeople, and even if you don't like the music you can't help but catch onto the star quality that has the more enthusiastic fans dashing up to the stage and snapping photos in such numbers that when a really popular character comes on stage the popping of the flashbulbs almost comes across like a giant strobe flickering over the audience. All in all, it's quite a show.

Consequently, it is hard to get tickets to the Opry, which plays on Friday at eight, and on Saturday at six-thirty and nine-thirty; by May, all reserved-seat tickets may be gone through October. A limited number of general admission tickets are available beginning on the Tuesday before that weekend's shows at the Opry box office: to get them, you have to show up just as soon as they go on sale at 10:00 A.M., or, during the summer, queue up even before the box office opens. At Opryland, the theme park that shares ownership and a pretty wooded site on the outskirts of Nashville, there are regular mini-Oprys, and some of the stars put in appearances. If you can't snag tickets to the Opry, you might want to take in one of these shows—but without the commercials and the hordes and their popping flashbulbs, it's not quite the same.

For all the details, write the Opry at P. O. Box 2138, Nashville 37214.

More Country Music in Nashville
It's a great place for music—no matter when you go. Even if there are no tickets for the Opry, you can hear your

fill. The Nashville Chamber of Commerce publishes an annual Visitor's Guide that lists the current hot spots; it's about $2, but good company for a Nashville visit since it also lists places to stay, eat, sightsee. As for music, some of the good ones include the Blue Grass Inn at 1914 Broadway (615/327-9974); Colonel Jackson's Picnic in the Woods and Country Music Jamboree at Hermitage Landing on Percy Priest Lake on the outskirts of town (P. O. Box 15014, 37215, 615/383-6720 for reservations); the Four Guys Harmony House at 407 Murfreesboro Road (615/256-0188); the Ernest Tubb Record Shop Saturday Night Jamboree at 1530 Demonbreun, with Opry stars coming in to perform (615/255-0589); George Jones' Possum Holler at Third and Commerce, huge and very lively (615/254-1431); the Old Time Picking Parlor at 105 Second Avenue North (615/256-5720); The Station Inn at 104 28th Avenue North (615/297-5796); and Tootsie's Orchid Lounge, a hole in the wall that is an institution (615/251-9725).

Some of them are fancy, some are real back-alley places and look as if they might go out of business any instant—but the music is terrific. Call ahead for show times, opening and closing hours, and information about cover charges and reservations, which may be required.

Caribbean Folklife

It varies with the island, but there are some spectacular, exotic goings-on in the islands because of the mix of peoples who have settled them and whose customs and cultures have blended in subtle ways that are fascinating to behold.

Voodoo

Not a witchery, but instead the religion of Haiti. Masses are held on Saturday nights in partly open-air shacks called *hounfours*. You can wander the streets of Port-au-Prince, the main city, and listen for the thin-skinned drums, which seem to set the air to throbbing the moment they're touched. You listen, and then you follow your ears. And, because voodoo is a religion, you ask permission to watch. Highly symbolic things happen. Chalky designs are drawn onto the floor. Singers sing. Dancers are possessed by the voodoo gods. Europeans and some tourist officials recommend against watching the real thing: this folk religion is a powerful one and you could, they say, end up in a situation considerably more involved than you bargained for when you followed those drums.

However, even the hotel spectacles, somewhat toned down, are something else again. Both the ritual and the drumming are authentic enough.

For more information, contact the Haitian Tourism and Public Relations Association at 30 Rockefeller Plaza, New York, New York 10020.

Puerto Rico's LeLoLai

Not exactly a festival in the usual sense of the word, but instead a holiday package available except in winter, LeLoLai gives you the chance to take in some of the folkloric activities of an island whose traditions go back to the days of the conquistadores—which is something you might otherwise forget if you're staying in the big air-conditioned hotels. The most interesting of the activities are the Bomba Show featuring African-derived dances and music at El Convento Hotel in Old San Juan, and a performance of the Areyto Folkloric Ballet. El Convento used to be a Carmelite convent; the former chapel, with an organ gallery, stained glass windows, tapestries, and wrought-iron chandeliers, is now the dining room—it's so spectacular that one enraptured writer called it the most impressive dining room in the Caribbean. You can get details about the packages from Puerto Rico's Tourism Development Company at 1290 Avenue of the Americas, New York, New York 10019.

What's Doing on the Crafts Scene

Crafts in the Mountains

Long after the rest of the country had turned to premolded plastic and 100 percent acrylic, America's mountain people were still living by their handicrafts—making their own rocking chairs and fashioning the wood shavings into artificial flowers; peeling oak branches, shaving them into strips, and weaving the strips into baskets for collecting eggs; stitching up scraps of cloth into quilts. It was in the thirties that outsiders, seeing the products of mountain hands as art, began convincing the highlanders to see that selling their baskets would help pay the bills a lot quicker than accumulating pennies gotten from other sources. Since then,

especially in the last few years, things have changed. Sometimes, going into the mountains to shop for crafts or visit the fairs, you can't help but think that it's not coming from the heart any more. No matter, though. Watching an object take shape in someone's hands, and inspecting the products of handwork, never fails to amaze.

"Art when really understood is the province of every human being. It is simply a question of doing things, anything well. It is not an outside extra thing. . . . [One] does not have to be a painter or sculptor to be an artist. He can work in any medium. He simply has to find the gain in the work itself, not outside it."

—Robert Henri

The Big Fairs

Fair-going has gotten to be such a popular sport that during the summer, there are sometimes as many as two or three fairs a week in the southeastern part of the United States. Heaps of food and near-nonstop music and the crowds you find at most fairs assure a good time no matter where you go.

The Craftsman's Guild of the Southern Highlands, biggest and oldest of the craft guilds that sponsor many of the fairs, was responsible for infusing many mountain artisans with the aesthetic consciousness that marked the very beginning of America's appreciation of its crafts heritage. At the Guild's two annual fairs, you can view spinning, blacksmithery, weaving, stitchery, potting, whittling, pewter-spinning, vegetable dyeing, chair canning, and the making of brooms and cornhusk dolls. The Knoxville, Tennessee fair begins on the third Tuesday in October and continues through the following Saturday; the fair in Asheville, North Carolina runs from the second Monday in July through the following Friday. In Knoxville, traditional mountain musicians, folksingers, and clog dancers perform about six times a day. But it's not for that reason alone that the two fairs are among the best in the nation: they're juried, and in addition to looking at the quality of the craftsmen's work, the judges also evaluate the quality of the booths and the quality of the hospitality extended to fairgoers. A craftsman who is impatient, snappish, or high-handed will not be asked back. These fairs are first-rate all the way. For more information, write the Craftsman's Fairs, P. O. Box 9145, Asheville, North Carolina 28805.

West Virginia—little touched by the last half-century despite its economy's dependence on tourists—has a strong tradition of mountain crafts, a strong state crafts guild to go with it, and plenty of crafts fairs, generally held in places that would be interesting to visit even if there were no fair. Some are held at times of year that make strolling from booth to booth under an open sky the most delightful way you could possibly think of to spend a weekend.

The biggest, by all accounts, is the Mountain State Art and Craft Fair in Ripley, West Virginia, a two-and-a-half-hour drive from Columbus, Ohio, and twenty-five miles from Charleston, West Virginia. It is held over the July Fourth weekend, usually Friday through Monday, at the Cedar Lakes Conference Center. The assortment of baskets alone (eighteenth-century service baskets; fancy baskets; egg baskets; baskets made of broom sedge, split white oak strips, honeysuckle vines, or river cane) gives you an idea of the variety you can expect to find in each category—from bee-handling to pewter-spinning, coal carving, and the making of churns, cedar buckets, puppets, and bobbin lace. A folk-medicine man named Catfish Gray is usually on hand to recommend herbs for what ails you; an extraordinary minister-whittler turns a single billet of wood into chains of foot-high fat men. And there are quilts, pillows, and patchwork dresses. The belt-loosening Deep South cooking is as plentiful as the good craft work, and the delicious smells—as well as the sounds of equally traditional mountain music—are everywhere. As if that weren't enough, there's that wonderful West Virginia countryside—all hills and hollows and forests. For details,

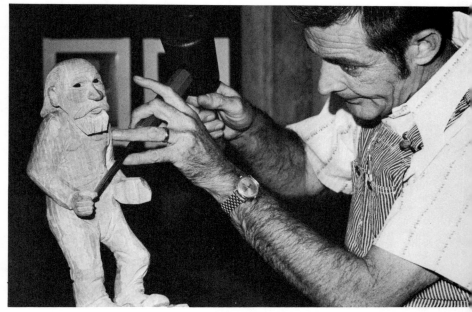

write the festival directors at Cedar Lakes, Ripley, West Virginia 25271.

Another good West Virginia festival is held in June in Glenville, one of those minuscule hill villages that doze through the year and wake up only for an annual festival, when the townspeople pull out all stops for an orgy of crafting, eating, dancing, listening, and such. Still another, held in October, is in Harpers Ferry, a nifty little town, much of it restored by the National Park Service because of its importance in pre-Civil War history. The old brick buildings climb a vast hill that rises at the confluence of the Potomac and Shenandoah rivers, and, from the Harper's Cemetery, or from the ruins of the old St. John's Episcopal Church, or from Jefferson Rock you get a view over the rivers so spectacular that Thomas Jefferson, who journeyed there in 1783, called it "worth a voyage across the Atlantic." At both the Glenville and the Harpers Ferry fair you'll see old-time down-home mountain craftings—with a sprinkling of somewhat more contemporary work. For details about both, write the Arts and Crafts Division of the West Virginia Department of Commerce, 1900 East Washington Street, Charleston, West Virginia 25305. This organization can also fill you in on other crafts festivals that take place just about once a month in some part of the state or other, and can send a directory of state craft workers whose studios are often open to visitors.

A Real Live Shur 'Nuff National Crafts Festival

Silver Dollar City, a re-creation of an 1870s Ozark mining village, is one of the smaller U.S. theme parks, but it is also one of the most interesting. Because it is a theme park, there are rides—a flooded-mine train ride, an Ozark float trip in which you're imperiled by a whirlpool, a steam-train excursion in which the train gets robbed. But because it is supposed to be an Ozark village, there are crafts and more crafts. And they're not mechanized or in the least bit hokey. Ropes are made of cornhusks and then woven to make chair seats. Wheat is threshed. Rails are split. Dulcimers are made. One Ozark gentleman in his sixties crafts knife blades from raw steel. Log houses are constructed. The ladies of the Christian Church in Branson, Missouri—the town nearest the park—get together every week, as they have for the last half-century, for quilting bees, and their work is sold at Silver Dollar City. Proceeds of their sales go to the church.

As all this constitutes a sort of American tradition, it's not entirely unfitting that one of the two annual festivals at the park—for which yet more craftsmen are brought in to demonstrate and sell—is called the National Festival of Craftsmen. It's held in the fall, which is a glorious time in the Ozarks. Sustenance and domestic-type crafts predominate at the festival. For example: a donkey-powered treadmill threshes grain; mules power a sorghum mill; a Conestoga wagon is constructed; meat is smoked; shingles and apple butter and tintype photographs are made. You can buy seed pictures, lead shot, wicker chairs, duck calls, dog-hair baskets. The festival goes on for two weeks, Wednesdays through Sundays, starting at the end of September or the beginning of October.

The second festival is held in the spring, one week in May. This one emphasizes woodworking and the crafting of rocking chairs, cradles, grandfather and grandmother clocks, churns, decoys, and musical instruments. Some of these items are made without nails, and one of the workers who is usually on hand even gets the wood he uses right out of the Ozark forests.

For particulars about both of these interesting festivals, or for information about visiting the area's lakes and resorts, write the Chamber of Commerce, Silver Dollar City, Missouri 65616.

The Fair of 1850

Some public-spirited citizens of the area around Lumpkin, Georgia—peanut country—got together some years ago and decided to start rescuing the crumbling old buildings of the neighborhood. To this end, they founded Westville, a restoration village which tries to show you the unsung side of life in the antebellum South—not the life of parties and Grand Tours of Europe, but the life of hard work on the farm, of raising chickens, ginning and spinning cotton and weaving it into cloth, making baskets. There were middle and lower classes as well as an aristocracy.

At Westville, weaving and blacksmithing and potting and spinning are the order of the day, every day. But several times a year there are special fairs at the restoration and more craftsmen come in to demonstrate still other crafts—woodcarving and soapmaking and candle molding. The Fair of 1850—which is the biggest and is held the first week in November—is not the sort of fair where you can buy directly from the craftspeople (though you can pick up attractive carved wooden toys and other items at the gift shop just outside the entrance gate). But it does offer a chance to see an astonishing variety of crafts that you don't see in too many other places, and to meet some really memorable old southerners. The quiltmaker, for instance, is a wizened broomstick of a woman who will talk your ear off with fifty years of county gossip. And the basketmaker is an ancient black man who tells the tale of his trade in the singsong tones of the best fire-and-brimstone sermons. There's no question about where *he's* spent his Sunday mornings for the last seventy-five years. Thirty miles away, in Eufaula, Alabama, there are some spectacular antebellum homes, and Lake Eufaula, on the way there, has some very good bass fishing. For more information about the area, write Westville, Box 1850, Lumpkin, Georgia 31815; the Eufaula Chamber of Commerce, Box 347, Eufaula, Alabama 36027; and the Historic Chattahoochee Commission, P. O. Box 33, Eufaula, Alabama 36027.

Arkansas' Fantastic Crafts Center (and Its Fair)

You'll find a big crafts festival, of sorts, just about any time you visit the Ozark town of Mountain View, Arkansas. Some years ago, the state legislature put $3 million behind their enthusiasm for the region's arts and constructed the Ozark Folk Center.

Well established and going strong by now, it's one of the best places around to see cabin crafts. In fifty-nine native stone and cedar buildings, you can watch quilters, basketmakers, spinners, smiths, saddlemakers, and broom- and furniture- and dollmakers at work, and you can buy the products at either of two shops on the grounds. Musicians of the Rackensack Folklore Society perform on the dulcimer, autoharp, banjo, fiddle, guitar, and mandolin—instruments made by the musicians themselves or handed down over the years. There's dancing too—jigs and reels and waltzes. Granny Rainbolt, one of the jig dancers, has been dancing since she was just a kid, and she's sixty-three now. A veteran of hoedowns that lasted from late afternoon until sunup, she has, in her time, literally danced the soles off her shoes.

The Folk Center is open from the end of May through October. Every October there is a festival—additional craftsmen cram the free space in the studios and spread out around the grounds, and the Rackensack Folklore Society puts on extra concerts. Since October is also foliage time in the Ozarks, this is a great season for visiting the region. For more information about the lake-dotted, river-laced national forest area that provides plenty of other things to do in the area, write the Arkansas Department of Parks and Tourism, State Capitol, Little Rock 72201.

More Arkansas Octoberfests. There are three: the Ozark Folk Festival in Eureka Springs, the Ozark Frontier Trail Festival and Craft Show in Heber Springs, and the War Eagle Mills

Ozarks Arts and Crafts Fair on War Eagle Mills Farm near Hindsville.

The festival in Eureka Springs, which features a barefoot ball, is especially nice because of the town in which it's held—a gingerbready little relic of the Victorian age that climbs a steep Ozark mountainside in the northernmost part of the state. You can find out more from the Chamber of Commerce at 5 North Main Street, Eureka Springs 72632.

The Frontier Trail festival, held the second weekend in October, offers you lots of mountain music, a pioneer parade and historical pageant, a working blacksmith, and a horse-drawn sorghum mill—in addition to the crafts demonstrations. It's sponsored by the Ozark Foothills Handicraft Guild (808 Sugar Loaf, Heber Springs 72543), which also puts on the festival at the Ozark Folk Center.

The festival at War Eagle Mills is very large, nearly thirty years old, and held on a decidedly pleasant old farm; details can be had from the Ozarks Arts and Crafts Fair Association, Route 1, Hindsville 72738.

Kentucky's Finest
The state's Guild of Artists and Craftsmen stages a freewheeling spring festival every year at the Indian Fort Theater in Berea, Kentucky—a craft-happy town at any time. There's some Appalachian basketry, quilts, and such, but more than half of what you find is contemporary and up-to-date. Puppeteers, bluegrass musicians, and folk dancers entertain you between trips into the craft worker's bright-colored tents. For details, write the Guild at Box 291, Berea 40403.

The Life Behind These Mountain Crafts
Foxfire—a tiny organism that glows in the dark and is frequently seen in the shaded coves of the mountains around Rabun Gap, Georgia—is also the name of a magazine that an inspired high-school teacher concocted to combat the army of paper airplanes with which unruly students greeted his efforts to teach Shakespeare. Supported by sales and by grants from the likes of the National Endowment for the Humanities, the publication grew into a best-seller, *The Foxfire Book*. Let the table of contents put some ideas into your head: "This Is the Way I Was Raised Up"; Aunt Arie; Wood; Tools and Skills; Building a Log Cabin; Chimney Building; White Oak Splits; Making a Hamper out of White Oak Splits; Making a Basket out of White Oak Splits; An Old Chair Maker Shows How; Rope, Straw, and Feathers Are to Sleep on; A Quilt Is Something Human; Soapmaking; Cooking on a Fireplace, Dutch Oven, and Wood Stove; Daniel Manous; Mountain Recipes; Preserving Vegetables; Preserving Fruit; Churning Your Own Butter; Slaughtering Hogs; Curing and Smoking Hog; Recipes for Hog; Weather Signs; Planting by the Signs; The Buzzard and the Dog; Home Remedies; Hunting; Dressing and Cooking Wild Animal Foods; Hunting Tales; Snake Lore; Moonshining as a Fine Art; Faith Healing; Hillard Green. Each chapter gives a detailed, simple account of the subject it covers. Some chapters are written in the words of the mountain men and women themselves: "Y'ever eat any lye hominy? Boys, 'at's th' best stuff ever you eat in yore life. It sure is. Boys, I've made many a pot full. And soap, law, I've made many a pot'a soap too. Had th' ash hopper, oak ashes. And bottomed chairs—I guess I bottomed 'bout ever'one a'these. He'ped to do it. I can't make th' splits. I bottom 'em with white oak splits. Some people bottoms 'em with bark, but I never did. Bark does easy t'what th' wood does. Course it don't last like wood. Tain't good like wood...."

Cram-packed with fascinating bits of lore, with tales of people like your grandmother or your grandmother's grandmother, *Foxfire* is oral history—the history of the frontier—put down on paper. But you know that the "relics" are still around, and all you've got to do is go out and be friendly in the right places and you can meet the tellers, or their peers, in person. Anchor Books/Doubleday, 245 Park Avenue, New York, New York 10016; $8.95.

More on Mountain Life and Crafts
Written by Allen Eaton, who helped found the Southern Highland Handicraft Guild, published in 1937, and now reissued by Dover, *Handicrafts of the Southern Highlands* gives yet another look at the life of the mountain people—this time the life they lived during the Depression; it was one of the first important studies of the subject. The descriptions are detailed and exact: "Mountain cabins . . . have been built without windows, many with but one door, and earth has frequently taken the place of wood for the floor; but every cabin, however simple and bare, has its fireplace. It was usually made of rough, native stone in dimensions as found, though there are in a con-

siderable number of the well-finished houses examples of stone cut to regular shapes and sizes, with careful masonry used in the construction." It is almost as if the author is telling you about a strange and exotic culture—and since he was not from the mountains himself, it probably was strange and exotic to him. Remarkable old photographs of the mountain people at work and of their craft works illustrate the book. Dover Books, 180 Varick Street, New York, New York 10014; $5.00.

Pennsylvania Dutch Crafts

The Pennsylvania Dutch country of the southeastern part of the state is a busy and popular area all year—but in late June and early July, things really go wild in an orgy of shoofly pies and mashed-potatoes-and-peanut-butter candy, barn raisings and hoedowns, soapmaking and food-canning and hay-raking. All these are part of the big Pennsylvania Dutch Folklife Festival in Kutztown, Pennsylvania. There's a country auction, a whole batch of crafts demonstrations, and a series of seminars dealing with things Dutch—Plain Dutch (Amish and Mennonites) and Worldly Dutch (Lutherans, Church of Brethren)—at which you can learn about Pennsylvania Dutch snake lore, religion, music, and witchcraft.

In the fall, at the Pennsylvania Farm Museum in Landis Valley, about four miles from Lancaster, about two dozen craftspeople set up shop to show you more about life in Pennsylvania Dutch country: pots, brooms, quilts, butter, and soap are made, corn is ground, fruit is preserved, and there's whittling, blacksmithing, walnut-hulling, cigar- and cidermaking, tinsmithing, bed-roping, and lots more.

For more information about both festivals, and about other things to see and do in this lively area, contact the Pennsylvania Dutch Tourist Bureau, 1800 Hempstead Road, Lancaster, Pennsylvania 17601.

Craftings in the Northeast

Just as almost everything you find craftworkers producing in the Southeast is as old-fashioned as the sunbonnets that some of them wear, the output in the Northeast is contemporary. Craftspeople are more likely to be improvising on their ancient techniques, experimenting with new forms, and turning out objects that have no earthly use except as ornaments.

Southern New York's Big June Bash
The place to tune into what's happening is at the Northeast Craft Fair in Rhinebeck, New York, held every year at the end of June. It's huge. There are over five hundred exhibitors in some forty-four different media. In the fiber arts alone, you'll find pieces that are crocheted, batiked, and silk-screened, as well as trapunto work and soft sculpture. The quality is uniformly high, since the exhibitors are chosen from some two thousand applicants. The ones who make it go all out, building mini-boutiques with carpeted floors and walls in which to show off their wares to the thousands of fairgoers (who include buyers from all the big New York department stores). There are also glassblowers, potters, carvers and, for kids, craft workshops. And always plenty to eat. This is *the* big crafts event in the East.

For details on getting there, and about the country inns in the area (including the ancient Beekman Arms in Rhinebeck), write Box 10, New Paltz, New York 12561.

Also in the New York City area: the Guilford Handcrafts Exposition (about which you can get information from the Chamber of Commerce, 669 Boston Post Road, Guilford, Connecticut 06437), which is held in July; the fair in Danbury, Connecticut, also in July (contact the Chamber of Commerce, 20 West Street, Danbury 06810); the Atlantic Coast Exposition in Old Greenwich, Connecticut, in October (contact the Chamber of Commerce, 35 Field Point Road, Greenwich 06830); and the Cancer Care Harvest Festival Art Show in Bedford, New York, in October (details available from Lydia Ward, R.D. 1, Box 218, Bedford 10506).

Old-Timey Crafts in New York
If you're not looking to buy but just to see how life was lived in the good old days, you should visit the Autumn Crafts and Tasks festival, a seasonal celebration held at Van Cortlandt Manor, a twenty-acre estate at Croton-on-Hudson, New York. The manor is a part of Sleepy Hollow Restorations, a trio of Hudson River Valley estates now open to the public. The festival brings extra craftsmen to the estate, and you can watch blacksmithing, tinsmithing, flax processing, coopering, vegetable dyeing, corn husking, hewing, rail splitting, quilting, hog dressing, meat and fish smoking, fruit and vegetable preserving, meat grinding, butter churning, baking, and the making of medicines, soap, cheese, and such. In the spirit of the fall "frolics" that kept the early Hudson River Valley settlers entertained, there are games, musical entertainments, and dancing.

You'll also want to visit the houses on this estate and at the rest of the complex, then wander over to Bear Mountain State Park to shuffle through the leaves on one of the hiking trails or just take in the magnificent Hudson River views. For more information, contact Sleepy Hollow Restorations, P. O. Box 245, Tarrytown, New York 10591.

If you miss Autumn Crafts and Tasks, there are similar goings-on elsewhere in the area, most notably at the Museum Village in Orange County (Monroe, New York 10950), on three Sundays in October. What you'll see varies from year to year, but mostly it will be activities like cooking over an open hearth, stuffing sausages, making soap or apple butter, splitting wood, making cider—whatever people would have done in the nineteenth century to get ready for winter.

Craft Fare in New Hampshire
In this state, where the main power on the crafts-marketing scene is the League of New Hampshire Craftsmen, the major fair of the year is the Annual Craftsman's Fair at Mount Sunapee State Park, near Newbury. There's a section for members—whose work must be accepted by a jury before they are admitted to the League—and a "general selling" area, where craftspeople who don't produce enough to stock a whole booth may exhibit. That means that in addition to crafts of a very high quality, you'll also see the work of newcomers, amateurs, and part-timers. Demonstrations are a part of the show, as is music—mainly music by the craftspeople themselves—and there are special programs for kids.

For more information about the fair, and about the League's several excellent New Hampshire crafts shops, write the office at 205 North Main, Concord 03301.

Downeast
The United Maine Craftsmen's Fair, held annually at Cumberland, Maine, in mid-August, ranks among the top ten events in the state and attracts thousands of visitors and some two hundred exhibitors. The show is non-juried, so newcomers as well as established craftsmen can exhibit their work. This makes for a good deal of variety among the exhibitors, and some of what you see is really good, while some is merely earnest. But the exhibitors are always interesting to talk to, and there is lots to see. For more information, contact the fair sponsors, the United Maine Craftsmen, at R.F.D. #2, Litchfield, Maine 04350.

Vermont's Best
When Frog Hollow, in Middlebury, Vermont, opened as a privately sponsored crafts center aiming to carry the highest-quality work being produced in the state, the work of 85 craftsmen was represented. Now, seven years later, some 250 artists exhibit, and Frog

Hollow has been designated a State Crafts Center. Housed in an old mill building are shops where various craft workers teach and produce; a gallery; and studios where classes are given for adults as well as for the local grade schoolers. In addition, every August, a craft festival fills the gallery and the outdoor balcony to overflowing with the most imaginative crafts being made in the state. And there are demonstrators—blowing glass, making pottery, enameling, sculpting, and so on. As a service to both craftspeople and buyers, the gallery maintains a directory of craftsmen, listing their names and addresses alongside a photograph of a representative work. For more information, write the Frog Hollow State Craft Center, Middlebury 05753.

Vermont's other state craft center is on Main Street in Windsor (zip 05089), in the Connecticut River Valley in the central part of the state. And there are plenty of other crafts fairs in the fall—in Montpelier, at Stratton Mountain, and at Mount Snow. You can get further information by writing, respectively, the Central Vermont Chamber of Commerce (Box 336, Barre 05641); the Stratton Arts Festival (Stratton Mountain 05155); and the Mt. Snow Development Corp. (Mt. Snow 05356). Anything else you need to know about Vermont crafts can probably be provided by the Vermont Council on the Arts (Montpelier 05602).

The Best Fair in the Midwest

The Ann Arbor Street Art Fair, held every summer in Ann Arbor, Michigan, is one of the biggest, and one of the most selective—with some sixty places filled from around six hundred applicants. For details, write the Fair Committee, P. O. Box 1352, Ann Arbor 48106.

An Around-the-World-in-One-Afternoon Crafts Spectacular

Williamsburg, Virginia, that bastion of colonial Americana, isn't exactly the place you'd expect to find a major international crafts exposition—but there it is. The recent appearance of the big, beautiful Busch Gardens theme park, the Old Country, has brought a lot of changes to that staid old town. What you'll see here is a far cry from the usual baskets and contemporary silver jewelry of most U.S. crafts fairs. Once a year, in the fall, the Busch people import from Europe makers of Hummel figurines; an Austrian who turns wood shavings into ornaments; another old fellow who demonstrates metal enameling; a silversmith from London; a potter from the Wedgwood factory; an enamel artist from Limoges; husband-and-wife teams making French folk dolls; reverse glass painting; a dollmaker from Italy; leatherworkers from Italy who stamp and burnish their products; and a Polish woman who does paper cutouts. You'll see bobbin lace, sporrans for kilts, silk-screen work, wooden shoes, needlepoint and crewel, hand-painted Easter eggs, and so on. The craft workers on hand vary from year to year, but so far, every year has brought more varied assortments—some available for purchase, some not. At any rate, it's quite a show. Afterward, you can enjoy the pleasant woods-and-ravines scenery on boat cruises, sky rides, and such, then make merry in the park's immense beer hall, which is something like what you'd find in Munich only bigger.

For details about the festival, which lasts three weekends, usually in September, contact the park at P. O. Drawer FC, Williamsburg, Virginia 23185.

Canadian Crafts

In a province-by-province fashion, Robert Kane tells you where you'll find the best craft outlets for all kinds of artisans working on the north side of the U.S. border. It's all in his *Canada A to Z* (Doubleday, 245 Park Avenue, New York, New York 10016; $3.95)

Crafts in the Caribbean

There is a naive quality to some of them that is very appealing, but in general, the naiveté is most attractive when the crafts come from the less populated islands. However, there are plenty of exceptions.

A Sampler

Haiti has some of the most imaginative and exotic crafts of all the islands: not just the bright-colored art (which had you not seen the emerald-city countryside yourself, you might think to be surreal), but also the hand-spun, hand-loomed cottons; rugs woven and dyed by hand and other textiles; embroideries; sisal and straw items. The Haiti Office of Tourism, 30 Rockefeller Plaza, New York, New York 10020, can send some details.

In Puerto Rico, look into the Institute of Puerto Rican Culture in the Old Dominican Convent on Norzagaray Street; the restored early sixteenth-century building contains a museum and a small shop, where you can buy high-quality carved wood, tortoiseshell items, woven straw, silk screen and ceramic work—all made in the area. In the mountain town of Barranquitas, one Sunday in mid-July, the Institute sponsors a craft show. For more information, write the Puerto Rico Tourism Development Company, 1290 Avenue of the Americas, New York, New York 10019.

Montserrat, mountainous and tiny, is good for hand-woven baskets, mats, and hats woven of palm fronds, pandanus grass, rope, or twine.

In St. Vincent, you can buy rugs of khuskhus, a West Indian grass—lacy and tropical—as well as bamboo, wood, and tortoiseshell knickknacks. For details on both islands, write the Eastern Caribbean Tourist Association, 220 East 42nd Street, New York, New York 10017.

St. Kitts has pottery, baskets of willow, and pins made of tortoiseshell—especially at the Curio Shop on Fort Street and the Lotus. For more information, write the St. Kitts-Nevis Tourist Board, 39 West 55th Street, New York, New York 10020.

In Trinidad, you can get African figurines; sandals of leather or rope; little bamboo boxes for trinkets; tote bags of palm fiber; and steel drums, small and large. Check at the Trinidad & Tobago Handicraft Cooperative, the Blind Welfare Association, V. Kacal in the Hilton Hotel in Port-of-Spain. For information on the island, write the Trinidad and Tobago Tourist Board, 400 Madison Avenue, New York, New York 10017.

In the Caymans, also great for beaches, there are tortoiseshell items: there's a turtle farm here. There are also hand-woven hammocks. For more information, write the Cayman Islands Department of Tourism, 420 Lexington Avenue, New York, New York 10017.

On Dominica, there are wonderful inexpensive grass rugs, waterproofed Carib baskets in all sizes (some as big as suitcases) and shapes, and shellwork. The Eastern Caribbean Tourist Board at 220 East 42nd Street, New York, New York 10017, can send more information about this small, picturesque island.

Puerto Rico's Santos

Carved statues of saints have been a tradition here for nearly three centuries, ever since Catholic priests taught the islanders to carve out their own religious objects when they weren't obtainable from abroad. Each family has had its own and has handed it down from generation to generation throughout that time. Recently, films and exhibitions of santos in the United States have made them a big deal, on the order of some New Mexican Indian crafts. They are available, and the Galeria Botello, in an eighteenth-century Spanish mansion floored with old bricks brought over as ballast in sailing vessels, is one of the best places to buy them or just to look. Also, there is a museum of santos in the

Casa de los Contrafuertes in Old San Juan. For details, write the Puerto Rico Tourism Development Company at 1290 Avenue of the Americas, New York, New York 10019.

Renaissance Crafts

Until Oliver Cromwell closed them down in the mid-seventeenth century, the great country fairs—outgrowths of the celebrations held by merchants and traders when their paths crossed—were the great social event of each season in England. So it's entirely appropriate that the first major twentieth-century revival of these joyful affairs takes place not once a year but twice—in the San Francisco Bay area in the fall, and in Agoura, near Los Angeles, in the spring. Both these Renaissance Pleasure Faires, founded and organized by Phyllis and Ron Patterson, have been carefully researched over and over for the last fifteen years, so that everything you see is authentically sixteenth-century. There may be no giants, unicorns, dromedaries, camels, dragons, or naked boys—all of which were prescribed for a fair in a document concerning a 1564 English midsummer pageant—and you will hear some very American music of the Appalachians. But you won't find Cokes or hot dogs—instead steak-and-kidney pies, Danberry tarts, bangers, cheeses, beef ribs, "rotten pot" (a sort of ratatouille in a custard sauce), sweetmeats, juices, gingerbread, fowl, and ale. Even the signs are phrased in antique terms: "Show Thy I.D., Please," or "Prithee, Wash Not Thy Dishes Herein."

But that's only part of what makes this fair such a clangorous, lusty spectacle. All the craftspeople, entertainers, cooks, and other personnel wear costumes; a good many fairgoers do, too. (For some years the fair management has been distributing a booklet, "The Compleat Guide to Compleat Costuming for Faire Folke.")

As at the fairs of the period the Pleasure Faire is re-creating, there is plenty of entertainment—here, on one main stage and a half-dozen or so satellite stages. There are puppet shows, mimes, dancers, singers, and musicians to keep things on the stages lively, while around the grounds stroll jugglers, troubadours, flowermongers, acrobats, assorted vendors, and, for atmosphere, long-robed friars. Some two hundred of the state's best craftsmen sell flowers, stained glass, leather work, period musical instruments, Punch-and-Judy puppets, apple-head dolls, peasant dresses, blown glass, pull toys, pots, and a myriad of other rustic items. There are jousts, beanbag toss games, a Tweizlie Wop or "King of the Log"—pillow fights in which the

participants balance on logs afloat in a sea of straw—and archery and ring-toss competitions. All the world's a stage. For information and dates—each one runs six consecutive weekends—write the Renaissance Centre, P. O. Box 18104, San Francisco, California 94118; or P. O. Box 46066, Los Angeles, California 90046.

Similar but by no means identical Renaissance fairs are held in Shakopee, Minnesota, at the end of August or the beginning of September (for information: Route 1, Box 125, Chaska, Minnesota 55318); in Fall City, Washington, at the Forest Theater near Snoqualmie Falls, in the autumn (information from the Snoqualmie Falls Forest Theater, 14240 S.E. Allen Road, Bellevue, Washington 98006); and at Skunk Hollow Meadow, near Morrison, Colorado, at the end of August (details from the Renaissance Arts Faire, 1395 South Humboldt Street, Denver, Colorado 80210).

Learning-a-Craft Vacations

When, after you've looked at enough pots and handwovens, you decide to learn to do it yourself, you can plan a vacation around a course at one of the good crafts schools. You'll end up feeling comfortable with your chosen equipment and your medium, and, more important, about yourself as well—not just because of the restorative powers of the rural areas in which most of the crafts schools are located, but also because of the camaraderie that develops among the students: in real life you may be lawyers, businessmen, housewives, college students, secretaries, whatever; for the duration, though, you're all just learners.

The schools:

Penland, old and big, with a 370-acre, 40-building campus, 53 miles northeast of Asheville, North Carolina. You can study photography, graphics, sculpture, lapidary, weaving, tapestry work, ceramics, wood- and metalworking, and enameling. Courses last two and three weeks, and usually begin in June, July, and August. Tuition is about $75 per week, room and board up to about $150 per week. Details are available from the school in Penland, North Carolina 28765.

The John C. Campbell Folk School, in Brasstown, North Carolina, is almost as old as Penland, and just as fine. On 365 acres of rolling hardwoods, pines, dogwood, rhododendron, and mountain-laurel forests in the westernmost part of the state, the school teaches weaving, spinning, vegetable dyeing, enamel work, pottery, blacksmithing, woodcarving, and woodworking.

Courses generally begin in July, August, September, and November. Tuition is around $70 per week, room and board about $100 and up. For details, write the school in Brasstown 28902.

The Arrowmont School of Arts and Crafts, in the Great Smokies in Gatlinburg, Tennessee, has been offering courses in things like ceramics, macrame, textiles, jewelry, and vegetable dyeing since the Pi Beta Phi Settlement School was established around the first decade of the century. For details, write P. O. Box 567, Gatlinburg, Tennessee 37738.

The Haystack Mountain School of Crafts, in a handsome modern shingled building that sits up on a wooded slope above East Penobscot Bay near Deer Isle, Maine, offers courses in ceramics, glass work, graphics, jewelry, photography, fabric work, weaving, sculpture, batik, stained glass, and papermaking; the orientation is contemporary. For details, contact the school at Deer Isle 04627.

The Naples Mill School of Arts & Crafts, in Naples, New York, in the Finger Lakes, offers an excellent course in ceramics, but you can also study weaving, fibers, fabrics, glassblowing, stained-glass work, photography, fine arts—sculpture, painting, and drawing—modern dance. The Finger Lakes region is wonderfully hilly country, full of interesting wineries, waterfalls, historic sites, and tiny villages. Tuition, a room for two, and board usually run under $150 per person per week. Two- and three-week sessions are offered from June through August. For details, contact the school at Box 567, 33 Academy Street, Naples 14512.

Peters Valley Craftsmen, in Layton, New Jersey, is a village center for instruction in crafts in the Delaware Water Gap National Recreation Area, in wooded, rolling, northwestern New Jersey. Blacksmithing, ceramics, jewelry, textiles, wood, photography, and glassblowing courses are aimed at professionals as well as beginners, and courses emphasize the finer points of the various techniques. You might learn, for instance, glass glaze chemistry and glazing techniques, or cloisonné, or enamel grinding, or the use of gold foils in jewelry production. Classes last two to seven days. For a schedule, contact the school in Layton, New Jersey 07851.

The Summer Arts Study Center of the University of Minnesota, held at the Quadna Mountain Lodge in Hill City, Minnesota, is surrounded by some fourteen hundred acres of woods, lakes, and meadows, so it would be a pleasant place to spend some time even if it weren't for the very interesting courses—in needlepoint, nonloom fiber sculpture, pottery, jewelry casting, fine arts, theater, music, and so on. Most courses run five days; tuition is about $75. Room and board (two meals a day) is about $100 for the one-week sessions, double that for two-week classes. For details, contact the Summer Arts Study Center, 1128 LaSalle Avenue, Minneapolis, Minnesota 55403.

The Truro Center for the Arts at Castle Hill, on Cape Cod, Massachusetts, offers courses which generally last just four or five days, but you spend three hours a day at them. Courses offered include, in ceramics, ceramic sculpture and hand-building techniques, raku (the use of found materials), and kiln building; in textiles, Ikat (a technique used to partially dye the warp before weaving), belt weaving, Peruvian weaving, dyeing from nature, basket weaving, and traditional and contemporary techniques for weaving rugs and wall hangings. Fees range from $85 to $125. For details, write Castle Hill in Truro 02666.

"Weaving, hit's the prettiest work I ever done. It's a-settin' and trampin' the treadles and watchin' the pretty blossoms come out and smile at ye in the kiverlet."
—Aunt Sal Creech, of Pine Mountain, Kentucky; quoted in *Handicrafts of the Southern Highlands,* by Allen Eaton

---

Weaving
Almost all crafts schools offer courses in weaving—but there's one where weaving, spinning, dyeing with chemical and vegetable dyes, and such similar subjects are the school's raison d'être: The Mannings, in East Berlin, Pennsylvania.

It's a fascinating place, for not only does it provide instruction in weaving for beginners, but it also teaches intermediate and advanced weavers, dyers, and spinners and sells the specialized equipment necessary for the activities. You can, for instance, buy rug warp, hooks and needles, all sorts of rug wool, looms, bobbins and bobbin winders, shuttles, tapestry beaters, and a half-dozen different kinds of spinning wheels.

Spinning fibers? Three kinds of silk, wild goat top, raw wool, ginned cotton. You'd like some cashmere goat hair? They've got cashmere goat hair. Angora rabbit? Opossum? Mohair? Alpaca? Flax? They've got it all. And more kinds of looms than you ever imagined existed.

Every year, there's a national weaving show in the spring, a spinning seminar in June, and a weaving seminar in August. These last two are especially interesting. In the spinning seminar, for instance, you can learn about shearing sheep and grading wool; flax scutching; vegetable dyeing with local plants and lichens; making rainbow fleece; casserole dyeing; spinning silk, cotton, camel hair, yak hair, mohair, dog hair, and wool (and mixing them); and the difference between spinning with vegetable and animal fibers. There are also costume contests, spinning contests, and various kinds of dyeing contests.

In addition, there are weaving programs for beginners. You start with a fully warped loom and begin weaving right away. Then, when you're used to the loom, you learn how to set it up, how to dress the loom, how to warp it in a couple of different ways, thread it, tie up, draft designs, and plan warps. In addition, you're taught all you need to know to start experimenting on your own with sleying, threads and sett, and texture and design. About $200 a week covers five days of room, board, and tuition.

For more information, write the Mannings at R.D. 2, East Berlin, Pennsylvania 17316.

More Handweaving
The Handweavers Guild of America (998 Farmington Avenue, West Hartford, Connecticut 06107), publishes an annual education directory that lists and briefly describes hundreds of schools and studios offering handweaving courses. "The Suppliers Directory," a separate booklet, provides an equally exhaustive list of weaving-supply stores throughout the United States and Canada and in some foreign countries. Both are full of fascinating advertisements for strange and exotic-sounding items like Moby Dick Wool. Write the Guild for the current prices.

Tiles

The tiles that edge the fireplaces at the Isabella Stewart Gardner Museum in Boston and at the Rockefeller estate at Pocantico Hills, New York, were produced at the Moravian Pottery and Tile Works, founded by an eccentric rich man named Henry Chapman Mercer. Recently restored, the big Doylestown, Pennsylvania, establishment is open for tours—and producing the decorative tiles as they were made in Mercer's day, around the turn of the century. After you've seen the building—a strange modern structure that seems a cross between California missions and the architecture of Antonio Gaudi—you can visit a gift shop where the products are sold. They're interesting pieces, embossed with motifs borrowed from the cultures of Europe, the Aztecs, and the Moravian stoves of the Pennsylvania immigrants. For more information about a visit to surrounding Bucks County and its quaint towns, inns, and antique shops, contact the Moravian Pottery and Tile Works, Swamp Road, Doylestown, Pennsylvania 18901; and the Bucks County Historical-Tourist Commission, Fallsington, Pennsylvania 19504.

Crafts Museums

Aside from the Carborundum Museum of Ceramics in Niagara Falls, New York—where the collections deal mainly with historic ceramics—one of the most important museums in the field is the Museum of Contemporary Crafts of the American Crafts Council in New York City. The permanent collection is very small, and it's usually not displayed all at once. Instead, the museum space is given over to changing exhibitions of contemporary American crafts in textiles, metal, clay, wood, glass, fiber, and related areas of design, architecture, and new technologies. There's always some sort of innovative exhibition on display: in the past, they've dealt with subjects like grass and decorative objects made from grass; Indian basketry; jewelry in thread; American blacksmithery; bags —from Burma, Scotland, Tibet, France, and so on; innovative dyeing; and the new American quilt. For details on what's on, write the museum at 29 West 53rd Street, New York, New York 10019.

On a par with the Museum of Contemporary Crafts is the Renwick Gallery on Pennsylvania Avenue at 17th Street N.W. in Washington, D.C. An ornate Victorian building in the French Second Empire style, the Renwick gets quite a few of the same exhibits as the Museum of Contemporary Crafts.

Carving is the focus of two museums—the National Carvers Museum (14960 Woodcarver Road, Monument, Colorado 80132) and the considerably smaller Warther Museum in Dover, Ohio. The National Carvers Museum contains the work of many different whittlers. There are carved figures with simple sayings emblazoned on the bases, as well as carved fish and birds and such. One of the more impressive exhibits is the massive carved doors. The Warther Museum is a monument to one skillful Swiss-born whittler, Ernest Warther, who has whittled some of the most ornate pieces you'll probably ever see— Casey Jones's engine, for instance, is carved in ivory, as are fifty-five other operating miniature locomotives, all the work of this one amazing old man. Nearby, there are plenty of other things to see and do—Schoenbrunn and Zoar

Villages are in the area, along with Devil's Den State Park. For more information, write the Ohio Department of Economic & Community Development, Box 1001, Columbus, Ohio 43216.

Native American Indian Crafts

"There are more practicing craftsmen among Indians than in any other racial group in America," says Jamake Highwater in his fascinating *Indian America*, one of the Fodor's Guides. "Almost every member of the tribes practices some kind of art or craft with a very high level of proficiency. . . . Among the finest achievements . . . are the pottery and jewelry of the Southwest; the beadwork and quillwork of the Plains; the weaving of the Navajo

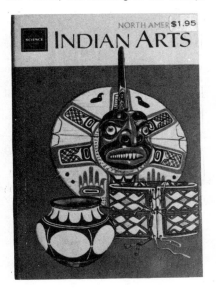

and the Pueblo Indians; and the basketry of the Cherokees of North Carolina, the Papagos and Hopis and Pimas of Arizona, and the Eskimo and Tlingit of Alaska." Highwater tells you what each means in the context in which it is produced, talks about how you can tell frauds, fakes, and trademarks—about how you can go about developing an eye to distinguish the fine work from the cheap imitations. He talks about pottery, about grass, plait, coil, and wicker baskets, about weavings and rugs, about silver work and turquoise, beadwork and quillwork, featherwork and skinwork, and art in stone and wood. He tells you what to look for. "Authenticity is not simply a matter of snobbery—it's a question of worth and beauty and truth." All of this is absolutely fascinating. If you've seen native American work and not had any satisfactory answers as to what is authentic

and what isn't, you won't be able to put the book down. The book would be worth $10.95 if the craft section was the beginning and the end of it.

But there's more. Highwater talks about ceremonials, music, Indian galleries and museums, dwellings, costume, and then discusses the Indian nations region by region. The attention to authenticity—to what is esteemed by the Indians themselves—stays with you throughout the book, and so when you take Highwater's advice, you are bound to come out understanding more about these important cultures than you did before. David McKay, Inc., 750 Third Avenue, New York, New York 10017; $10.95.

More on Indian crafts. Write the Indian Arts and Crafts Board, Room 4004, U.S. Department of the Interior, Washington, D.C. 20240, for information in impressive quantity.

Also see *North American Indian Arts* by Andrew Hunter Whiteford. This is a book for people who know absolutely nothing about the Indian culture that existed in the United States long before the arrival of the European settlers, and that has co-existed, if not always peacefully, with the rest of American culture ever since.

Like the rest of the Golden Guides, this one on Indian Arts packs a good deal of information into a very small space; a look through the chapters on pottery, baskets, textiles, skinwork, applied decorations, woodwork, stonework, shellwork, metalwork, and featherwork familiarizes you not just with the basic techniques but also with regional variations in the products and with modern techniques. Oversimplified? Perhaps. But fascinating reading nonetheless, and a good thing to peruse before you go on to study more detailed works on the subject—or visit a museum of Indian artifacts or crafts area. Golden Books, Western Publishing, 1220 Mound Avenue, Racine, Wisconsin 53404; $1.95.

More Crafts

Of the thousands upon thousands of less nationally renowned crafts fairs and sidewalk arts shows, the following are some of the most interesting. Each has its charms, and if you're in the area you owe it to yourself to write the state tourist office for the details.

In the Midwest. The Parke County Maple Fair in Rockville, Indiana (in late February or early March); the Newton, Kansas, Mennonite Folk Festival, usually in early April; Canal Days at Roscoe Village Restoration, in mid-August in Coshocton, Ohio; the Clothesline Art and Craft Fair at Prairie Grove, Arkansas; the Petersburg, Illinois, Land of Lincoln Crafts Festival at the New Salem Carriage Museum, in late September.

In the South. The Heart of Florida Folk Festival in Dade City, Florida, in late February; the Cedar Key, Florida, Sidewalk Arts and Crafts Festival, in late April; the Annual Carolina Designer Craftsmen Fair at the North Carolina State Fairgrounds in Raleigh, North Carolina, in late April; the Virginia Highlands Festival in Abingdon, Virginia, during the first two weeks in August; the Pendleton, South Carolina, Foothills Arts and Crafts Festival, in mid-August; the Horse Pens 40 Crafts Festival in Oneonta, Alabama, in the middle of October; the Macon, Georgia, Southeastern Arts and Crafts Festival, the first weekend in November.

In the West. The Laguna Beach Winter Festival in Laguna Beach, California, in February; the Los Angeles, California, Westwood Village Sidewalk Art Show, in May; in Longview, Washington, the Lower Columbia Arts and Crafts Festival, held the third weekend in June; the Dinosaurland Art Festival, in mid-June in Vernal, Utah; All-American Indian Days in Sheridan, Wyoming, in late July; the Pacific Northwest Arts and Crafts Fair in Bellevue, Washington, in July; the New Mexico Arts and Crafts Fair in Albuquerque, New Mexico, the last weekend in July; the Park City Art Festival in Park City, Utah, in mid-August; and the Red Lodge, Montana, Festival of Nations, the third week in August.

The Contemporary Crafts Market Place

A big book compiled by the American Crafts Council, this is the most comprehensive guide to the U.S. crafts scene—not only crafts schools and fairs, but also colleges and universities offering crafts courses, sources of materials, and much more. R. R. Bowker, Box 1807, Ann Arbor, Michigan 48106; $14.95.

A Potpourri of Vacation Ideas and Activities

On the Road

How to Read the Highway Route Signs

There's a method to the numbering of Federal highways. As for the interstates, the east-west routes have one- or two-digit numbers that are even and that get higher the farther north you go. (I-4 in Florida, for example, is south of I-10 through Louisiana and Texas, which in turn is south of I-96 in Michigan.) North-south route numbers are odd, and get bigger as you go east. (I-95 runs up and down the east coast; I-5 is in California.) Three-digit numbers belong to routes near large cities. When the first digit is even, the route will go through or around the city; if odd, the route is a spur that will end downtown.

Federal highways other than interstates are similarly numbered, except that the lower numbers belong to roads on the east coast and along the Canadian border.

The Every-25-Miles Game

A New Mexico photographer faced with the prospect of a dull two-hundred-mile drive one Sunday afternoon a couple of years ago decided to make a game of it. Starting just outside Las Vegas, he would stop to take a photograph every 25 miles.

In accordance with the rules he made up, he spent only 5 minutes for each picture, took each photo within 50 yards of the roadside, included a bit of roadside fence in every picture, and used only a normal or a close-up lens. He came home with some interesting pictures.

"A dull stretch of road? There is no such thing," he concluded.

An FM Radio Guide

One of the facts of life of long-distance driving is that you get an intimate acquaintance with all the songs on the top 40; for years after, whenever you hear one of the songs, it will take you back to that drive. Most of the time, the music will be just one other reminder—like photos or tape recordings—of the pleasant times on the road.

Which is all well and good: you go traveling to get memories.

But while you're actually there, the drone of the DJs who sound more or less alike no matter where you are can get so monotonous that you'd gladly listen to just about anything else, and if it's jazz or good rock or classical music, so much the better. There aren't enough stations playing this sort of music to get you across the country, but if you have a choice of routes, the balance might be tilted by the radio fare available. Here are cities that have jazz, classical, or good rock radio stations and where you'll find the stations on the dial.

Albany: WQBK, 103.9 (rock). *Austin*: KLBJ, 93.7 (rock). *Baltimore*: WDJQ, 104.3 (rock). *Boston*: WBCN, 104.1 (some classical, plus rock, folk, jazz). *Buffalo*: WBLK, 93.7 (R&B, gospel, jazz), and WBUF, 92.9 (country, rock, folk, jazz, classical). *Chicago*: WBMX, 102.3 (soul); WEFM, 99.5 (classical); WSDM, 97.9, and WXRT, 93.1 (both rock). *Cleveland*: WLYT, 92.3 (rock, jazz, latin music). *Columbus*: WCOL, 92.3 (rock). *Dallas*: KAFM, 92.5 (rock and folk) and WRR, 101.1 (classical). *Denver*: KLAK, 107.5 (country) and KVOD, 99.5 (classical). *Detroit*: WABX, 99.5 (rock); WGPR, 107.5 (R&B, jazz, gospel); WJZZ, 105.9 (jazz); WQRS, 105.1 (classical); WWWW, 106.7 (rock). *Eugene, Oregon*: KZEL, 96.1 (jazz, rock, classical, folk). *Houston*: KLOL, 101.1 (rock, blues, jazz, folk). *Indianapolis*: WTLC, 105.7 (rock, jazz). *Jacksonville*: WAIV, 96.9 (rock). *Kansas City*: KWKI, 93.3, and KYYS, 102.1 (both rock). *Las Vegas*: KORK, 97.1 (some classical). *Los Angeles*: KFAC, 92.3 (classical); KUTE, 101.9 (jazz, blues); KGBS, 97.1 (country). *Memphis*: WMPS, 97.1 (classical). *Miami*: WINZ, 94.9 (rock). *Minneapolis/St. Paul*: KQRS, 92.5 (rock) and KTWN, 107.9 (classical). *New Orleans*: WNOE, 101.1, and WRNO, 99.5 (both rock); WXEL, 105.3 (R&B). *New York*: WBLS, 107.5 (jazz, black music); WNCN, 104.3, and WQXR, 96.3 (both classical); WRVR, 106.7 (jazz); WLIR, 92.7 (rock). *Omaha*: KFMQ, 101.9 (rock) and KQRQ, 98.5 (jazz, folk, rock). *Philadelphia*: WCAU, 98.1 (jazz); WDAS, 105.3 (rock); WFLN, 95.7 (classical). *Phoenix*: KDBK, 93.3 (rock, folk, jazz, and some classical) and KNIX, 102.5 (country). *Pittsburgh*: WAMO, 105.9 (R&B, rock); WYDD, 104.7 (rock). *Portland, Oregon*: KINK, 101.9 (folk, rock). *St. Louis*: KADI, 96.3 (rock); KKSS, 107.7 (blues and jazz); KSHE, 94.7 (jazz, folk, rock); WIL, 92.3 (country). *San Francisco*: KDFC, 102.1 (classical); KRE, 102.9 (R&B, jazz); KSAN, 94.9 (jazz, folk, rock, some classical); KTIM, 100.9 (classical, R&B, rock, jazz). *Seattle*: KZAM, 92.5 (jazz, folk, rock). *Washington, D.C.*: WHFS, 102.3 (jazz, folk, blues, and rock); WKYS, 93.9 (rock, jazz); WMAL, 107.3 (rock, folk, country); WWDC, 101.1 (rock).

A Thinker's Answer to CB

Conceived on the West Coast a few years back as an answer to the "cerebral atrophy" that sets in on long-distance drives, Books on Tape offers you around a hundred recorded works —from classics like *Walden* to works by Joseph Wambaugh, Ring Lardner, James Thurber, and George Plimpton. Each book takes about ten hours of listening time; rentals for a month run $6.50–$7.50.

For details, write Books on Tape, P. O. Box 71405, Atlantic Richfield Station, Los Angeles, California 90071.

Truck Stops

At truck stops, in addition to fuel, you can get food, repairs, and sometimes even lodging, showers, and a haircut. As *Business Week* said recently, "the truck stop business has entered the million dollar phase. . . . The new truck stops are loaded with so many services that they are virtually smaller scale shopping centers." The *24-Hour Full-Service Auto-Truck Stops Directory* lists some five hundred of them along or near interstate highways and codes them according to the services you get. If you do much night driving, it can be useful. Reymont Associates, 29 Reymont Avenue, Rye, New York 10580; $2.50.

The Diesel Stop Directory

Listed in this handy guide are over eight thousand locations where you can buy diesel fuel in the United States and Canada, plus lists of authorized Mercedes-Benz dealers, maps, and brief notes of the sights to be seen along the way. In the introduction is a rundown on the various state statutes requiring operators of diesel-powered autos to have a permit to buy gas: Arizona, Colorado, Massachusetts, Michigan, Montana, New Hampshire, New Mexico, Oregon, and Wyoming. Hammond, Inc., Maplewood, New Jersey 07040; $4.95.

Landforms

by George Adams and Jerome Wyckoff

"For an interested observer, landforms always raise questions. Why are the hills and valleys where they are? Why does the river take that turn? Why is this region riddled with caves, while others are not? Why does the valley have a steep wall on one side, a gently sloping wall on the other? What makes this terrain a badland, that one a land of rolling hills?"

Questions like these, posed in the early part of the book, are the kind that come up naturally when you're covering distances in a car. This book provides some of the answers. A map sketches the physiographic regions of the United States, while subsequent paragraphs talk about the processes that shape landforms (igneous activities, solid movements, gradation and weathering, and so on). A fascinating little book. Golden Books, Western Publishing, 1220 Mound Avenue, Racine, Wisconsin 53404; $1.95.

In the Rockies and California

David Alt and Donald Hyndman of the University of Montana discuss landforms and geological formations that can be seen from the highways in *Roadside Geology of the Northern Rockies* ($6.95) and *Roadside Geology of Northern California* ($5.95). The books discuss rock collecting as well. Both are published by the Mountain Press Publishing Company, 279 West Front Street, Missoula, Montana 59801.

Parkways of the Canadian Rockies: An Interpretive Guide to Roads in the Mountain Parks

by Brian Patton

There should be more books like this. Going on the premise that Canada's Banff, Jasper, Yoho, and Kootenay National Parks are "the largest area of mountain parkland in the world"—a single parkland whose boundaries are quite artificially constructed—the author takes you along the Yellowhead

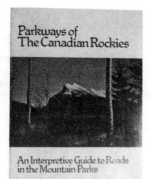

Highway, the Icefields Parkway, the Trans-Canada Highway, and the Banff-Windermere Highway, and explains the flora, fauna, and geological formations that "run oblivious of man-made boundaries." There's a general chapter explaining wildflowers, animals, rock

formations, and such, as well as the human history of the area. Then (and this is the bulk of the book) there are mile-by-mile accounts of features visible from roadside viewpoints, picnic areas, and campgrounds. It's like having an exceptionally entertaining park ranger right there in the car with you. It would be a mistake to drive these magnificent roads without it. Summerthought, Ltd., Box 1420, Banff, Alberta TOL OCO; $6.95.

Twenty-Eight Great Drives

At the end of one of those marathon drives you sometimes have to endure in order to get someplace, your teeth are gritted, the muscles in your shoulders and your arms are in knots, and your back feels as if someone just sliced it in half.

But driving can also be terrifically enjoyable. There's a special feeling of excitement—and freedom—that goes with getting into a car and taking off that only gets better when you're driving through exhilarating scenery.

Now, you don't have to go very far away from home to find one of those little bends in a country road that sets your heart alight and fuels the home fires for another hard week at the old grind. Various road maps indicate particularly scenic stretches, and you can bet that almost any secondary road in a lightly settled part of the country will offer pleasant—if not grand—scenery. But some stretches of road are so extra special that they're worth traveling a long way from home to experience. They're long or short, historic or merely scenic—but each offers its particular view of America and Americans.

To the End of the Road in Newfoundland

As you head northward on Route 430 off Canada-1, the Long Range Mountains loom up on your right; the sea foams onto the beaches and forested shores on your left. The road is graveled, and settlements are few and far between, but there are plenty of woods, flower-covered meadows, and heaths. There are also two National Parks—the Gros Morne, all dune-fringed beaches, lakes, salmon streams, nature trails, and splendid wildlife (moose, caribou, black bear, lynx, beaver, mink, otter); and, close to the end of the road, 225 miles from the Trans-Canada, l'Anse aux Meadows National Park, where a Viking settlement of a thousand years back has been excavated.

For more information, write the Department of Tourism, Confederation Building, St. John's, Newfoundland A0L 3E0; and the Director General, Parks Canada, Department of Indian and Northern Affairs, Ottawa, Ontario K1A OH4.

New Brunswick's Saint John River Valley

The 92 miles between Fredericton and Saint John, on Route 102, string together nearly a half dozen small towns (Evandale, Hampstead, Queenstown, and Gagetown); bypasses some fine textile-and-weaving studios; and in the process gives you such magnificent river views that some ecstatic fans of the area dubbed it the Rhine of America.

At Saint John, there's one sight you won't see in Germany, however—the famous "Reversing Falls": when the tide comes in, every twelve hours and twenty-five minutes, some hundred billion tons of salt water surge up the four-hundred-fifty-foot-wide gorge at the point at which the river plummets fifteen feet into the ocean, and those waters whirl and foam with such ferocity that the rapids of the river seem to do an about-face. Tide tables are widely available in Saint John; be sure to get one and schedule your visits to other sites in this handsome old provincial capital with your visit to the reversing falls in mind. For more information, write the Department of Tourism, P. O. Box 12345, Fredericton, New Brunswick E3B 5C3.

The Sublime Trans-Canada

What better way to take the measure of the continent? Between Victoria, British Columbia, at the southernmost tip of Vancouver Island, and St. John's, Newfoundland, there are 4,877 miles. In those many miles, the Trans-Canada takes in not only ten provinces, six time zones, major cities, national and provincial parks, the Laurentians and the Rockies, but also countless coastal fishing villages, rippling wheat fields, campgrounds, service stations, waterfalls, unspoiled lakes, forests—*a mari usque a mare*, from sea to sea, in the words of the Canadian coat of arms' slogan. Count on a month of driving to take it all in.

For more information, write the Canadian Government Office of Tourism, in Ottawa, Ontario, or any of its branches in major U.S. cities.

Road's End in Saskatchewan

Drive straight up Saskatchewan Routes 6, 3, and 2 from the North Dakota border and you'll see the wheat fields and swelling prairies give way to muskeg swamps, thick bright green forests of fir and spruce, and royal blue lakes that are deep and cold and full of trout, walleye, and pike—good eating if ever there was good eating. About 200 miles before you get to the end of the road, you hit 1,500-square-mile Prince Albert National Park, and you may not want to go any farther. On the one hand, there are comfortable motels and cabins where you can spend the night (and

play tennis or go riding) and on the other, there are rental canoes that you can paddle deep into the woods and trails that you can hike to miraculous little lakes. The forests are full of deer, moose, elk, black bear, caribou, mink, marten, fox, lynx. And there's some good fishing.

But push farther into the wilds down this road. There, at the end, is beautiful Lac La Ronge, whose fabulous fishing has been drawing anglers for years. In the days before the road was finished, they flew up in airplanes.

For more information, write the Saskatchewan Department of Tourism, Box 7105, Regina S4P 3N2.

Prince Edward Island's Lady Slipper Drive

Acadians and Indians; fishing villages and Irish moss; clay roads and paved ones that skirt coves, red-sand beaches, and bays. This day-long drive at the west end of Prince Edward Island covers 150 miles. The island, home of the famous Malpeque oysters, is a pastoral place with lots of dairy farms and spic-and-span villages. It's far less wild than most of the rest of Canada. The Lady Slipper Drive is marked on the roads with special signs at key intersections and on maps available from the Tourist Information Division of the Department of Environment and Tourism, Box 940 Charlottetown, Prince Edward Island C1A 7N5.

Cape Breton Island's Celebrated Cabot Trail

One of the most stunning drives in Canada, this 184-mile highway takes you along a rugged bluff-edged shoreline. On one side there are great sweeps of green forests and meadows; on the other, there are rocky little coves and sandy beaches—and endless, stupefying views of the Atlantic. From Margaree Harbor to Ingonish, where this highway-in-the-sky finally slumps to water's edge, there are also some nifty little Gulf of St. Lawrence fishing villages where the islanders speak French or Gaelic. A magnificent side trip takes you from Cape North up to Capstick, where the island ends. The Keltic Lodge in Ingonish—one of the province's best hostelries—is another Cape Breton Island pleasure.

For details, write the Nova Scotia Department of Tourism, Box 456, Halifax B3J 2R5.

Alberta's Icefields Parkway

Surging nearly one hundred fifty miles through the great peaks of the Rocky Mountains between Banff and Jasper National Parks, crossing countless rivers and streams, passing bluer-than-blue Lake Louise (which is every bit as jewellike as you've probably heard) and the fine Johnston Canyon Falls, the

Icefields Parkway gives up some truly stupendous views of the glaciers on the Continental Divide—the Waputik and Wapta Ice Fields and the fantastic Columbia Ice Field, largest body of ice south of the Arctic Circle. At the end of the road: Jasper townsite, sitting in the mountains like a picture-postcard Alpine village. For details, write Travel Alberta, 10065 Jasper Avenue, Edmonton T5J OH4.

The Alaska Highway

Some of the most beautiful scenery in the world is here—and there are fifteen hundred miles of it. Fifteen hundred miles of forests, snow-capped mountains, lakes, fish, moose, caribou, trading posts, and good conversation (though not too much of it). When you come up to enjoy all that, you'll also find one of the finest gravel highways in the world. Gravel. Fifteen hundred miles, according to some, of dust, chuckholes big enough to get called gravel pits, and mud. A fifteen-hundred-mile-long washboard. The Alcan Highway, which stretches from Dawson Creek, British Columbia, to Fairbanks, Alaska, is all of that—and then some. The hot springs, historic sites, fishing opportunities, and other activities and points of interest you can enjoy along the way are all written up in *The Milepost*, a mile-by-mile log of the highway that also tells you about places to stay and wildlife and wildflowers. You can order it for $5.95 from the Alaska Northwest Publishing Company, Box 4-EEE, Anchorage, Alaska 99509.

The Only Road to the Arctic Ocean

For what it's worth, Canada is the only country in the world where you can drive to three oceans—that, because of the recent completion of the Dempster Highway, which begins twenty-six miles east of Dawson City in the Yukon and ends down the road some three hundred miles—and many adventures —later, on the Arctic Ocean at Inuvik. All but the first fifty miles carry you through the breathtaking tundra—above tree line. North of the Blackstone Pass in the Ogilvie Mountains, you're on the north slope of the continent, where all streams drain north. Get *The Milepost* ($5.95 from Alaska Northwest Publishing Company, Box 4-EEE, Anchorage 99509) for a mile-by-mile rundown of the sights to see along the way. Also write the Yukon Department of Travel and Information, Box 2703, Whitehorse, Yukon Y1A 2C3.

The Klondike Loop and the Top of the World

Branching off the Alaska Highway, the Klondike Loop Road and the Taylor Highway take you first east along craggy ridge tops, then south between the Ogilvie Mountains and the Dawson

Range, along Fortymile River and through old gold-rush country, tundra, past strange rock formations, in a country of plentiful animals, big fish, and birds. Dawson City, at the intersection of the Klondike Loop Road and the Top of the World Road (as the Taylor Highway is sometimes called for the feeling you get when you drive on it) is slightly down at the heels, but plenty lively in summer. The cabin of author Robert Service, who wrote "The Shooting of Dan McGrew" and "The Cremation of Sam McGee," is open for visitors, and there are "mellerdramas," museums, festivals, shops, and such. For more information, write Travelarctic, Yellowknife, Northwest Territories X1A 2L9; and the Tourism Division of the Alaska Department of Commerce and Economic Development, Pouch E, Juneau, Alaska 99811. Or get *The Milepost* ($5.95 from the Alaska Northwest Publishing Company, Box 4-EEE, Anchorage 99509).

The Yellowhead Highway
At Regina, Saskatchewan, the Trans-Canada Highway forks. One branch heads west through Calgary and over steep mountain grades through Banff to Victoria, British Columbia. The other

angles northward through Edmonton, Alberta, and Jasper National Park toward Prince Rupert, a salmon and halibut fishing village just south of the Alaskan border. That's the Yellowhead. From Edmonton, those prairie lands and farms that you thought would never disappear give way to foothills, forests, lakes, and streams—then soar to the skies in a real symphony of alpine peaks, mountain meadows, rushing streams. You can make side trips, along the way, to a hot springs, or to 11,033-foot Mount Edith Cavell and its Angel Glacier. At Hazelton, which is also on the way, you can visit the Ksan Indian Village, where totems are carved, displayed, and explained on the spot at the Pacific Northwest's only existing school of Indian art. Members of the Gitksan and Hagwilget Carrier Indians, who founded the village, demonstrate carving and tell you about the lives of the tribes in the area before the arrival of the white man. In summer, there are weekly performances by Ksan dancers and feasts of Pacific Northwest Indian foods.

Also along the Yellowhead: old churches, gold-rush towns gone bust, lakes, streams that are great for salmon fishing.

From Prince Rupert, you can get

cruise ships to Alaska or the Queen Charlotte Islands—splendid trips full of fjord-like scenery.

For more information, write the British Columbia Yellowhead 16 Travel Association, Box 1659, Prince George, Brtish Columbia; or any Canadian Government Travel Office. (The one in New York City is at 1251 Avenue of the Americas, zip 10020.)

British Columbia's Fjord Roads
Whether the spires of the Mackenzies are outlined sharply against a bright blue sky or wrapped in pale swirling fog, this land of mossy rainforests, four-thousand-foot-high mountains, inlets, sheltered coves, and sea lions might remind you of Norway, especially when you drive along the coast roads and the green rugged hills soar on one side and the sea gleams like a sheet of silvered blue on the other. There are three good routes to explore: British Columbia Route 19, which takes in some 200 miles of coast between Victoria and Kelsey Bay, about two thirds of the way up Vancouver Island; Route 4, a spur off 19 that heads west through lake-dotted forests of western red cedar and a section of the Pacific

Rim National Park to the town of Ucluelet; and, on the mainland, up the Squamish Highway, Route 99 out of Vancouver, along Howe Sound. For more information, write Tourism British Columbia, 117 Wharf Street, Victoria V8W 2Z2, and the superintendent of the Pacific Rim National Park in Ucluelet. You should also get a ferry schedule: write British Columbia Ferries, 816 Wharf Street, Victoria.

Oregon's Columbia River Scenic Drive
You can charge through the Columbia River Gorge on I-8ON in no time flat—but then you would miss the cliffs, the canyons, the ferns, the mosses, and the stunning forests (their greens looking almost electric when the sun filters through the leaves). Far more pleasant is to drive the old Columbia River Highway, one of those superscenic routes that has made a name for itself because of its pathway high above the river and for the occasional glimpses of the big stream. En route, you can stop in any number of state parks with woods paths to myriad waterfalls, some so lovely they've been called the most beautiful on the continent. At Latourell Falls, for example, a straight and narrow ribbon of water tumbles into a shadowy pool; at Mist Falls the water disappears into its own mist, then collects to form a second breathtaking cataract. And there are many more, among them 620-foot-high Multnomah Falls, Oregon's highest.

Starting at Crown Point, the river is always in view; and after the Bonneville Dam, where you can visit the powerhouse and the fish ladder, you're at river level. The trip on this road is only about twenty-five miles; if you feel like continuing, turn off at Hood River and follow Route 35 through the foothills of the fruit-growing country around Mount Hood. To get back to Portland, take U.S. 26 (which offers a spectacular display of daffodils every April).

For more information, contact the Travel Information Division of the Oregon State Highway Department, Salem 97310.

California's Highway 1
This stretch of road south of San Francisco between Monterrey and Morro Bay is one of the single most beautiful bits of road on the continent: twisting and climbing and swooping along a shelf of road cut into the sides of the Santa Lucias, it towers over the rocky shores. On one side, there's always sea—as far as you can see. Breakers. Whitecaps. The wild blue yonder of the briny deep. On the other side, incredibly lush redwood forests alternate with swelling grasslands, which, most of the year, seem like gray green bolsters. En route, you can stop at

Point Lobos Reserve, clamber out onto the rocks of the point, and watch the sea lions; sometimes they'll flip over on their back and bang abalone shells open on rocks they put on their stomachs. San Simeon, William Randolph Hearst's castle full of carvings, marbles, alabasters, and art treasures beyond belief, is also along the way. For further information about it, write the Area Historical Monument, San Simeon 93452.

The Northwest Pacific Coast
Between Pacific County, Washington, and Del Norte County, California, the United States' western coastline is just one continuous five-hundred-mile stretch of public beach divided up, occasionally, by dramatic headlands and dotted with jagged boulders. The whole thing makes for splendid tripping because there are so many ways to disport yourself en route. You can go out and comb the beach for agates, shells, driftwood, glass fishing floats, or a flotsam and jetsam of objects broken off offshore wrecks. You can go fishing. Salmon fishing charters are offered in almost every one of the small seaside communities along the road. Fifty miles of the road cut-through the Oregon Dunes National Recreation Area and Honeyman State Park, where kids use snow-saucers to slide down the immense Sahara-like dunes. And there are literally dozens of other state parks and roadside stops where you can admire the view or, in season, the wild azaleas and rhododendrons that are as common here as dandelions in the Midwest. There are gray mornings, all misty and quiet, and sparkling

white-and-blue mornings when the gulls are out wheeling through the sky and the whales are spouting offshore. The crashing winter storms, which uncover the agate beds and pile mounds of driftwood in the windrows, are also an experience worth waiting around for.

To get details on the many things to see and do en route, write the Oregon Coast Association, Box 670, Newport 97365.

Idaho's Lewis and Clark Highway
Two hundred twenty-nine miles of roadway take you through some of the ruggedest of Idaho's rugged Bitterroot countryside between Lewiston, Idaho, and Missoula, Montana. First you're hugging the banks of the Lochsa River; then (after the Lochsa's confluence with the Selway), you edge along the Middle Fork of the Clearwater, then the Main Clearwater (a tributary of the Snake) then, finally, the big Snake itself. Lewis and Clark's real trail was up the mountainside along what is now a gravel road known as the Lolo Trail, which runs about a hundred miles between Kooskia and Powell. For more information, contact the Clearwater National Forest, Route 3, Orofino, Idaho 83544.

Hell's Canyon
Seventy-nine hundred feet deep, this gorge, cut by the Snake River on the border of Idaho and Oregon, is quite a spectacular sight—all the more so because it's so wild: there aren't just dozens and dozens of roads leading to it. Route 71, off U.S. 95 not far from McCall, takes you through the Boise National Forest toward the Canyon. Cross

the border and continue west on Route 86 to Homestead, where a tiny road crosses the canyon and forks—one branch footing it in the shadows at the base of the cliffs, 23 miles to Hell's Canyon Dam; the other climbing steeply—2,600 feet in six miles—to Cuprum, in Idaho, where you can get a road back to U.S. 95 or follow a narrow corkscrew of a spur road into the mountains for 15 miles and some of the most dramatic views over Hell's Canyon.

For more information, write the Idaho Division of Tourism & Industrial Development, Capitol Building, Boise 83720.

Southwestern Colorado's Million Dollar Highway
The legend that says U.S. 550 got its name when construction crews discovered too late that they had used gold-bearing gravel to surface the road probably isn't true—but the "Million Dollar Highway" is an apt title all the same, because of the scenery along its seventy-five miles between Ouray and Durango. The peaks of the San Juans, of volcanic origin, are broken and shattered by deep crevices and sharp pinnacles; they're so jagged that the Rockies look like worn down horses' teeth in comparison. Then there are the forests, the ten-thousand-foot passes, the mountain streams (as clear and cool as the thin high air). This part of the state has also escaped the onslaught of construction and development crews, so for the most part it's almost as unspoiled as it was a quarter century ago. For more information about the highway and about this wonderful part of the state, contact the Travel Marketing Section, 500 State Centennial Building, Denver 80203.

Oklahoma's Superscenic Talimena Drive
Real honest-to-goodness mountains—not just very high hills, but actual mountains, with peaks colored deep blue and purple with pine, oak, and cedar. Off in the distance, small patches of blue lake reflect the mountains and the sun. As you drive the Talimena Drive, from Talihina, Oklahoma, through the Ouachita National Forest across the Arkansas line to the little town of Mena, you can't help but wonder whether this is the Oklahoma you've always thought of as flat and boring. For fifty miles, you're in the mountains, and they're lush and lovely.

For further information, contact the Oklahoma Industrial Development and Park Department, 500 Will Rogers Memorial Building, Oklahoma City 73105, and the Arkansas Department of Parks and Tourism, State Capitol, Little Rock 72201.

The Great River Road
The Great River Road is not actually a single road, but instead it's a fifty-six-hundred-mile stretch of highways along the Mississippi that have been marked to form a single route through the ten states and two provinces near the river. From the bluffs and through the forests along the way, the big river is a constant marvel with its islands, its procession of barges and pleasure cruisers, and its almost imperceptible current. The associations with Mark Twain and Huck Finn and those wonderful days back when childhood was childhood are so strong that you can't quite look at the river without dreaming. For more information, write the state tourist departments in Ontario, Manitoba, Minnesota, Wisconsin, Illinois, Iowa, Missouri, Kentucky, Tennessee, Arkansas, Mississippi, Louisiana. Or write the Great River Road Association in Cassville, Wisconsin 53806.

The Natchez Trace
First an animal trail, then an Indian pathway, then a wilderness road between Natchez and Nashville—the northward route of the boatmen who had floated southward on the mighty Mississippi—this four-hundred-fifty-mile parkway through the forests, swamps, meadows, and fields of Mississippi is, as a Mississippi matron recently observed, "the way God meant highways to be." To wit: limited of access, lush of vegetation, full of nature trails and picnic areas, and entirely void of commercial vehicles and advertising. Some high points among the historic sites and points of interest along the way are the Ruins of Windsor, six miles west of Gibson, a rectangular procession of forty-foot-high Corinthian pillars that look for all the world like something out of Greece except for the lush vegetation around them; Natchez, on the Mississippi, full of stately antebellum mansions; and some remaining sections of the old Trace, sunken roads worn deep into the soil and edged by tall trees bearded in Spanish moss.

For more information, contact the Travel Department of the Mississippi Agricultural and Industrial Board, Box 849, Jackson 39205.

South Carolina's Ashley River Road
One of the oldest roads in South Carolina, this curling ribbon of asphalt between Charleston and Middleton Place is the sort of road you go south to experience: giant oak branches are twined overhead to form a nearly unbroken archway, veiled in Spanish moss. In the spring, dogwoods, jessamine, goldenrod, and wildflowers bloom through the green. Route 61, as

the Ashley River Road is officially named, takes you to Ashley Hall Plantation, Magnolia Gardens, and some other similarly exotic Deep South experiences. For more information, contact the South Carolina Department of Parks, Recreation and Tourism, Box 113, 1205 Pendleton Street, Columbia, South Carolina 29201.

Georgia's Richard Russell Scenic Highway
A mere eighteen miles from one end to the other, this lovely road through the Blue Ridge curls and climbs and plunges its way, in narrow switchbacks, from just south of Blairsville to Robertstown, and, in the process, carries you past a hundred gorgeously lush, hill-behind-Appalachian-hill vistas. If you're in the area, you ought not to miss it.

For more information about the area, write the Georgia Bureau of Industry and Trade, Trinity-Washington Building, P. O. Box 38097, Atlanta 30334.

The Blue Ridge Parkway
The Southern Highlands are exquisite during the lush green summers, breathtaking during the pink-and-white springs, bright as a polished copper kettle in the sun during the autumns. No wonder the 469-mile Blue Ridge Parkway, which takes in the best of the Highlands, is such a joy to drive.

Throughout the length of the road there are quiet stretches of meadowland, vistas of forests and farmlands, rhododendron and azalea stands, streams, boulders, wildlife galore—and nary an ugly road sign to spoil the view. When you get tired of riding, you can get out and stretch your legs on trails in the forest that lead to overlooks from rocky outcrops or more good views from a ridge. Or detour off the road into the picturesque little mountain towns where there are crafts to inspect, country stores to visit, fairs and festivals where you can celebrate the local heritage with the natives. When the sun goes down and the stars come out, you can understand why the Indians called these mountains the *Shenandoah*, the daughter of the stars.

For more information, write the Blue Ridge Parkway Association, P. O. Box 475, Asheville, North Carolina 28802; the Superintendent, Blue Ridge Parkway, P. O. Box 7607, Asheville 28807.

Massachusetts' Rugged Mohawk Trail
Blazed by Indians a century ago, this route takes you sixty-three miles from the New York border to Millers Falls on the Connecticut River, over rugged mountains, through wooded valleys, and past old Colonial villages, lakes, antique shops, old museums, historic restorations, maple-sugar shacks, and

acres and acres of forested state parks. It's beautiful in the spring and summer—and spectacular in the fall.

For more information, write the Massachusetts Department of Commerce and Development, State Office Building, Government Center, 100 Cambridge Street, Boston 02202.

New Hampshire's Kancamagus Highway

Crossing the White Mountains between Conway and Lincoln, up north and up high where the air is clear and cool, these thirty-four miles are among the most scenic in an area full of super-scenic drives: on either side of you in the distance are the peaks of the White Mountains—Chocorua, Mt. Paugus, Mt. Osceola, Big Attitash. Close at hand is the Swift River, and, after you've climbed the pass over Mt. Kancamagus, the Hancock and East Branches of the Pemigewasset River.

For more information, write the Forest Supervisor in the White Mountains National Forest, Laconia 03246.

Vermont's Route 100

Stretching from the Massachusetts line into Canada, this winding little Vermont highway takes in rolling hills, red barns, babbling brooks, white steeples, brindled cows grazing in pastures rimmed with elms—in short, pure Vermont scenery. Now there are other roads that are perhaps less traveled, and Vermont has about eight thousand miles of graveled roads that are in some ways more scenic. But few in the state are so consistently scenic over a long haul, or so consistently equipped to delight you with antique shops, working craftsmen, factory outlet stores, inns, and such. Especially notable are the Woodstock Inn in Woodstock (a town so chi-chi in its Vermont propriety that the power lines are buried); the Original Vermont Country Store, in Weston, which is well provided with other points of interest and a restaurant where you can snack on crackers and milk and hunks of Vermont cheddar; and, in Plymouth Union, Calvin Coolidge's neat-as-a-pin hometown. Stowe, a very fancy ski and summer resort town, is in the north.

For more information, contact the Vermont Agency of Development and Community Affairs, 61 Elm Street, Montpelier 05602.

Maui's Hana Highway

It's just fifty miles from Kahului, at the waist of the hourglass-shaped island of Maui, to Hana, at the eastern end of the island, but those fifty miles will take you two hours to drive. The road itself—hilly, narrow, and so full of torturous hairpin bends that it's sometimes called the road of a hundred turns—is one reason. The other reason is the scenery. Sometimes you're hugging the beach; sometimes clinging precariously to fern-fringed, pandanus-laden cliffs that bottom out in the deep blue. Inland—uphill—are jungles of mango trees, ginger, guava and giant a'pe leaves, paper-bark trees, breadfruit, bamboo, and waterfalls with fern-banked pools where you can jump in—if you can find space to pull off the road. However, there are little parks all along the way where you can take in views of the ocean and the crater of Haleakala, the dormant volcano, or picnic, or go for a walk. In Waianapanapa State Park, four miles before you get to Hana, you can go for a spooky swim in one of the lava tube caves; from the black sand beach nearby you can hike over a stone-paved trail built as a highway in the sixteenth century right along the shoreline, about twenty minutes into Hana. Drive a little past Hana and you'll come to the famous Seven Pools at the base of two wonderful cascades. Spur roads nearby will take you to the Haleakala crater. There's lots of exploring to be done, and you couldn't find a more beautiful site to do it in.

For more information, write the Hawaii Visitors Bureau, 2270 Kalakaua Avenue, Honolulu 96815.

The Best of the Regional United States

As a sort of Bicentennial project, *Better Homes and Gardens* magazine sent its editors out exploring the United States to pick out the best of New England, the mid-Atlantic states, the Deep South, and the West, and to map it all out into tours that would be accomplishable in one-, two-, and three-week vacations. Ambitious as it was, the project was immensely successful and the mapped-out tours that resulted are really good.

You can order back issues of the magazine from 1716 Locust Street, Des Moines 50336.

Colorado Road Log Atlas

An interesting idea, this series of five logs of the highways in southwestern, west central, northwestern, northeastern, and southeastern Colorado. Each log presents small strip maps for about a dozen highways in the region covered in the volume; a mile-by-mile log of the other highways, landmarks and campgrounds en route; and, on the opposite side of the page, are discussions of history, resources, economy, and anything else that might be notable about some of the more interesting towns. If you're one of those people who is always wondering what this or that is over at the side of the road, these books are for you—you'll end up wishing for similar volumes on other parts of the country. Robert Taylor, the author, is a professional geographer. The Filter Press, Palmer Lake, Colorado 80133; $1.50 per volume.

Bridges

Why They Covered the Bridges

" 'Keeps 'em dry,' an old Pennsylvania carpenter always answered. Not the travelers, not the horses, or the wagonloads of hay, or the sweethearts halted in the fragrant shadows; nor was he referring to the plank roadways of the old landmarks. The roofs were put on our old covered bridges to keep the great main beams and arches dry. Staunch as these supporting timbers are, they rot if left exposed to be alternately wet by rains and snow and then scorched by sun. Builders in Maryland and the Virginias put the facts less bluntly but they felt the same way about it. 'Our bridges were covered, my dear Sir, for the same reason that our belles wore hoop skirts and crinolines—to protect the structural beauty that is seldom seen, but nevertheless appreciated.'"

So begins *Covered Bridges of the Middle Atlantic States* ($6.50), one of a pair of books about covered bridges by Richard Sanders Allen.

Why visit covered bridges? Because, for one thing, the heavy, dusty bridge trusses possess the same curious beauty that you find in carpenters' tools or in Shaker artifacts or in old barns. They are spare and handsome. And each one is different: there were kingpost designs, queenpost designs, multiple kingposts, Burr-kingpost arches, Town lattices, Long, Howe, Paddlefords, simple laminated arches, Pratt adaptions thereof, Haupts, Tecos, and so on. Look under the covering.

You visit these bridges, too, for their nostalgia value. In his other book, *Covered Bridges of the Northeast* ($10.00), Allen elaborates on this second aspect of the pleasures of covered bridges: "More people than you'd suspect can recall the covered bridges they knew and delighted in during their youth. . . . The smell in the darkened tunnel was a delicate aroma of wood shavings, ammonia, hay, and horse manure—hardly Chanel No. 1, but a scent that, once sniffed, could never be forgotten. After a trudge in the hot sun, bare toes sifted the cool dust on the bridge floor and knew a won-derful feeling. Light, reflected from the water below, would flicker up through the floorboards to make dancing spots on the rafters, shimmering and ever-changing. A worm-baited fishline dangling down through a hole in the floor sometimes produced a whopper. . . . A rainy day and little traffic brought a game of 'one-o'-cat' to the bridge. If you slammed the ball beyond the sheltering portals you were out. When the game grew tiring there were always hundreds of initials to be examined and chalked notes of import to their inscribers to be deciphered: 'S.E.C. 1880-W.C. 1885—BL-FM 1900—F. Brown, August 1892—I Hugged Polly P. in this Bridge—Liar—Did too—Didn't Didn't Didn't. F.B.'s a Liar!—Did too.'"

Both of Allen's books contain state-by-state listings of the bridges that are still standing, along with anecdotes about them and photos past and present. Also included are general discussions of the state of the art in the areas covered, and maps. In addition to being a good background book, a fine armchair travelogue, and a nifty history book, each of Allen's works also has a practical use. You'll enjoy visiting bridges all the more if you know the stories behind them. If you get hooked on Allen, you'll want to try to locate copies of *Covered Bridges of the Midwest* and *Covered Bridges of the South*, both now out of print. From the Stephen Greene Press, Brattleboro, Vermont 05301.

Where Have All the Bridges Gone?

Fires, ice, and floods have claimed many of them. However, in the eastern part of the United States and Canada, about a thousand still stand. Pennsylvania boasts close to 250, the Northeast about 200 (nearly half of which are in Vermont). Ohio has some 150, Indiana about 100. There are exceptionally large concentrations in Parke County, Indiana; in Franklin, Lamoille, Grafton, Merrimack, Orange, Washington, and Rutland counties, Vermont; in Adams County, Maryland; and in Bed-ford, Chester, Columbia, Greene, Lancaster, and Washington counties, Pennsylvania. If you don't have Allen's books, you can get the precise locations by contacting local, state, or provincial tourist offices. Or write the National Society for the Preservation of Covered Bridges, Inc., 44 Cleveland Avenue, Worcester, Massachusetts 01603. The Society publishes a *World Guide to Covered Bridges* ($3.50), which pinpoints the locations of all the covered bridges in the *world*. The Society also compiles technical and historical data, legends, and folklore about the bridges; works to preserve them; and issues a bi-monthly bulletin to keep members posted. Dues are $10 per year.

The Great Parke County Covered-Bridge Bash

Approaching the beginning of its second quarter-century, the annual October Parke County Covered Bridge Festival is everything you would expect to find in a corner of farming country that somehow never got made into farms. It is down-home, home-grown, unslick, quaint, sometimes (it seems) disorganized, unsophisticated, unpretentious—in a word, a very Hoosier affair. Because the area is so far off most people's beaten track, the landscape might take you back forty years or so—but the festival won't, because of the crowds. The goings-on have become so famous, in fact, that there's not a room to be had in the area during the festival. On weekends, you won't even get a bed in a private home unless you've planned well in advance.

But the crowds just add to the good-time feelings that come naturally given this fine mix of scenery (the Indiana foliage is at its flaming October best), sights (thirty-six covered bridges in a single small county), and activities (driving tours through the countryside, hymn sings, quilting demonstrations, and eating). The food is of the thresherman's feast variety. Imagine a pancake breakfast, barbecued chicken, ham and beans simmered in a mammoth black kettle so big you wonder how they ever got it to the courthouse square, home-baked cornbread, persimmon-and-vanilla ice cream, cinnamon delights, crullers, smoke-cured hams and bacon, corn on the cob, gingerbread, biscuits fresh out of the oven, sandwiches, fried apple pies, and just about any other kind of pie you can name. The town of Montezuma, in some years, roasts a whole pig. Water? In Mecca, it's from a "witched well"—located by a certified water witch. In Billie Creek Village, a "village" concocted of nineteenth-century buildings moved to the site, there are crafts demonstrations. Above the hum of the crowds, the clack of the looms, and the whir of the spinning wheel, you can hear the shrill little whistle of the antique popcorn-and-peanut-roasting wagon that is the source of the best of the smells in the air of the Indian country autumn. For dates and information about places to stay, contact the Tourist Information Center, Box 165, Rockville, Indiana 47872.

The Longest Covered Bridge in the World

Nestled in among the trees, spanning a tiny stream hardly worth calling a river, covered bridges look great. The proportions, however, are all wrong once you put the bridge atop a major waterway

like the Delaware. Yet in the days that men could build bridges only with wood, if you crossed the Delaware at all, you crossed it on a covered bridge, simply because covered bridges lasted at least half a century longer than any other variety. The longest bridges across the Delaware, built in 1806 and 1814, measured 1,008 feet and 1,050 feet respectively.

These giants have long since succumbed to the ravages of the years. But you can get an idea of how incongruous bridges of this length must have looked when you visit New Brunswick and the covered bridge across the St. John River at Hartland, which is a whopping 1,282 feet long and consequently is listed in the *Guinness Book of World Records* as the longest covered bridge in the world. That's one record that probably will stand for a long time to come.

For details on the other things to see and do in New Brunswick around Hartland, contact the New Brunswick Department of Tourism, P. O. Box 12345, Fredericton E3B 5C3.

More Bridge Notes

The highest suspension bridge in the world spans the Royal Gorge over the Arkansas River, near Canon City, Colorado. The bridge is more than a thousand feet above water level; the Chamber of Commerce in Canon City 81212 can provide details on other activities in the area.

North America's longest single-span suspension bridge, the Verrazano-Narrows Bridge, crosses the mouth of New York Harbor. It used to be the world's longest. Before the Verrazano was built, the world's longest suspension bridge was the Brooklyn Bridge, the first of the bridges across the East River and, at the time it was built in 1883, an engineering feat. It is a beautiful bridge, worth walking across for the views of the East River and Manhattan at your back. The New York City Convention and Visitors Bureau, 90 East 42nd Street, New York, New York 10017, can provide details on both.

Measuring length another way (that is, from anchor point to anchor point), the Mackinac Bridge between St. Ignace and Mackinaw City, Michigan, is the longest suspension bridge in the world. The Mackinaw City Chamber of Commerce, Mackinaw City, Michigan 49701, can send you information about AAU-sanctioned races and general recreational walks across the bridge.

The longest steel-arch bridge in the world crosses the New River Gorge near Fayetteville, West Virginia. It's a spectacular leap of a bridge that you can't fully appreciate when you're driving across it—you're too captivated by the scenery. You can get your best look at it on raft trips down the New River, which are about as adventurous an undertaking as building the bridge was ambitious. For information about these trips, contact Wildwater Expeditions Unlimited, P. O. Box 55, Thurmond, West Virginia 25936.

And an old-fashioned floating bridge: 380 barrels held in place by cables support a Vermont floating bridge near Brookfield. The Green Trails Inn, Brookfield, Vermont 05036, right next to the bridge, is a jumping-off point for cross-country ski tours and walks and year-round back-road trips.

In the Caribbean. The Queen Emma Pontoon Bridge over St. Anna Bay connecting Willemstad's busy Punda section and quieter Otrabunda, in the Netherlands Antilles island of Curaçao. The water is blue as you'd expect to find in this part of the world and the miniature Holland of a town is a pretty backdrop. Depending on the traffic in the channel, the bridge may be opened or closed; if it's closed, you've got to take a ferry across. The Curaçao Tourist Board (30 Rockefeller Plaza, New York, New York 10020) can send you more information about the island.

The Circus and Other Fun Stuff

The Greatest Show on Earth

Showmen were showmen back then. Big bright posters—which appeared as if by magic on every flat surface within sight—were the harbingers. Then there was the parade, a magical procession of promises, spangled beings, strange humanoid creatures, gilded wagons carved into rococo fantasies of animals and goddesses. The circus was so strange—so different from everyday existence—that it seemed to have descended from Mars to inhabit that tent city that appeared, as if by magic, on a lot you knew as a field or a no-man's-land of rubble. The big top soared over a host of smaller tents and trailers and cages and strange contraptions—and then the whole thing vanished as quickly as it had appeared.

Not all the circus museums in the world can bring back those days. But some of them come close.

Recapturing the Magic

When the aerialists and tightrope walkers climb so high that you can scarcely see their faces and then start flying through the air, flipping and spinning as they do—well, then, there's magic to the circus.

But most of the time, the pomp and the pageantry don't overwhelm you as legend says they should; and you end up with a nagging so-what feeling. Time to go get popcorn. And, when the ringmaster sings off key, and the PA system goes on the blink, it's not hard to start wondering why everybody gets so excited about the circus.

One brief fifteen minutes at the Sears Circus Exhibit at the Museum of Science and Industry in Chicago will give you back your faith. For, at the end of a spiral hallway full of marvelous miniature circus exhibits, old photos of circus folk (sitting around the mess hall, getting ready to perform), and brilliant posters, you come, quite by surprise, on a tiny auditorium, more wide than deep, with a screen that towers over you so that you've got to bend backward to see the screen. As

you sit there in the half dark, waiting for the show to start, you don't know quite what to expect. Even though this Museum of Science and Industry is quite an extraordinary place, not everything, to be quite honest, is as wonderful as it could be.

But suddenly the lights go out, and the red-coated ringmaster, who first appears as a tiny speck at the bottom of the screen, starts to grow and grow like something out of Alice in Wonderland, until he's occupying the entire screen, and he keeps on swelling until you

can see just his head and shoulders—and then, conjurer that he seems, he brings on his acts, which included some tightrope walkers balancing on chairs—photographed from underneath—and flashing lights and crowd sounds that put you right into the circus of your imagination. Magic? When you leave, you feel as if you've been zapped to the moon and back.

Other than that, the museum is such a big place that it's hard to spend just half a day there. Some of the other nifty exhibits include one about nutrition that has you talking to computers and learning dozens of interesting, obscure facts about the foods you eat every day; a walk-through human heart; a real fairy-tale doll house; a Rube Goldberg-like contraption of a flying automobile; a coal mine; a submarine; and more. For more information, you can write the museum at 57th Street and Lake Shore Drive in Jackson Park, Chicago 60616 or the Chicago Convention and Tourism Bureau, 332 South Michigan Avenue, Chicago 60604.

The Best Collections of Circus Memorabilia

The two biggest and most complete are at the Circus World Museum in Baraboo, Wisconsin, and the Ringling Museum of the Circus in Sarasota, Florida.

The Ringling Museum of the Circus, established in 1948 on the grounds of John and Mable Ringling's magnificent mansion Ca' d'Zan, contains memorabilia from many circuses, and more than any other circus museum, emphasizes the fact that this form of entertainment has been around since the Circus Maximus in Rome in 329 B.C.: there are rare prints, drawings, and engravings dating from the mid-sixteenth century, plus recent posters, lithographs, performance rigging, and costumes. A special vast hall houses those ponderous carved-and-gilt parade wagons from the late nineteenth and early twentieth centuries—and there are reconstructions—to scale and full size—of a circus backyard with its baggage wagons, blacksmith shop, and cookhouse; a big top at the peak of its glory; and a circus parade. In the background: constant band and calliope music.

The 30-acre Circus World Museum, which focuses on the history of the circus in America, is bigger than the Ringling Museum; in addition to the collections of parade wagons and posters and all the other gilt-and-spangled memorabilia you'd expect to find in six buildings, there's a real circus presentation under canvas several times a day. Outside, a tightrope walker teeters above the Baraboo River, and student acrobats work out around the lots. For kids there are rides on the circus wagons and in goat- and llama-drawn carts. The musical accompaniment to the big shows comes in the form of calliope music, unafons, and the like. For details, write the museum in Baraboo 53913, or the Chamber of Commerce, Box 245, Baraboo 53913.

Small but Mighty

Like the museum at Baraboo—which used to be circus winter quarters—the smaller museums are located in towns whose history was touched by the cir-

cus. Peru, Indiana, for example, was, in addition to being Cole Porter's hometown, the largest circus winter quarters in the world, for a while; and Bridgeport, Connecticut, can claim Phineas T. Barnum among its former mayors.

The P. T. Barnum Museum at 804 Main Street in Bridgeport remembers the showman's contributions with a collection of memorabilia of Jenny Lind, whom Barnum coaxed to this country, and Tom Thumb—the twenty-nine-inch-high son of a Bridgeport carpenter who was thrice presented to Queen Victoria and developed a taste for the high life of the Gilded Age as Barnum's first, and one of his most celebrated, money-makers. On display in the museum are Tom Thumb's Masonic uniform, his brown velvet jacket, some of Jenny Lind's clothing—plus fantastic photos of Thumb; miniature circus wagons; and a circus ticket wagon.

In Peru, Indiana, the Puterbaugh Museum at 11 North Huntington, and the Miami County Historical Society Museum in the county courthouse in the center of town, display some twenty-two elephant statuettes, posters, old photos, dozens of models of circus wagons, spangled clothing, ticket posters, whole sides of circus wagons—and the elephant hook and the skull and tusks of Charlie, the Hagenback-Wallace elephant who killed his keeper, Henry Hoffman, in 1901.

For more information, contact the P. T. Barnum Museum at 804 Main Street in Bridgeport 06604, and the Puterbaugh Museum at 11 North Huntington, Peru 46970.

A Fantastic Miniature Circus Parade

This one is so long that a whole

building had to be built to house it. The "winding, dazzling river of silver and gold"—which is how Barnum described his circus parades—stretches 518 feet around the horseshoe-shaped building. There are 450 prancing, plodding, snorting, trotting horses—no two alike. Plus elephants, seals, clowns, giraffes, musicians—and everything else that ever made a circus parade glitter. A poster collection occupying the same building represents all the major road shows, and, out front, there's a display of forty carousel figures. Where? The Shelburne Museum in Shelburne, Vermont 05482, in the northern part of the state.

Two other miniature circuses are on display at the Toy Chest, a child's joy among the antique shops of Nashville, Indiana 47448, which is in the hilly, scenic southern part of the state, and at the Dorothea B. Hoover Historical Museum at Schifferdecker Park, in Joplin, Missouri, off I-44 between St. Louis and Oklahoma City. At the Hoover Museum, there are literally hundreds of figures: horses, bandwagons, elephants, camels, wagon cages, barkers, a menagerie of animals in cages or eating hay, Wallendas, Cordonas, an airborne Man (just shot from a cannon), clowns, freaks, and more. Recordings of circus music and circus sounds—the ringmaster describing acts, the elephants trumpeting, the seals squealing, dogs barking, and lions roaring—make you feel as if you've stepped into another world. The whole thing occupies two platforms, one four feet square and one ten feet square. Quite a lot of circus.

A Circus in a Casino

High-wire artists and trapeze stars fly through the air above you as you shoot craps, feed the slots, or gamble at the roulette wheels at the Circus Circus, one of the more unusual of the casinos on the Strip in Las Vegas. For information about other doings in this glittery town, write the Convention and Visitors' Authority, P. O. Box 14006, Las Vegas, Nevada 89114.

Circus Festival
Peru, Indiana, and Bridgeport, Connecticut, both have municipal festivals, but instead of devoting them to the appreciation of a pioneer heritage or a revolutionary war heritage—or any of the other historical matters to which municipalities usually devote their annual wingdings—these towns celebrate their place in the grand old age of ballyhoo. At Bridgeport's Barnum Festival, there are parades, concerts, art shows, clowns, fireworks. Kids compete in Tom Thumb and Jenny Lind contests, and Barnum is remembered at a memorial service at his grave in the Mt. Grove Cemetery. At Peru's Circus City Festival, there are food and game booths, carnival rides, a parade, and an amateur circus. For details, write the festival directors at 804 Main Street in Bridgeport 06604 and Box 482 in Peru 46970.

Clown for a Day
You can get your face whited up and painted like a clown's. Or walk a tightrope, swing on a trapeze, jump on a trampoline, or ride an elephant—with traditional circus gear, and the safety devices always used in training. It's all part of a theme park called the Ringling Brothers and Barnum & Bailey Circus World, near Haines City, Florida. Like other theme parks, it has some rides (the most notable of which is the Zoom-erang, one of the steel-tube roller coasters that takes you forward, backward, and upside down) as well as singing-and-dancing shows—but here, since everything is on a circus theme, there are circus performances galore: a lion rides a motorcycle, for example, elephants dance, and, in a film on a stupendous six-story-high movie screen, circus people perform on the high wire, put the big cats through the air on trapezes. The big screen gives a you-are-there feeling that will have your stomach turning somersaults right along with the high-wire artists. For more information, write Box 2006, Haines City, Florida 33844. Haines City is in Central Florida, about halfway between Tampa and Orlando.

Clowning
The Clowns of America, a 3,000-member organization, is devoted both to teaching the fine art of clowning and the discussion thereof by amateurs,

semiprofessionals, and professionals. A monthly publication called *Calliope* talks about costumes, props, makeup, and various tricks. For details, write 2715 East Fayette Street, Baltimore, Maryland 21224.

Circus Fans
An association of grown-ups who as kids carried water for the elephants or followed the red circus wagons down the winding roads—or wanted to—the Circus Fans Association of America furthers the cause of the circus ("We fight anything that fights the circus," in the words of one member), encourages the work of circus museums around the continent, and generally works to make it a little easier for the circus to come to town. There are a couple of conventions a year at which there's much ado about the state of the circus, and a publication, *White Tops*, keeps members posted on the latest circus news. For information about joining, write Box 69, Camp Hill, Pennsylvania 17011.

How the Ball Bounces
The International Jugglers' Association, organized in 1947 "for jugglers and friends of juggling" is worth mentioning if only for the conventions. Held once a year, you'll see juggling, juggling, juggling, juggling, and more juggling, anytime, anyplace—four or five days of it, in shows, competitions, and impromptu juggle-ins. For information about the convention—or about joining the association, in which case a newsletter will keep you posted on juggling weekends and seminars in your area—write the membership secretary at 129 Fourth Avenue, Bartlett, Illinois 60103.

Everybody Loves a Parade

Every small town has one for precisely that reason. But if you're a real connoisseur of parades, it's inevitable that you think along the lines of bigger is better, and certainly there is something exciting about parades that just keep on coming, one wave of bandspeople and drummers following another, in a joyous manifestation of the old cast-of-thousands mentality.

New York might well be called parade city for the preponderance of big ones that jam up traffic—and bring joy to the hearts of pedestrians—several times a year. Macy's Thanksgiving Day Parade—the curtain raiser of the Christmas season that brings out balloon-toting kids in mittens and mufflers and their parents—is the biggest. But there are others. There are parades for the West Indian American Day Carnival, Steuben Day, Pulaski Day, United Hispanic American Day, Columbus Day, Veterans Day, plus the one spon-

sored by the Federation of Turkish American Societies—and those are just the events scheduled during the fall. The St. Patrick's Day Parade—the big deal in the spring—is followed by parades for Loyalty Day, Salute to Israel Day, Armed Forces Day, Greek Independence Day; and, in the summer, there is a parade for Puerto Rican Day. Routes and dates change from year to year; the Convention & Visitors Bureau, 90 East 42nd Street, New York, New York 10017, can provide you with details.

Gambling

Never mind about laying eight to five on the outcome of Congress's latest squabble with the president, or putting down fifty cents on a lottery ticket, or betting on the horses. Big-time casino gambling is something else—fascinating whether you're looking for an atmosphere of elegance in which to drop your bundle, or just a chance to see for yourself what it's like. Here's where you'll find the casinos.

Lake Tahoe, Nevada. You can scarcely hear yourself think above the din of the slot machines. Keno runners dash through the crowds around the craps and blackjack and roulette tables. Croupiers call out just like in the movies. The only difference between Nevada gambling and the movies, in fact, are the crowds of tourists, little old ladies bused in from Dubuque, as well as handfuls of men and women here and there who really look as if they know what they're doing. Tahoe's particular characteristic among the three principal Nevada gambling centers is that skiers, skaters, sailors, swimmers, and assorted other sportsmen, recognizable by their suntans, are much in evidence. The fact is that Tahoe's gambling is, for most people, a sidelight to another sort of vacation entirely. For information about what goes on in the waters and forests around the lake, and the resort activities, contact the Travel Division of the Nevada Department of Economic Development, Carson City 89710.

Reno, Nevada. Full of marriage chapels, and famous for the wedding rings tossed into the Truckee River and the divorces granted in the Washoe County Courthouse, this "Biggest Little City in the World" has a sort of frontier ambience that filters into the casinos. For more information, write the Chamber of Commerce at 133 North Sierra Street, Reno 89501.

Las Vegas, Nevada. Mecca for gamblers. Shiny, full of hotels that are decorated to within an inch of good taste. The pace of the gambling is about what you find around New York at rush hour: dawdlers don't win the popularity contests. Most hotels have casinos—both downtown, in a three-block area that is, incredibly, home to twelve hotels and casinos, and along the Strip, a five mile stretch of U.S. 91. The hotels along the Strip also feature nightly big-name entertainment. It will be a while after you leave Las Vegas before your eyes and ears get used to the silence of a room without slot machines and the dimness of a room without dozens and dozens of crystal chandeliers. For details on hotels and gambling, contact the Las Vegas Convention and Visitors' Authority, P. O. Box 14006, Las Vegas 89114.

The Bahamas. The Caribbean is full of places to gamble. The Bahamas have two giant Las Vegas-style casinos—El Casino, in the town of Freeport on Grand Bahama Island, and another on Paradise Island, a tiny cay connected to New Providence Island by toll bridge. Lots of high rolling. For details, write the Bahamas Tourist Office, 30 Rockefeller Plaza, New York, New York 10020.

Puerto Rico. Most casinos are in the hotels around San Juan and out on the island at Cerromar and Dorado Beach. The Puerto Rico Tourism Development Company, 1290 Avenue of the Americas, New York, New York 10019, can send details on the island.

Haiti. There are slot machines in hotels and restaurants, and one big casino—Mike McLaney's International Casino in Port-au-Prince. To find out more about Haiti, write the Haitian Tourism Association, 30 Rockefeller Plaza, New York, New York 10020.

Netherlands Antilles. Casinos are such a big deal here on Aruba and Curaçao that planeloads of properly bankrolled gamblers are flown down on a regular basis. There is also gambling on Bonaire at the Hotel Bonaire near Kralendijk, but on a smaller scale: there are no junkets, and no bets higher than $25 are allowed. For details about the trio, contact the Aruba Tourist Information Office at 685 Fifth Avenue, New York, New York 10022; the Curaçao Tourist Board at 30 Rockefeller Plaza, New York, New York 10020; and the Bonaire Tourist Board, at 685 Fifth Avenue, New York, New York 10022.

And more gambling. You'll find it on Dutch Sint Maarten, Antigua, the Dominican Republic, and Martinique. For details write the tourist offices: the Sint Maarten Tourist Bureau, c/o Sontheimer and Company, 4 West 58th Street, New York, New York 10019; the Antigua Tourist Board, at 101 Park Avenue, Suite 913, New York, New York 10017; the Dominican Republic Government Tourist Office, 64 West 50th Street, New York, New York 10020; and the French West Indies Tourist Board at 610 Fifth Avenue, New York, New York 10020.

Perhaps the most unexpected places that you'll find legal gambling are the two big luxury ferries between Portland, Maine, and Yarmouth, Nova Scotia, and in the Yukon, at Diamond Tooth Gertie's Gambling Hall, in Dawson City, where cancan dancers dance, and a motley assortment of tourists and flannel-shirted locals play poker and roulette. For information about the ferries, call the Prince of Fundy Line at 207/775-5616; to find out about Dawson City and its many other historic gold-rush remnants, write the Klondike Visitors Association, which operates the saloon, in Dawson City, Yukon Territories.

Atlantic City, New Jersey. To find out about gambling here, and all the changes that this recent development has wrought, contact the Convention Bureau at 16 Central Pier, Atlantic City 08401.

Magic!

Think back on the last time you saw a card trick—and how mystified you were. Then imagine yourself in a place where magic tricks—each one thrice as mystifying as that last bit of prestidigitation with the cards—go on and on nonstop, and you've pretty well got an idea of what it's like at the Magic Get-Together in Colon, Michigan, a little town of about 1,100 people in the south central part of the state not far from the Indiana line.

Perhaps you'd expect something small and insignificant in a town of that size. Not so.

After the great illusionist Harry Blackstone moved to Colon in 1925, the town became sort of a magicians' colony, and magicians came from all over to settle near Blackstone. Among the pilgrims was Percy Abbott, who subsequently started Abbott's Magic Company, which has, in turn, been bringing magicians from all over the world for the Get-Togethers for nearly fifty years. They get together in private homes, in recreational vehicles, and at picnic tables outside the Elementary School, where a magic bazaar is set up. And while they talk new tricks (or "illusions," as they're called in magical company) and exchange ideas about the patter that goes with them, they're changing doves into silk scarves or little American pennies into big English ones, and using the most innocent of passersby as their guinea pigs. A guy will swipe your $10 bill, for example, tear it up, throw the pieces over his shoulder, then pull another—undamaged—from your shirt pocket. At the bazaar, you can buy rabbit hats, temples of toads, or, for $2,500, order a vanishing elephant (you supply the elephant) trick. There are ventriloquists on

hand, too, and you can imagine the noise that that adds to the fracas. Colon's tricky time is the third week in August. You can find out more from Abbott's Magic Company in Colon 49040.

Another Magic Festival
The Wizard, a very modern magic store at 1136 Pearl Street in Boulder, Colorado 80302, usually sponsors some kind of summer celebration, the dates of which you can get by writing the store.

Magic Conventions
Magic is big business these days, and the ways that new magicians get to be old hands are practicing, reading, and talking with their fellow conjurers anywhere they can. It's the sort of sport that lends itself quite naturally to clubs, and so there are clubs. And where there are clubs, there are conventions. You can pretty much watch your fill of magic tricks—even if you're not a member. However, membership brings all sorts of benefits including newsletters that keep you posted on regional conventions as well as the big national ones.

For information about the Society of American Magicians, write the International Secretary at 66 Marked Tree Road, Needham, Massachusetts 02192.

Free Magic in the Stores
Say you can't make it to the get-togethers but you're in the mood for a little prestidigitation. Then the thing to do is wait until a Saturday and head for the nearest magic store—for magicians always seem to head like homing pigeons to magic stores on weekends, to talk shop, exchange ideas, try out routines, learn new tricks, work out the kinks, loosen up. There are the really ancient places, holdovers from the age of vaudeville that are at once a little shabby, a little sad, and a little elegant; and the spiffy modern palaces where everything is neatly laid out so that you can figure out what's what even if you don't know much magic. Either way, establishments like Lou Tannen's, the world's largest magic store, at 1540 Broadway in New York City, are fun to visit. And there are plenty like it.

In New York: Al Flosso's, a slightly eerie place at 304 West 34th Street (212/BR 9-6079). In Boulder, Colorado: the Wizard, at 1136 Pearl Street (303/449-7252). In Chicago: Edward Drane and Company, at 1400 North Halsted (312/664-6635). In Los Angeles: the Magic Corner at 6338 Hollywood Boulevard, in Hollywood (213/462-3385). In Minneapolis: the Eagle Magic Store, at 708 Portland Avenue (612/333-4702). In Washington, D.C.: Al's Magic Shop, 1205 Pennsylvania Avenue

(202/638-4241).

For a complete list of magic stores around the country, you can order the *Mister E List* (about $5) from P. O. Box 8883, Rochester, New York 14624.

The Magic Table

There exists, in New York City, a sort of Round Table at the Algonquin for magicians. Lovers of magic, whether prestidigitators in their own right or merely fans, are welcome. But if you go, be prepared to get a live dove when you ask for salt to put on the melon (inside which you just found a playing card). Magicians back from Europe are often on hand to relate their experiences with ghosts. You may play magician's assistant to some of the world's greatest—it depends on who's around when you go. The Magic Table is at the Scandia Restaurant in the Piccadilly Hotel at 227 West 45th Street in New York—from about noon until two.

The Magic Castle

The Magic Castle, a turreted Victorian construction at 7011 Franklin Avenue, hidden away in Hollywood, California, is open only to members and their guests, but as the magic goes on all night, every night, it's worth your while to hang out at the Magic Corner in Los Angeles (6338 Hollywood Boulevard) to find someone who will make you a guest. Some of the best of the world's magicians show up there to perform in the hundred-seat auditorium or do close-up illusions at the tables in the bar. However, this is no ordinary place where you just sit and watch: from the minute you say Open Sesame to the owl who guards the door, you can expect strange things to happen to you (stools that sink into the floor, mysterious vanishings and appearings, and such). Good fun.

A Pair of Magical Restaurants

You can see shows and tricks —sometimes very good, sometimes purely fantastic—in San Francisco at Earthquake McGoon's Magic Cellar Saloon (630 Clay Street, 415/986-1433), which is full of ancient theatrical trunks, and in New York City on weekends, at buffets at the Magic Towne House (1026 Third Avenue, 212/752-1165), a magic store and occasional restaurant set up in an old town house.

Good Reading for Magicians

After a while magicians tend to specialize. They'll get interested in card tricks. Or doves. Or sleight of hand. Or billiard balls—or any of a dozen other areas. And there are magazines for almost all of them. One of the best, though, for generalists who are just beginning, and for nonmagicians as well, is *Genii, the International Conjurors' Magazine*, which is going on fifty years old. Subscriptions are $12 per year: write P. O. Box 36068, Los Angeles 90036.

As for learning, there are dozens of books—some clearer, some more comprehensive than others. *The Amateur Magician's Handbook*, by Henry Hay, now in its third edition, gives a good overview; there's information about tricks with and without cards, coins, billiard balls, thimbles, cigarettes, silks, and standard gimmicks—for stage performance and close up (from the New American Library, 1301 Avenue of the Americas, New York, New York 10019; $1.95).

Great American Amusement Parks: Where to Find Them and What They're Like

There's nothing quite like a roller coaster for making you feel like a kid again, and nothing quite like an old-fashioned carousel for putting you back into Edwardian times.

So it's no wonder that a business like the amusement-park industry—which makes these feelings its stock in trade—would flourish. What's fascinating are the variations on the theme.

At first amusement parks were merely adjuncts to picnic groves set up by trolley and interurban companies in an effort to compete for customers; as time went on rides became a part and parcel of the seaside or lakeshore experience. Many of these establishments fell into decay. The people who operated them were as odoriferous as the hot dog stands, and considerably less appetizing. Litter proliferated. Disneyland changed all that: Walt Disney pioneered the idea that an amusement park should offer good clean fun for the entire family. One of his major contributions was the fresh-scrubbed cleanliness of the kids-next-door who guided visitors in and out of the rides. Once Disney's success was assured, other promoters caught on—and the theme park as we know it today (at places like Opryland, Six Flags over Georgia, and dozens of others) was born.

Meanwhile, the people who ran the old amusement parks were fixing up and painting up and putting up hanging baskets of petunias to set the mood for good clean fun. And so today carousels and roller coasters and those good old-time feelings are easy to find. Here's a rundown of what's what, and where you'll find it.

Opryland, Nashville.

The New Amusement Parks

Theme parks, they're called, because of the management's proclivity for grouping attractions together, slapping labels on the groupings ("France," "New Orleans," and so on), and then naming everything within sight accordingly, whether or not the item itself has anything to do with the theme. The sandwich served in the German area may be just a plain old all-American burger, but you can almost count on seeing it on the menu as "Der Oompah," "Der Grossvater," or "Der Grossmutter," or something equally improbable.

Because once-seedy old amusement parks (realizing that cleanliness was next to wealth as well as to godliness) have gone on a clean-up-and-paint-and-tell-the-world-about-it campaign, and because they have been adding attractions like live shows, strolling entertainers, and shops purveying something besides the hokeyest of souvenirs, use of a theme is the main feature distinguishing the old parks from the new parks. If you have seen one park, you haven't seen them all.

The McDonald's of the Business
The Marriott Corporation, the motel and hotel chain, got into the theme park business a couple of years ago as a sort of Bicentennial project. The idea

was to go all the others one better—to offer something for everyone, but to do it better than anybody else. The ultimate goal was a chain of theme parks and mini-theme parks across the United States. Rides, shows, and administration specialists from every other theme park were brought into the Marriott machine.

The result? Thrills. Chills up and down your spine. Music-and-dance entertainments that make you get all misty-eyed and put a lump in your throat. There are two sky rides, two flumes, one of which has the longest single drop in the country. There's a spectacular double-decker carousel, specially made for the Marriotts. It looks something like an oversized wedding cake in bright-painted wood plopped down in the middle of a reflecting pool. The roller coaster, whimsically named the Turn of the Century, hurtles you silently up and down, then upside down through a corkscrew; it is twice as long as garden-variety steel-tube-corkscrew coasters, and extra high.

The food is among the best offered at any park. In addition to hamburger and hot-dog stands—which is about all you'll get at some parks—there are food boutiques selling Swedish waffles, fresh fruit, tacos, egg rolls, Belgian waffles, pizza, and some of the crunchiest French fries you'll find anywhere.

And the entertainment is equally varied. Not just song-and-dance shows (though there are plenty of these, and most of them are worth seeing several times in a summer), but also log rollers, greased-pole climbers, and a "Merry Mardi Gras" floats-and-bands parade over which Bugs Bunny reigns.

So far, the chain has only two links—one in Gurnee, Illinois, just outside Chicago, and the other in Santa Clara, California. Eventually they'll be identical; right now, because they don't always get new rides at the same time, one park may have more rides than the other.

For details, contact the parks at P. O. Box 1976, Gurnee, Illinois 60031; or Box 1776, Santa Clara, California 95052.

The Park with the Best Music
That it's Opryland, in Nashville, Tennessee, is almost a truism among theme-park owners. Why? The quality of the talent, for one thing—mainly kids from the mid-South, who are singing their hearts out in the hope that some record-company talent scout is out in the audience. There's also something in the quality of the music. Almost all of the eleven shows are made up of snippets and snatches of the century's favorite songs from Broadway, the pop charts, the mountain country, and New Orleans—the

toe-tappers and sing-it-in-the-shower numbers that you can't get out of your head. The affection you feel for those old songs rubs off. You go away just loving those shows. The rosy glow gets some extra fuel from the site—lush, forested, on the banks of the Cumberland River. Trees that were there before the park was built were usually left standing, and dozens more were planted during construction. Every year, garden crews put in hundreds of wonderful flowers like pansies and petunias and care for the lavish baskets of flowers that are hung throughout the park. Rides are not the main attraction here, though there are a couple of thrillers. But there is a pavilion where you can dance to big-band sounds, polka music, and rock. The food: crepes, frozen yogurt, soft pretzels, sausage-on-biscuit sandwiches, tacos and other Mexican treats, Creole specialties, and Belgian waffles heaped with strawberries and whipped cream.

Lest there be any confusion in your mind, Opryland is *not* the same as the Grand Ole Opry. The Opry only shares the premises and the management with the theme park. At the Opry, you will hear *only* country music; there's all sorts of music at Opryland. You can just walk into Opryland once you've paid your admission fee. To see the Opry (an experience, even if you don't like country music) you must write for tickets months in advance.

For details about the park and the Opry, write to P. O. Box 2138, Nashville, Tennessee 37214.

The Prettiest Park
Opryland fans say it's Opryland; a lot of other people will tell you it's Six Flags over Georgia in Atlanta. With a theme based loosely on the six countries whose flags have flown over Georgia, Six Flags climbs a forested hillside on the western edge of the city. Because this is Georgia, there's watermelon to eat, and plenty of strolling paths and white gazebos edged with frilly woodwork. The Great American Scream Machine, an apparition of white latticework that encircles a mirror of a lake, is as scary as it is pretty. And there are forty-two other rides for grown-ups plus nightly parades, eight shows, magicians and musicians who stroll the grounds, jugglers, puppeteers, and fireworks. All the ingredients, in other words, of a wholesome good time.

Six Flags over Georgia is the biggest of a quartet of parks under the same ownership: Six Flags over Mid-America, in Eureka, Missouri (near St. Louis), and Six Flags over Texas, in Arlington, Texas (halfway between Dallas and Fort Worth), have similar themes and are similarly set up. The Texas park—

next to Disneyland the oldest of all of the new family parks—pioneered the rides-shows-attractions combination after which almost every other theme park in the United States is modeled. Because this is Texas, everything is tunneled through with air-conditioning ducts, even the grape arbors. The Missouri park, though the smallest of the four, has one of the two highest and fastest roller coasters in the world. The Screamin' Eagle, installed in 1976 to the tune of $3 million, is 110 feet high at its highest point; the highest single drop is 92 feet; and cars often reach a speed of over 60 miles per hour. (Even the highest roller coaster of all time—the now demolished Blue Streak of Woodcliffe Pleasure Park in Poughkeepsie, New York—only got up to 57 mph.) The fourth Six Flags park, Astroworld, in Houston, Texas, is a recent addition to the stable. One of the first moves the new management made was to construct a replica of the Coney Island Cyclone, one of the most loved of all roller coasters.

For details: Six Flags over Georgia, P. O. Box 43187, Atlanta, Georgia 30336; Six Flags over Texas, P. O. Box 191, Arlington, Texas 76010; Six Flags over Mid-America, Box 666, Eureka, Missouri 63025; and Astroworld, P. O. Box 1400, Houston, Texas 77001.

Best Rides
While all the other theme parks were concentrating on beefing up their shows, following Disney's models, and making entertainment for the whole family, Magic Mountain in Valencia, California, was putting in steel-tube roller coasters and other chillers with such alacrity that for a while Magic Mountain looked as much like a refinery as an establishment meant for the entertainment of families. Only when the landscape architects came in and started planting trees and hanging baskets of ferns and petunias did the effect begin to soften, so that by the time the latest new ride was added, the place was a regular Black Forest among theme parks.

As it happened, the latest ride was also one of the most frightening ever to appear in any amusement park—a devastating plunging-and-climbing coaster with a hairy 90-foot vertical loop right in the middle. The Revolution, as it is called, prompted the motion picture men to set a movie—*Roller Coaster*—in the park. In the summer of 1977, when the movie premiered, Magic Mountaineers were moving again, this time installing a nifty rough-around-the-edges crafts village, Spillikin Corners. Here you can watch craftsmen demonstrating, then go shopping. Lots of trees, lots of folksy diversions here and there, plus the big-name entertainers who appear periodically on evenings in the summer make the park well worth visiting.

For details, contact the park in Valencia, California 91355.

The Most Romantic
The people who bring you Budweiser beer nearly out-Europe Europe at their idyllic park, The Old Country, in Williamsburg, Virginia. The site itself is densely forested, cut through by ravines and streamlets, and only a small part of the total acreage is given over to the shops, rides, and food stands that represent the countries of Europe—the theme of the park. Most of the best rides are the ones that show off the landscape—Rhine cruises, steam-train trips, sky rides. But there are some thrills, too—a corkscrew coaster, for instance—and some very special places that really do smack of the Old Country. Das Festhaus was planned to resemble the party halls of Munich and actually does, except that it's larger (twice the size of a football field). Instead of hamburgers, you can munch sausages, rouladen, sauerkraut, schnitzel, and such, and wash them down with wine and beer. An International Crafts Exposition held in the fall brings makers of Hummel figurines, glassblowers, weavers, and other hand workers to Virginia. For details about the park, write P. O. Drawer FC, Williamsburg, Virginia 23185.

The Antiqueyest Park
Once upon a time, Knott's Berry Farm in Buena Park, California (just down the road from Disneyland) really *was* a berry farm. Then, to supplement the family income, Mrs. Walter Knott started serving chicken dinners to passers-by. Soon the chicken dinners got so popular that visitors were lining up for them, and Mr. Walter Knott had to devise entertainments to amuse the waiting guests. And before anyone knew it, the amusement program was more famous than the fried chicken that started it all.

The restaurant is still there, and so are the lines to get to the grub. But the entertainments, designed around an America-of-bygone-days theme, are some of the best in the West, largely because of the slightly rough-around-the-edges, comfortable-as-an-old-shoe atmosphere produced by the scattering of old things around the grounds: weathered wagon wheels, split-rail fences, antique airplane parts keeping company with displays of San Francisco cable cars, and three antique merry-go-rounds (one powered by mules). There's a famous collection of miniatures, and scaled-down reproductions of Independence Hall and a Mississippi River steamboat. The Old

West ghost town is something else again.

Entertainment? The rousing square dance that welcomes you to the park gives you only a small taste of what's to come: Hollywood stunt men, cancan dancers, marionettes, bands of all persuasions. There's an ice spectacular. There are fireworks. There are singing-and-dancing extravaganzas. And about seventy-five rides. A flume carries you through an old sawmill where you're regaled with old logging tales before the plunge. The penny arcade is the largest west of the Mississippi. In and around the corners of these good times, you can stuff yourself on fast foods and gargantuan meals of Sicilian pizza, spaghetti, extra-juicy hot dogs with a special Knott's topping, salads, and so on. Every night, there's dancing to top it all off.

For details, write the park at 8039 Beach Boulevard, Buena Park, California 90620.

More Good Ones
Stop for a visit at one of these well-rounded big ones when you venture nearby: Great Adventure, Box 120, Jackson, New Jersey 08527; Hersheypark, at Hershey, Pennsylvania 17033; Kings Island, Box 400, Kings Mills, Ohio 45034, near Cincinnati; Kings Dominion, P. O. Box 166, Route 1, Doswell, Virginia 23047, near Richmond; Carowinds, P. O. Box 15514, Charlotte, North Carolina 28210; and Worlds of Fun, 4545 Worlds of Fun Avenue, Kansas City, Missouri 64161. Kings Island, Kings Dominion, and Carowinds all have double racing wooden roller coasters. Carowinds and Kings Island both have terrifying versions of the loop-the-loop coaster known as the shuttle loop—the one that takes you upside down and backward. Hersheypark has the only up-and-down loop-the-loop coaster (like Magic Mountain's Revolution) on the East Coast. Great Adventure has a fifteen-story Ferris wheel. They're all rides worth going out of your way for.

The Great American Amusement Parks

by Gary Kyriazi

Gary Kyriazi traveled to just about every amusement park in the United States. He saw big ones, little ones, expensive ones, down-at-the-heels ones, not-enough-money-to-pay-the-rent parks, and parks that spend as much on their stationery as others pay their manager. The book that he wrote about his travels is a joy. Not only does he tell you all about the big theme parks, but he also describes the smaller, old-fashioned ones that don't

get much publicity outside their home-towns. In addition, there are pages of antique pictures documenting the history of the amusement park from the pleasure gardens of the seventeenth century, through the Coney Islands and Steeplechase Parks of the 1880s, and on to the present-day theme parks. There are hundreds of photos, including one of the ride known as the Human Roulette Wheel, one of the Human Whirlpool, and one of the Steeplechase ride. In one photo of a booth from a nickle arcade at Coney Island, you see a couple of 1920-era men in coats and ties and their lady friend, complete with hat and pearls, aiming missiles at shelves of china. "You Fully Relieve Your Primitive Instincts Here—Destroy! Destroy!" says one sign. And another: "No Prizes Given—See How Much You Can Damage." Not all the photos are quite that amusing, but most come close. It's a good book. Citadel Press, 120 Enterprise Avenue, Secaucus, New Jersey 07094; $14.95.

A Super-Duper Old-Fashioned Amusement Park

The midway at Cedar Point, near Sandusky, Ohio, really looks like a midway. Not a little Italy, or a little Germany, or a little anything. This is a midway, no mistake about it—and a big one at that.

Cedar Point has been around ever since the days that trolley and interurban companies competed with ever-more-elaborate picnic groves. And because this fixture of the Great Lakes summer scene was long ago rescued from the decay that hit almost all such parks back in the 1950s, *this* midway is clean, green, and flowering. And Cedar Point's ride capacity is bigger even than Disney's—in other words, it's *very* big.

The dozens of rides include the tallest Ferris wheel in North America, five roller coasters, two flumes, and four carousels. Movies shown at the $2 million Cedar Point Cinema, whose 67 x 88-foot screen is the largest indoor screen in the world, give you a you-are-there feeling that fairly takes your breath away. A big plus: the park is located on the shores of Lake Erie.

For details, contact the park at Box 759, Sandusky, Ohio 44870.

Some Other Good Old-Fashioned Parks
There are still a few of these around: the Santa Cruz Beach and Boardwalk in Santa Cruz, California 95060; Elitch's Gardens at 4620 West 38th Avenue, Denver, Colorado 80012; the Lakeside Amusement Park at 4601 Sheridan Boulevard, Denver, Colorado 80212; Pontchartrain Amusement Park and Beach, Elysian Fields Avenue and Lakeshore Drive, New Orleans, Louisiana 70122; Riverside Park, in Agawam, Massachusetts 01001; Bob-Lo Island Amusement Park, in Detroit, Michigan 48226; Fairyland Park, 7501 Prospect Avenue, Kansas City, Missouri 64132; the six amusement piers at Wildwood, New Jersey, about which you can get further information from the Chamber of Commerce, Wildwood, New Jersey 08260; and the Crystal Beach Amusement Park, in Crystal Beach, Ontario, near Buffalo, New York.

Also: Geauga Lake Park, Route 43, Aurora, Ohio 44202; Idora Park, Route 62, Youngstown, Ohio 44511; Bell's Amusement Park, New Haven at 21st Street, Tulsa, Oklahoma 74114; Dorney Park, 3830 Dorney Park Road, Allentown, Pennsylvania 18104; West View Park at West View, Pennsylvania 15229, near Pittsburgh; Kennywood Park at 4800 Kennywood Boulevard, in West Mifflin, Pennsylvania, near Pittsburgh.

Coney Island, in Brooklyn, New York, is seedy-looking, but for rides it still ranks with the best. The New York Convention and Visitors Bureau, 90 East 42nd Street, New York, New York 10017, can send you information.

A Little Merry-Go-Rounding

The gentle ups and downs of the elaborately carved and painted carousel beasts, and the sweeping and swooping feeling you get when you ride a carousel, have their aficionados. Just as there are people who travel the country collecting rides on roller coasters, so also some lovers of carousels pay visits to the shrines of carousel construction. One of the things they look at is the carving: the animals executed by the master carvers stamp impatiently, their

nostrils flaring. They're wild stallions in painted woods, mustangs, steeds fit for a horse-loving emperor. Some carousels are National Historic Landmarks.

Real carousel buffs belong to the National Carousel Association. The $10 annual dues buy four quarterly issues of *The Merry-Go-Roundup*, which contains news of carousels restored, burned, bought and sold and, once a year, a carousel census. The NCA also has an annual three-day convention with lectures about—and by—carousel makers; tours of the antique carousels in the area in which the convention is held; tale-telling by old-time amusement park owners; reports from communities that are saving their carousels; films on carousels; talks about how to restore carousels and where to get parts; and trading areas. For details about joining, write the NCA c/o Mrs. Eva Landers, Honesdale, Pennsylvania 18431.

As of the 1977 census, there were about 350 carousels in the United States and Canada. Barbara Charles, who runs a design office and devotes nearly all her spare time to saving carousels, pinpoints her favorites:

California. Tilden Park, Berkeley; and the Los Angeles County Fairgrounds, Pomona.

Colorado. The County Fairgrounds, Burlington; Elitch's Gardens, Denver; and Lakeside Park, Denver.

Connecticut. Lake Compounce, Bristol.

Georgia. Six Flags, Atlanta; and Lake Winnepesaukah, Rossville.

Illinois. Kiddieland, Melrose.

Maryland. Glen Echo Park, Glen Echo.

Massachusetts. Riverside Park, Agwam; Paragon Park at Nantasket Beach, Hull; Oak Bluffs, Martha's Vineyard; and Salem Willows Park, Salem Willows.

Minnesota. Valleyfair, Shakopee; and St. Paul Fairgrounds, St. Paul.

Mississippi. City Park, Meridian.

New Hampshire. Canobie Lake Park, Salem.

New Jersey. Clementon Lake Park, Clementon; Great Adventure, Jackson; and Freeman's Carousel Arcade, Seaside Heights.

New York. Coney Island, Brooklyn; Roseland Park, Canandaigua; Sherman's Amusement Park, Caroga Lake; Half Moon Beach, Crescent; Storytown USA, Lake George; Central Park, New York; Dreamland Park, Rochester; and Playland, Rye.

Ohio. Geauga Lake Park, Aurora; Kings Island, Kings Mill; Gooding Zoo Park, Powell; Cedar Point, Sandusky; and Idora Park, Youngstown.

Oregon. Jantzen Beach Center, Portland.

Pennsylvania. Dorney Park, Allen-

town; Lakemount Park, Allentown; Conneaut Lake Park, Conneaut Lake; Knoebel's Grove, Elysburg; Hersheypark, Hershey; Idlewild Park, Ligonier; The Ghost Town in the Glen, Moosic; Mainline Park, West Chester; and Kennywood Park, West Mifflin.

Rhode Island. Crescent Park, Riverside; and Watch Hill Beach, Watch Hill.

South Carolina. Grand Strand Amusement Park, Myrtle Beach.

Tennessee. Libertyland Amusement Park, Memphis.

Texas. Six Flags, Arlington; and State Fair Park, Dallas.

Virginia. Kings Dominion, Richmond.

Washington. Fun Forest Park, Seattle; and Expo Grounds, Spokane.

In Canada. Crystal Beach Amusement Park, Crystal Beach, Ontario; Centreville Park, Toronto, Ontario; and Belmont Park, Montreal, Quebec.

For details about each of these establishments, write the chambers of commerce in the towns listed. The International Association of Amusement Parks and Attractions at 7222 West Cermak Road, North Riverside, Illinois 60546, has a directory of amusement parks, in which you'll find most of those listed above.

"It was something dreadful. I was never so frightened in my life and if the Dear Lord will forgive me this time, I will never ride it again."
—Agatha Wales, 1912; inscription on the back of a postcard of the Venice, California, roller coaster

---

The World's Steepest, Highest, Longest, Meanest Roller Coasters

Robert Cartmell started riding roller coasters back in the forties, when he was six, and he just never stopped. To date, he's dropped and swooped along nearly 150 tracks—no mean accomplishment, since there are only about 200 coasters in existence today. In addition to being one of the best-traveled roller-coaster freaks, Cartmell is also one of the most scholarly and has made such a name for himself as a student of the genre that the Smithsonian Institution commissioned him to put together its "Coast to Coast Coasters: A Thrilling Exhibition on American Roller Coasters," which toured the United States for two and a half years starting in November 1975.

Not all coasters are the same; hills, curves, drops, height, and speed are combined and paced differently on each to make a ride more or less exciting than its counterparts. Of course, Cartmell has his favorites:

Giant ice slides built in Russia in the 16th century are generally considered the first roller coasters.

A French "roller coaster" at the Bellfort Fair, 1904.

"America's first roller coaster," a transformed mining device,
near Mauch Chunk, Pennsylvania, 1870.

The "Texas Cyclone" at Astroworld in Houston.

The Texas Cyclone at Astroworld, Houston, Texas. A mirror image of the Cyclone that has been devastating riders at Coney Island in Brooklyn, New York, for over fifty years, this relative newcomer starts off with a chilling 53-degree, 92-foot drop, then churns stomachs some more with such a startling series of plunges and round-house curves that many people consider it the greatest thrill ride built since the golden age of roller coasters in the twenties.

The Thunderbolt at Kennywood Park, West Mifflin, Pennsylvania. The most frightening parts of this 1968 expansion of a 1920s oldie—two perilous drops, a tunnel, and a series of brutal turns—are hidden by shrubs, fences, and a natural valley. The final plunges—80 and 90 feet—come just when you're breathing sighs of relief and thinking it's all over—and make the Thunderbolt's finish one of the most chilling among coasters.

Mister Twister at Elitch's Gardens, Denver, Colorado. Ninety-six feet high at its highest point, and crammed with treacherous hills and curves.

The Cyclone at Coney Island, Brooklyn, New York. Still fast and nasty after fifty years of operation, the Cyclone was one of Charles Lindbergh's favorites. The first hill seems nearly vertical.

The Great American Scream Machine at Six Flags over Georgia, Atlanta, Georgia. The reflection of the coaster in the lagoon below makes you feel even higher than the terrifying 105 feet you actually are when you get to the top. The downhill swoops that follow are so smooth that it almost seems as if the tracks are waxed.

The Comet at Crystal Beach Park, near Buffalo, New York. The world's tallest steel coaster, the Comet seems even higher than its 104 feet because Lake Erie is an extra twenty feet lower than the ride's lowest point. The first hill, though, is only the beginning of an all ups-and-downs 4,800-foot-long nightmare of 96- and 70-foot drops.

The Giant Coaster in Paragon Park, Nantasket Beach, Massachusetts. Extremely fast and steep, with one staggering 98-foot drop.

The Racer at Chapultepec Park, Mexico City, Mexico. At 110 feet, the Racer shares the place of world's highest with the Screamin' Eagle at Six Flags over Mid-America, near St. Louis. The Racer, 4,000 feet long, is one of the few coasters that require both a lap belt and a seat belt.

The Giant Dipper at Santa Cruz, just south of San Francisco. Built in 1923, and still one of the most beautiful. Harrowing curves are its strong point.

The Coaster at Dorney Park, Allentown, Pennsylvania. Most riders liken the first drop to falling off a cliff.

If you'd like to share your coaster experiences with Cartmell, write him at Box 189, Altamont, New York 12009.

A Perfect Ride

You'll probably get it on a hot summer night just after a rainstorm. Why? Says Cartmell: "The night eases the friction caused by the drying sun; the heat loosens the heavy grease on the wheels and the track; and the rain wets the tracks for smoother gliding." As for where you ought to sit, that's a matter of taste. "The front seat heightens the floating sensation, allows the smoothest ride, and gives a sense of being alone on the ride," explains Cartmell. "The rear seat is like the tail end of a giant whip, provides the roughest trip, and gives the sense of a group of strangers caught together inside a tornado." Another tip from Cartmell: ride with your eyes closed. The plunges, the grueling twists and turns—all coming before you're visually prepared for them—will be that much more terrifying.

Disney's World Apart

For a long time there was no place on earth quite like Disneyland. It was cleaner, brighter, friendlier, and generally happier than any of the old carnival parks. It was life with the rough edges smoothed; life seen through rose-colored glasses, without the glasses. It was the end-of-the-rainbow pot of gold.

No wonder Disney wanted another one.

Walt Disney World is even more ambitious than Disneyland. The Magic Kingdom—the main rides-and-attractions section of the World, and nearly identical to the California park—is the most fantastic theme park imaginable. The Hall of Presidents, the Haunted Mansion, the Cinderella castle, the Pirates of the Caribbean, and other favorite Disneyland attractions—all of which are here, arranged pretty much as they are at Disneyland—are every bit as good as you've heard they are. There are marvelous displays of fireworks, and in summer there's a nightly Main Street Electrical Parade, in which a half million tiny lights outline 140 animals, butterflies, people. All that shines and glitters and twinkles is here, just as if Tinkerbell had been fluttering around with her magic wand, strewing fairy dust.

But at Walt Disney World, the Magic Kingdom is only a part of what's offered. The ultimate something-for-everyone vacation destination, Walt Disney World has a campground, a shopping village, resort hotels, and a swimming hole, all of which are, in their own way, nearly perfect. The idea,

of course, is to transport you out of your workaday world and into another, whether that world is the world of the campground, the world of the shopping center, or the world of the pirate-infested waters of the Caribbean. The best of the experiences you take vacations to find are here. All you've got to do is come and get it.

For more information about Disney World, contact P. O. Box 40, Lake Buena Vista, Florida 32830. For information about Disneyland, write the Guest Relations Office at 1313 Harbor Boulevard, Anaheim, California 93803.

Great Adventure, Jackson, New Jersey.

A Collection of Collections

The Acquisitive Syndrome

The urge to accumulate leads people to hoard, if nothing else, their own personal memorabilia; nearly everyone collects *something*. However, some people impose a system on their instincts, and specialize. They collect Kewpie dolls, Depression glass, antique autos, armor, air guns, barbed wire, insulators, art. It all depends on their means. The financiers, the industrial magnates, and their progeny —the ones who don't devote their fortunes to good works—usually collect, then bequeath their collections to museums like the Smithsonian, the Metropolitan Museum of Art, the Field Museum, or the Philadelphia Museum of Art. As a result, these institutions have most of the best collections of just about everything imaginable. But there are plenty of smaller museums with fine collections of just one sort of object— and that's what you'll find in this section.

The World's Largest Air-Gun Collection

Some version of the BB gun has been around at least since the seventeenth century. Royalist party members in England attempting to assassinate Oliver Cromwell in 1654 described their weapon as a gun "which shewts with wynde only a bullet at 150 paces and that 7 times one after another." Later, Napoleon so feared the Austrian army's air rifles that when he invaded the Tyrol he ordered the death sentence for anyone owning an air gun. Lewis and Clark killed some deer and amazed the Indians with their "smokeless rifle," and improved versions were widely used in commercial shooting galleries at fairs and carnivals in the late 1800s. The Daisy Air Rifle, a variation of the shooting-gallery model, was one of the air guns inexpensive enough for average people. Within ten years of its introduction there were Bulls Eyes, Deweys, Heroes, Dandies, and Atlases

competing with the Daisy Red Ryders, Buck Joneses, and Number 25s. All of the above are part of the large collection at the Daisy International Air Gun Museum in Rogers, Arkansas. Next door to the museum, at the Daisy BB Gun plant, you can watch BBs being produced at the rate of 65 million a day.

Rogers is in the northwestern corner of the state, in the Ozarks, near Beaver Lake—where you can fish, swim, go boating, and rent just about anything you need to enjoy those activities—and Eureka Springs, a tiny town whose gingerbready Victorian frame houses cling precariously to a mountainside so steep that you wonder how anybody ever picked it for a townsite to begin with.

For infomation about the BB gun collection, contact the Daisy Manufacturing Company, Rogers, Arkansas 72756. For particulars about the area, write the Chambers of Commerce at Box 428, Rogers, Arkansas 72756, and 5 North Main, Eureka Springs, Arkansas 72632.

Archery Artifacts

Fred Bear, founder of the Bear Archery Company, has in his time killed a thousand-pound Kodiak bear with bow and arrow. The collection of artifacts he has made during his career as a bow-hunter is the world's largest. There are unusual native knives from

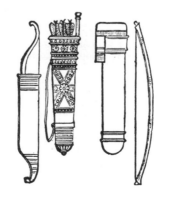

around the world—strange serrated objects, curvy-bladed daggers, sinister-looking daggers, and ornate Oriental warheads. His museum is in Grayling, Michigan, in the north-central part of the state. Grayling and the nearby Au Sable River are superb canoeing territory. For details on the area, contact the Chamber of Commerce, Grayling, Michigan 49738, and the Oscoda-Au Sable Chamber of Commerce, Box 67, Oscoda, Michigan 48750.

Barbed Wire

Sunderland Kinks, Triangle Lines, Four Points, Hold Fasts, Ric-Racs, Untorn Ribbons, Kelly's Diamonds, Corsicana Clips, Underwood Tacks, Nadel Twos, Saber Points, Brink Twists, Wrap Arounds and nearly five hundred other varieties of barbed wire are on display at the Barbed Wire Museum at 614 Main Street in LaCrosse, Kansas 67548. Barbed-wire collecting is a big deal in certain circles, and there are whole societies devoted to it. For information, contact the Texas Barbed Wire Collectors Association, 1019 Cedar Trail, Cedar Hill, Texas 75104.

The Great Beer Collection

Kermit Dietrich, who founded the World of Beer Memorabilia Museum in Barnesville, Pennsylvania, displays one of the best beer-can collections you'll see anywhere. Not only are there about 150 flattop cans, but also the early cone-top cans, some in remarkably good condition; a beer delivery wagon, once used to ship beer by the Weaver Brewery in western Pennsylvania; a beer delivery truck; beer openers, mirrors, pocket knives, coasters, bottle caps, matchbooks, menus, and fans; a beer pocket watch; beer knobs and foam scrapers; bottling equipment; leaded-glass advertising equipment. There are also scores of advertising signs: tin, paper, wood, canvas, lithography on milk glass, leaded-glass windows, and hundreds of trays and calendars. And if that isn't enough, there is even some paraphernalia relating to whiskey, wine, tobacco, and Coca-Cola.

Barnesville is in the Poconos, about ten miles south of Hazleton and about fifteen miles north of the Appalachian Trail. You can get more information about the museum from Mr. Dietrich at RD #2, Kempton, Pennsylvania 19529.

Just Buttons
Sally Luscomb has been editing and publishing a magazine by that title for some thirty-five years, has written two books on the subject, and now runs a small museum devoted to buttons at 45 Berlin Avenue, Southington, Connecticut.

The museum contains thousands of buttons, many in frames on the walls. Here you will find the largest collection of Armed Forces buttons in the country; prehistoric stone buttons; eighteenth-century buttons made of hand-wrought copper, brass, tombac, silver, steel, sulphides, and jasperware; American pewter buttons; gilt buttons from the first half of the nineteenth century. There are buttons of glass, ivory, bone, tortoiseshell, horn, rubber, pearl, shell, and wood. And there are early campaign and presidential buttons. You can see the museum only by appointment, and Sally Luscomb herself will always be on hand to tell you what's what and answer your questions. For details, write the museum or phone 203/628-6337.

Campbell's Collection
Soup tureens, of course.

Make no mistake about it, though. The collection you'll see at the Campbell Museum in Camden, New Jersey, contains some very elegant objects. Just think back to the Georgian silver tureens of the eighteenth century, or the faience pieces of western Europe you've seen scattered in small historical museums around the country, and you'll have some idea of what you'll see here—in quantity. There are silver tureens—embossed, cast, finialed, gadrooned, engraved, and otherwise ornamented; silver-gilt tureens; rococo Meissen tureens of hard-paste porcelain; antique tureens and modern ones—and on, and on, and on.

For further information, contact the museum in Camden, New Jersey 08101.

Ceramics: The Compleat Potter
A huge institution devoted just to pots, the Carborundum Museum of Ceramics in Niagara Falls, New York, takes you through twelve centuries of the potter's art.

There are, in the collections, mud bricks made along the Nile before the time of Moses, classical Greek pots from ancient Athens, heating ducts

and water pipes from Roman times, Chinese jars, pre-Columbian sculpture, Persian pots that Marco Polo brought to Italy from the East, Italian earthenware from the time of Michelangelo, Ming vases, Spode, Spanish earthenware, and German stoneware. On loan from the Smithsonian is a lidless teapot. How do you fill it? Through a hole in the bottom that runs up a tube and into the collection chamber. When the pot is filled and turned right side up, gravity keeps the tea in the chamber so that you can pour only from the spout.

After you've finished touring the exhibit areas, not only will you know what bone china looks like (and how it differs, say, from porcelain), but you'll also have seen it being made: among the exhibits are the Claymasters, working potters from Staffordshire who, using the techniques and

materials of Josiah Spode II, turn out reproductions of his teapots, creamers, sugar bowls, cups and saucers, and dessert plates—all decorated in a design from Spode's own pattern book. Their products are on sale in the gift shops, along with the one-of-a-kind works of other potters in yet another studio.

Outside, of course, the falls roar and the city teems with activity. For more information, contact the museum at P. O. Box 746, Niagara Falls, New York 14302; the Niagara Falls Area Chamber of Commerce, 224 First Street, Niagara Falls, New York 14303; and the Niagara Resort and Tourist Association, 5433 Victoria Avenue, Niagara Falls, Ontario L2G 301.

The Fine Art of Collecting Time
Clock museums are fun to visit, for several reasons. Clocks seem to be one utilitarian object on which makers exercise their imagination. One clockmaker, for instance, would produce a batch of ordinary clocks, and then, on another occasion, would let himself go by ornamenting the face with beaming moons and chortling sun-faces, landscapes, trees—or by adding mechanical figurines, or by creating variations on the sounds his chimes would produce. Visit a museum where the clocks are wound up and working and you're surrounded by a symphony of ticking and tocking as mesmerizing as a chorus of crickets. It's a tranquil, soothing sound. Here are some good museums to visit.

How French Lick ticks. Not far from the famous French Lick resort hotel in hilly southern Indiana, you'll find the House of Clocks Museum. From the looks of the place, you might well think that the owners, Bob and Golda Cardwell, had traveled the country in search of items for the collection. Actually, most of the grandfather clocks, cuckoo clocks, wall clocks, mantel clocks, and pocket watches came from within fifty miles of French Lick—but then, since French Lick was always the sort of spa to which gentlemen and their ladies traveled from many miles away, it could be said that the clocks came to French

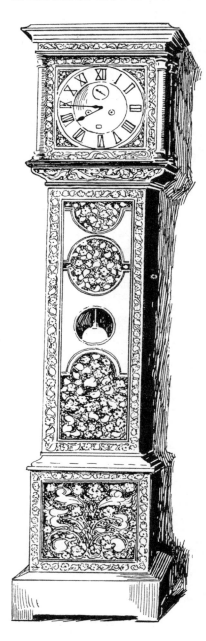

Lick. Some of the most telling items in the collection are the "gambler's watches"—pocket watches on whose faces playing cards replace the numerals. The collection also includes Swiss music boxes, an 1898 Edison gramophone, an old reed organ, prayer books, shaving stands, postcards printed on leather, an antique typewriter, old photographs, and even a player piano. Saturday is usually winding day at the museum. For information, write 225 College Street, French Lick, Indiana 47432; the Chamber of Commerce can send you more information about the town.

The clocks of Spillville. This small Iowa town—settled by Czechs, surrounded by woods and fields, and once the summer home of composer Anton Dvořák—was also the home of Frank and Joseph Bily, two Czech brothers whose clock-carving hobby brought them fame as they carved intricate figures of mechanical bands, pioneers, apostles, and so on, to ornament their clocks. The works they executed between 1913 and 1956 are on display in the building that Dvořák occupied in 1893. Also in the area is a museum of Norwegian-American items, one of the largest in the country devoted to a single immigrant group. For details on the area, contact the Chamber of Commerce, Decorah, Iowa 52101.

A world's largest. The Time Museum in the Clock Tower Inn in Rockford, Illinois, in the northeastern part of the state, calls itself the world's largest museum devoted exclusively to a historical display of timekeeping pieces. Whether that's true or not, what you'll see is spectacular—first, because of the museum's unmuseumlike decor (emerald carpeting and cushiony velvet settees), and also because of the sumptuousness of the collection, which contains items dating from 2000 B.C. Arranged in chronological order, they'll give you a brief history of the fine art of measuring time—beginning with the days of water clocks, sand glasses, and astrolabes and sundials, moving through the development of watches and clocks as we know them during the Renaissance, and continuing through to precision clocks from some of the greatest of the European makers, such as Berthoud, Janvier, and Breguet. There are some truly marvelous-looking gilt clocks and silver clocks, and a massive oak construction of Christian Gebhard: the figures on the clock have some twenty-six different movements. In addition, there are American clocks, watches from nearly every watch company in the United States, the first digital clock, early electric clocks, clocks powered by atmospheric changes and solar cells, marine and pocket chronometers, the most complicated mechani-

cal astronomical clock in the world, plus any number of clocks with moving figures, and enameled watches. Clocks in ships and models of various sorts, as well as other unusual timepieces, make the collection interesting to noncollectors as well as to cognoscenti.

Rockford and its environs is not the sort of place you'd expect to be a great weekending spot, but it turns out to be full of interesting sights, including the Illinois Railway Museum, about thirty miles out of town in tiny Union, and the towns of Oregon and Grand Detour, where you can visit the restored homestead of John Deere, who invented "the plow that broke the plains." Area information: Black Hawk Hills Tourism and Promotion Council, 815 East State Street, Rockford, Illinois 61101.

Clocks for the common man. The American clockmaking industry—once one of the most important manufacturing endeavors in the country—became world famous because it produced clocks so cheaply that for the first time nearly everybody could afford one.

And so it is that the American Clock and Watch Museum, in a square white clapboard mansion as old as the clocks it houses, in Bristol, Connecticut (a major clockmaking center in the old days), presents you not with a collection of timepieces owned by kings and queens but one made up mostly of what were once just ordinary clocks. The collection includes a lantern clock made about 1680 by one Henry Webster, in England, and, on an antique table in a low-ceilinged, plank-floored summer kitchen that also contains a lineup of 1840–1860 Bristol shelf clocks, an unusual four-hundred-year-old sand-glass. Most of the clocks in the collection were, however, made in America during the eighteenth and nineteenth centuries. There are some handsome dome clocks, some banjo clocks, some tall inlaid clocks; most are notable for their movements as well as for their cases. "The clock," says the curator, "is actually the movement, and the case is merely a piece of furniture to keep the movement clean and to appeal to the owner." This is not the biggest, most valuable collection you will encounter as you clock it around the country, but it is one of the finest, and it is the most extensive assemblage of Connecticut-manufactured clocks. In all, the museum contains some eight hundred clocks, and a similar number of watches and watch movements. For more information, write the museum in Bristol, Connecticut 06010.

The world's second largest clock. The Colgate-Palmolive Company, in Clarksville, Ohio, has it. Louisville, which the clock faces across the Ohio, calls it the city's "Big Ben." You can tour the plant; call 812/283-6611.

North America's oldest clock. It's in Montreal, at the St. Sulpice Seminary, founded in 1657 and the oldest structure still in use in the city. On the Place d'Armes, where the seminary is located, don't miss Notre Dame Church, a rather plain Gothic structure that blazes with the rainbow colors of some of the most elaborate stained-glass windows extant.

Clocks, clocks, and some more clocks. Besides these good one-subject clock museums, you'll find very good collections at Old Sturbridge Village (Sturbridge, Massachusetts 01566); at the Henry Ford Museum (Dearborn, Michigan 48121); at the Smithsonian's National Museum of History and Technology (12th and Constitution Avenues N.W., Washington, D.C. 20560); at Old Mystic Seaport (Mystic, Connecticut 06355); at the Museum of Connecticut History (231 Capitol Avenue, Hartford, Connecticut 06115); and at the National Museum of Science and Technology (1867 St. Laurent Boulevard, Ottawa, Ontario, Canada).

A club for clock collectors. The time-conscious—and the timepiece-conscious—may want to consider membership in the National Association of Watch and Clock Collectors. Fifteen dollars a year gets you six bulletins full of articles on the technical, artistic, and historical aspects of timekeeping; reviews of horological books; and information about Association activities. Six times a year, too, you'll get copies of *The Mart,* in which members, and members only, announce their intent to buy, sell, or trade parts of their collections. A national convention held at some location of horological interest usually includes seminars and lectures where you can learn still more. For further information, contact the association at 514 Poplar Street, Box 33, Columbia, Pennsylvania 17512.

Decoys

To someone who knows them, decoys are as distinctive as paintings are to an art historian. The collector can tell you whether the carver hailed from New England, the eastern shore, New Jersey, the Midwest, or North Carolina simply by inspecting the markings on the head and body; sometimes these will even reveal the name of the carver.

So it's not surprising that there are decoy collectors, and given the fact that there are collectors, that one of them turned his collection into a museum devoted to the subject.

Mr. Roy Bull, who owns about three thousand decoys, has one of the largest decoy collections open to the public. Most on display are wood, but there are also some covered with canvas and some made of iron. One, an Italian bird, is constructed of reeds.

To get to the museum at Magothy Bay, one of the inlets that lie between the Virginia barrier islands and the mainland, continue north for about three miles on U.S. 13 after leaving the Chesapeake Bay Bridge-Tunnel, then turn right on Route 645 at Cedar Grove, left on Route 600, right on Route 655, and left on Route 696. The museum is on the right at the first country lane. It's hard to find, so it's important that you call before you go, especially since Mr. Bull is not always at home. Telephone him at 804/331-2130. To contact him by mail, write him at Townsend, Virginia 23443.

More decoys. Among the large museums with fine decoy collections, the Shelburne Museum—a "village" constructed of buildings moved to Shelburne, Vermont, from all over the state—has an excellent collection: headless ducks that seem to be feeding, gulls, cranes, feeders, and sleepers by people like Joel Barber, Shang Wheeler, Lem Ward, Harry Shourdes. For details, write the museum in Shelburne, Vermont 05482.

Two Really Spectacular Dollhouses

The world's largest dollhouse is in the Victorian Room of the rambling, imposing old Empress Hotel, in more-British-than-Britain Victoria, British Columbia. The dollhouse's thirty-five rooms, courtyard, flower gardens, and hand-carved coaches reproduce exactly the English residence of Queen Victoria, who inhabits the dollhouse along with Prince Albert.

Another breathtaking dollhouse is in the Museum of Science and Industry in Chicago. Colleen Moore's Fairy Castle has, in its yard, a weeping-willow tree that "weeps" diamonds; and, inside, crystal chandeliers whose crystals are more diamonds. The Convention and Tourism Bureau (332 South Michigan Avenue, Chicago, Illinois 60604) can send you more information about the museum and the city in general.

Antique Fire Apparatus

Usually ornate, but always functional, firefighting apparatus and firemanic memorabilia have their ranks of aficionados and collectors just as antique autos do. For the casual spectator, however, fire apparatus is perhaps even more interesting than old cars are—first because so few people know very much about it, second because the machines are so much more elaborate. Here are a few of the best collections.

A museum on the Hudson. Every item in the American Museum of Firefighting at the Firemen's Home of the State of New York has a colorful history. Take Barnum's Museum Flag, circa 1865, which is acquisition number 135. Its rescue from the great conflagration that destroyed Barnum's museum full of "wonders of the world" was just one of the heroic acts performed during the extinguishing of that fire. The flag became an object of pride for every member of the old New York City Volunteer Fire Department. Also in the museum, besides numerous lithographs and oil paintings depicting famous fire departments and fires: the curious-looking little wagon that was America's first fire engine; a bucket carrier used in the 1840s to carry up to forty leather buckets at a time; fire hats; company slogans and mottoes that convey the spirit of volunteer firefighting; wooden hydrants; firemen's shirts; parade banners; and badges. All of the floor space in each of two 100 x 65-foot Engine Halls, as well as the wall cases, are filled with similar exhibits. For information about the museum, contact the Curator at Harry Howard Avenue, Hudson, New York 12534. The Hudson River Valley Association, 105 Ferris Lane, Poughkeepsie, New York 12603, can provide more information about local attractions.

Maryland's superfirehouse. Parades and fire-prevention demonstrations highlight the routine of the Fire Museum of Maryland, at 1301 York Road in Lutherville, about a block north of the Baltimore Beltway. The building is vast—eighteen thousand square feet. The engines displayed include quite a few that are new enough to be recognizable as firefighting equipment—1917, 1922, and 1933 Ahrens-Fox pumping engines, a 1933 Mack tractor with an 1898 water tower and a 1928 Mack pumper, a 1941 American La France pumper, and a 1908 American La France horse-drawn ladder. They're all shiny, massive contraptions that look not unlike Rube Goldberg inventions. For details, write the museum in Lutherville, Maryland 21093. For information about other things to see and do in Baltimore—which has some very interesting museums devoted to railroad memorabilia, Babe Ruth, Edgar Allan Poe, and art—contract the Baltimore Promotion Council Information Center, 22 Light Street, Baltimore, Maryland 21202.

The Indiana collection. The fire service collection at the Children's Museum in Indianapolis is small, but its home in the brand-new building is designed to show it off well. A firehouse of the horse-drawn era has been faithfully reconstructed, right down to the sliding pole, the antique fittings, and the doors and moldings. An 1892 Ahrens steamer with a two-horse hitch harness stands ready to go. All that's needed is a sound of the alarm from the watch room, a working Gamewell Fire Alarm Telegraph System that was originally constructed

for the fire department in Muncie. In another room there's a dazzling American La France water tower with a sixty-five-foot ladder—fire-service-equipment buffs say it's worth the trip just to see this. Most of the time, you can climb into the drivers' seats of the engines and check out the view. For details about this museum, the biggest children's museum in the world, contact the curator at 30th and Meridian Streets, Indianapolis, Indiana 46208.

The firehouse on Cape Cod. The New England Fire and History Museum in Brewster, Massachusetts, has thirty-five of the most historic fire engines in the United States including the deep green Volunteer of Leeds, a metal pumper with brass fittings that goes back to the 1600s. It's small enough so that kids can pump it comfortably, which gives you an idea of how short people were three hundred years ago. Youngsters can also ring the fire alarms donated by the town of Falmouth and then see what happens inside the alarm boxes to make the bells ring in the firehouse. In addition, there's a reconstruction of Benjamin Franklin's first firehouse; a sound-and-dialogue diorama of the 1871 Chicago fire; an assortment of axes, hooks, ladders, and leather buckets from the days of the fire brigade; and old-time fire hoses, prints, books, and documents. There is also a re-created Victorian apothecary shop containing one of the largest displays of apothecary bottles east of the Mississippi. For further information about the museum, write the curator at Route 6A, Brewster, Massachusetts 02631. For information about beaches, fishing, and resorts on sea-swept Cape Cod, contact the Cape Cod Chamber of Commerce, Hyannis, Massachusetts 02601.

Conflagration memorials. On September 1, 1894, a fire destroyed most of the town of Hinckley, Minnesota. The Northern Pacific Depot was one of the buildings destroyed, immediately after the railroad's telegrapher called for help. To memorialize the fire, the depot built on the site of the original one has been restored and furnished as it was in 1894, with the agent's living quarters upstairs and the office and two waiting rooms downstairs. One of the waiting rooms contains a diorama showing the city before the fire. There are audio tapes that tell you stories of the fire survivors. Details about the area, near the St. Croix River and about halfway between Duluth and Minneapolis, can be had from the Minnesota Department of Economic Development, Tourism Division, 480 Cedar Street, St. Paul, Minnesota 55101.

The Chicago Historical Society has an impressive exhibit commemorating the Chicago fire. The heat of the fire fused buttons into shapeless lumps, and dinner plates into strange columns. Miraculously, a few ginger-snap cookies survived, only slightly charred. All are on display here, along with a great many photos that tell of the town's rebuilding and a diorama that tells the frightening story of how it all happened. The Convention and Tourist Bureau (332 South Michigan Avenue, Chicago, Illinois 60604) can send you more information about that museum.

Most people don't know, though, that on the day that the Chicago fire claimed 250 lives, a fire was raging in Peshtigo, Wisconsin, as well. This huge conflagration claimed eight hundred lives on October 8, 1871. The Peshtigo Fire Museum (400 Oconto Avenue, Peshtigo, Wisconsin 54157) can send you information about the collection of relics that tell the dramatic story.

A bit of fire trivia. The first fireproof building in the United States was the Burlington County Prison. It is now a museum at 128 High Street, Mt. Holly, New Jersey 08060. Designed by Robert Mills, a student of Thomas Jefferson and designer of the Washington Monument, the museum contains a good deal of local historical memorabilia, including an old bicycle used on a monorail that once went to Smithville.

Antique firefighting equipment in action. Seeing the equipment actually working beats watching a caravan of old cars by a long shot. The fire trucks throb and roar and make the air fairly vibrate with the sounds of their engines.

Where to see all this? At special firemen's musters sponsored by the Society for the Preservation and Appreciation of Antique Motor Fire Apparatus in America (SPAAMFAA). You can find out about the equipment, how it worked, and how it was used; reminisce with collectors who have reminisced with old-timers, and maybe even talk with the old-timers yourself.

If you get enthusiastic enough about the equipment, you might even want to join the SPAAMFAA. You don't have to own an engine to belong; active membership costs $8 a year. For information about that, or about the locations of musters in your area, contact the SPAAMFAA at Box 450, Eastwood Station, Syracuse, New York 13206.

Funnies

Classic comic strips of this century, plus original cartoons by Thomas Nast, Charles Dana Gibson, and even Charles M. Schulz (the creator of "Peanuts"), are on display at the Museum of Cartoon Art and Hall of Fame at 384 Field Point Road in Greenwich, Connecticut 06830. For more information, write; or call 203/661-4502.

Glass

Peculiarly fascinating, this substance—not just because of its chemistry (which is odd enough; glass is one of the few solids without an apparent crystalline structure), or because it is made by the same methods that have been used for hundreds of years, but

also because it's relatively common in the United States, and the simpler, newer forms of it are fairly easy to collect.

Among the best public collections to be seen is the one at the Corning Museum of Glass in Corning, New York, in the Finger Lakes area of New York State, a pleasant area of hills and clean lakes and woods. The collection contains some thirteen thousand items spanning thirty-five centuries—from the earliest glass beads to present-day pieces. In addition, in the Corning Glass Center, of which the museum is a part, you can study other aspects of glass. For instance, in the Science Hall, you can experience the interesting properties of glass through animated demonstrations: you can bend a sheet of glass; flex a glass spring; interrupt the flow of high voltage with glass; give a glass an acid bath. In the same area, you learn that depending on how it's made, glass can be lighter than cork, heavy as iron, fragile as an eggshell, soft as cotton, hard as precious stones. There are also films, including one that shows you glassblowing machines turning out 2,200 light bulbs per minute. Nearby there's a display of ninety-six varieties of light bulbs—everything from decorative bulbs to imitation flickering candles.

The third part of the Corning Glass Center is the Steuben Glass Factory, where amazing professional teams of three or four men each group together to begin making the elaborate Steuben pieces. You can also watch the engravers at work.

For more information, contact the Corning Glass Center, Corning, New York 14830; for information about the area in general, contact the Finger Lakes Association, 309 Lake Street, Penn Yan, New York 14527.

Glass capital of the world. Glassmaking came to Toledo, Ohio, in 1888 with Edward Drummond Libbey, who brought his glass company from the Boston area. His company prospered, and at about the turn of the century Mr. Libbey founded the Toledo Museum of Art and began collecting glass for it. Between his own collecting, and purchases of various private glass collections, he amassed more than five thousand items in the museum. They've recently been installed in their own area in a new gallery, some arranged chronologically in a special study area (to which members of the public are admitted). Glass is arranged by group (the Ancient World, the Islamic World, the Byzantine Empire, the Orient, Europe, and the United States), and each piece has an identification number that refers to pages in a notebook where you can read about the date, site, and method of manufacture of the item. For more information about the museum or its glass collection, contact the Curator of Glass, Box 1013, Toledo, Ohio 43697.

Some other big museums with good glass collections: the Henry Ford Museum (Dearborn, Michigan 48121); the Metropolitan Museum of Art (Fifth Avenue at 82nd Street, New York, New York 10028); the Museum of Fine Arts (Huntington Avenue, Boston, Massachusetts 02115); the Art Institute of Chicago (Michigan Avenue at Adams, Chicago, Illinois 60603); the Smithsonian Institution (1000 Jefferson Drive, S.W., Washington, D.C. 20560); the New Orleans Museum of Art (P. O. Box 19123, New Orleans, Louisiana 70179); and the Currier Gallery of Art (192 Orange Street, Manchester, New Hampshire 03104).

Some all-American glass. The Sandwich Glass Museum, part of the Sandwich Historical Society on the lower part of Cape Cod, tells you a good deal about the evolution of Sandwich glass in its three-thousand-item collection; at the same time it also tells the story of the evolution of American glass. In the same way that Connecticut Yankees put clocks within the purchasing power of the common man, Massachusetts man Deming Jarves cut the price of glass by making it in molds rather than blowing each individual piece. When the "lacy glass" he originally made fell from favor, he switched to a plainer sort of three-mold pressed glass. From then on, he rolled with the punches, so that the glass that came out of Sandwich comes in colors, many patterns, and was made into many sorts of objects. Eventually, though, Jarves went back to blown, cut, and engraved glass, and the fact that the Sandwich Factory finally ceased production makes those items that it did produce still more valuable, and the museum—at least to collectors—all the more interesting. To noncollectors, the important features are the size of the collection and the beauty of the pieces covered with trefoils, palmettes, oak leaves, thistles, daisies, beehives, and other elaborate designs, in shades of amethyst, canary, blue, and ruby red. For more information about the museum, contact the Sandwich Historical Society, Sandwich, Massachusetts 02563; the Cape Cod Chamber of Commerce (Hyannis, Massachusetts 02601) can send more information about vacation activities on Cape Cod.

Seeing how glass is made. The carnival glassblowers you see give you just an inkling of how glassblowing really was in the old days. To get the true picture of the skill required to make blobs of molten liquid into utilitarian objects, you can visit the Corning Glass Center in the Finger Lakes, described above. Or, in

Liberty Village in Flemington, New Jersey, in the west-central part of the state just north of Trenton, see the gaffers working with their blowpipes, which look something like the trumpets used by heralding angels. The furnace roars—it's so hot inside that you can't stay around too long if it's summer—but the sight is spellbinding. A similar operation can be viewed at the Glass House at the Jamestown section of the Colonial National Historical Park. For information about Flemington, write to Liberty Village, 2 Church Street, Flemington, New Jersey 08822. For information about the Jamestown Glass House, contact the Colonial National Historical Park, Yorktown, Virginia 23490. Glassblowing in this way is worth traveling a long way to see.

Then, too, there are any number of glass factories that are open to tour—also noisy, hot places. West Virginia is full of them: there are glass companies in Milton, Williamstown, Moundsville, Ceredo, Huntington, Morgantown, New Martinsville, and Weston. For hours and information about the tours and the factory stores, contact the Travel Development Division of the West Virginia Department of Commerce, State Capitol, Charleston, West Virginia 25305.

The Steuben glass book. Next best to owning a piece of Steuben yourself is looking at pictures of the best of it—and, in *Steuben Glass,* a monograph by James S. Plaut now in its third revised and enlarged edition, there are seventy-two glorious black-and-white pictures plus a list of the museums in the United States and around the world in which Steuben glass is displayed. Dover Books, 180 Varick Street, New York, New York 10014; $3.50.

Guns

The fact that amassing antique firearms consumes the energies of such a large number of collectors is bewildering to a lot of people who can think of guns in none but psychological terms. But, in the words of one aficionado, "The field . . . involves many other things than just guns and shooting. Art, for instance, in no small amount. And the life and times of frontier days, living in tipis, and a whole lot of other activities." Quite a few private collections are open to the public. Once you've seen some of them, you'll realize the truth in the assertions.

These guns were used by Jesse James, Cole Younger, Pancho Villa, Captain Quantrell, Billy the Kid, Cherokee Bill, Annie Oakley, Belle Starr, and Three-Fingered Jack. The collection in the Saunders Memorial Museum in Berryville, Arkansas, in the northwesternmost part of the state near Beaver Lake and Eureka Springs, is notable for reasons other than these celebrities' guns (which, for the most part, are well used and quite utilitarian). One case shows the evolution of firearms, beginning with a replica of an Oriental twelfth-century hand cannon and continuing through the ages of matchlock ignitions, mechanical wheel locks, flintlocks, percussion caps, rim firers, to the center-fire model which is in use today. Among the other outstanding exhibits: the four cases of Colts that show that brand's development; a brace of double-barrel flintlock pistols, circa 1735, that belonged to the Prince of Wales; an elegant pair of gold-inlaid dueling pistols, circa 1848, in their original velvet lines case, with all the original accoutrements.

Burton Saunders, who assembled the collection, also gathered objets d'art from around the world—including a sheik's quilted silk tent, Sitting Bull's headdress and battle jacket, antiques from the Holy Land, Persia, and the Orient—to which Mr. Saunders and his wife traveled about the turn of the century. It is interesting to contemplate, when you visit this modern building, the fact that it all belonged to one person. For further information, write the museum at 314 East Madison, Berryville, Arkansas 72616. The Department of Parks and Tourism (State Capitol, Little Rock, Arkansas 72201) can send material about the outdoor activities and sightseeing opportunities in the area.

More celebrity shooters. Visit the Stage Coach Museum in Shakopee, Minnesota, just outside the Twin Cities. Guns owned by Buffalo Bill, Annie Oakley, some of the members of the James Gang, and John Brown are part of a collection that also includes Sioux and Chippewa buckskins, weapons, headdresses, and scalp locks; and a veritable symphony orchestra's worth of mechanical musical instruments, including band organs and an orchestrion. It is all displayed in a Western village re-created on the site of a former stagecoach stop. For further information, write Osborne and Marie Klavestad, Route 1, Box 1033, Shakopee, Minnesota 55379.

Colts, mostly. The gun to which Wild Bill Hickok and Bat Masterson both owed their lives—the Colt—was the world's first practical revolver. When you think of the dramatic effect that this single creation has had on American history, it's astonishing to think that at first the invention didn't succeed. It was only because one Captain Sam Walker of the Texas Rangers insisted that General Zachary Taylor order some of Samuel Colt's pistols that the .44-caliber six-shooter took off. Subsequently, Samuel Colt visited the crowned heads of Europe, presenting them with ornately engraved models, and, later, produced about 508,000 muskets, revolvers, and rifles for the Union forces during the Civil War.

The Colt Collection at the Museum of Connecticut History (231 Capitol Avenue, Hartford, Connecticut 06115), one of the most famous collections of firearms in the world, tells much of the story with an exhibit of about five hundred specimens, including the Whitneyville-Walker that Colt produced for the Mexican War; the Third Model Dragoon of 1848, beautifully engraved and inlaid, presented to European officials before the Civil War; Gatling guns that fired up to a thousand shots per minute; Browning Automatic Rifles; the Vickers; the M2 and M3 aircraft machine guns; and more.

For details about other sightseeing you can do in Hartford, contact the Chamber of Commerce at 250 Constitution Plaza, Hartford, Connecticut 06103.

Another world's largest. John Monroe Davis, born in 1887 on an Arkansas plantation, was given his first shotgun by his father, as a reward for his obedience. He had no idea then that that shotgun would be the beginning of a collection he would spend the better part of his life amassing.

In its original location, in the Mason Hotel, in Claremore, Oklahoma, the collection jammed the ballroom, lobbies, hallways, and seven guest rooms. Now properly housed for the first time as the state-maintained J. M. Davis Gun Museum, the remarkable collection has at last been given the space it deserves. The twenty thousand guns, rifles, pistols, and other items are displayed along a full mile of aisles. The collection is noteworthy not only for its vastness, but also for its variety. You'll see the smallest pistol ever to be factory-produced, an Austrian model two and five-eighths inches long and weighing only two and a half ounces; a twenty-one-pound wheel lock, one of the largest ever to be fired from the shoulder; and an amazing ornate rifle with a barrel made of watered steel and a stock inlaid with more than fifty thousand pieces of natural and stained ivory and brass in intricate designs. There are also Winchesters, Colts, and muzzle-loading rifles that saw action in the French and Indian War, the Revolution, the War of 1812, the Mexican War, and the Civil War.

In addition to the guns, there are about a thousand beer steins, from a one-ouncer to one that holds nine gallons; plus saddles, mounted animal heads, steer horns, early Oklahoma cattle brands, World War I posters, Indian artifacts, swords, knives, and even musical instruments.

For further information about the museum, write P. O. Box 966, Claremore, Oklahoma 74107. The Tourist Association (Box 1254, Claremore, Oklahoma 74107) can give you more information about the town, which inspired the play *Green Grow The Lilacs*, on which Richard Rodgers based his *Oklahoma!*

The L. L. Bean of antique rifles. Like J. M. Davis, Turner Kirkland, who runs the Dixie Gun Works in Union City, Tennessee, in the northwesternmost part of the state, has been collecting since he was a tyke. But instead of running a hotel to support his habit, Kirkland went into the business of manufacturing rifle parts, bullet molds, and the like, which led him into the mail-order business. His four-hundred-page biannual catalogue is as eagerly greeted by cognoscenti as the L. L. Bean catalogue is by outdoorspeople. It provides fascinating reading: exhortations to check out passages in the Bible; tips on shooting and enjoying firearms, on tempering a Hickory Ramrod, on case hardening your frizzen, on tanning animal hides, and on making Civil War-style hardtack. You can order everything from a Civil War cannon, complete with a trailer for transporting it, to a $450 gold-leaf-trimmed Colt replica, to three-cent lead balls, to

swords, lances, tomahawks, and scalp locks. Much of the merchandise advertised in the catalogue is on display in the Dixie Gun Works showrooms, along with some items that are not for sale—Turner Kirkland's personal collection of expensive Derringers.

The Union City area also happens to be a great place to go fishing—bass-rich Reelfoot Lake is nearby. For information about the town, contact the Northwest Tennessee Tourist Development District, P. O. Box 63, Martin, Tennessee 38237. For more information about the showrooms, write the Dixie Gun Works, Union City, Tennessee 38261.

Muzzle loaders in action. These venerable rifles saw action in the French and Indian War, the Revolution, the Mexican War, and the Civil War, as well as on the frontier, and you can see examples of them on exhibit at many historic sites; usually at National Historic Sites there are firing demonstrations. There's lots of smoke and a whopper of a bang that scares you even when you're expecting it.

However, for seeing the most smoke and noise at one time, you can't beat the muzzle loaders' festivals in Friendship, Indiana, a small town in the southeastern part of the state. Twice a year, in spring and fall, muzzle-loading rifle buffs costumed as frontiersmen, Indians, and soldiers from the Revolution and the Civil War bring their teepees, tents, and rifles and settle in, across from the national headquarters of the organization of muzzle-loading aficionados to which they all belong, for some serious selling, swapping, and shooting. The Historic Hoosier Hills Office (Versailles, Indiana 47042) can send you dates and more details about this exceptionally scenic, hilly part of the state.

Books about rifles. One publisher specializing in books about rifles and related things antique is George Shumway. For a catalogue, write R. D. 7, York, Pennsylvania 17402.

Cameos, Coins, and Kewpie Dolls

They're all part of the 800,000 specimens in the collections at the Ralph Foster Museum in Point Lookout, Missouri. The cameos are part of the Schmidt collection. The Kewpie dolls are accompanied by the original works and models, first-draft sketches, and molds made by Rose O'Neill, the Kewpie doll lady. And coins: there's a room filled with coins, currency, tokens, bonds, medallions, and bills from all over the globe.

For details on these collections, and for information about the museum's exhibits of science, firearms, Ozark celebrities, Middle Mississippian pots, Meerschaum pipes, and so on, write the curator at the School of the Ozarks, Point Lookout, Missouri 65726.

Miniatures

Perhaps the most spectacular collection anywhere is at the Art Institute of Chicago. The Thorne Rooms, originally intended to provide a background for the study of European and American decorative arts, are truly fabulous in their detail; it is almost as if Mrs. James Ward Thorne, who worked for many years planning the rooms, had taken whole chambers from rooms like the Harrison Gray Otis House in Boston (1795), No. 1 Bedford Square, London (1775), or any number of French châteaux and Tudor mansions, and immersed them in a magical solution that shrank them in perfect scale. When you see a picture of one of these miniatures, you'd swear it was the original room. Even under close examination, the details are amazing: every curlicue in the brass fender is there, every scroll in the Chippendale chair. Through doors left slightly ajar, you can glimpse still other, equally perfect rooms. The lighting perfectly simulates morning sunlight, afternoon sunlight, twilight.

The closest thing you'll see anywhere to the Thorne Rooms are not the miniatures displayed in Marshall Field's toy department nearby—fabulous, and expensive, though they may be—but the full-size originals at the Metropolitan Museum of Art in New York or at the Winterthur Museum in Delaware.

For further information about the Thorne Rooms, contact the Art Institute, Michigan Avenue at Adams, Chicago, Illinois 60603; or the Convention and Tourism Bureau, 332 South Michigan Avenue, Chicago, Illinois 60604.

Music Boxes

Captain Nye's Sweet Shop in Roscoe Village, a restored canal town near Coshocton, Ohio, is a Babes-in-Toyland sort of place. All rosy pink and white, from the enameled walls to the cellophane-wrapped candies in the glass jars and the gingham costumes of the ladies who scoop out ice cream cones and serve up the sundaes, Captain Nye's is a delight. What makes it the ultimate sweet shop, however, is not the decor or the food, but the Vox Regina, the grandest of music boxes, which, when fed with quarters, tinkles away with a richest sort of round sound you can imagine, a sound like no other. As you sit there spooning up your peppermint ice cream, you might well be sitting on the set of a Walt Disney movie for the story of a Becky Thatcher childhood. The Vox Regina is the voice of another age, a sweeter time.

Why do people collect music boxes? When you've heard the Vox Regina, you can understand the enchantment without any trouble at all. It can be safely said that once you've heard one music box, you'll make a detour to hear another—and that you'll travel miles out of your way to see and hear a museum of them.

In California, there are two good collections to see: one at the American International Galleries in Irvine, the other at Merle Norman's San Sylmar, in Sylmar. One highlight at the American International Galleries is the Taj Mahal 101-key Mortier dance organ, which measures 24 x 18 x 15 feet, contains hundreds of pipes, and is said to be the most ornate automatic instrument in existence today: when it plays, a thousand light bulbs on three circuits flash; torches flicker; statues move; colors change. In addition to this dazzler, there's a Weber "Maestro orchestrion," a device that plays everything from jazz to symphonies and sounds like a fifteen-piece orchestra (with piano, xylophone, mandolin, bass, violin, flute, cello, jazz trumpet, woodblock, kettledrum, snare drum, clarinet, tambourine, and so on). Another orchestrion on display, a Wurlitzer style 30A Mandolin Pian-Orchestra, was once used in the waiting room of a Salida, Colorado, bordello. For details on the American International Galleries, write to 1802 Kettering Street, Irvine, California 92714 (714/754-1777).

To visit San Sylmar, you've got to make an appointment. Don't fail to, if you're in southern California. The collection, which also includes some of the most luxurious classic cars you'll ever hope to see, is displayed in an elegant carpeted mansion. The musical instruments on exhibit include small cylindrical disc players, a magnificent 1926 theater pipe organ with some seventeen hundred pipes, a ten-foot-high orchestrion, a mechanically played violin, and some art nouveau masterpieces like the 1923 Popper Gladiator, straight from the restaurants of thirties Berlin. The setting makes it all special: San Sylmar is one of the most elegant marbled, gilt, and velvet-curtained mansions you'll see for a while to come. To make an appointment, write San Sylmar Tours, 15180 Bledsoe Street, Sylmar, California 91342 (213/367-1085).

In Iowa, there's Tom Fretty's Corner Market at the intersection of Highways 9 and 65 (near Manly, Iowa 50456). There are some 165 different music-making mechanisms here: mechanical xylophones, pianos, violins, band organs, nickelodeons, orchestrions, even motorized bands whose members are coordinated by perforated rolls. Quite a few of the mechanical music machines are in the buildings of a nineteenth-century country town that has been re-created on the site. For instance, in a reproduction of an old-time theater, a mechanical organ and piano accompany the silent movies. One building is a mechanized music museum, and it's there you'll see the bulk of the collection—which is heavy on Wurlitzer band organs. Fretty says he thinks he has one of the most comprehensive collections of Wurlitzer band organs in the world. There are also early nickelodeons, a tiny band organ, an accordion jazz player, and a fancy Leipzig-made orchestrion.

In Maine, you can visit the Musical Wonder House, a private museum of antique musical instruments set up in an immense old former sea captain's house by the Konvalinka family. When you visit—in the summer only—you'll see some 250 instruments—barrel organs, Austrian birds that chirp and whistle when you flick a switch; puppets that do magic tricks to the accompaniment of roundelays; musical furniture; and a mechanical music-hall-entertainer doll that tap dances, raises and lowers its head, turns from side to side, and winks in time to the music. The largest piece is the Steinway player piano. This can be played like an ordinary piano, from the keyboard, or played by ordinary music rolls. It also takes special "expression" rolls, which were recorded by great concert artists and composers themselves in a special way that would catch the nuances of their phrasing and dynamics. The Konvalinkas also own a store that sells music boxes, the Merry Music Box, in Boothbay Harbor. For information about both establishments, write the Musical Wonder House, 18 High Street, Wicasset, Maine 04578 (207/882-7163).

In New York, look for the Musical Museum in Deansboro. Among the oldest items in the collection is a prehistoric whistle, but the museum's main purpose is to show how far the world of entertainment had come by the turn of the century. The museum, which started out in the thirties as a family collection and was opened to the public in 1948, includes a number of Regina music boxes, a panoply of reed and pipe organs, plus music boxes that feature feathered caged birds that move their bills, flit from limb to limb, or pop in and out of a trap door. There is also a German-made Welte player piano that plays expression rolls, and a couple of Violano Virtuosos (mechanical violins that are activated by a punched roll: rotating wheels move along the strings; frets under the string raise and lower according to what pitch is desired).

One of the niftiest things about this museum is that you can play nearly all of the instruments yourself. Some people actually sit there making music all day. For information about hours, write the Musical Museum, Deansboro, New York 13328.

Also in New York, there's the Born- and Music Box Company in Pelham. The Bornands had been in the music box business for generations when, in the late 1800s, Joseph Bornand brought some of his workmen to America, where the new disc players had just replaced the old cylinder machines. Joseph's son's widow now runs the company, and she has opened up the family collection to the public. One of the most spectacular machines is a giant ebony model made for the Czar of Russia and elaborately decorated with bronze in 1874. There are also musical chairs, musical grandfather clocks, key-wind music boxes, cylinder-powered music boxes, disc-type boxes, and more. It's not only a very large collection, but a very fine one as well—everything is gleaming and in perfect working order. For information about seeing the collection, contact Mrs. Ruth Bornand at the Music Box Company, 139 Fourth Avenue, Pelham, New York 10803 (914/PE8-1506).

Where can you buy them? Music boxes are getting scarce. You just have to haunt the antique shops and hope you find something. Or you can go to Rita Ford, Inc. This store, at 812 Madison Avenue, New York, New York 10021 (212/535-6717), is full of music boxes of all sizes and types. Even if you're not looking to buy—and at prices that often start at $750 and go on up into the thousands, you might not be—Rita Ford's small store is a delight to visit. If you're desperate to buy a Regina and can't visit the store, write for the descriptive price list issued regularly throughout the year.

You don't have to own a music box to join a society. There are two societies you can join if you're interested in the subject: AMICA International (P. O. Box 666, Grand Junction, Colorado 81501) is mainly devoted to roll-actuated instruments, specifically pianos, but also orchestrions and nickelodeons. In addition to receiving a regular bulletin, members are given access to a mail auction at which members and members only can buy and sell rolls and related items, and are invited to conventions, where there are speakers, exhibits, and so on.

The Musical Box Society International is devoted to all mechanical musical instruments. Membership, open to anyone interested in the field, gets you a subscription to the bulletin, which contains technical information, a newsletter that informs you of chapter meetings, an annual meeting, and a mart. For details, contact the Society at Box 202, Route 3, Morgantown, Indiana 46160.

Paper

Crane & Co., Inc., has been owned by the same family since 1801. Crane made currency for use in the United States immediately after the Revolution, and it has made currency for South and Central American countries. It has also made paper for use as bonds, stock certificates, and stationary. Crane paper has been used for more different purposes than you would probably imagine. The company's history is delineated in the exhibits at the Crane Museum in Dalton, Massachusetts, on the Housatonic River in the Berkshires. You will not learn the history of papermaking, but you will learn how all-rag papers are made now, learn about the progress of papermaking from Revolutionary times to the present, and get to know the history of one papermaking family. Most of the artifacts are displayed in simple glass-topped trestle tables that stand on the polished floors of the old paper-mill building. For information about hours, write the museum in Dalton, Massachusetts 01226.

Another good paper museum is the Dard Hunter Museum at the Institute of Paper Chemistry, which is attached to Lawrence University (Appleton, Wisconsin, 54911). This museum is stocked with early handmade papers and rare books and manuscripts to illustrate the history of papermaking. You'll learn what watermarks really are and how they're made, and see the tools of the papermaking trade.

Historic Pharmacopoeia

Few subjects are so close to a person's heart as his health, or so quick to bring out his prejudices, quirks, and phobias.

So museums devoted to medical and pharmaceutical history, far from being the fusty, musty bastions of boredom that some people might think they are, are actually fascinating, even when the dioramas are amateurish (as they sometimes are) or the display techniques fairly crude. You learn about practices and remedies on which the people in days of yore relied every bit as fervently as their twentieth-century counterparts believe in yoga, yogurt, and jogging; about men, doctors mostly, who had to overcome the prejudices of their day to get people to accept new curative techniques; about women pharmacists and doctors, who, in ·addition, had to overcome prejudices against members of their sex working outside the home; and more. There are a few particularly interesting small museums that are worth visiting.

Hook's Historical Drug Store, on the state fairgrounds in Indianapolis, Indiana, is stocked with all sorts of herbs, patent medicines, pills, and powders. It also has a soda fountain where you can buy real chocolate sodas.

The Indianapolis museum's New Orleans counterpart, La Pharmacie Française (514 Chartres Street, New Orleans, Louisiana 70130), offers an even more complete view. The wall cabinets hold tincture and syrup bottles; wide-mouthed ("Salt-Mouth") bottles for powders and crystals; proprietary medicines containing herbs, tree barks, medicinal leaves, minerals and salts; and, in the prescription area, suppository molds, pill-rolling slabs and machines; cork-compressors used to make corks fit the uncapped bottles of the day; and early prescription books and filing systems. Here, too, there are plenty of patent medicines whose labels proclaim them to be positive cures for everything from consumption and scrofula to asthma or venereal disease. Godfreys Cordial and similar preparations contained opium, but they were on the shelves right along with the leech jars, the gris-gris (voodoo) items, and the rouges and powders. There are also some instruments on display: a scarificator, used to make the gashes necessary to bleed a person, is one of them.

In Chicago, an interesting museum is the International College of Surgeons Hall of Fame at 1524 North Lake Shore Drive. Even in a city full of museums, this one, installed in four floors of an old mansion, is a standout. There are paintings; old examining tables; antique artificial limbs; an amputation set that dates from Revolutionary War days; a "bone crusher" used for correcting bow legs; and an exhibit on trepanning (one surgeon did the operation with some prehistoric tools to prove that prehistoric men had probably used the tools he had in hand for that purpose). Not all the exhibits

are exciting, and the place does have a sort of musty cold smell to it, but you'll find plenty to hold your attention. The Convention and Tourism Bureau (332 South Michigan Avenue, Chicago, Illinois 60604) can give you details.

St. Louis has a similar establishment, the St. Louis Medical Museum, which you'll find in the St. Louis Medical Society Building. Some of the exhibits deal with St. Louis medical lore—herbs used in the area, for example, or locally famous physicians like Dr. Antoine Saugrain, a French immigrant who lived the last twenty years of his life in St. Louis, and Dr. Tom Dooley, who practiced his own brand of missionary medicine in the early days of the Vietnam War. There are exhibits of a nineteenth-century doctor's office, of an old pharmacy, and of Robert Wadlow, a young man studied by doctors at the Washington University Medical School. Wadlow was the tallest person in recorded history—nearly nine feet tall at the time of his death at the age of 22 in 1940. Another noteworthy part of the museum is its National Museum of Medical Quackery, set up with help from the U.S. Department of Health, Education and Welfare's Food and Drug Administration. Exhibits include items deemed useless for the purposes for which they're intended and are sometimes even dangerous. You may recognize a few of them: the Absorber Ad, the Inductoscope, De Ans Mittens, copper bracelets, the Ion-Lite Lamp, the Uranium Ore Sack, the Master Violet Ray & Helios Irradiator, Magnetic Ray Belts, the Morse Electric Belts, the Relax Acizor, the Slenderoll, and the Therapax Magnetic Wave Helmet. For details, write the museum at St. Louis Medical Society Headquarters, 3839 Lindell Boulevard, St. Louis, Missouri 63108.

Philadelphia medica. The historical places of health interest in Philadelphia—a good many that are interesting to visit, and some hospitals that are not—are discussed in a handsome illustrated little book, *Philadelphia Medica*, published by Smith-Kline Corporation as its Bicentennial project. Stackpole Books, Cameron and Kelker Streets, Harrisburg, Pennsylvania 17105; $4.95.

Tools

People who like to work with their hands often start collecting antique tools, and before they know it, they've opened a museum. Frank Wildung collected enough tools to fill the 86 x 40-foot Shaker Shed at the Shelburne Museum (Shelburne, Vermont 05482). The same thing happened to Wayne Phipps, of Burton, Ohio, except he added a wing onto his house to accommodate his fifteen hundred tools.

Also in Burton are the Geauga County Historical Society and the Western Reserve Pioneer Village. Then there's the Sloane-Stanley Museum—another situation entirely. At this institution, a cooperative venture undertaken by artist Eric Sloane and the Stanley Works of New Britain, Connecticut, tools are displayed as works of art rather than simply the tools they were. Write the Connecticut Historical Commission, 59 South Prospect Street, Hartford, Connecticut 06106, for further information about the museum, which is on the outskirts of the town of Kent in the southern Berkshires. After you've seen it, you'll look at tools in a different way. look at tools in a different way.

Collecting tools yourself. The spirit behind Eric Sloane's museum was the same spirit that moved the Shakers to make the objects of their everyday life so beautiful. It is entirely fitting, then, that one company that reproduces Shaker artifacts also sells antique tools. The company is the North Family Joiners, in the town of Housatonic in Massachusetts' Berkshires. For the details, write Box 567, Housatonic, Massachusetts 01236.

The City of Many Totems

Near Ketchikan, Alaska, you'll see one of the world's biggest assemblages. At Saxman Totem Park, about three miles south of Ketchikan, twenty-two totems tell such stories as the tale of the Raven and the Sun, the legend of the founding of the Eagle clan, and the legend of the hunter who winters in the wilds far from his tribe. Nearby, there are thirteen more totems at the Totem Bight Community House and Totem Park (Mile 9.9 of the North Tongass Highway), and, at the Totem Heritage Cultural Center (601 Deermont Street, Ketchikan), there are thirty-three totems and totem fragments. For further information, contact the Chamber of Commerce, 414 Mission Street, Ketchikan, Alaska 99901.

Toys

They're there in numbing profusion—at the Museum of Yesterday's Toys, 52 George Street in St. Augustine 32084; at the Museum of the City of New York in New York City; at the Shelburne Museum in Shelburne, Vermont 05482; at the Perelman Antique Toy Museum, 270 South Second Street, in Philadelphia. It's a subject that holds such fascination for so many people that you'll find some sort of display in almost every area that gets any visitors.

World Records

The people who gave you the Guinness Book of World Records have transformed their facts into photos, videotapes, and other displays that you can see at the Guinness World Records Exhibit Hall in the lobby of the Empire State Building in New York City. On a video screen, for example, you can watch as fifteen thousand dominoes fall; watch Babe Ruth and Lou Gehrig hit home runs; see the woman with the smallest waistline (thirteen inches—she is Mrs. Ethel Granger, an English actress, who, during her twenties and early thirties, reduced her waistline

from its normal twenty-two inches). There are photos of the longest mustache, the longest beard, a sword swallower, a bed of nails, and so on. To find out more, you can write the Exhibit Hall at 350 Fifth Avenue, New York, New York 10001. For details about New York City, contact the Convention and Visitors Bureau, 90 East 42nd Street, New York, New York 10017.

Some Collections of Collections of Americana

Quite a few of the major collections of Americana are in museum villages set up to show what life was like in a given period in American history. However, there are some major museums set up to show objects as objects.

The Shelburne Museum in Shelburne, Vermont, near Lake Champlain, is a far bigger establishment than you would expect to find in such a remote area. It is at once a collection of buildings and other large structures—a gleaming white side-wheeler, a lighthouse, a one-room schoolhouse, a general store, a church, and so on—and a collection of collections of objects. Carousel horses. Decoys. Cigarstore Indians. Ships' figureheads. Weathervanes. Woodworking tools and brass castings. Dolls—tiny ones made of seashells, bigger ones with stuffed bodies and porcelain heads. Quilts—including one that is intricately stitched with fruit and flower designs and was commissioned by the Singer Sewing Machine Company to show what its newfangled product could do. In each category (and this is just a sampling of the categories) there are *hundreds* of examples on display. The rural setting serves only to make your visit more pleasant. For further information, contact the Museum in Shelburne, Vermont 05482.

The Winterthur Museum, devoted almost exclusively to eighteenth-century American decorative arts, has few peers. The collection, assembled

by Henry Francis du Pont, is simply one of the greatest ever assembled. There are 195 rooms containing 40,000 items. Just to walk through quickly would take a couple of hours or more. The rooms are set up not so much to show how people lived during the eighteenth century—few had as much furniture in their rooms as you'll see in those at Winterthur—as to show off the individual pieces to best advantage. There are wing chairs, wing sofas, and Queen Anne, Chippendale, Hepplewhite, and Sheraton items by the score. Clocks. Silver. Candelabra. Paintings. Highboys. That you must make an appointment for a group tour of the main museum makes a visit there that much more meaningful. Each guide knows the pieces backward and forward; she can give you a standard talk about each of the gleaming rooms you visit, or she can emphasize items that particularly interest you—clocks, furniture, silver, whatever. If you don't want to take one of the three-hour tours, you can view fourteen rooms in the South Wing without an appointment. But that's only a tiny taste of what's in the other 181. In addition, there are special subject tours that cover the seventeenth century and the William and Mary period, the Queen Anne period; Chippendale, Federal, and Empire furniture; American silver; English ceramics; Chinese export porcelain; glass; American needlework; textiles; floor coverings; Pennsylvania German folk art; paintings; and interior architecture. These special-subject tours are for groups of four; the regular tours are for groups of six. The museum will put together the group if there aren't enough people in your party.

The spectacular gardens that are part of this thousand-acre estate—planted to look as if they'd grown up naturally—are really dazzling in the spring. Huge banks of azaleas and other flowering plants transform the woods into studies in pinks and reds and lavenders.

For information about the museum and the gardens, contact the Henry Francis du Pont Winterthur Museum, Winterthur, Delaware 19735.

A Special Note about Visiting Museums

Whenever you plan a trip around a visit to one specific site, call ahead to make sure that whatever it is you're going to see is still on display: occasionally objects are taken down for cleaning, or the museums are closed for remodeling or repairs. This is especially true of smaller museums. If they don't know you're coming, the proprietors may not be home when you get there.

Some Publications for Collectors

Every widely collected artifact has its collectors' society, and nearly every one of those societies has its newsletter, bulletin, or magazine. There are, for example, societies devoted to comic books, popular culture, model airplanes, circus memorabilia, barbed wire, clocks and watches, old lace, pencils, automatic musical instruments, carriages, air-cushion vehicles, music boxes, mechanical banks, and so on. Should you get interested in collecting something you see in a museum or an antique shop and want to find out more, you can generally find the names of the associations that can provide the information in the *Encyclopedia of Associations*, a giant reference book available in most libraries.

In addition, there are general publications for collectors.

Century House (Watkins Glen, New York 14891) publishes a number of specialized books and booklets about Americana: about collecting post cards, matchbook covers, toys, Victorian silver, old lamps, and so on. Many of the books have become collectors' items in their own right because each is printed in limited quantity. The publishers can send you a list of what's available at any given time.

Collector Editions Quarterly (170 Fifth Avenue, New York, New York 10010; $8.50 a year) covers contemporary collectibles like porcelains, plates, prints, paintings, stamps, coins, glass, paperweights, and various types of figurines. A good many of the items are "limited editions" about which you may receive information in the mail. The magazine is large, printed on slick paper, and is full of ads about yet other items you can collect.

The American Collector (Box A, Reno, Nevada 89506; $8 for one year, $14 for two years) is a monthly magazine that covers all sorts of collecting—everything from George III silver to matchbook covers. The format—close to tabloid size, on newsprint, big and thick.

Foreign and Ethnic Affairs

International Travel at Home

If you can't go to the foreigners, get them to come to you. A number of organizations will get you in touch with foreigners who are anxious to visit Americans: write COSERV, 1630 Crescent Place, N.W., Washington, D.C. 20009; People-to-People International, 2201 Grand Avenue, Kansas City, Missouri 64108; Servas, P. O. Box 790, Old Chelsea Station, New York, New York 10011.

Learn a Language on Your Vacation

Sweating it out at your local university extension isn't the only way to go. In two or three weeks in an intensive language-learning course, you can master the vocabulary and grammar well enough to get you through most social conversations in the country—when you do get to go. Besides, learning can be fun.

Where to go?

Berlitz can teach you just about any living language in just about any corner of the world. You can study French in Quebec, for instance. But even apart from the variety of languages you can learn, Berlitz rates high among instruction programs because there are no earphones, tapes, film strips—or English. From the moment you walk into your lesson, your teacher speaks the language you're supposed to learn. And you do learn. Classes are available, along with tutorials and two-to-four-student semiprivate lessons. Figure on about $300 for 40 semiprivate lessons in a popular language like French or Spanish, but the cost will vary depending on where you go and what you study. For more information, contact your local Berlitz school or write Berlitz Schools, Research Park, Building O, 1101 State Road, Princeton, New Jersey 08540.

The Experiment in International Living, in Brattleboro, Vermont. Three times a year—in July, August, and January—the School for International Training of this private nonprofit organization sponsors language programs emphasizing speaking and listening comprehension of Arabic, French, German, Greek, Italian, Japanese, Mandarin, Portuguese, Russian, and Spanish. You spend 25 to 30 hours a week in small, informal classes—the equivalent of a year of college language study. Cost: about $350; $115 extra for room and board on campus. Also available by special arrangement are tutorials in nearly 40 other languages—everything from Bengali to Swiss-German, Gujarti, Hiligaynon, Ilokano, Twi, Urdu, or Wolof—among others. Instruction costs $275 per person per week, based on a two-person class; room and board about $50 per person per week.

For details and up-to-date prices, contact the Department of Language Education at the School for International Training of the Experiment in International Living, Brattleboro, Vermont 05301.

The New School's Guadeloupe Courses. The New School for Social Research, New York City's school for continuing education, offers an intensive week-long program in French on the Caribbean island of Guadeloupe. Mornings and evenings are devoted to lessons. The rest of the time is free for exploring. The fee has always been about $600 per person based on double occupancy, including tuition, lodging, recreation, breakfasts, and round-trip air fare from New York. For details, contact the school's language division at 66 West 12th Street, New York, New York 10011.

Around the World— without Crossing an Ocean

You don't have to go very far to be

reminded that North America was settled by people from all around the world. There are communities in which the customs are still what they were in the Old Country; there are places where the citizenry tries hard, against considerable odds, to preserve the local heritage with festivals and fiestas of various degrees of spontaneity and authenticity; there are places with buildings that recall the Old Country.

Sounds of Music—Stateside

Not a few Europeans came to New England and then went back home again impressed with how similar the White and Green Mountains were to their Alps back home-sweet-home. A few stayed on in America and promptly built chalets—whether to stave off homesickness or to capitalize on their accents no one can say. Nevertheless, there they are, those chalets, brooding over the American mountains to this day.

Some of the more notable spots include the Trapp Family Lodge, in Stowe, Vermont, a ski and summer resort in the northern part of the state, and the Mittersill Alpine Inn in Franconia, New Hampshire. The Trapp Family Lodge, built by the Trapp Family of *Sound of Music* fame, is a cozy, low-ceilinged, curlicue-trimmed old chalet more Austrian than most you find in Austria. The Austrian fingers in the kitchen have made the schnitzels-and-kartoffeln menu among the most popular in the area. In summer, it's almost impossible to get a reservation. Meanwhile, at teatime, the cafe is jammed with sightseers drawn to the establishment by tales of buttery pastries mounded with whipped cream and cunningly contrived concoctions that meld flavors not often seen together on American menus. The Trapp Family Lodge also sponsors a wonderful and unique Christmas celebration. For details, contact the lodge in Stowe, Vermont 05672.

Another resort, the Mittersill Alpine Chalets, while not quite so authentically Austrian looking, still does a close resemblance to the real thing (when you close your eyes to the American cars in the parking lot), and the White Mountains are pleasant enough. From some points of view, it really does look like Austria. For details, write the Chalets in Franconia, New Hampshire 03580.

The Caribbean in Canada

A ferry-boat cruise, a ball and a dance, a parade and a lot of Caribbean music all along make up the Caribana Festivals held annually at the end of July in Toronto, Ontario. For information and ticket request forms, contact the Caribbean Cultural Committee, 632B Jonge Street, Suite 1, Toronto, Ontario, Canada M4Y 1Z8.

Chinatowns

Almost every large city in the United States has its Chinese community—invariably one of its most exciting corners. The food in the groceries and markets is different from what you find elsewhere. You can't read the labels on the cans or the packages, and you don't recognize the contents unless you know the cuisine. In the markets hang dried fish and crisp roasted ducks. The vegetables are only vaguely familiar looking. The talk in the shops and in the streets is a firecracker of baffling sounds. The old customs die hard. Western and Oriental ways are so different that an even slightly occidentalized Chinatown still seems terribly foreign. If you're curious, you can spend hours and hours taking it all in.

Chinatown in San Francisco is the largest Oriental community outside Asia. In school, the kids learn calligraphy and Chinese language and history. Drug stores dispense herbal compounds rarely found outside China. There are dozens of restaurants and shops, especially along Grant Avenue, the so-called Street of Twenty-Five Thousand Lanterns. The Chinese Historical Society of America Museum, at 17 Adler Place off 1140 Grant Avenue, tells the story of the Chinese in America with artifacts and photos. The Chinese New Year celebration is among the most raucous and lively anywhere on the continent. Firecrackers sputter and cherry bombs explode against the near-constant drone of cymbals, gongs, and brass percussion instruments. Groups of ceremonial lion dancers nod their grotesque papier-mâché heads as they whirl and hop through the narrow streets. At the main event, the Night of the Dragon Parade, a colorful, glittering 120-foot-long human-powered dragon twists and writhes down Grant Avenue, weaving from one sidewalk to the one opposite, dodging firecrackers and bobbing its ritual of a dance. Spangles, feathers, and beads encrust the costumes of still other fabulous creatures which, with the press of the crowds, make it almost impossible to move.

Afterward, there are special New Year's banquets in all the restaurants: the foods are supposed to bring good fortune for the New Year. For details, write the San Francisco Convention and Visitors Bureau, 1390 Market Street, San Francisco 94102.

All the other Chinatowns ring variations on these themes; the bigger the Chinatown, the more exotic and foreign it will seem.

Second in size to San Francisco's Chinatown is that of Vancouver, British Columbia, concentrated west of Main and East Pender. For more information, write Tourism British Columbia, 1117 Wharf Street, Victoria V8W 222. Chinatown in New York City is also vast; concentrated along Mott, Pell, and Doyers streets, shops, restaurants, markets, and grocery stores crowd every crannied side street. A recent change in immigration laws has resulted in still more expansion of the Chinese community, and a still more diverse assortment of eateries and wares. A good source of information for the schedules of Chinese New Year's events is Emile Bocian at the Chinese Post, 11 Allen Street, New York, New York 10002. General information about Chinatown and the city is available from the Convention and Visitors Bureau, 90 East 42nd Street, New York, New York 10017. *New York's Chinese Restaurants*, by Stanley and Arline Miller and Rita and James Rowan, published by Atheneum in July 1977, has so far proved itself an excellent guide to the best food in an area that is full of it. At the end of the book there are fascinating sketches of the changing immigration patterns that produced the sudden boom in Szechuan restaurants. They tell you about *Dim Sum*—the tea lunches on Sunday mornings for which Chinese and occidentals are now turning out in droves. When you go, you'll be served from steel carts laden with pastries, dumplings, bean curd skin delicacies, and dozens of other foreign specialties that will leave you feeling something like an English explorer meeting an Indian for the first time. In addition, the authors sketch Chinatown's produce markets, butcher shops, fish markets, food factories, bakeries, and such—on Bayard Street, the Bowery, Canal, Catherine, and Division streets, East Broadway, Mott, Mulberry, and Pell streets. Atheneum, 122 East 42nd Street, New York, New York 10017; $4.95.

More Chinatowns: in Boston, write the Convention & Tourist Bureau, 900 Boylston Street, Boston, Massachusetts 02115. And in Chicago, details are available from the Convention and Tourism Bureau, 332 South Michigan Avenue, Chicago, Illinois 60604.

Chinatown in Honolulu, downtown, is the typical pastiche of fish, meat, and produce markets, herb shops, tea shops, noodle factories, confectioners —but here the buildings are mainly two-storied affairs trimmed in turn-of-the-century gingerbread, and there are lei stands as well as restaurants. The Chinese Chamber of Commerce (42 North King Street, Honolulu, Hawaii, 96817) offers tours, usually on Tuesdays, and can tell you about noodle factories and confectioners that welcome onlookers.

A Chinese Museum. The amazing cultural heritage of China is displayed in almost every large museum in the United States and Canada. Devoted entirely to artifacts from the Orient is the Oriental Institute Museum, 1155 East 58th Street, Chicago, Illinois 60637.

Czech Fests
One of the biggest is the Oklahoma Czech Festival, held every year on the first Saturday in October in Yukon, the Czech capital of the state. Men, women, and children haul out their fanciest native costumes. Folk dancers do the *beseda* to the accompaniment of a polka band. *Kolbasy* are on the menu, along with plenty of *kolaches*—sweet rolls with fillings of poppy seeds or jams. In the early evening, the action moves to the Yukon Czech Hall for Czech bands and more dancing. For details, contact the Oklahoma Czechs, Inc., Box 211, Yukon, Oklahoma 73099.

Variations on this theme can be found in Prague, Oklahoma, where a Kolache Festival is held in early May every year; in Montgomery, Minnesota, just south of Minneapolis, besides a *kolache*-eating contest, there's a parade that brings in the state's top bands and drum corps, and plenty of

polka dancing Wilson, Kansas, is the Czech capital of that state and the site of the Wilson Reservoir where you can go camping and boating after you've had your fill of food and music.

For details, contact the Chambers of Commerce in Prague (Box 223, zip 74684), Montgomery (100 East Elm Avenue, zip 56069), or Wilson (zip 67490).

Florida's Little Cubas
There are two. The Ybor City area of Tampa, Florida, has been a sort of little Cuba ever since the 1880s, when a series of fires and labor troubles brought the cigar industry up the coast onto the mainland from Key West. Wrought-iron balconies illuminated by gaslights look down on antique brick sidewalks and malls. Local bakeries turn out long loaves of Cuban bread on palmetto fronds. There are cigar factories, Spanish restaurants, Spanish coffeehouses, and heavenly aromas to go with them. You wouldn't think you were in Florida.

There are big festivals in mid-February as part of the 74-year-old Gasparilla Celebration in Tampa. People dress up in costumes, watch the pirate invasion, dance in the streets, and enjoy the *Fiesta Sopa de Garbanzo*, the Spanish bean soup festival, for its free soup, Cuban coffee, and bread. For details, write the Ybor City Chamber of Commerce, 1509 Eighth Avenue, Tampa 33605.

Even larger is the more recently established community in Miami. Well over half of Miami's population of seven hundred thousand is Cuban-born; in the phone book there are more columns of Rodriguezes than Smiths. Walking around the Cuban sector, which is centered at S.W. Eighth and Flagler streets, you can buy religious items, books, greeting cards in Spanish, oil paintings, guitars, filigreed jewelry, mantillas, comic books (in Spanish), and Scrabble games (in Spanish). Coffee stands sell *cafe y leche*, coffee and milk, or *cafe tinto*, black coffee that is locally described as "black as the devil, hot as Hades, pure as an angel, and sweet as love." There are markets where mangos and plantains keep company with avocados and more kinds of beans than you ever imagined. And restaurants: some two hundred Latin establishments, including some that are very fancy and some that specialize in home-style cooking, *comidas criollas*. You can eat oysters with lemon and salt, black beans and saffron rice, pickled fish, foot-long Cuban subs, paella, and pastries filled with custard or almond paste (baked or deep-fried, then covered with a sifting of sugar). After dinner, there are Spanish movies, swish Spanish supper-club shows—pageants of pulchritudinous females done up in feathers and spangles and not much else. For more information, contact the Greater Miami Chamber of Commerce, P. O. Box 4219, Miami, Florida 33101.

A Danish America

The little town of Solvang and the surrounding Santa Ynez Valley go all out for Danish Days, an annual event in mid-September and one of the biggest bashes on the southern California events calendar. Solvang is fairly Danish to begin with: the roofs of the buildings, though not made of real thatching, sometimes look as though they were. The walls are half timbered. The sidewalks are cobbled. There are four windmills.

But for the festival, it almost seems that the most Danish things about Denmark are moved in for the moment. Hans Christian Andersen, that great Danish literary figure, is remembered in special window displays in the shops and there are readings of his stories. There are folk dancing exhibitions, showings of Scandinavian movies and exhibitions of spear riding. More people wear Danish costumes than are worn in Denmark. Perhaps the most popular events, though, are the *aebleskiver* breakfasts at which people from all over the town cook up batches of these Danish specialties, which are a little like pancakes and a little like waffles and which, here, are most often topped with raspberry jam and a sifting of powdered sugar. For details on other events, contact the Solvang Business Association, P. O. Box 465, Solvang, California 93463.

Dutch Treats

Believe it or not, the heaviest concentration of windmills in the United States is around East Hampton, Long Island. However, for a little Holland, you want to visit Holland, Michigan, or Pella, Iowa. Both towns were settled by Dutch refugees from religious intolerance; both still retain quite a bit of Dutch character—a lot of which seems surprisingly genuine. Pella, the boyhood home of Wyatt Earp, has a historical village that tells the story of the Dutch settlers in eleven buildings (pottery and blacksmith shops, a log cabin, gristmill, museum, etc.). At a craft house there you can watch a descendant of the original Hollanders chipping out wooden shoes with tools brought over by the town's first shoemaker. Holland, a town of about twenty-five thousand, has more going on. The most celebrated attraction, a two-hundred-year-old De Zwaan windmill, the last working mill the Netherlands government allowed out of the country, was shipped in some seven thousand pieces, then reassembled by a Hollander. The mill, surrounded by a vast tulip bed, grinds graham flour when the wind is right, and the sight of those eighty-foot arms sailing through the air, reaching as high as a twelve-story building, is pretty impressive. Costumed guides give you tours of the mill, then introduce you to the Klompen Dancers. In the Netherlands Museum, rooms have been set up in nineteenth-century Dutch style; the Poll Museum is jammed with antique autos, trains, carriages, and fire trucks. And that's just the beginning.

Both towns are at their best at the height of the blooming seasons in early to mid-May—when the fields are bright with tulips as far as you can see—and it's then that all the townspeople turn out in the costumes of their grandparents and great-grandparents, dance in the streets, march in parades, and make more ado than usual about Dutch eats like *Uitsmijter* (roast beef or ham laid on bread, then topped with fried eggs) or *Erwtensoep* (split pea soup served with Dutch rye bread). In Pella —and in Orange City, in the northwest part of the state—the townspeople even get out and scrub the streets. For details, contact the Chambers of Commerce in Holland (3 East Eighth Street, zip 49323), Pella (507 Franklin, zip 50219), and Orange City (125 Central Avenue, S.E., zip 51041).

Tour a Wooden Shoe Factory

Then take home a pair. The De Klomp Wooden Shoe Factory is at 257 East 32nd Street in Holland, Michigan; another establishment, the Wooden Shoe Factory, is at U.S. 31 at 16th Street, Holland, Michigan. The zip for both is 49423, in case you want to write ahead.

Some Looks at English America

Described by one English visitor as "a distorted dream of home concocted by homesick Englishmen who spent their lives supervising the Empire," Victoria, British Columbia, is as determinedly English as nearby Vancouver is American. Consider the Empress Hotel, an elaborate pile of stonework; the Conservatory full of potted palms; the elderly dowagers in wicker chairs, and the afternoon teas. Or the double-decker buses. Or the dazzling Butchart Gardens. Victoria would feel more than slightly English even without the assorted bits of Shakespeariana installed for the benefit of visitors who want their days filled up with "attractions."

Then, of course, there's Stratford, Ontario, the home of the immense, important, and excellent Shakespeare festival. It also has some wonderful grounds and gardens on either side of the Avon River.

For further information, contact the Chambers of Commerce in Stratford (38 Albert Street, N5A 3K3) or Victoria (1020 Government Street, V8W 1X7).

The Basques

The first weekend in July every year the population of Elko, Nevada, in the northern part of the state on I-80, nearly doubles as campers, sightseers, and assorted other merrymakers come to join the fun at the National Basque Festival. After the obligatory all-American small-town parade (led by the oldest Basque to be found in the town), the assembled throngs chorus the Basque National Anthem, and the festival really gets underway with Basque games and contests that in one way or another occupy everybody for the rest of the weekend. Fifty pounds in each hand, contestants attempt the walking weight carry; youngsters have a wood-chopping contest and their elders compete to see who can lift 250-pound cylinder weights the most times in a minute. There's a tug of war and a sheep-hooking contest. And a granite-ball lift: the real strongarms of the town see who can lift this mammoth ball to the shoulder, then circle it around the neck. The program lists the activities as "Euzkal jokoak; arrijasotze, txing-aeroate, ardi txakurrak, soka tira, aizkora . . ." There's a handball tourney, a contest in baking sheepherder's bread, and a competition in Basque yells—long, wavering hollers that are part laugh, part shriek, part horse's neigh. Sunday morning is celebrated with an outdoor mass; that afternoon there's an enormous Basque meal. And throughout the weekend, there's some of the fastest dancing ever: Basque folk-dancing groups from all over Nevada and Idaho take their turns twirling, spinning, and leaping to the accompaniment of flute, accordion, and tambourine. In the evening, Basque bands play for everybody.

To find out more, contact the Chamber of Commerce, P. O. Box 470, 1601 Idaho Street, Elko 89801. As there are also many Basques living around Boise, Idaho, you can also see Basque festivals there. For a list, contact the Idaho Department of Tourism and Industrial Development, Capitol Building, Boise 83720.

A Little France in Missouri
The oldest settlement west of the Mississippi, Sainte Geneviève, Missouri—now a town of about five thousand—was founded in the early eighteenth century by Frenchmen who were mining lead in the region; at one time the town competed in size with St. Louis not far away.

The French language has long since disappeared from the town, except on menus, where words like *quiche* and *oeufs* appear. But quite a few of the old buildings are still standing along the placid streets, and the townspeople remember their heritage as proudly as DAR members look back on theirs. Once a year, in honor of the town, they celebrate the Jour de Fête à Sainte Geneviève—which is as good a time as any to see the points of interest. In addition to touring the homes, though, you can visit a French market, browse for antiques, and watch the townspeople perform "La Guignolée," an ancient French song and dance that dates from the Middle Ages.

For more information, contact the Foundation for Restoration, 34 South Third Street, Sainte Geneviève, Missouri 63670.

Germany
If it's Germany you want to visit, you'll have only one trouble: deciding just where you want to go. There are the restaurants in Milwaukee—Karl Ratzch's, especially, where, though the atmosphere is a little fancier than what you might find across the Atlantic, the food is nearly identical. The Rhine? Try the Rhine of America—the St. John River Valley between Fredericton, New Brunswick, and Saint John. A version of Oktoberfest? The Wurstfest around New Braunfels, Texas—where the drinking and the sausage-eating and the dancing go on for 10 days, until everyone has loosened his belt as far as it'll go and staggered home so many

times he doesn't really want to repeat it. And there's always the Old Country, the Busch-operated theme park in Williamsburg, Virginia: the beer hall there is modeled after the party halls of Munich and differs from them only in that it's bigger.

The Schuplatte dancers, oom-pah bands, flags, shields, beer, and German food by the platterful that you find in Williamsburg also are part of the goings on at other German festivals: the Maifest, held in mid-May in Hermann, Missouri, for instance; or the Bavarian Summer Festival, an annual July event in Barnesville, Pennsylvania. In Barnesville, there are also tons of soft pretzels, amusement-park rides (including a nifty old hand-crafted carousel), Maypoles, flowers. The Budweiser Clydesdales—immense and handsome horses—make an appearance; and a team of other powerful Belgians pulling an old-fashioned beer wagon periodically takes a turn around the grounds. The German Alps Festival in the Catskills, Hunter Mountain, New

York, lasts about three weeks and, during that time, the Clydesdales make another appearance, along with zither and accordion players, hot-air balloonists, wood carvers, hang-gliders, puppeteers, antique collectors, and hundreds of spectators who wander through the grassy fairgrounds, stop at the enormous beer hall in a tent, and toast their friends and perfect strangers and go home happy as clams. At the Frankenmuth, Michigan, Bavarian Festival, in June, hundreds of thousands line up for the kickoff-day parade, admire the Bavarian Inn's thirty-five-bell glockenspiel, carillon, and its *wetter haus*, weathervane. And there's a five-thousand-square-foot dance floor for polkaing. Also: crafts displays, historic tours, and acrobatics exhibitions. Biggest of all these events, perhaps, is the Kitchener-Waterloo Oktoberfest, held in the twin cities of Kitchener and Waterloo, Ontario—for in addition to everything you find at each of the others, there are big sports contests. For example,

Canada's biggest running marathon—the Canadian answer to the United States' Boston marathon—is there. And there are hockey tourneys, motor-cross races, handball demonstrations, and speed-skating championships.

Here are sources for more information: the Milwaukee Convention & Visitors Bureau, 808 North Broadway, Milwaukee 53202; the New Brunswick Department of Tourism, Box 12345 Frederickton, New Brunswick E3B 5C3; the Wurstfest Association, Box 180, New Braunfels, Texas 78130; the Old Country, P. O. Drawer FC, Williamsburg, Virginia 23185; the Maifest, c/o the Hermann Chamber of Commerce, Hermann, Missouri 65041; the Bavarian Festival Society, Inc., Box 90, Kempton, Pennsylvania 19529, for the Barnesville affair; the German Alps Festival, P. O. Box 297, Hunter, New York 12442; and the K-W Oktoberfest office at 77 Ontario Street, P. O. Box 1053, Kitchener, Ontario N2G 4G1.

Odyssey

The Greeks have been pulling up sponges since the time of Aristotle. They made it their livelihood in Greece, then moved to the waters around Tarpon Springs, Florida, where the substances they used in Greece to pad the breastplates of warriors came to be sold to tourists to take home for washing cars, dishes, and babies. Although they've been in the United States for over three-quarters of a century, the Greeks have retained their national identity more than most other ethnic groups. When you visit Tarpon Springs, you can't help but be impressed with the Greekness of the place. To be sure, Tarpon Springs is no Greek island paradise. But the food is Greek, the coffee is Greek, the seafood is cooked with Greek flair. The people that you see as you stroll up the seawall—the main drag—are brawny, olive-bronze, dark-eyed. There is ouzo and retsina. And, of course, the sponges: tiny sponges and giant sponges a foot across and shaped like a cup, and sponges strung on ropes and hung as rings.

Tarpon Springs is interesting just about any time you go, but special super-Greek festivities are scheduled at Easter, Christmas, on Apostles Day at the end of June (heralding the return of the spongers), and at Epiphany, when the Archbishop blesses the fleet, divers dive after a cross, and a dove is freed—all symbolic.

For more information, contact the Greater Tarpon Springs Chamber of Commerce, 112 South Pinellas Avenue, Tarpon Springs 33589.

More Greeks. In Chicago's Greektown, there are lots of Greek restaurants serving retsina and flaming cheese and more Greek specialties than you've probably heard of unless you've lived Greek before. For details, contact the Convention and Tourism Bureau, 332 South Michigan Avenue, Chicago 60604.

Iceland West

North America's largest Icelandic settlement is in Gimli, Manitoba, near Winnipeg, on the shores of Lake Winnipeg. Islendingadagurinn is the name for the settlement's annual festival in celebration of the area's heritage; it takes place every year at the beginning of August or the end of July. You can get dates plus the latest information about ethnic events, entertainments, and contests from Manitoba Government Travel, 200 Vaughan Street, Winnipeg, Manitoba R3C OV8.

Little Italy

There's hardly a city on the continent without its Italian population and at least a handful of Italian restaurants, if not an Italian market as well. Baltimore, Maryland, for instance, has a street full of Italian restaurants; Providence, Rhode Island, has a huge, if scattered, Italian population, whose influence is felt almost everywhere in the metropolitan area.

But for real Italian ambience, you can't beat the Little Italys in Boston, Massachusetts, New York, New York, and San Francisco, California, where the Italian neighborhoods just go on and on, in an amazing parade of blocks and blocks of Italian groceries, Italian bakeries, Italian butchers—all of them stacked, piled, and stuffed with items in counters and bins and on shelves. There are shiny vats of salty olives, espresso, Tuscan peppers, homemade pasta, prosciutto, rounds of provolone, and glistening, burnished wheels of parmesan.

If there's any adulteration of the Italian character of these neighborhoods, it's more by other encroaching ethnic groups than by garden variety American culture. New York's Little Italy, for example, is hard put to hold its own against a growing Chinatown.

For more information, contact the respective city tourist offices: the Baltimore Promotion Council Information Center, 22 Light Street, Baltimore 21202; the Rhode Island Development Council, One Weybosset Hill, Providence 02908; the San Francisco Convention and Visitors Bureau, 1390 Market Street, San Francisco 94102; the New York Convention and Visitors Bureau, 90 East 42nd Street, New York, New York 10017; and the Convention & Tourist Bureau, 900 Boylston Street, Boston 02115.

Some Outposts of Japan

San Francisco is the town for Japanese culture: not only is there a whole five-acre Japan Town (albeit one established by dint of a big urban redevelopment project), but there is quite a lot of Japanese business transacted in the area. The Miyako Hotel, all fourteen stories, has sunken tubs and Japanese bathrooms. You can get Japanese-style rooms with mats and mattresses on the floor, or Western-style rooms. The Japan Center is focal point for a Cherry Blossom Festival featuring a tea ceremony, Japanese films, dance, exhibits of origami, and exhibits of flower arranging, every year in April; the harvest time is celebrated in the fall with more tea ceremonies, folk dance and judo exhibitions, cooking and karate demonstrations. For details, contact the Convention and Visitors Bureau, 1390 Market Street, San Francisco 94102.

In New York, one of the most Japanese of Japanese restaurants outside Japan is Hatsuhana at 17 East 48th Street (212/355-3345).

A Japanese garden: in Vancouver, British Columbia, on the grounds of the University of British Columbia, there's the Nitobe Memorial Gardens. The narrow graveled pathways take you through a world of very studied understatement: instead of masses of bright blossoms, there's a stalk of iris here, a sprout there against a hulk of a dark boulder whose form is mirrored in a lake. Quite a peaceful place. For more information about it, you can write the Botanical Garden at the University of British Columbia, 6501 N.W. Marine Drive, Vancouver V6T 1W5.

The Lithuanians

More ethnically diverse than most other American cities, Chicago has its Lithuanians as well as its Poles, Swedes, Germans, Greeks, Ukrainians, Mexicans, Puerto Ricans, Serbs, Chinese, Japanese, Italians; the Lithuanians have their museum: the Balzekas Museum of Lithuanian Culture at 4012 South Archer, 60632. One room is dedicated to famous Lithuanians, and there are lace displays, a set of armor, many paintings by and of Lithuanians, and a display of medals. The museum can send you more information; the Convention and Tourism Bureau, 332 South Michigan Avenue, Chicago 60604, can send city information.

Mexican

You don't even have to cross the border to savor that mañana mentality or the exhilarating spirit of a Latin celebration: there are fiestas in Chanute, Kansas (zip 66720), in September; in San Juan Capistrano, California (zip 92675), in May; and in Marysville, California (zip 95901) in September. For details, contact the Chambers of Commerce.

All That Is Polish

The Polish Museum, at 984 Milwaukee in Chicago, has a fantastic collection of everything, but everything, relating to the history of the Poles in America. For details, contact the museum, zip 60622.

The Scandinavians Celebrate

The Syttende Mai in Norway was the day that the Norwegian constitution was signed; in the United States, it's the occasion for a good deal of celebrating, in towns like Poulabo, Washington, and Spring Grove, Minnesota. Spring Grove's festival is especially interesting. The streets are decked out with Norwegian flags and the stores put up signs identifying themselves in Norwegian. Norwegian is still commonly heard in coffeeshops and taverns; English is spoken with an accent. During the festival, the Sons of Norway and the elementary-school children, all in costume, demonstrate Norwegian folk dances. *Everyone* dances in the street on Friday and Saturday nights. On Sunday, there's a church service in Norwegian, and afterward, a big feed: *lefse, krumkake, søtsuppe,* and *rømmegraut* are all there, in delicious quantities.

For more information, write the Minnesota Department of Economic Development, 480 Cedar Street, St. Paul 55101.

The Scots' Gatherings

At a Highland Games, you can buy meat pies, scones, strawberry tarts, tartans, and plaids by the yard. Or you can pick up a pot of heather to plant in your yard, buy some bagpipes, or investigate your family background.

In one corner of the field where the games are held, a solitary piper paces back and forth. Above the high throaty whine of the bagpipes rises the roar of the crowd: a man in kilt, undershirt, knee socks has just tossed a 4-foot 2-inch 22-pound wooden hammer farther than all the other competitors. Later, the caber toss begins. The judges start off with a trimmed tree trunk too big to be thrown, and they keep sawing off chunks until someone will try it. Another man in a kilt and undershirt steps forward, grasps one end of the pole, then, in a flurry of grunts and groans and grimaces, he heaves! And the caber goes end over end through the air. The Highland Pentathlon moves on. There are shot puts; 56-pound weight throws. There are competitions in Highland dancing. Little girls, agile as elves, wearing kilts hardly bigger than a sleeve on their brawny fathers' shirts, leap and swirl through the intricate steps of sword dances, *seann triubhas,* sailor's hornpipes, Irish jigs. There may also be competitions in solo dancing, demonstrations with sheep dogs, and tugs of war (more grimacing, more grunting). Or Celtic fiddling. The pipes whine, the dogs yap, the fiddles play merrily, the colors swirl. The Highland Games are part three-ring circus, part high-school track meet. Before you know it, the kilted pipers and drummers have massed together on the field, and in a huge swelling of sound and a glinting of silver buttons against dark doublets, they're piping the grande finale—and an invitation to come back. Grand? That's just the half of it.

Not all the Highland events are featured at every Highland gathering, but the good ones—and those that are listed here are a few of them—will give you plenty to see and do.

The Stone Mountain Highland Games in Atlanta, Georgia, are held in mid-October. A special feature is a series of Scottish cultural seminars

that cover tartans and Highland dress and its symbolic meaning, the history of Highland dancing and how it's judged, the history of the bagpipe, how it's played and how competitions are judged. For details, contact the Games at 1090 Lanier Boulevard, N.E., Atlanta 30306.

The Ligonier Highland Games and Gathering of the Clans of Scotland, in Ligonier, Pennsylvania, outside Pittsburgh, are held in September. Events and band competitions follow each other fast and furiously; there's a Scottish fair, too. For details, contact the games' sponsors at 1208 Twenty-fourth Avenue, Altoona, Pennsylvania 16601.

The Grandfather Mountain Highland Games and Gathering of Scottish Clans, in MacRae Meadows, on the slopes of Grandfather Mountain near Linville, North Carolina, are held every year on the second Saturday and Sunday in July. In addition to the highland dancing, the sheep dog demonstrations, the piping competitions, the side-drumming and tenor-drumming, the variety show, and the country dancing, there are AAU-sanctioned track-and-field events, and a marathon run (26 miles, from Boone, North Carolina, to MacRae Meadows). This is Appalachian mountain country—not quite Scotland, but beautiful nonetheless. For details, write the games c/o Linville, North Carolina 28646.

The Dunedin Highland Games and Festival, in Dunedin, Florida, about 15 miles from Tampa, are held in March and are one of the biggest in the United States. In addition to the competitions, there's a fair of Scottish goods; a *ceilidh*, variety show, in which the dances you see at the competitions are done as exhibitions; and an evening ball at which everyone gets to try Scottish country dancing—something like square dancing. For details, write P. O. Box 507, Dunedin 33528.

The Highland Games of Nova Scotia, in Antigonish, Nova Scotia, held every July, are large and famous; the people there, some say, are more Scottish than the Scots themselves. There are other noteworthy games, though, in nearby St. Ann's on Cape Breton Island. Even in normal times the Gaelic college there, the only one in North America, is a hotbed of Scottishness; you can see for yourself just about any time if you drop in on one of the classes in Gaelic language, dancing, singing, or piping. But there's yet more activity during the annual Gaelic Mod, for in addition to games there are all sorts of Scottish folk art exhibitions. Afterwards, you can visit the school's handcrafts center and museum, where there are displays of memorabilia concerned with one Angus MacAskill—a 7-foot 9-inch giant. And Cape Breton

Island is, as any good Scotsman will tell you, just like the highlands of his home. For details, write the Department of Tourism, Box 456, Hollis Building, Halifax, Nova Scotia B3J 2R5.

Swisstown

There are Swiss towns and there are Swiss towns. On the one hand, you've got those whose Swissness goes only skin deep: the architecture is about the extent of it. Helen, Georgia, in the northern part of the state, in one of the greenest parts of the Blue Ridge, is one such town. Pretty as those red roofs are against those evergreen hillsides, clean-looking as the buildings' white-stuccoed walls are, it's not Switzerland. Nor is the ski village of Schuss Mountain, near Mancelona, Michigan. Same goes for Vail, Colorado. Similar, yes, but not the real thing. You'll come a little closer in one of the several "Switzerlands of America." There is Ouray, Colorado, where the mountain peaks are as craggy and irregular as the Alps, and in the "American Alps," the local appellation for the Sawtooth range where the famous resort of Sun Valley, Idaho, is located.

But the real Switzerland is a pastiche of all of these places, plus those where a version of the Swiss culture really does flourish because they were settled by Swiss whose descendants, at special festivals, carry on the traditions: yodeling, blowing those 15-foot-long alpenhorns, eating Swiss food such as *nusli*, *bierenbrot*, and *lebkuchen*. New Glarus, Wisconsin, is one of the most tenaciously Swiss of these Swiss-settled towns: most of the townspeople still have Swiss names, and a good many still speak the dialect of Swiss-German that was spoken in Switzerland at the time of the emigration. Three festivals a year rouse the citizenry to holiday fervor: the Heidi Festival, in June, in which the big event is a reenactment of the famous story by Johanna Spyri; the Wilhelm Tell Festival, of which the main feature is a rousing outdoor drama that tells the story of the thirteenth-century hero's struggle against his country's Austrian overlords (on Labor Day weekend); and the Swiss Volksvest, which includes the folk dancing, flag throwing, yodeling, and alpenhorn blowing that were sidelights at all the other events (in August). New Glarus, in southern Wisconsin not far from Milwaukee and Chicago, is quite a pleasant rural place, surrounded by fields full of Holstein and Brown Swiss cattle, neat farms with giant silos, and green rolling hills; it's also the home of the Swiss Museum Village that tells you all about the Swiss settlement in this neck of the woods, and the Chalet of the Golden Fleece, a replica of an old Swiss chalet. For more information, contact the Chamber of Commerce in New Glarus 53574.

There are other festivals—the Berne Swissfest, at the Zwingli Church in Berne, West Concord, Minnesota, held every year the second Tuesday in August, and the Ohio Swiss Festival in Sugarcreek, Ohio, held usually at the end of September or the beginning of October. Both feature events such as *steinstossen*—heaving a huge stone for distance—and *schwingfest*, Swiss wrestling. The Swissfest usually begins with a parade in which costumed people wave the Swiss and American flags, plus flags from each of the Swiss cantons; there's a program afterwards at which some of the singing, dancing, and yodeling groups from New Glarus perform. And plenty of food. The Ohio Swiss Festival, in a cheese-producing area, devotes a lot of its activity to cheese, and lots of people eat lots of cheese. For details, contact the Berne Swissfest in West Concord, Minnesota 55985; or the Ohio Swiss Festival in Sugarcreek 44681.

Melting Pot Festivals

When you've had your fill of tamales and falafel, you can wander over to where they're stuffing up pita bread sandwiches or dishing out helpings of curried chicken. Or get some lasagne or a Danish open-faced sandwich, or a Latvian roast goose, or Polish doughnuts. At the Holiday Folk Fair in Milwaukee, Wisconsin, members of dozens of national groups start cooking and freezing as early as September for the November event, and there are between two and three hundred different kinds of foods available. Around seventy thousand people come every year for the food alone.

But in addition to the gustatorial diversity, there are folk-dance shows, pageants, exhibits about life styles in various countries—and dancing, some to watch, and some to do yourself. To buy: Spanish castanets, Italian pottery, little German figurines, Czech cut glass, Danish blue Christmas plates, Japanese lacquer, Japanese puzzle boxes, Swiss music boxes, Greek woolen shoulder bags, wooden shoes, pins from east India, and on and on: this is one of the biggest events in the Midwest. For details, contact the Holiday Folk Fair, 2810 West Highland Boulevard, Milwaukee 53208.

More fairs, not quite so big. In Detroit, the summer is full of fairs (you can get details from the Public Information Department, 1008 City-County Building, Detroit, Michigan 48226); in Pittsfield, Massachusetts, an Ethnic Fair draws about twenty thousand to the Berkshire town in late August (the Central Berkshire Chamber of Commerce, 107 South Street, Pittsfield 01201, can send details). Also, for nine days every August in Red Lodge, Montana, there's a Festival of Nations, which features pageantry, dancing, food (the Chamber of Commerce, Red Lodge, Montana 59068, can provide the details).

Around the World— in Trinidad

Trinidad. African Ashanti, Ibo, Yoruba, Hausa, Mandingo, and Rada tribes, English, Spanish, French, Bengalese, Parsees, Madrassis, Dutch, Portuguese, Lebanese, Syrians, Venezuelans, Chinese, East Indians, and a thousand other races give the country its strange culture. The calypso and steel drum culture that grew up can be seen around Carnival time; the cosmopolitan nature of the country can be felt in the architecture of Port-of-Spain, the capital: the buildings are modern, Victorian, Gothic, Arabian, and there are monasteries, mosques, synagogues, minarets, and such. In the spring, the Moslems celebrate Hosein, three days of chanting, drum-beating, ritual stick-fighting, and parades. The Hindus light votive oil lamps for a festival of lights that also has them plunging into the sea for a purification ceremony. There is an equal variety of food. For more information, write the Trinidad and Tobago Tourist Board at 400 Madison Avenue, New York, New York 10017.

The West Indies as They Used to Be

Ruins, sleepy villages that are slightly tumbledown, a mountain shrouded in mist, feathery coconut palms, coral reefs, and beaches—the sand as fine as talcum powder, but eerie and coal-black: that's Nevis, at the northern end of the British Leeward Islands. You can spend the night on the estate first owned by William Nisbet, whose beautiful young widow, Fanny, was later wooed and won by Horatio Nelson. St. Kitts, across the Banana Bay, is full of cane fields and is topped off with the immense Brimstone Hill Fortress—uncrowded, gentle, and very, very grand. There are fine places to stay: the Golden Lemon, as exquisite as you'd expect of a holstery set up in a seventeenth-century French stone manor house by a man who reigned at *House and Garden* for fifteen years ("for the discriminating few who like to do nothing in grand style"), and Rawlins Plantation, a guesthouse-inn on a working plantation that sits in the middle of cane fields on top of a three-hundred-fifty-foot-high hill with a spectacular view across the Caribbean to eight-mile-distant St. Eustatius.

For more information, write the St. Kitts-Nevis Tourist Board, 39 West 55th Street, New York, New York 10020; the Nisbet Plantation Inn, Nevis, West Indies; the Rawlins Plantation, Box 340, St. Kitts, West Indies; and the Golden Lemon, Dieppe Bay, St. Kitts, West Indies (110 West 15th Street, New York, New York 10011, during the summer).

Spice, banana, and coconut plantations, and exotic tropical flowers—bougainvillea, oleander, hibiscus, flamboyant, orchids, lilies—are part of what makes St. Lucia such an interesting place to visit. Fire has destroyed the main town, Castries, a couple of times, so it has a modern, glossy shine. But the houses have a sort of garden villa look that is pleasant, and the landscape—the vegetation plus the mountains and the volcano Soufrière—have a very Caribbean feel. There's a fascinating twisting road to Soufrière, whether you go along the West Coast or the East Coast. The town of Soufrière, right at the volcano's base, is a picture-postcard affair, full of pastel houses, golden strands, quaint fishing boats, pretty children. From there, you can drive up to the volcano, and, surrounded by vast clouds of steam, explore the caldera. The St. Lucia Tourist Board can answer questions and provide details; write c/o the Eastern Caribbean Tourist Board at 220 East 42nd Street, New York, New York 10017.

Fairs and Festivals

State Fairs (Etc.)

The rural life comes to the city at the state fair; it's the biggest Saturday night in town of the year for the farmers and their spouses and their offspring who bring their prize livestock, their prize baked goods, their exhibits on how to freeze properly (and how not to freeze), their Grandmother's Blue Ribbon Chocolate Swirl Cakes, their Christmas decorations, their art work, their quilts, and their year's best sewing projects. The city dweller (wandering from exhibit hall to shed to midway, stopping en route to munch corn on the cob or pizza or footlongs—with or without a cornmeal mush wrapping that makes them corn dogs—or snow cones or soft ice cream) gets a very intimate glimpse into what people are *really* doing in their spare time. Sometimes it doesn't bear much resemblance to what magazines make you think that just *everybody* is doing. Between the home shows and the livestock, and the midway and the food and the manufacturers' exhibits of just about anything you can name, and the horse races and the live big-name entertainment, it's a straight-across-the-board picture of the Real America, better than anything you'll ever see on TV in a thousand years. State fairs and county fairs—they're worth planning a trip around. Write the state and provincial information offices for dates of the big ones in your area.

Big Fairs in the Midwest and the East

Every midwestern state has its giant state fair, as often as not straight out of a Pat Boone movie of the fifties. Those in Indiana and Wisconsin are among the biggest.

However, there are also a few approximations thereof in the northeastern and mid-Atlantic states—more than you'd expect. Except for the Big E, in Springfield, Massachusetts, they're smaller, to be sure, but they serve: the Great Danbury State Fair, in Danbury, Connecticut, in October; the Delaware State Fair, in Harrington, Delaware, in July; the Skowhegan State Fair, in Skowhegan, Maine, and the Northern Maine Fair, in Presque Isle, Maine—both in August; the Great Cumberland Fair, in Cumberland, Maryland, in August, and the Maryland State Fair, in Timonium, Maryland, during the first half of September; the Topsfield Fair, in Topsfield, Massachusetts, in October; the Hopkinton Fair, in Contoocock, New Hampshire, in early September; the Great Allentown Fair, in the Pennsylvania Dutch Country, in Allentown, Pennsylvania, in August; the Reading Fair, in Reading, Pennsylvania, in June; the Rocky Hill State Fair, in East Greenwich, Rhode Island, in August; and the Vermont State Fair, in Rutland, Vermont, in September. The Tunbridge World's Fair in Tunbridge, Vermont, is a boisterous, even rowdy county fair—one of the biggest in the state.

Fairs in the West

The endless displays of combines and harvesting equipment from John Deere and International Harvester—all shiny red and grass green—give way in the West, for the most part, to ranching equipment, fruit-picking equipment, and such: the Maricopa County Fair, in Phoenix, Arizona, in April; the California Exposition and State Fair, in Sacramento, California, from late August into the first week in September; the Western Idaho Fair, in Boise, Idaho, in late August and early September, and the Eastern Idaho State Fair, in Blackfoot, Idaho, in early September; the Multnomah County Fair, in Portland, Oregon, in early August, and the Oregon State Fair, in Salem, Oregon, held late August through early September; the Utah State Fair, held in Salt Lake City, Utah, in September; and the Western Washington Fair, in Puyallup, Washington, in September. The Los Angeles County Fair, held in Pomona, California, every September, is the largest such event in the nation.

The World's Largest Annual Exhibition

The Canadian National, held annually in Toronto, Ontario, at the end of August, is more than a state fair: to keep the nearly 4 million visitors happy over the 6 days of the event, the operators have got to do something. And so they set up exhibits of the latest developments in home care products. Exhibits of fashions for kids. Of electronics, transportation, communication. Of agriculture. There's an international shoppers' market. There are big-name entertainers every evening; the grandstand in which they perform holds twenty-five thousand spectators. One day, free food samples are given away. And the midway is a mile and a half long. For information, write the Canadian National Exhibition, Toronto, Ontario, and the Toronto Convention & Tourist Bureau of Metropolitan Toronto, 112 King Street West, Toronto, Ontario.

The Last Camptown Fair

The races that we all doo-dahed about in the Stephen Foster song probably took place at a camptown not much different from the one you find on the outskirts of Philadelphia, Mississippi, as part of the Neshoba County Fair. This annual August event is in many respects like many other county fairs: there are arts and crafts shows, gospel sings, high school band concerts, beauty pageants, musical stage shows, square dances, a midway, livestock exhibitions, and harness racing (the only harness racing in the state, in fact). What makes the Neshoba County Fair different, however, is its camptown. When the number of days of the fair was increased from one to three, back in 1890, fairgoers began to build small cabins where they camped during the event—and they kept on building them over the years until today there are about 350 of these rather rickety two-story structures arranged along walkways shaded by immense oaks that were planted by a beautification committee in 1898. The atmosphere in the camptown during the festival is about as close as the South will ever see to Woodstock. Here, it's a distillation of the summer evenings' porch life, the warm and friendly best that small towns can offer. The food available to day visitors on the grounds is not much to jump up and down about—it's your basic hamburger-and-hot-dog menu. But the people who own the cabins do their own cooking, and once you get to talking to one of them, you can almost count on getting asked back for some fried chicken. It's that friendly.

Besides the cabin life and the racing and the gospel singing and such, politics is the lifeblood of this festival. You've always heard that Southerners like politics—well, here's the proof. Everybody sits around in the big pavilion for what seems like hours on end listening to speaker after speaker—candidates for tax assessor and collector, county attorney, chancery clerk, circuit clerk, county superintendent of education, constable, state senator, state land commissioner, commissioner of insurance, secretary of state, state treasurer, attorney general, and so on up the line until you get the candidates for lieutenant governor and governor. The political wisdom in this part of the world is that if you don't make it here, you're not going to make it, brother. So there is, besides the considerable speechmaking, considerable handshaking, backslapping, baby kissing, and button pinning. It's a show that has few equals these days. The Neshoba County Fair Association, 207 Beacon Street, Philadelphia, Mississippi 39350, can send you the details about "the world's largest house party."

Fat Tuesdays and Other Mad Carousings

car'ni val, n. (Fr. carnaval; It. carnevale; from, LL. carnelevarium, from hyp. carnem levare, to remove meat; associated by folk etym. with ML. carne vale, "Flesh, farewell!" from L. caro, carnis, flesh, and vale, farewell, from valere, to be strong.) 1. the period of feasting and revelry just before Lent: Mardi Gras is the last day of this festival. 2. a reveling or time of revelry; festivity; merrymaking. . . .

For centuries, Europeans have been celebrating the Carnival season with general abandonment to masked orgies of dancing, drinking, loving. There's a method in this madness: the old saw that if everyone could enjoy carnival at least once a year, there'd be no need of psychiatrists, has its measure of truth. Through the hangovers that are part and parcel of the frenzy, you're purged. Cured of what ails you. Inhibitions that keep you from letting go, barriers that keep you from knowing people that are different from you, and all the mannered ways that keep society hanging together in a more or less orderly fashion the rest of the year simply have no place in the brightly colored, glittering never-never land come to earth that is Carnival.

The Wild Ones

They're in New Orleans, Louisiana; in Port of Spain, Trinidad; and in Quebec City, Quebec.

The New Orleans Mardi Gras celebration actually gets moving just after Christmas with a string of balls so private that some New Orleans high-society ladies may only sit and watch, and a series of weekend parades. But that's not what you go for.

What you go for are the last few days before Fat Tuesday, when parades full of wondrous floats glittery enough to drive a magpie mad jam the narrow streets of the Vieux Carré and a motley crowd of collegians, sightseers, and various and sundry other merrymakers mill around brown-bagging beer and cheap wine or sipping hurricanes—a potent fruit-and-booze drink sold at a place called Pat O'Brien's. On the balconies of hotels in the French Quarter, hoydens in low necklines and ropes of costume jewelry toss kisses to the hoi polloi below. The streets get filthy with all the people and all the drinking. One of the more reputable of the jazz bars in the area closes down during the wildest period. But it's all good fun, and you can't help but feeling that if there is a place on earth where peace reigns, with good will to men, it's New Orleans. You should plan months in advance for lodging; for details and for information about the parades (Bacchus, Proteux, Rex, Comus, and the all-black jivey Zulu), contact the Greater New Orleans Tourist and Convention Commission, 334 Royal Street, New Orleans, Louisiana 70130.

Some good books about Mardi Gras.

Mardi Gras: A Pictorial History, by Leonard Huber ($4.95), jammed with photos that illustrate the festival's long history; *Mardi Gras*, by Robert Tallant ($4.95), which gives anecdotes and some how-to; and *Bacchus*, a pictorial volume by Myron Tassin ($12.50), which traces the development of the krewe of Bacchus, sponsor of one of the parades (the book has an introduction by New Orleans author Frances Parkinson Keyes). All three are published by Pelican Books, 630 Burmaster Street, Gretna, Louisiana 70053.

In or out of the Mardi Gras season, visit the Mardi Gras Museum at 516 Wilkinson Street in the French Quarter, to see, close up, the elegant costumes worn by the parade participants.

Jouvay—and Afterward—In Trinidad

From the Jour Ouvert—*jouvay*, in Trinidad talk—until midnight of Shrove Tuesday, Port of Spain is a madhouse, a kaleidoscope of bobbing bodies costumed in pink, red, blue, green; of black faces and white faces, and faces that are coffee colored and faces that you can hardly see for the feathered, sequined headdresses. The costumes here—for which Trinidadians will spend a year's savings—are all coordinated by a *mas camp*, a planning center for the masquerades, the *mas*, which are at once the center and the background for the carnival in Trinidad.

It lasts more or less two days. The masquerade—which is combination masque, parade, and street dance—is presented in five acts. The parade on Tuesday elaborates the themes of the masquerade, and unmasked revelers join the mummers. Steel bands—they're called panmen here—beat the time to the chipping—the mincing parade step-dance. The air throbs with the music. Trinidadians leap into the air, over and over and over, working

themselves into a rapture and putting on such a show that the staidest American throws his self-control to the trade winds. The dancing gets faster and faster, moving in a massive crescendo that takes the throngs into ecstasy. It ends with the stroke of midnight that signals Ash Wednesday—the end of Carnival and a return to business as usual that is so sudden that, but for the broken costumes heaped in the streets and the litter, you might think it all a dream. For details and the information you need to plan far in advance, contact the Carnival Development Commission, 76 Queen Street, Port of Spain, Trinidad, West Indies.

Quebec and Bonhomme Carnival

This giant papier-mâché snowman reigns over the old city from January until Ash Wednesday, during which time the city is a mob scene. There are ice sculptures to inspect, a terrifying toboggan slide near the Château Frontenac (the Rapunzel-towered hotel that dominates the town's skyline), curling bonspiels, skating and skiing contests, a dogsled derby, masked balls, floats, parades, and a boat race across the iced-over St. Lawrence. Every chunk of cobblestone, it seems, is crowded with high schoolers, college kids, and other visitors. The great treat is a ride in one of the open horse-drawn carriages, cabrioles, decked with sleigh bells and buffalo lap robes, through the snow-covered streets—and there's always snow. For details on places to stay, contact the Carnaval de Quebec Organization at 290 Rue Joly, Quebec, Canada.

A *caveat about Carnival*. You won't find an atmosphere of total abandonment without crowds, and in cities that are designed to accommodate lots of people anyhow, crowds mean so many

people that service in hotels and restaurants—as well as traffic—reaches its most unpleasant. If you're looking to enjoy the city, don't go at Carnival time.

Some More Saturnalia

You'll find Carnival madness in Grenada; for details, contact the Grenada Mission, 866 Second Avenue, New York, New York 10017.

Also in Haiti; for details, contact the Haiti Government Tourist Bureau, 30 Rockefeller Plaza, New York, New York 10020.

There's a carnival in the Virgin Islands; for details, contact the Virgin Islands Government Tourist Office, 10 Rockefeller Plaza, New York, New York 10020.

For details about Mardi Gras in Louisiana's Cajun Country, contact the Lafayette Parish Convention and Visitors Bureau, P. O. Box 51352, Lafayette, Louisiana 70501.

Details about the Mardi Gras festivities in Georgetown, Colorado, are available from the Chamber of Commerce, zip 80444.

Contact the Tourist Department of the Mobile Area Chamber of Commerce, P. O. Box 2187, Mobile, Alabama 36601, for information about that city's Mardi Gras.

The Biloxi Chamber of Commerce, P. O. Box CC, Biloxi 39533, can send a schedule for the Carnival goings-on of the Mississippi Gulf Coast.

RaRa

Between Ash Wednesday and Easter, RaRa, another mad African-touched carnival, is held in the town of Leogane, Haiti, about 20 miles from Port-au-Prince. Judas Iscariot is burned in the pageantry. For more information, contact the Haiti Government Tourist Bureau, 30 Rockefeller Plaza, New York, New York 10020.

Merry Christmases

For a while there, it didn't look as if Christmas was going to get very far in the New World. Up in New England, the Puritan fathers were scowling furiously at any hint of seasonal frivolity. Down in New Amsterdam, which had fallen on hard times, old Peter Stuyvesant had gone so far as to dispatch night watchmen to snoop around his colonists' houses, just to make sure that nobody was wasting energy having a good time.

But by the middle of the nineteenth century, the Puritans had lost their stranglehold, and crotchety Peter Stuyvesant and his wooden leg had gone the way of Christmas past. The St. Nicholas/San Nicolass/Sinterklaas of the New York Dutch and the jolly white-bearded, red-cloaked Father Christmas of the English had become a single, fabulous figure. Washington Irving had invented a Santa Claus who hauled parcels down chimneys; scholar Clement Clarke Moore had rhymed of the "little round belly/That shook, when he laughed, Like a bowl full of Jelly"; and Thomas Nast, political cartoonist, had portrayed the ringleted, pipe-puffing elf in a way that still puts each and every street-corner bell-ringing imposter to shame.

Add all that to the tradition of feasting and jollity and wassailing and Yule logs that got started in England and never really expired in Virginia, and you've got a fair portrayal of how we arrived at Christmas today and what sort of ingredients you'll find at Christmastime happenings in country inns, hotels, resorts, and cities around the country.

Plan well in advance—some of the more elaborate affairs book up as much as a year ahead.

An Austrian Christmas with the Trapp Family

Along with sleigh rides, Christmas tree hunts, rosy cheeks, and friends whooshing in from the cold and stomping the snow off their feet, Maria von

Trapp will remember, when she thinks back on the Christmases she knew in her Austrian homeland, the old custom of marking a room off-limits to the children. The kids weren't admitted until Christmas Eve, by which time the tree was decked, the packages were wrapped and stacked under the tree, and the candles—real candles—on it were lit. When the doors were flung open, the youngsters would charge in like hounds after a squirrel. Unwrapping the gifts waited until after the family had caroled a round of "Silent Night" and exchanged wishes for a blessed Christmas.

Maria and her son Johannes, the youngest of the Trapp crew when the family fled Austria in the forties, share the holy customs (with only a few variations) with Christmas guests at their Trapp Family Lodge, a cozy old low-ceilinged, pine-paneled chalet more Austrian than many you find in Austria. The lodge would be festive even without snow on the ground or fir branches and wreaths greening every paneled window, lamp post, and scrollworked nook and cranny.

On Christmas Eve, Maria von Trapp relates the story of her Christmases once again, and Johannes rings a little bell at the proper time, a signal that the Christmas angel has just left the living room. Guests who have deposited their presents at the desk on arrival retrieve and open them after the carol. There are real candles on the tree, and cookies, straw snowflakes, and other old-fashioned ornaments. Christmas dinner? A bounty of schnitzels, smoked pork chops, and Austrian pastries mounded with buttery frosting and whipped cream. And afterward—skiing downhill at Mt. Mansfield or cross-country on some sixty miles of over-the-golf-course-and-through-the-woods trails. You'll come sliding back through the fading afternoon with an appetite as big as Vermont's great outdoors. The after-dinner glow and good friendship that follow are the sort you'd expect to find at a gathering of some larger-than-usual family clan.

The reason for the warm feelings is, at least in part, a peculiarity of the reservation system worked out to deal with the Lodge's popularity: before November 1, reservations are accepted only from previous guests. To get a place the first time around, you have to be among the first callers on November 1, the day reservations are opened to the public. Details: the Trapp Family Lodge, Stowe, Vermont 05672.

An Elegant Christmas at the Greenbrier Hotel

If you can imagine a resort that makes details its fetish, then imagine how it would go about staging the most stupendous Christmas ever. Then imagine something thrice as magical, and you've more or less pinned down the holiday celebration at the Greenbrier Hotel in White Sulphur Springs, West Virginia. For it's at Christmas that this grand resort hotel's unflagging attention to the little things works its most dazzling effects.

Not a single lobby, parlor, sitting room, or ballroom escapes the blizzard of red and green. Wreaths, swags, candle rings, poinsettias, red velvet bows and baubles are hung, piled, and massed on walls, tabletops, and mantelpieces. A twenty-foot-high tree towers over the lobby; life-sized Santa Claus and reindeer—carved in ice—glisten at the entrance; an ice angel surrounded by tiny white lights sparkles at the rear door.

By nature, the Greenbrier is sumptuous without being even slightly nouveau riche, genteel without being hidebound, and old-fashioned without being antiquated; it is the embodiment of good taste and good manners. And since good manners involve allowing other people their privacy, the Greenbrier is generally somewhat formal.

At Christmas, the hotel loosens its stays.

On Christmas Eve, even the grown-ups go out and comb the acres of manicured grounds for a Yule log, haul it back, and hover like mother hens until it's burning. After the candlelit dinner, Santa arrives in a real sleigh to pass out stuffed animals to the kids. Christmas Day, there's eggnog and brunch and a mammoth dinner: suckling pig, pheasant, plum pudding; a boar's head is paraded around the enormous dining room, and at the appropriate time, madrigal singers carol "Oh Bring on the Figgy Pudding."

What else to do? Tennis, swimming, massages, and other spa activities. For details, contact the hotel at White Sulphur Springs 24986.

A Nantucket Christmas

Christmases on Nantucket Island, Massachusetts, are seldom white, but once the summer people have gone, there's a wild wind-swept feeling to this Atlantic landfall that makes a fire-warmed parlor seem just that much cozier. The Jared Coffin House, an inn installed in one of the finer Federal homes lining the island's cobbled streets, has some of the snuggest salons this side of the mainland. This can be attributed as much to the house itself (a marvel of high ceilings, gleaming antiques, elegant chandeliers) as to the cranberry wreaths and evergreen ropes entwining the carved moldings and swoop of the spiral stair-

case: there's no overkill here—just enough decoration to remind you what season it is.

As if you could forget. The house is crammed to the rafters. There are punch parties, cocktail parties, wassail parties, large and small, planned and impromptu, which fill the house with companionable banter and the spicy smells of cloves and brandy and citrus and cinnamon. Guests exchange jokes; tales of politics in their cities and small towns; views on the future of Christmas, Nantucket, God, Mankind, America. "Singles," says innkeeper Philip Read, "soon become doubles and triples, triples become parties of four, parties of four become parties of six." It's all like some exceptionally jolly house party—except that there's never any pressure to join the group. When and if you please, you can go off and stroll the trackless beaches, admire the salty weather or the Christmas trees along the main street. As for the food, it's abundant and arresting. No "it's-so-easy-to-fix" at *this* house party. The lighting of the Yule log and the Christmas candle, appropriately solemnified, a boar's head procession, and a splendid banquet (all on December 21 or thereabouts) kick off a "Twelve Days of Christmas" gala menu that will have you banqueting on roast goose, venison, and such. You can get steaks and seafood from the main menu if you want, and when the big day comes, there's turkey on the table and fixings as traditional as the Christmas Eve services at the Congregational Church down the way. For reservations for the antiquey doubles, write the inn at 29 Broad Street, Nantucket 02554.

The *Nantucket Whole Island Catalogue*, by Dick Mackay (Sankaty Head Press, Box 18, Siasconset, Massachusetts 02564; $3.95 plus 50¢ postage), is the best guide to other island goings-on, places to eat, things to see.

Beefeaters on Parade

During the Christmas season, the famous museum village of early nineteenth-century New England life—Old Sturbridge Village in Sturbridge, Massachusetts—goes about business as usual, because in the days that the restoration represents, celebrating Christmas was one of those things that you just didn't do. Were you to stroll along the dirt streets of Sturbridge this season, you'd see potters at their wheels, farm laborers joisting bales of hay, a blacksmith at his anvil. The delectable odors filtering out of the farmhouse are those of an ordinary midday meal. Down the road, the Publick House, a vast rambling clapboard inn old enough to have welcomed General Lafayette and his son, is serving quiet Christmas dinners.

So what's the fuss about Sturbridge at Christmas?

Actually this town's bows to the customs of the mother country come before Christmas, on the Saturday and Sunday of the second and third weekends in December. The innkeeper pulls all stops for one of the most sumptuous Christmas pageantries this side of Edwardian England, one of those meals that makes gluttons of even the most prudent eater. Minstrels sing, wenches dance, and there are tales about the meaning of the Christmas candle and Christmases far and near. Toasts are offered to health and fortune. And Beefeaters—in their scarlet and gold uniforms—pour the wassail, then shoulder the roast suckling pig, the goose, the turkeys, the hams, roast beef, and the boar's head to parade them underneath a greenery-draped balcony and present them to the innkeeper whose duty it is to taste the meat, pronounce it fine and fit to eat, and invite his guests to present themselves at the festal board. In addition there will be venison, tongue, crab, rosemary-roasted chicken, shrimp, and more different kinds of salads and side dishes than even Henry VIII, that great gourmand, would have expected at one table at one time. For dessert: a proper English pudding and a very up-to-date ice-cream pie. Rooms in the inn, with tip-tilted doors and primitive antiques, go for about $28 a night; the feast, for which you'll want to reserve a year or more ahead, costs about $20. For details, contact the Publick House, Sturbridge, Massachusetts 01566.

Celebrate Christmas in Yosemite with Washington Irving's Squire of Bracebridge

It's hard to say which stands out more in Yosemite at Christmastide—the white-on-white mountain scenery of snow-tufted trees, white-blanketed meadows and waterfalls frozen into lacy sculpture, or the Bracebridge Dinner, which for over fifty years has been an institution as important as the Ahwahnee Hotel where it's presented.

Part pomp and pageantry, part concert, part six-course feast, the Bracebridge Dinner is based on the Squire of Bracebridge, a character first met in Washington Irving's *Sketch Book*. With members of his family, all in satins and velvets and furs, Bracebridge offers up a holiday dinner to some three hundred fifty guests in a dining hall half the size of a football field.

"Nourish laughter! Gloom destroy! Bright pleasure to this feast is bidden.

And he with frown best keep it hidden!" With this the cue is given for the start of a string of rhymes, stirring carols, and a procession of courses— the fish, the peacock pie, the boar's head, the baron of beef, the flaming plum pudding, the wassail—that has everybody sitting at table for three and a half hours. It's all so splendidly theatrical that even at $40-plus a head you don't mind very much that the "peacock" in the pie is but ordinary fowl.

To get reservations, make sure your check arrives on the second Monday in January; any later than that and you won't get a spot. For details, write the Yosemite Park and Curry Company, Yosemite National Park, California 95389.

An English Christmas in Williamsburg

When Yuletide rolls around, Williamsburgers deck their halls and their doors in the manner of their eighteenth-century forebears, with holly, braided branches, pinecones, tawny lemons, scarlet berries, and apples. White tapers stand like silent benedictions in the paned windows. Walk tranquil Duke of Gloucester Street, absorbing the feeling of peace on earth that

seems especially strong in this outpost of the past, and you encounter groups of carolers, cloaks flapping in the brisk winter breezes, on their way to the Governor's Palace, to Bruton Parish Church, or the Capitol, where there are concerts nearly every day.

Though Christmas Day itself was quietly celebrated as a holy day, the season that preceded it was a time of merrymaking and revelry. And so, in Colonial Williamsburg, there are Colonial Games, pie-eating contests for kids, hoop rolling, bag and foot races, penny pitching, quoits, cannonball throwing, and lawn bowling. Another day, there might be festive militia musters with fifers, drummers, and musketeers. Williamsburg at Christmastide is also a gastronomic blowout with its Fish House Punch Reception and Groaning Board Banquet; the Old Dominion Dinner, on Christmas Eve; the Chesapeake Bay seafood feasts and the champagne breakfasts. For reservations and rooms, contact Colonial Williamsburg Visitor Services, P. O. Drawer B, Williamsburg, Virginia 23185.

City Christmases on Both Coasts

The harbinger of Christmas in New

York City is the arrival of the Christmas tree at Rockefeller Center, just after Thanksgiving. But for a while, nothing much happens. The tree stands there dark and empty. Though the counters and racks in the stores are jammed, nobody's buying. There's a concert, an evensong in a church somewhere, and someone at one of the corporate headquarters buildings along Park Avenue drapes some strings of white lights on a couple of the plane trees outside his building. Near Bloomingdale's, a solitary Santa Claus clangs his bell.

When does it happen? One day, workmen on scaffolds festoon the Rockefeller Center tree, and dozens of others around the fountains at its base, with tiny jewel-lights and enormous balls; the Channel Gardens are empty. And the next day, it seems, the tree is a blaze of lights, the wire-sculpted angels in the gardens are trumpeting "Christmas!" to the city.

The trickle of shoppers becomes a flood. The bells of dozens of Santa Clauses make a din at every street corner. Barricades are set up around Rockefeller Center to direct celebrants flocking to Radio City's big Christmas show. On Park Avenue, all the plane trees are covered with white lights. Can you help but catch your breath? Can you resist the spell the city is spinning?

Visit FAO Schwarz, which has furnished the booty underneath the tree at the red-and-green bedecked Plaza Hotel, and watch the kids in this most splendid of toy stores. Or stop at St. Patrick's or St. Bartholomew's or any of a dozen other churches where choral concerts seem to echo from the earth to the heavens. Or travel to the Metropolitan Museum and hunt up the Medieval Hall for a look at the Baroque Christmas Tree, all hung with angels and cherubs carved by some of the finest artists of eighteenth-century Naples. The stores of Fifth Avenue, all asparkle and ashine with seasonal glitter, open up on Sundays; the Avenue is a pedestrian mall where jugglers, madrigal singers, carolers, street musicians, and other performers dispense more of the good cheer you've already found at the museums, the puppet theaters, the churches, the tiniest boutiques and craft shops—each of which does something special to toast the holidays. The spirit of Christmas willing, the New York City Ballet presents the *Nutcracker*.

Check the winter calendar of the New York Convention and Visitors Bureau, 90 East 42nd Street, New York, New York 10017, for the latest information.

If any other city can come close to New York City's charms at Christmas, it's San Francisco. There are twice-daily performances of the *Nutcracker* by the San Francisco Ballet, baroque music and carol concerts in the Grace Cathedral, a Christmas party for the gorillas at the zoo, and the tableau of the Nativity set up in Golden Gate Park. Carolers, some of them in costume, ride the cable cars. If you think it might not be Christmasy because of the fine, mild weather, think again. The St. Francis Hotel (Union Square, 415/397-7000) sets up an elaborate gingerbread-and-marzipan fairy castle; at the Fairmont there are carolers, a thirty-foot tree, and a Christmas dinner that features Crab Louis, ham, Long Island duckling, turkey and chestnut dressing, and an English plum pudding with hard sauce (California and Mason streets, 415/772-5000). For more information, contact the Convention and Visitors Bureau, 1390 Market Street, San Francisco, California 94102.

A Southwestern Christmas

The celebration in Santa Fe, while not a traditional white Christmas scene but a meld of the Southwest and Indian elements of the culture, says "Christmas" to the people of the region quite as strongly as Christmas lights on the tree at Rockefeller Center mean "Christmas" to other Americans.

Thousands upon thousands of *luminarias*—the brown paper lunch bags half filled with sand in which lighted candles are planted—flicker along sidewalks, roads, roof lines, patios, especially on Christmas Eve, in a sort of Southwestern version of the electric-light displays in the East. During the season, the Cochiti, Jemez, Picuris, Santa Ana, San Felipe, San Juan, Taos, and Tesuqe Pueblos hold elaborate dances, processions, feasts. San Miguel Mission, an old Spanish church that is supposedly the oldest in America still in use, reenacts "Las Posadas"—the search for the inn—from mid-December until a few days before Christmas.

There is more of the same—and somewhat bigger displays of *luminarias*—in Albuquerque; there, in addition to the reenactment of "Las Posadas," "Los Pastores" is performed.

For specific dates and times and information about where to stay and eat, contact the New Mexico Department of Development, 113 Washington Avenue, Santa Fe 87501.

Some Currier and Ives Christmases

For a picture-postcard Christmas—Trapp Family Lodge Christmases minus the Austrian accent—look into some of the tiny New England inns. Some examples:

The Inn on the Common, in the Northeast Kingdom of Vermont has an ultraquaint setting on a town common presided over by a handsome clapboard church; plus Christmas trees, homey ornaments, and lots of natural greenery. The bedrooms in the annex across the street have fireplaces and wood-burning stoves that make snuggling down after the walk back from the midnight service all the cozier. Getting up on Christmas morning, after that, would be a chore if it weren't for the promise of that day's feast: cornbread stuffing, apples and cabbage, brussels sprouts in cream and cheese, and a special native Vermont turkey, grown for the occasion, which is juicier than the ordinary variety. For details, write the Inn, at Craftsbury Common, Vermont 05827.

The Inn at Sawmill Farm, in West Dover, Vermont, in the southern part of the state, is a converted barn. This inn has made a tradition of its Christmas Eve scenario—a seven-course roast-beef-and-Yorkshire-pudding dinner, a tramp across the snowy fields to a midnight service at the village church, tree trimming afterwards over sparkling Burgundy and Christmas cookies, caroling, and a late-night walk in the woods. Write the inn in West Dover, 05356, for details.

The Homestead, in Sugar Hill, New Hampshire, is made extra-special by the energetic kindness of Mrs. Serafini, the incredibly capable whirlwind of a lady who owns the place and sees to it that the silver napkin rings are polished, the linen cloths are unwrinkled, and the greenery and the Nativity scenes on all the antique tabletops are just so. She also directs the preparation of a gigantic Christmas feast; many far larger establishments would do well to equal it. For details, write The Homestead, Sugar Hill 03585.

Foreign Christmases at Home

The Highlands Inn in Carmel Highlands, California, celebrates Christmas in a way that is doggedly faithful to Scottish holiday traditions. Pipers pipe, choirboys sing, as the Yule log is hunted and brought back to the Inn. Five feet long and three feet in diameter, the log is so huge that a dozen men are needed to carry it. For details, write Box 1700, Carmel 93921.

The Santa Barbara Biltmore, in Santa Barbara, California, does a Mexican-type Christmas, with a reenactment of "Las Posadas," a fiesta with Mexican singing and dancing in groups and solo, and the breaking of two pinatas, each of them four feet high. The lobby is decorated to the nines with poinsettias, greens, swags, and berries. For details, write 1260 Channel Drive, Santa Barbara 93102.

Two Other Grand Feasts

A version of the side-splitting banquets at the Ahwahnee and the Publick House (the feasting minus the pageantry) unfolds on Christmas Day at the Arizona Inn, a relatively small Tucson establishment (built circa 1930) with gardens and Mediterranean-style architecture that sometimes makes you think of Italy. The three-hour dinner is the highlight of the season. There's a boar's head, a pheasant, a baron of beef, plum pudding, and more. To reserve, write the Inn at 2200 East Elm Street, Tucson 85719.

In Charlottesville, Virginia, the Boar's Head Inn stages a three-day Merrie Old England Christmas Festival where carolers, recorder tooters, drummers, and krumhorn players, minstrels, tumblers, jugglers, and sundry other jolly pranksters disport themselves before, during, and after banquetings like the "Feast Before Forks." Unless you insist on being anachronistic, you eat your seven courses—fish, salad, Cornish hens, beef, ribs, wild boar pie, mutton, plum pudding, and accoutrements—with a knife and spoon and your fingers. Plus: caroling, mummers' plays. For reservations, contact the Inn in Ednam Forest, Charlottesville 22903.

Skiing Christmases

The Homestead (near the White Mountains in New Hampshire), and the Inn at Sawmill Farm (near Mount Snow in Vermont) are good places to go, as is the Trapp Family Lodge, in Stowe itself, and the Ahwahnee, which has its own smallish downhill area. The best Christmas place in the ski country of the Western United States is, however, Timberline Lodge in Timberline, Oregon, near Multorpor Ski Bowl, Mt. Hood Meadows, and the Timberline ski areas. There are two traditions at the Timberline Lodge, a mammoth 1930s-vintage establishment built of logs and fieldstone: there's the solemn Christmas Eve when one staff member

carries a lighted candle down the stairs, with other employees following, everyone singing and each person lighting his neighbor's candle until there are a hundred blazing. The light is as warm as the spirit of Christmas that everyone feels. Then Santa arrives from the North Pole in a sleigh pulled by real reindeer (among them a Rudolf with a red light on his nose). Because this is the Pacific Northwest, there's salmon on the menu on Christmas Day, along with turkey and prime rib. For details, write the Lodge in Government Camp, Oregon 97208.

For more help picking a ski area. See I. William Berry's thorough, entertaining, and highly original *Where to Ski* (New American Library, 1301 Avenue of the Americas, New York, New York 10019; $1.95). He tells you about terrain, snow conditions, lifts, accommodations, and transportation at each one of a terrific number of ski areas all over the U.S. One of the best chapters is his "Choosing a Ski Area"; he talks about basic things you ought to consider in planning a ski trip, such as the length of time you plan to stay, the kind of terrain you like (narrow or wide trails, steep or just tip-tilted); the kind of accommodations you like (rustic, elegant, cozy); the overall feel you'd enjoy (say, lonely or modern or cluttered and busy); and the kind of people you like to have around you—and then talks about a couple of well-known resorts in those terms. There are plenty of where-to-ski books on the market, but so far this one is the most helpful.

Food, Glorious Food

The Culinary Institute of America

Everybody likes to think of himself as different or special in some way—and so do institutions. As for the Culinary Institute of America, it pats itself on the back for being "the largest private nonprofit post-high-school institute in the United States offering an educational program to persons desiring to become professional cooks." It's a twenty-month course, so unless you want to be a cook in a restaurant, you can't consider it a "cooking school." But it's fun to visit because while you're eating your meal—in a sort of large refectory room that will probably remind you of college days—you're served by young men and women who are learning how to wait tables—properly—and their instructors will come over and correct them if they make a wrong move. If you have exceptionally bad service, you may learn quite a lot about what makes good service good. For further information about a visit to the Institute, which is in the Hudson River Valley along with Roosevelt's mansion and any number of other interesting destinations, write the Culinary Institute of America, Hyde Park, New York 12538. The Hudson River Valley Association, 105 Ferris Lane, Poughkeepsie 12603, can provide helpful information about what to do and see in the area.

Big Feeds

Here's your chance to eat more than your fill, go back for seconds—and still feel good about it. Each of the following festivals features some local food specialty in a big way.

Apple Butter Stirs

While the craftspeople demonstrate, the fiddlers fiddle, the banjo players pick, and the kids race their turtles, the rest of the citizens of Berkeley Springs, West Virginia, and their visitors, will be checking up on the progress of the apple butter, simmering, and being

stirred in big iron kettles on the grounds. The steamy sweet smell of it is everywhere. Dates: mid-October. Further information: the Morgan County Chamber of Commerce, Berkeley Springs 25411.

Bananas

They've come a long way since their official debut in the United States at the Philadelphia Centennial Exhibition, where they were wrapped in tin foil and sold for a dime apiece: they're specially handled, treated with special chemicals to protect them against disease on their way to market, and, like tomatoes, treated with gas by the wholesalers to bring them just to the proper ripeness. Each man, woman, and child in the United States consumes an average of eighteen pounds of bananas a year. And there's even a festival devoted to the fruit in the town that earned itself the nickname "Banana Crossroads of the United States," or, sometimes, "the Banana Capital of the World" for its role as a shipment inspection checkpoint during the days when bananas were shipped by rail in refrigerator cars that had to be reiced en route. Nowadays, that's getting to be a memory, but the people of Fulton, Kentucky, and South Fulton, Tennessee, celebrate those days anyway, with beauty contests, banana eating contests, a banana bake-off, the welcoming of Latin American dignitaries and teenagers, and a one-ton banana pudding. The recipe: in a 3-foot-tall bowl which is about five feet across, slice three thousand bananas,

add 250 pounds of vanilla wafers, and spread them both in alternating layers with 950 pounds of boiled custard.

For exact dates, contact the International Banana Festival, P. O. Box 428, Fulton, Kentucky 42041.

Maine's Best Saturday Night Bean Feed

Baked bean suppers are a way of life in Maine, but the annual Bean Hole Bean Festival in South Paris is by far the biggest. Three thousand people make their way to the local fairgrounds, and they gobble twelve hundred pounds of red kidney and pea beans cooked, with water, sow belly, white pepper, dry mustard, and molasses, in immense black iron kettles buried in pits with six cords of burning hardwood. Only one man knows the exact proportions, but everyone in town gets into the act—the people who aren't helping to crank the kettles down into their pits are baking bread, getting out the pickles they put up, or buying the supplies. For details, contact the Oxford-Norway Chamber of Commerce, 163 Main Street, Box 268, Oxford, Maine 04268.

A Recipe for Bean-Hole Beans. The Maine Department of Agriculture (Augusta 04330) gives the following information for doing it yourself: "Dig a hole in the ground at least 3 feet deep and 2 feet wide, or larger if your kettle takes more space.

"Get a special iron kettle, with legs, and a cover that fits down over the top of the kettle at least 2 inches, with slots at the two opposite sides to allow the kettle handle to be raised.

"The chances are that your first beans will not be as tasty as later cookings until after the hole has been 'burned out'. Place a flat rock at the bottom of the hole; add any old scrap iron or good sized rocks. Lacking these, the woodsmen use old logging chains. Fill the hole with hardwood and keep a fire for half a day for this 'burning out' process. After good coals are formed, the hole is ready for cooking the beans.

"Soak or parboil the State of Maine Beans as for oven baking; place in kettle with salt pork, molasses, salt, and plenty of boiling water. Cover the kettle and attach a long wire, 1½ or 2 feet long, to the kettle bail. Now remove all scrap iron, rocks, or chains from the hole. Lower the kettle of boiling beans into the hole. Then surround the kettle with the coals and the rocks or scrap. Fill the hole with earth. Pack the earth tightly and tread on it to seal the hole. One tiny opening may allow the air to get in and result in burned beans. The following day, dig off the earth, pull out the kettle by the wire and eat!"

Black Walnuts

The festival that honors them is an annual October event in Spencer, West Virginia. For details, write Route 1, Box 85B, Spencer, West Virginia 25276.

Blueberries

Pie-eating contests, sales of fresh and frozen blueberries and blueberry products, free blueberry pies, Blueberry Queens, and/or dancing, flea markets, and all the other country-fair activities —are the order of the day in late July at the South Haven, Michigan, National Blueberry Festival; in August at the Maine Blueberry Festival, at Union, Maine; in September, in Amherst, Nova Scotia, at the Blueberry Harvest Festival. For details: the Greater South Haven Chamber of Commerce, 602 Phoenix Street, South Haven, Michigan 49090; the Union Chamber of Commerce, Union, Maine 04862; the Nova Scotia Travel Bureau, Box 456, The Hollis Building, Halifax, Nova Scotia B3J 2R5.

Barbecued Buffalo

While not quite as large as the Brisbane, California, barbecue at which seven buffalos were roasted in 1973, buffalo roasts are a common thing at the small-town celebrations of the West. The Fiesta de la Primavera in Old Town San Diego State Historic Park in San Diego, California, in May, usually features a buffalo barbecue along with fiddling and banjo-picking contests, mariachi playing, and arts and crafts exhibitions. There are buffalo barbecues in Manitou Springs, Colorado (early September) and in Grand Lake, Colorado (mid-July); and in Teton Valley, Idaho (mid-August). For the exact dates and details, contact the San Diego Convention and Visitors Bureau, 1200 Third Avenue, Suite 824, San Diego 92101; the Manitou Springs Chamber of Commerce, 354 Manitou Avenue, Manitou Springs 80829; the Grand Lake Chamber of Commerce, Box 57, Grand Lake 80447; and the Idaho Division of Tourism & Industrial Development, Capitol Building, Boise, Idaho 83720.

Don't feel guilty about eating buffalo. Since poachers on Colorado's Lost Park shot the last wild buffalo in 1897, leaving just the small protected herd in Yellowstone as a reminder of the species, a few ranchers have been raising buffalo as scientifically as other ranches raise cattle. There were only a handful at first, but with growers now raising them in forty-three states, buffalo aren't what you'd call an endangered species.

If you want to cook it yourself, you can order the meat by mail from places like the Triple U Enterprises, Pierre, South Dakota 57501; and the Durham Meat Company, Box 4230 San Jose, California 95126. The American Buffalo Association, Box 643, Coffeyville, Kansas 67337, can give you a rundown on other sources. A buffalo cookbook? A dollar, from the National Buffalo Association, Hermosa, South Dakota 57744.

How does it taste? "Like beef wished it tasted," quipped a rancher.

Burgoo

The exact ingredients are a closely guarded secret, but this pioneer settler stew contains scores of vegetables and many kinds of meat chopped and sliced and cooked from twilight until noon the next day. You can taste it at the Burgoo Festival in the Illinois River Valley town of Utica, Illinois. While the stirrers are stirring and the eaters are eating, wood carvers, glassblowers, hand weavers, quillers, spinners, smiths, butter churners and cream separators, leather crafters, china painters, quilters, and wool workers are all intent upon their respective tasks. It's all part of a fund drive and a pioneer heritage show put on by the La Salle County Historical Society, which can also send you dates. Write c/o P. O. Box 278, Utica, Illinois 61373.

Cereal

The smell in the air might be Froot Loops. Or maybe Corn Flakes. Or Grape Nuts. Or Cheerios, Wheat Chex, Rice Krispies, Wheaties, or Special K. All of these are products of the factories in the Breakfast Capital of the World—Battle Creek, Michigan. When you visit, you never know what'll be cooking (and only the natives can tell by the smell). To celebrate its considerable stature in the hall of fame of great American products, each June the city of Battle Creek sets up the World's Longest Breakfast Table—four blocks of end-to-end picnic tables— and serves up tons of the stuff along with other products made by the Big Three (Kellogg's, Post, and Ralston-Purina) such as Pop Tarts. Afterwards, there're plenty of other activities— Tony the Tiger and Smokey the Bear are on hand, and you can tour the

Kellogg's plant. For details, contact the Chamber of Commerce, Box 16, Battle Creek, Michigan 49016.

Swiss Cheese

The Swissfest, held annually in Sugarcreek, Ohio, is as much a taste of old-time Switzerland as it is a bacchanale devoted to the holey stuff. As part of the celebration, strongarms play a game called *steinstossen*, in which they toss a 138-pound stone. The one who throws it farthest is the winner. Anyone who has a mind to can give it a try. Then there's *schwingfest*—Swiss wrestling. As well as free street dancing, yodeling, and a parade with floats like the white-crepe-papered "Winter in the Swiss Alps," or the "Swiss Express No. 1: Swiss Cheese Energy." Along with huge quantities of bologna, Swiss cookies, ice cream, and French fries, visitors down 22,000 pounds of Swiss cheese, most of it made at the area's seventeen Swiss cheese factories. For details, write the Ohio Swiss Festival, Sugarcreek, Ohio 44681.

Cherries

Seventy percent of the world's red cherries are grown in Michigan, and the largest concentration of cherry trees in Michigan is on the Old Mission Peninsula in the area around Traverse City. So it's entirely fitting that the National Cherry Festival should be held here. Over fifty years old, this annual July event is important enough that Gerald Ford served as Grand Parade Marshal in 1975.

Cherry activities: cherry sundaes at the ice-cream social, a cherry pancake breakfast, a cherry smorgasbord luncheon that features a slew of cherry deserts made by local cherry growers' wives, frozen cherry ice-cream desserts at the Cherryland Band concert, cherry-pie eating contests for kids, cherry-pie baking contests, cooking with cherries contests, and, along the grand parade route (which is decorated with cherry motifs), cherries and cherry products for sale at the food stands. For area information, contact the Traverse City Area Chamber of Commerce, 202 East Grandview Parkway, P. O. Box 387, Traverse City, Michigan 49684. For festival information, contact the National Cherry Festival, P. O. Box 141, Traverse City 49684.

Another cherry festival is held in Bellevue, Ohio, in late June every year. All the stores on Main Street decorate their windows; in the Tasty Bakery, there's always a fifty-inch cherry pie made with five thousand (thirty-six quarts) of tart Bellevue cherries. That cherry pie is portioned out on the last day of the festival. Until then, there are auctions of the cherry pies that won prizes in other events, pit-spitting contests, cherry-inspired foods at booths

on the funway—and plenty of cherries to eat. For the details and dates, write Box 166, Bellevue 44811.

Chili

Who cooks the best bowl of red? That's what the Chilympiad in San Marcos, Texas, is all about. Chili is a subject dear to the heart of Texans, and they come from all over the state for this event. There are chamber of commerce cookoffs, collegiate cookoffs, even a kids' cookoff. Since prizes are awarded for showmanship as well as taste, and since all the cooking must be done on the site (and no electric outlets are furnished) the spectacle of all those cooks lined up with their peppers and meat and tomatoes is quite a sight. When you get tired of watching, there's plenty to eat. Plus a midway, an arts and crafts show, a parade, a fiddlers' contest, and lots of beer. The prize-winning dishes are auctioned off. For details, contact the Chilympiad, Box 188, San Marcos, Texas 78666.

Chitlins

Boiled deep-fried hog intestines: "You've got to get 'em down fast, stay ahead of em," said Southern novelist William Price Fox, who knew about this poverty food of the South, which is now the center of a huge festival in Salley, South Carolina, the town that calls itself "the chitlin' capital of the world," and even chooses a Chitlin Queen—as if to convince you that this festival is just as good as the next, even though it does concern chitlin's. This is your chance to come and get it. November, when the festival is held, is a fine pleasant time to be in South Carolina. For information about other goings on besides the 8,000 pounds of chitlin's served, contact the Town of Salley's Mayor, in Salley, South Carolina 29137.

Citrus Fruit

One of the oldest fairs in the state, the Citrus Fair in Cloverdale, California, in the hilly Russian River Valley, is an all-out village fiesta, with parades, gem shows, flower displays—and a very fancy exhibition of oranges and lemons grown in the area, which is claimed to be the northernmost commercial citrus-growing area in the United States. Cloverdale is also the home of the Italian Swiss Colony Vineyards, where you can see the what must be the world's most enormous redwood vat—it holds eighty thousand gallons. That's big enough to hold an entire infantry platoon.

For details, contact the Cloverdale Chamber of Commerce, Cloverdale, California 95425.

Coon Stew, Rabbit Roast, and Other Game

Church suppers always give you the chance to sit down with the natives and eat local specialties the way the locals cook them. In sea country, you will get fresh fish at a church supper, and in bean country, you can be sure you won't get beans out of cans. The church supper at the United Church of Christ in Bradford, Vermont, however, is different: on the table are not old-fashioned specialties like fried chicken, but really old-time goodies like beaver, boar, bear, coon, moose, pheasant, rabbit, venison, and sometimes antelope, duck, and elk. To go with these are cabbage salad, carrots, mashed potatoes, and squash—most of it donated by parishioners. There are several sittings of the dinner, which usually takes place in late November, but you should make your reservations early. Write the church in Bradford 05033, for the latest dates and prices.

Corn

Nobody has contested Hoopeston, Illinois', claim to being the Sweet Corn Capital of the World: this food canning and industrial machine center in the east-central part of the state is home to Joan of Arc Company, Stokely-Van Camp, the American Can Company, FMC Corporation, and John Deere—all of which are involved in some phase of getting the corn from the cob to the can. They all support the National Sweet Corn Festival, and the National Sweetheart Pageant (a sort of Miss America Pageant, with swimsuit, formal wear, and talent competitions), and the big sweet-corn feed that is a part of it: eight tons of sweet corn, cooked in a 1919 Minneapolis steam engine, is served each day of the Labor Day weekend, which is when the festival is held. In addition, there are tractor pulls (classes: five thousand pounds stock, nine thousand pounds Hot Rod, twelve thousand pounds N.D. 18.4 Tires, twelve thousand pounds N.A. Open, six thousand pounds S-4 W.D.T., seven thousand pounds Hot Rod, and twelve thousand pounds Stock), and if you don't know what that means now, you will after you've seen it, for the tractor pull is an Illinois Tractor Pulling Association sanctioned event.

After this, almost any other sweet-corn festival is bound to be anticlimactic. However, if you're not in the area and have a yen to eat corn, consider the Sweet Corn Festival in Ortonville, Minnesota, in August (corn from a steam engine, a fiddling contest, and fireworks). For the dates and details, contact the Civic & Commerce Association, 33 N.W. Second Street, Ortonville 56278. Or the Sweet Corn Festival in Mendota, Illinois, about 15 miles north of I-80 halfway between Moline and Chicago. For details, contact the Chamber of Commerce in Mendota 61342.

Crawfish

You can get them baked, boiled, broiled, fried. In gumbo. Etouffe. Served in booths. At restaurants. In eating contests. You can eat crawfish —sweet tiny shellfish that bear some, but only some, resemblance to lobsters, until they're coming out your ears. This crawfish affair is so massive that the citizens of the town that puts it on take two years to rest up before repeating the performance. Breaux Bridge, on the bayou, is tiny, neat, lush with the live oaks of the surrounding Cajun countryside. The Festival is held during even-numbered years. For the exact dates, contact the Louisiana Tourist Development Commission, P. O. Box 44291, Capitol Station, Baton Rouge, Louisiana 70804.

Eggs

The incredible edible egg has its festival in Pittsfield, Maine, every year toward the end of July. A gold-plated chicken, the world's largest, is on display, watching over the world's largest frying pan, where fifty dozen eggs are scrambled together at regular intervals between 5:30 A.M. and midnight. There's also an egg contest and an egg princess contest (for kids twelve to sixteen).

The Maine Department of Commerce and Industry, State House, Augusta 04330, can send you the details.

Grapes

Italian immigrants of Tontitown, Arkansas, in the northwestern part of the state, used to have a big picnic every year, and the picnic simply grew like Topsy. After about eighty years it is huge. The ladies of the parish, descendants of the original settlers—who were stoned when they arrived—cook up one of the biggest spaghetti dinners you'll ever see, and also one of the weirdest, because along with the spaghetti there's very southern fried chicken and very southern-style home-baked rolls. The festival makes a nod to the fruit it honors with a Grape Judging contest and plenty of grapes for dessert. For the details about the other nifty things to do in the area, and for information about the exact dates in the August you decide to attend, contact the Festival Chairman at Box 36, Tontitown, Arkansas 72770.

Ham

Country ham breakfasts in the streets,

country-style soup, beans, and cornbread dinners, country ham sandwiches, and ham-and-biscuit snacks are all part of the offerings of the late September Kentucky Country Ham Days, in Lebanon—along with bluegrass, a costume contest, square dancing, arts and crafts shows, and a flea market. Lebanon is in the central part of the state, close to Stephen Foster's "My Old Kentucky Home" at Bardstown, and Lincoln's b thplace at Hodgenville. For more information, contact the Lebanon Area Chamber of Commerce, zip 40033.

Huckleberries

There's a huckleberry auction and free games and ice cream for all comers in the hills of northeastern Oklahoma, every year in July. For details: the Chamber of Commerce, Box 608, Jay 76346.

Picking huckleberries. In the Gifford Pinchot National Forest in Washington, thousands and thousands of gallons of huckleberries are harvested every year, and despite the fact that the campgrounds fill up on weekends with pickers, many thousands more go unharvested. There are just too many acres. September—a beautiful time of year anyway—is the berriest month. For details, contact the Forest Supervisor at 500 West 12th Street, Vancouver, Washington 98660.

Molasses

The Arnoldsburg, West Virginia, Molasses Festival is a pleasant little country fair with enough going on that visitors don't get bored. There are pancake suppers, greased-pig races, a greased-pole climb, old-time molasses-making demonstrations, a few arts and crafts, sales, 4-H exhibits—but there's not too much that people don't have time to be neighborly. It's always held the last weekend in September. For details, contact the Festival Chairman at Route 3, Box 510, Arnoldsburg, West Virginia 25234.

A Big Pancake Flap

Pancake-eating contests and a pancake feed are just small parts of the International Pancake Day goings-on in Liberal, Kansas, a town of about fifteen thousand in the southwest corner of the state. The main event is a foot race in which women in house dresses, aprons, and headscarves run a 415-yard S-shaped course through the town while flipping a pancake in a skillet. It seems very strange, until you hear the legend behind it. About five hundred years ago, it was the custom on Shrove Tuesday, the day before Lenten fasting began, to use up accumulated cooking fats by baking pancakes. One housewife in Olney, England, got so involved with her baking that she lost track of

time until she heard the church bell calling parishioners to church to be shriven of their sins, whereupon, even more absentmindedly, she dashed off to church, her apron around her middle and her skillet and pancake in hand. For some reason the other women of the town thought the absentmindedness worth imitating. They called the lady the first pancake racer, and forever more—for the next five hundred years—they took Shrove Tuesday as their opportunity to race around the town wearing their house dresses and their aprons and flipping pancakes as they ran.

So what does that have to do with Kansas? Well, somebody in Liberal saw the Olney women charging around with their skillets in a photograph, thought the practice charming, and shortly thereafter arranged a parallel competition. The ladies of Liberal, similarly clad and equipped, run a similar course, then compare times with their English sisters. And so it goes.

The prize? A kiss from the local parson and a pancake griddle engraved with the winners' names, which travels from town to town from year to year, depending on who wins.

For details about eating pancakes in Liberal, contact the Chamber of Commerce, Box 676, Liberal 67901.

Peaches

To celebrate the harvest in the peach orchards that have been around Porter, Oklahoma, since the early 1900s, the Lions Club annually sponsors a Peach Festival the first Saturday in August. Porter is tiny, with less than a thousand souls—but they all outdo themselves to put on the parade of 25 floats, antique cars, Shrine motor patrols and horsemen. About forty townswomen spend more than a day preparing the peach desserts—ice cream, cake, and peaches. There is no eating contest, but to look at the serving line you might think there was, since so many kids go through as many as ten times and consume, in the process, a half gallon of peaches and a half gallon of ice cream. For more infomation, contact the Festival Chairman c/o the Porter Lions Club in Porter, Oklahoma 74454.

More peaches in quantity: at the Louisiana Peach Festival in Ruston 71270, and in Stonewall, Texas 78671, close to the Lyndon Baines Johnson National Historic Site. Both festivals are in June. For dates, contact the chambers of commerce.

Peanuts

The National Peanut Festival, an annual mid-October event in Dothan, Alabama, may be only marginally a big feed, but it is one of the few places that you can reliably get boiled peanuts—

that great southern specialty that you simply can't find, except in cans, outside peanut country: to make boiled peanuts you need fresh nuts. There are peanut recipe contests that are entered by as many as two thousand people. A hundred thousand, however, attend the festival, which is as much like a small-town bash grown to state-fair size as anything else, and there are very fancy parades, arts and crafts shows, rides, 4-H displays, greased-pig scrambles, and such. For the details, contact the National Peanut Festival Association, Box 976, Dothan, Alabama 36301.

The Great Pumpkins
They're in ice cream, pie, fudge, candy, milk shakes, cookies—even hamburgers—at the Pumpkin Show, in Circleville, Ohio. This little town really outdoes itself getting up the food and putting on the parade—and it sits back and reaps the rewards, too: crowds of up to half a million and a fame that just doesn't quit. Lots of people know it as "the greatest free show on earth." For the dates, contact the Chamber of Commerce, Circleville 43113.

Not quite so big, but pumpkiny enough are the goings-on in Morton, Illinois; Sycamore, Illinois; Owatonna, Minnesota; and Thornton, West Virginia. The state tourist offices are your best sources for the details.

Ramps
Old-timers swear that ramps, a wild vegetable peculiar to the shady slopes and coves of Appalachia, are the only known cure for the common cold. Why? Ramps are something like onions and, the old-timers say, if you eat a bit of ramps immediately upon feeling that first sniffle, no one will get close enough to you to catch it. All over the mountains in the spring, there are festivals devoted to ramps, among the most famous of which is the Ramp Convention, sponsored jointly by the Haywood Post 47 of the American Legion and the North Carolina Society of the Friends of the Ramp, held annually in early May in Haywood, North Carolina. The convention gets into full swing one Sunday noon with country music, square dancing, clogging, and plenty of ramps, ham, eggs, barbecued chicken, buttermilk, and cornbread; then moves along to the big event of the day, the Ramp Eating Contest. Competitors get fifteen minutes to down as many ramps as they can without benefit of side dishes. Said one winner, when asked how he felt after laying in fifty-one: "Fine, I just hope I can get a ride home."

For more information about the Convention and hiking, riding, fishing, and mountain drives in the area, contact the Chamber of Commerce in Haywood, North Carolina 28786.

Wild Rice

A supper featuring wild rice is one of the highlights of Wild Rice Day on the White Earth Indian Reservation in Mahnomen, Minnesota, in the north-central part of the state. For details, contact the Mahnomen Boosters, Mahnomen, Minnesota 56557. And there's another wild rice festival in July in Kelliher, Minnesota; contact the Upper Red Lake Area Association, Kelliher 56650.

Sassafras

Indiana people grow up with the pungent-sweet taste of the tea made from this root engraved in their memory; it's as pioneer a taste (if such a thing is possible) as the town of Vernon, Indiana, which holds a Sassafras festival every year the last Sunday in April, is down-home and unpretentious. The festival? Free cookies and hot sassafras tea and, for sale, sassafras roots. Mostly you go for the chance to see Vernon, a nifty old town that is just beginning to pick itself up by its boot-straps and restore the old buildings as shops, interesting restaurants, and such. For the details, contact the Heritage Association at Box 225, Vernon 47282.

Salmon

Salmon bakes are nearly an everyday thing in the Pacific Northwest—sort of a West Coast version of Maine's bean suppers. Wherever you go, keep an eye out for signs on telephone poles, fence posts, grocery store bulletin boards, and the like. The one in Depoe Bay, Oregon (Box 21, zip 97341) is, however, an annual September affair: fresh-caught fish are cooked Indian style before an open fire at Fogarty Creek State Park and served buffet style by the sea with all the trimmings.

Sauerkraut

The eat-it-up festival on the subject is a project every August of the town of Phelps, New York, just off the New York Thruway near Seneca Lake in the hilly Finger Lakes country. To get the exact date, contact the Town Clerk (14523).

A recipe for chocolate sauerkraut cake as served at the sauerkraut festival in the sauerkraut capital of the world. Sift together 2¼ cups flour, 1 teaspoon baking soda, and 1 teaspoon baking powder. Set aside. Cream 1½ cups sugar and ⅔ cup shortening or butter. Add 3 eggs. Mix well. Then add 1¼ teaspoon vanilla, ¼ teaspoon salt, and ½ cup cocoa. Add ½ cup chopped and drained sauerkraut. Bake in greased and floured pan in a 375-degree oven—45 minutes in 8-inch square layer pans, or 35 minutes in a 13 x 9 x 2-inch oblong pan.

Seafood

That peculiarly appealing atmosphere of a waterside community, and the chance to get out and enjoy the sea air and maybe even sit on the beach, make festivals devoted to seafood especially enjoyable—and they're all over the place. Alabama, for instance, has had an annual Shrimp Festival since 1971 in the town of Gulf Shores, a really nice place with a fine white beach and one of the best of the state resort parks. Though fairly new, the Shrimp Festival gets crowds of about seventy thousand for the seafood bash, which includes a Seafood Cooking Contest; booths serving up boiled and fried shrimp, gumbo, shrimp tacos, crab salad; a parade full of shrimp-colored floats; and a blessing of the fleet, plus sky-diving exhibitions, a midway, band concerts, a gun show, sand castle and greased pig contests. For the details and the dates in October, contact the Gulf Shores Tourist Association, P. O. Box 457, Gulf Shores, Alabama 36542. This is a good time, too, to visit the genteel, old-fashioned Grand Hotel at nearby Point Clear (36564).

In California, the northern town of Crescent City, in Del Norte County, sponsors the World Championship Crab Races, and, to go with it, a crab feed, at the Del Norte County Fairgrounds, in February. For the details, write the Chamber of Commerce in Crescent City 95531. The town of Pismo Beach boasts 21 miles of beach and a big three-day Clam Festival at which locals compete at what they do year-round anyway—fishing and clamming. Afterward, there's clam chowder for everybody. To get the exact dates, usually in late February or early March, write the town's Chamber of Commerce, 93449.

In Florida, Spanish-moss-hung live oaks surround you as you put away oysters, shrimp, and other seafood as part of the annual Seafood Festival held every October in Apalachicola, a sleepy little town on the northwest coast of the state—an idyllic place if ever there was one. For details on the boat parade, the seafood factory tours, the arts and crafts shows, and the fireworks displays that are also part of the event, contact the Chamber of Commerce, 90 Avenue E, Apalachicola, Florida 32320.

Downeast, one of the biggest festivals is in Rockland, Maine, where every year in early August thirty thousand start the day at special pancake breakfasts, then munch their way through a ton and a half of shrimp, a hundred bushels of clams (steamed, raw, and in clam cakes), and similar quantities of fried scallops, mussels, and crabmeat. The star of the show that calls itself "the original lobster festival" is *Homarus americanus*, some three to six tons of them, cooked to a flaming red in a 2,000-gallon copper kettle that is said to be the world's largest. The scene: the seawall next to the public landing. Between bouts of eating, people enjoy the entertainment—a Maine Sea Goddess contest and a flurry-of-fingers sardine-packing contest, the World Championship, at which women from the local canneries vie for the title of Super Snipper. For more information about the event, contact the Rockland Festival Corporation, P. O. Box 508 Rockland, Maine 04841.

Down the coast just north of Portland, in Yarmouth, Maine, the Yarmouth Clam Festival stars a giant clambake, a clam-shucking contest, booths purveying all manner of fried, boiled, and otherwise tasty Maine sea foods, plus a baked bean supper, auctions, arts and crafts shows, church bazaars, and a beauty pageant. The Yarmouth Chamber of Commerce, Box 416, Yarmouth 04096, can send details.

Flin Flon, Manitoba has its Trout Festival (bannocks and fillets, flour-packing contests, a Mermaid Queen's coronation, and dancing in the streets of this old mining town). Contact the Manitoba Government Travel Office (200 Vaughan Street, Winnipeg R3C OV8) for exact dates, which will be early in July.

Then, every year at the end of April, there's the Smelt Fry sponsored by the Commercial Club, Garrison, Minnesota 56450.

Pictou, Nova Scotia, which is one of the first two places to be settled by the Scots who came to Nova Scotia by the thousands in the early part of the nineteenth century, puts on an annual Lobster Carnival in early July; details are available from the Nova Scotia Department of Tourism, Box 456, Halifax B3J 2R5.

On the scenic, sea-swept Eastern Shore, Accomac, Virginia, has its own big feed, but it's not a carnival—just a simple $10-a-head dinner for 3,250 Virginia Assembly members, Representatives, Senators, reporters, Chamber of Commerce volunteers, spouses, North Carolinians, Pennsylvanians, New Yorkers, Delawareans, Marylanders, Tennesseeans, Californians—and even some other Virginians; no loudspeakers, no eating contests, no speeches—just good friends, good food, and the sound of the wind in the pines. Lest you doubt the quantity, here's the shopping list for 1977: 65,000 clams for steaming; 7,265 clams for eating on the half shell; 110 cases of clams for strip frying; 49 gallons of clams for fritters; 110 gallons of oysters for frying and 52 bushels for eating on the half shell; 632 pounds of scallops; 1,750 pounds of trout; 500 pounds of eel; 45 gallons of coleslaw;

401 dozen rolls; and 25 bushels of *sweet potatoes* for french frying; plus eggs, milk, flour, and cocktail sauce in similar quantities. All tickets to the event, which is held in May, go on sale the preceding October 1 and usually sell out within three hours. For details—and the latest ticket prices (times being what they are, you should expect a slight rise)—contact the Eastern Shore of Virginia Chamber of Commerce, Box 147, No. 1 Court House Avenue, Accomac 23301.

The same low-key good times can be found at the celebrated lobster suppers run by the St. Ann's Church in Hope River, Prince Edward Island, except that here, sing-alongs and martinis are part of the combination that has made St. Ann's the best known of all the church suppers in the area and, in the process, retired the mortgage on the church and helped construct a new parish school. The Tourist Information Division, Department of the Environment and Tourism, Box 940, Charlottetown, Prince Edward Island C1A 7M5, can send you information about it.

A real lobster bash. Cooked claw consumption zooms in mid-July in Shediac, New Brunswick, the Lobster Capital of the World. You probably won't see that many lobster claws in one place for a long time to come. For details, write the Shediac Lobster Festival, Inc., P. O. Box 487, Shediac, New Brunswick.

The biggest lobster ever. Caught in 1934 off the coast of Virginia, this 42-pound 7-ounce crustacean, measuring three feet from end to end, is on display in the Museum of Science in Science Park, in Boston—a really lively museum with lots of please-touch exhibits. For details, write the museum, Boston 02114, or the Convention and Tourist Bureau at 900 Boyleston Street, Boston 02115.

World's largest lobster pound. What better place to eat seafood? The pound is located on Deer Island, one of the three Fundy Isles, off the coast of New Brunswick. For details, write the New Brunswick Department of Tourism, Box 12345 Fredericton, New Brunswick E3B 5C3.

Strawberries

Fruitful good times devoted to this red berry, a member of the rose family, are what you find at the festivities in Glenwood Springs, Colorado (late June; 81601); Stilwell, Oklahoma (mid-May; Box 292, 74960); Manistee, Michigan (early July; 49660); Lebanon, Oregon (first full weekend in June; 712 Park Street, 97355); Montague, Prince Edward Island (in July); and Pleasant Grove, Utah (mid-June). For further information, contact the chambers of commerce. For details about the festival in Montague, write the Tourist

Information Division of the Department of the Environment and Tourism, Box 940, Charlottetown, Prince Edward Island C1A 7N5. For information about the Utah festival, write the Mountainland Travel Council, 160 East Center Street, Provo, Utah 84601.

The festival in Manistee is the *National* Strawberry Festival; it's held on the shores of Lake Michigan not far from the site of the National Cherry Festival. However, the Oregon Festival, nearly seventy years old, is bigger. Its main strawberry event is the world's largest strawberry shortcake. Sixteen feet long, twelve feet wide, eight feet high, it weighs 5,700 pounds, serves 16,000 and, for the record, contains 350 pounds of flour, 225 of liquid milk, 27 of baking powder, 325 of sugar, 125 of shortening, 4 quarts of flavoring, 3 pounds of salt, and 196 pounds of eggs. *Plus* 3,000 pounds of strawberries. And if you think that sounds wild, you ought to see it on a trailer leading a parade full of drum majorettes. Good fun, though, along with the rest of the goings on.

More berries. At the Florida Strawberry Festival (Box 832, Plant City, Florida 33566), a strawberry cookout, national horseshoe-pitching contest, diaper derby, and grand parade herald the strawberry season in this town near Tampa.

Suckers

Once a year every May, the entire town of Nixa, Missouri (population 900) up and goes fishing. What are they looking for? Suckers—fresh-water fish that are so plentiful in the crystal streams of the area at this time of year that all you've got to do is throw in a hook and snag them on the barb. A quick yank, and you've got him, and it doesn't matter where—gills, fins, mouth, body, or tail, though it's said that they really take off when you catch them by the tail. By the end of the day there are some three hundred pounds cleaned (by local high schoolers), cut into chunks, rolled in corn meal, and deep-fried, a bushel at a time, in Civil War-era iron kettles full of lard. To go with this are baked beans, bread, potato chips, and soda pop. For further information, contact the Missouri Division of Tourism, 308 East High Street, Jefferson City, Missouri 65101.

Sugar Cane

Nothing you can buy in the North will prepare you for the taste of it as it comes out of the fields—fresh and sappy sweet, chewy as honeycomb. No wonder they celebrate in Louisiana's Cajun country during the harvest time. For dates, usually sometime in late September, and more particulars about the fais do-do dancing, the fireworks, dances, and food that is a part of the

show, contact the Chamber of Commerce in New Iberia, Louisiana, where the festival is held (108 West Main, 70560).

Swamp Cabbage

The Sabal palm, or cabbage tree, from which they get swamp cabbage is the platter of honor every year in February at the Swamp Cabbage Festival in LaBelle, Florida, which is halfway between the Gulf of Mexico and Lake Okeechobee, toward the southern part of the state. There's music—gospel, country-and-western—square dancing, plus a beard-growing contest, a swamp-cabbage dinner, and a swamp-cabbage exhibit. For details, you can write the town's Chamber of Commerce at Box 456, LaBelle 33935.

Walleye

Music, dancing, contests, and such, are all part of the Annual Voyageur Day held in Crane Lake, Minnesota, one day in early July. But the world's largest outdoor fish-fry is what will interest you most if you like to eat. Next to small-mouth bass, walleye is one of the best eating fishes there is. For details, write the Crane Lake Commercial Club, Crane Lake 55725.

Watermelon

Free watermelon. Thousands of people slobber their way through thousands of pounds of it every summer, in Chipley, Florida (in the panhandle, third weekend in June; 32428); in Oxford, Kansas (in September; 67119); in Lucedale, Mississippi (in July; 39452); and in Rush Springs, Oklahoma (in May; Box 521, 73082). In Rush Springs, where 40,000 pounds are given away, there's also a rodeo, a terrapin derby, and a watermelon judging contest; the population of the town of 1,400 swells to 20,000. In Lucedale, there are some seed-spitting contests, thumbing contests (squeezing a seed between the fingers until it squirts skyward), and eating contests. For the exact dates, write the chairmen of the festivals c/o their chambers of commerce at the addresses above.

The Wurst

The wurst-packers in New Braunfels, Texas, stuff double-time to produce the forty tons of wursts gobbled up with "New Braunfels Ice Water"—local parlance for beer—at the town's annual early November Wurstfest. In its over fifteen years of existence, this sausage festival, started up by the descendants of the area's original German immigrant settlers, has swelled from an event at which around 10,000 people consumed about three tons of wurst, to an extravaganza that draws 150,000 to gobble mettwurst, bratwurst, blutwurst, leberwurst, wurst-burgers, wurstkabobs, wurst-on-a-stick, sauerbraten, potato dumplings, white pork hocks, stewed spare ribs, sauerkraut, dumplings, potato soup, potato pancakes, rye bread, sauerkraut cake, dried beef—and plenty of New Braunfels Ice Water. The scene—a vast rock-walled building that used to be used for grain storage, and two outdoor biergartens installed when the grain building got too crowded—is like something out of Munich in October, except that the metal folding chairs and the wooden tables are all-American small town. Up front there's dancing to the music of a series of bands—the Alpine Yodelers; Der Sauer Krauts; the Pumpernickels; the Wienerschnitzels; the Kein Bier in Himmel Bands; the Kinderchor; the Kadlecek Family; and Die Bergvagabunden, which in recent years featured Kevin Hatcher, the 1976 U.S. Yodeling Champion. This festival, too, has its royalty—Der Grosse Opa (Big Grandpa) and Miss Loverwurst. And there's a dog show (for dachshunds), a Heritage Exhibit where you can learn how they stuffed sausages in the old days, and all manner of non-wurst activities—garden displays, square dancing, tennis and bowling tourneys, and bike races. For the dates and the details, contact the Wurstfest Association at Box 180, New Braunfels, Texas 78130.

Yams!

Opelousas, Louisiana, holds its Yambilee every October in celebration of this cousin of the sweet potato. The town itself, in the Cajun country where you'll hear as much French as English, is a handsome old place, full of gracefully restored antebellum homes. For details and dates, contact the Opelousas Chamber of Commerce. 121 West Vine Street, 70570.

City Feeds

New Orleans has one every year in early July. For information about the tasting booths and the banquet (Cajun and Creole specialties), contact the Convention and Tourism Commission, 334 Royal Street, New Orleans 70130. And, in New York, there's the half-century-old San Gennaro Festival in Little Italy every September. You eat calzone, zeppoles, grilled sausage, gelati, and dozens and dozens of spicy, stick-to-the-ribs Italian specialties. For dates and details on eating in Manhattan, contact the Convention and Visitors Bureau, 90 East 42nd Street, New York, New York 10017.

Milk as Your Mother Knew It

It comes in glass bottles. It's not pasteurized. And not homogenized. Inches of yellow cream rise to the top

by the time you get it home—you can spoon it out onto strawberries or peaches. Where do you get it? The Merrick Guernsey Dairy, Merrick Road, in Ardena, New Jersey (201/938-2491).

How they made it in the good old days. The "dairy capital of the world," Fort Atkinson, Wisconsin, located in the county that used to be known for having more cows than people, tells the story of early dairying with an enormous assortment of utensils and equipment: milk pails, milking stools, separators, steam engines, troughs, vats, a milk safe, a churn, butter molds, paddles, cream dippers, a dry sink, enameled cans with lids, and pails belonging to families who didn't own their own cow. Even a barn has been reconstructed.

For details, contact the Fort Atkinson Historical Society, Fort Atkinson, Wisconsin 53538.

Great Popcorn

Connoisseurs recommend the fresh and crispy variety, specially popped by old-fashioned methods. You can find it at the Country Stores at Cox Municipal Airport in Dayton, Ohio, and at the airport in Cincinnati, Ohio. The source is the Shawnee Mission Velvet Creme Popcorn Company, near Kansas City, Kansas. The business (located at 2711 West 47th Street, Kansas City, Kansas 66025) has been in the same family for two generations; its only product is popcorn. From mid-November until mid-December, literally hundreds of gallons of the stuff—cinnamon, caramel, cheese, and just plain buttered—are shipped all over the world in 6½-gallon cans.

Chocolate

There's a chocolate aroma in the air almost any day of the year in Hershey, Pennsylvania, and if, for some reason, you've left one of the Pennsylvania Dutch restaurants of the area less than stuffed, the smell might drive you to madness.

Never fear. There's no trouble finding a chocolate bar: Hershey is just one step removed from being a company town. Once sated, you can tour the bean-to-bar Chocolate World, going from cacao plantations to candy kitchens in a moving chair.

Also in town: Hersheypark—a spiffy theme park that focuses not on chocolate, as you'd imagine (though costumed Krackles and Mr. Goodbars do roam the grounds), but on Pennsylvania heritage. Plenty of chocolate to eat here, too.

For details, contact the town's tourism office at One Chocolate Avenue, Hershey, Pennsylvania 17033.

In Wisconsin, you can tour a Nestlé

factory. Where? Burlington, in Racine County. For information, contact the state's Department of Business Development, Loraine Building, Box 7606, Madison, Wisconsin 53707.

Parker House Rolls

Feather light, yeasty, eat-a-dozen delectable, Parker House rolls were born at the famous old Boston hotel known as the Parker House. Recently renovated, the hotel looks inside just like an exceptionally nice, smallish downtown hotel; you'd never guess that those old walls had seen the history they have—and they've seen more than the invention of the rolls that accompany practically every Thanksgiving dinner in the United States. Malcolm X and Ho Chi Minh waited tables here, and before that, Willa Cather lodged at the Parker House for almost a year while gathering material on Christian Science for *McClure's* magazine. And before that, the Parker House was the first meeting place of the Saturday Club, whose members included Ralph Waldo Emerson, Oliver Wendell Holmes, James Russell Lowell, and Nathaniel Hawthorne.

For more information, write the Parker House, 60 School Street, Boston, Massachusetts 02108.

See Them Make It

Watching food go from raw material to the state in which you find it in the store is endlessly fascinating, if for no other reason than that the sheer quantity of food that parades before your eyes at one time is staggering. There are tons of fish, acres of beans, mountains of pineapples. If you're traveling and happen to come across a food factory, stop for a visit.

Snack Food

At the Made Rite Potato Chip Company in Bay City, Michigan, seventy thousand pounds of potatoes travel from the shortening to their packages at the rate of two thousand chips per hour. Seeing them go from potato to chip is something like a magical mystery tour. If you're in the area, have a look, but write or call ahead: 505 North Euclid, Bay City, Michigan 48706 (517/684-6271).

Some Hawaiian Examples

In Honolulu, the Lin Fong Company (1037 Maunakea Street, 808/538-6644) can show you how Chinese cakes and candied vegetables are made. The Kanai Tofu Factory (515 Ward Avenue, 808/538-1305) turns raw soybeans into tofu (bean curd). Leonard's Bakery (933

Kapahulu Avenue, 808/737-5591) makes Portuguese *malasadas*, doughnuts minus the holes, and *pao doce*, sweet bread, and does extravagant cake decorating. There are also good tours of the Dole Company cannery (650 Iwilei Road, 808/536-3411); after you see how the pineapple goes into the can, you're given samples of the fresh fruit. The Hawaii Visitors Bureau (2270 Kalakaua Avenue, Honolulu, Hawaii 96815) can tell you about other food-factory tours.

Maxim's Comes to America

The turn-of-the-century Parisian ambience that prevails in the French branch of this celebrated restaurant also makes the American establishment one of the most romantic around. All wine-colored silks and velvets, dark woods, glowing brass and glass, and sculptured mirrors, the decor is grand indeed. The waiters wear tuxedos. A string trio keeps you company at dinner. And while few people would tell you that the food at Maxim's is the very best in Chicago—Le Perroquet takes that prize in most books—it rates up there at the top with specialties like *pâte de grives au myrte* or *pâte de merles au cognac* (thrush or blackbird paté), salmon with sorrel sauce, delicate turbot, veal kidneys, dessert soufflés—and an elegant, expensive wine list. The Chicago Convention and Tourism Bureau (332 South Michigan Avenue, Chicago, Illinois 60604) can tell you more about the city. The restaurant is at 1300 North Astor, in the Astor Tower Hotel (312/943-1136).

The Fanciest Fast-Food Store

It's not called the Magnificent Mile for nothing: the shops along Michigan Avenue specialize in the kind of merchandise usually within the reach only of ladies who spend their days wondering what color nail polish to wear with their new tweed jacket while their husbands are over on La Salle Street transacting Big Business. On Michigan Avenue you find seersucker blanket covers that are meant to be monogrammed (with pillow shams to match) to the tune of more green stuff than most Americans spend on the mattress and box springs. That's Michigan Avenue. A great tourist promenade, a great working girl's promenade, and a great place to go and dream. So it was inevitable that sooner or later fast food would come to the Magnificent Mile.

What came as a surprise, though, was how elegantly it was presented. The Arby's Roast Beef Store didn't even have a Western hat—the chain's answer to Big Mac's golden arch. Instead, at the Water Tower Arby's, there are two rows of very tasteful Helvetica type in which the word "Arby's" appears, all told, four times. Below that there is a curtain wall of glass that curves inward around the door, where, on simple plastic strips, the business hours are stated. Indoors: exposed ductwork painted in bright colors; a panoramic view through the front windows; seating that makes the place look more like a health-food sandwich shop. In all, a nice place to be. Will the good design pay off? Therein lies the question—and the look of the fast-food shop of the future.

Some Great Eating in the Caribbean

On most Caribbean islands, you find more hotels than restaurants. Not so on Guadeloupe and Martinique, in the French West Indies, where the food you eat is some of the best on all the islands.

On Guadeloupe, look for redfish, lobster, turtle, roast wild goat, rabbit, raccoon, waterfowl, broiled doves, skewered larks, conch, octopus, and such—all seasoned with imaginative abandon. The restaurants themselves don't usually look like much, but there are a lot of them.

Martinique's food is similar, but, some say, subtler. Local specialties, in addition to those you find on Guadeloupe, include rabbit with prunes and stewed octopus. On occasion you'll encounter weird dishes like iguana or even bat cooked up in wine.

The French West Indies Tourist Board (610 Fifth Avenue, New York, New York 10020) can send details on the food scene.

Mountain Frogs

Distinctive and delicate are the words for this species of frog found only on the islands of Montserrat, a verdant, volcanic island not far from Antigua, and equally lush Dominica, halfway between Martinique and Guadeloupe. For information about the islands, write the Eastern Caribbean Tourist Association, 220 East 42nd Street, New York, New York 10017.

Guadeloupe's Cooks' Festival

Held every year on the Saturday nearest August 10—the feast day of the patron saint of chefs—the Fête des Cuisinières starts off with all the cooks, in their Creole finery, parading to the church, specialties in hand, to be blessed. This is in preparation for an enormous banquet that sometimes lasts six hours and has you downing quantities of fish, chicken, and a parade of Creole specialties. And it's free. The French West Indies Tourist Board (610 Fifth Avenue, New York, New York 10020) can send more information about the island.

Tastes from the Islands

In Haiti: *tassot* (strips of turkey, turtle, pork, or beef marinated in lime juice and cooked for a day in the sun); *griot* (charcoal-roasted pork); cat meat—raw, with lime juice and garlic, or deep-fried with onions and tabasco in batter.

In Puerto Rico: *forty* kinds of bananas, including *tostones* (deep-fried plantains); *jueyes* (land crabs); barbecued kid; *lechón* asado (roast suckling pig); and some incredibly sweet pineapples.

In the Bahamas: conch chowder with sherry; conch salad spiced with lime juice and hot peppers; red snapper fillets with anchovy sauce; and mango, breadfruit, papaya, and sweet pineapple from the Out Islands.

In Jamaica: good curries, especially goat; mackerel and bananas; boned and stuffed roast suckling pig with thyme, coconut, corn meal, rice, peppers, and yams; wonderful, exotic mangoes, sweetsop, rose apples, and custard apples; and mangoes in dry champagne.

And all over the Caribbean: *callalou*—a thick green soup.

Wines

The history of wine in America begins with the brown-robed Franciscan padres who came up to California from

Mexico in the late eighteenth century, bringing with them as necessities, in their creaky oxcarts, the equipment they needed to make wine. Fifty years later there was a Frenchman who brought vines to America from Bordeaux. But the real story of wines in California started a quarter of a century later, on the heels of the Gold Rush, with the arrival of Hungarian Colonel Agoston Haraszthy. He studied the soil and the climate, imported a hundred thousand vines from Europe, passed them out to farmers throughout the state, proved by example that vineyards in dry country didn't have to be irrigated to produce good wines, and became the Father of California Viticulture. With interruptions for the wars and for combating disease and Prohibition, California viticulture has been going strong ever since.

Meanwhile, in upstate New York, the wine making begun by the colonials was going through some major changes. The native American Vitis labrusca, to which the earliest producers had resorted when Vitis vinifera were killed by the cold winters, had never been held much in esteem. To connoisseurs, the wines made from labrusca tasted foxy.

The story of how the growers started experimenting, in the thirties, with various hybrid grapes that could make it through the winter, and how they were succeeding—well, that's just the sort of tale that dyed-in-the-wool wine buffs go to the wineries to hear. They go to hear about that and to learn about the technicalities that, taken together, make one wine taste different from another.

But even if you could care less about what gets the grape from the vine into bottle, visiting wineries can be fascinating. There is almost always something going on inside—if it's only the walls getting hosed down—or in the fields. The rows upon rows of vines are delightful to look at, and they're usually located in most scenic countryside—in the hilly Finger Lakes of central New York state, along the Hudson River, in the rugged rolls of California's Napa and Sonoma, in the Willamette River Valley of Oregon, as well as quite a few other areas where you wouldn't expect to find vineyards. When you visit a larger winery, there will usually be a slicked-up tour in which you'll see a good deal of the operation, from fermenting rooms and crushers to cellars. At tasting rooms you can taste. At the smaller wineries, there may be nothing to taste, or nobody to take you through the vineyards —but you'll probably get a chance to talk to the wine maker himself, and as they're ordinarily independent souls with lots on their minds and plenty to talk about, winery visits can be people

experiences as well as fact-finding missions and excursions into some very lovely country. Collecting wines and tasting wine can be as addictive as any other hobby, once you get started.

There are dozens of wineries around the country. How to figure out which one to visit? Pick an area you want to see anyway. Or pick a couple of kinds of wine you'd like to taste—a Chardonnay or a Chenin Blanc or a Zinfandel, say— and visit the wineries that produce them. Or taste only the best wines of each vineyard. An old rule of thumb about wine tours is not to try to visit more than three wineries in a day (a large one, a smaller one, and one that produces sparkling wines, for instance). Another old hand advises that you don't drink more than a half-inch in the bottom of your glass per type of wine.

Where to Find the Vineyards

There are vineyards—most producing remarkably high quality wines—in more than twenty states of the United States and several of the Canadian provinces. How can you find out where they are?

There are, first off, some good magazine articles: "The New American Wines" by Evan Jones, which appeared in the May 1977 issue of *Travel and Leisure* (available from the Back Issues Department at 1350 Avenue of the Americas, New York, New York 10019) and "Discovering All-American Wines," by Jose Wilson, from the February 1976 issue of *House and Garden* (350 Madison Avenue, New York, New York 10016) are two good ones. They pinpoint interesting wineries not just in California and New York, but also in Arkansas, Illinois, Indiana, Maryland, Missouri, New Jersey, Ohio, Oregon,

Pennsylvania, Virginia, and Washington. There are some brief descriptions of what's going on in American wine making today, and some information about what each winery is producing.

For a coast-to-coast and Canada guide, see "Wine Country USA/ Canada," published by Reymont Associates (29-W Reymont Avenue, Rye, New York 10580; $2). It lists some two hundred wineries and vineyards, with addresses and telephone numbers—which you'll need: proprietors of the smaller establishments occasionally take the day off in the off-season.

"California's Wine Wonderland," published by the Wine Institute (165 Post Street, San Francisco 94108) lists all the wineries in California—some 280 of them—open to the public. Listings are keyed to a large state map and to county maps with the wineries' exact locations marked. To order a copy, send a stamped self-addressed business-size envelope.

For a quarter, the Napa County Development Council, P. O. Box 876, Napa, California 94558, will send you a larger map of the region. On the back, area wineries are listed with exact addresses, hours, and telephone numbers; locations are pinpointed on the map.

"Winery Trails of the Pacific Northwest," by Tom Stockley (The Writing Works, 7438 S.E. 40th Street, Mercer Island, Washington 98040; $2.49) lists and describes wineries in Oregon, Washington, and British Columbia— three areas that are seeing a hand-over-fist growth in both the number of wineries and the quality of their product. For a list and maps of those in Oregon, contact the Winegrowers Council of Oregon, 816 S.W. First Avenue, Portland 97204.

The Best Wine Country Guide

The wine country of California is extensive enough that there's plenty to talk about, and the editors of Sunset Magazine, who have published and written *California Wine Country* for a decade now, have done a first-rate job with what's there. Region by region, you're given the rundown of the wineries, their product, and their facilities for visitors—in Sonoma, the Napa Valley, the East Bay, the Central Coast, the Lodi area at the gateway to the Gold Country, San Joaquin, and the twelve thousand acres of vines an hour from downtown Los Angeles. You're told how wine is made—helpful information that gives you background for what the winegrowers will subsequently explain. There are special features, too—suggestions for picnicking in the wine country, tips on tasting, a rundown of the various kinds of wine produced in California and their characteristics, and explanations of reading wine labels and of how champagne gets its bubbles. There are also lots of photos, maps, charts, and details about other things to see and do in the area around each winery. Sunset Books, Lane Publishing, Menlo Park, California 94025; $2.95.

The Northern Wine Country in Depth

"The Golden State produces more than 80 percent of all the wine made in the United States (340 million gallons in 1974 from fewer than 250 bonded wineries). Most of the premium wines are crushed within a few hours' drive from San Francisco, in an area generally referred to by the trade as the North

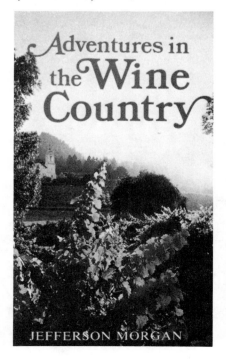

Coast." And for that reason, and because "the rivers, forests, hills, and valleys of the North Coast are prettier than the flat plain of the Valley or the freeways between Los Angeles and Cucamonga," Jefferson Morgan has written his wine country book, *Adventures in the Wine Country*, all about the North Coast. Most other wine country guides talk mainly about the wine, or at best about the wine and the other sights to see in the area, but Morgan also gives you the low-down on restaurants and the lodging situation, and he gives two sets of advice: one for traveling couples, and one for families. The tone is informal, almost chatty, and Morgan crams nifty little facts around the edges—things like the fact that San Francisco's sourdough bread tastes the way it does because of a certain kind of microscopic spore that is found in the air there and nowhere else. The whole thing is pretty interesting reading. Chronicle Books, 870 Market Street, San Francisco, California 94102; $2.95.

Wine Country Tours

You meet the owners of some of the out-of-the-way wineries whose names ring a bell in the minds of only the most knowledgeable; you eat French sourdough bread, quiche, fresh fruit, and cheese at picnics at wineries that are not ordinarily open to the public; and you're escorted by members of the Napa Valley Docent Council (some of whom are wine growers by profession) on excursions sponsored by Wine Tours International. For details, write P. O. Box 2536, Napa, California 94558.

Wine Museums

There are two—both very different—the Greyton Hoyt Taylor Wine Museum in Hammondsport, New York, and the Wine Museum of San Francisco, at 633 Beach Street, in San Francisco, California. The Greyton Hoyt Taylor Museum, whose founding in 1967 makes it the first of the genre, concentrates on giving you the history of wine making in the Finger Lakes of central New York. There are historical documents, exhibits of antique wine-making equipment, bottles and labels that illustrate the changing styles in packaging wines and champagne, and cooperage tools used for making white oak wine casks originally used in the Taylor winery. Outdoors is a "living grape library" in which two hundred separate grape varieties from all over the world are planted. For a brochure on the museum, write the museum on Bully Hill Road, R.D. #2, Hammondsport, New York 14840.

The Wine Museum of San Francisco

emphasizes the way in which wine has through the ages inspired artists—poets, writers, painters, sculptors, silversmiths, glassblowers—to create works in praise of wine. And so there are wooden sculptures, mugs, engravings, exquisite antique goblets, heads of Bacchus—as a cherubic apple-cheeked boy, a virile young man, an old codger who has been through the mill but has managed to keep laughing anyway. "Histowalls" in the museum contain dozens of photos and graphics. And there are special exhibitions. For more information, contact the Wine Museum, 633 Beach Street, San Francisco 94109.

" . . . In Spring I have hard work to do
With digging, pruning and with hoeing,
With grafting, planting, and bending,
With binding and cutting the vines,
Until in Fall the grapes give wine . . . "

—*Der Rebmann*
by Jost Amman
from a German sixteenth-century woodcut

Harvest Festivals

Harvest time is, first of all, a cooler time in the wine country. The heat that makes the cool interiors of the cellars as welcome for their coolness as for their fragrant, slightly musty smell has died down and there's a slight nip in the air. The leaves of the vines start turning tawny gold and scarlet with the season. The smell of the fermenting wine fills the air. And the pickers swarm through the fields and the wine makers themselves are just slightly harassed: it's a popular time to tour the wine country and stop to taste, and it's a busy time with the wine as well.

The excitement of the harvest, the feeling of satisfaction once it's done, comes out at any number of wine festivals. Most are impromptu affairs, but there are a couple of reliable annuals.

The Valley of the Moon Festival in Sonoma, California in late September. After a tableau at which the story of the Hungarian who brought the vines to California is presented, there are blessings of the grape harvest, more historical vignettes, folk dances, an art show, sidewalk games and food booths, barbecue stands, music, and wine sales and tastings. Details: Sonoma Valley Chamber of Commerce, 461 First Street West, Sonoma 95476.

The Sonoma County Harvest Fair, held at the Santa Rosa County Fairgrounds in Santa Rosa, California, about the first of October, is basically an ordinary county fair featuring fall produce, but one of the big events is the judging, displaying, tasting, and auctioning off of various wines from Sonoma, Napa, and Mendocino counties. Details: Harvest Fair, P. O. Box 1536, Santa Rosa 95402.

The Lodi Grape Festival and National Wine Show takes place all over Lodi, California, the first weekend after Labor Day. The biggest feature of the event, which also includes farm exhibitions, wine tastings, and winery exhibits, is a grape mosaic—a mosaic made entirely of grapes placed one by one on a wire mesh that may measure as much as five feet by ten feet. You'll be surprised just how many shades of grapes there are—not just purples and greens and reds, but enough other colors to make a scene depicting, say, early California. For details, contact the Chamber of Commerce in Lodi 95240.

More wine in California. At the Grape Festival at the Marin County Civic Center Fairgrounds in San Rafael. For details, contact the Redwood Empire Association, 476 Post Street, San Francisco 94102.

In Canada, the wine harvest around St. Catharines, Ontario—which produces more grapes than anywhere else in the nation—is celebrated from mid- to late September, with parades, winery and vineyard visits, wine and cheese parties, band competitions. For details, contact the Chamber of Commerce at P. O. Box 940, St. Catharines L2R 6Z4. Another harvest festival is held in Penticton, British Columbia, in the Okanogan Valley. For details: the Chamber of Commerce, Jubilee Pavilion, 185 Lakeshore Drive, Penticton V2A 1B7.

In the eastern United States, the Hudson Valley Wine Company, in Highland, New York, celebrates the harvest—and the simultaneous flaming of the foliage in the Hudson River Valley—with feasts, hayrides, and dancing. Call 914/691-7296 for reservations; the Hudson River Valley Association, at 105 Ferris Lane, Poughkeepsie, New York 12603, can send details about other area goings on.

A Wine Festival for Spring

In the valley of the twisting, turning Russian River, the town of Healdsburg celebrates the products of the hillside vineyards with a big wine-tasting bash one weekend during the first half of May. Concerts are scheduled, and if you get itchy to get out of the plaza where most of the tasting is going on, you can go out into the countryside to visit the ultramodern Cambiaso winery, Dry Creek Vineyards (where there are once-a-month tastings for which you must have reservations), the Geyser Peak Winery, the Italian Swiss Colony near Cloverdale at Asti (which is one of the best places in the state to find out how wine is made on a large scale), Korbel and Martini and Prati. On the Italian Swiss Colony tour, you'll see an eighty-thousand-gallon redwood fermenting tank that is big enough inside to accommodate an infantry platoon. For details about wineries in the area, and about the festival, contact the Chamber of Commerce in Healdsburg 95448.

"An old winebibber having been smashed in a railway collision, some wine was poured on his lips to revive him. 'Pauillac, 1873,' he murmured, and died."

—Ambrose Bierce

Winy Seminars

The Hudson Valley Wine Company—a beautiful old winery with about 325 acres of tip-tilted vineyards and handsome stone buildings, right on the Hudson River near Highland, New York 12528—holds annual grape-picking seminars in late September every year. For details, write the winery.

In the West, there are special Wine Appreciation Courses sponsored by the Napa Valley Wine Library Association several weekends in June and August in St. Helena, California. Staffs of the area wineries do the teaching. Applications are accepted first from members of the Wine Library Association (whose dues go to the purchase of books for the St. Helena Public Library's special collection on wine). To get details, contact the Napa Valley Wine Library Association, Box 328, St. Helena 94574.

For some in-depth reading on your own, see "Wines, Grape Vines, and Climate," in the June 1974 issue of Scientific American (415 Madison Avenue, New York, New York 10017).

The author, Philip Wagner, owner of the celebrated Boordy Vineyards in Riderwood, Maryland, addresses himself mainly to the matter of how climate makes wines different from one another.

Wagner, one of the eminent American winegrowers, has also written two books on the subject: *A Wine Grower's Guide* ($7.95) and *Grapes into Wine: the Art of Wine Making in America* ($5.95 in paperback). Both are published by Alfred A. Knopf, 201 East 50th Street, New York, New York 10022.

Buying Your Own Vines
When you're involved in the subject enough that you've had it with making your own wine out of commercially produced grape juice and don't want to waste your time making wine with labrusca grapes, the person to talk to is Philip Wagner. Stop at his Boordy Vineyards, if you can. It's in Riderwood, Maryland, just outside Baltimore. Or order vines of assorted types directly from the winery (Box 38, Riderwood 21139). You can order Baco No. 1 grapes, Foch, Joannes-Sevye 26-205, Landot 4511, Millot, Seibel 7053, Seibel 8357, Seibel 9549, Seibel 10878, Seibel 13053, Seibel 14596, Sevye-Villard 5247, Sevye-Villard 18-315—and that's just what's available if you're interested in making reds. The catalogue gives brief descriptions of characteristics of the grapes, the vine, the wine that results, and the care necessary. Example: "early, hardy, disease resistant, ultravigorous, moderate crops. When properly handled, its wine sometimes recalls red Bordeaux. Its great vigor can make it hard to handle in commercial plantings, but is no obstacle in family vineyards and makes it ideal for decorative trellis or arbor. Cane pruning." At $1, more or less, per vine, the booklet is enough to start you thinking about growing your own. Enclose a stamped self-addressed envelope with any request for information, and you'll get priority handling.

And a Wine Magazine
It's *Wine World*—information about kinds of wine, wine places, wine tours, doing it yourself, as well as interesting letters and ads. Subscriptions, $7.50 a year for six issues, are available from 15101 Keswick Street, Van Nuys, California 91405.

Distilleries
Distillers, just like wine makers, have very strong opinions about how to turn out the best product.

On any tour you might make of the country's distilleries, for instance, you'll encounter tour guides who tell you that their company uses stainless steel for the fermenting process because it is only by using tanks of this

scrubbable substance that they can get quality control. Then at the next establishment, you'll be told that stainless steel deprives the liquor of its character—that only fermentation in wood tanks can produce anything worth drinking. But quite beyond this very amusing quirk of distillers, the places where bourbon and whiskey and vodka are made are fun to visit. The smells—the brewer's yeast fermenting and giving off an odor like that of fresh-baked bread—are delightful, and there are all sorts of mysterious-looking tanks and tubes, dials and doodads. The Hiram Walker Distillery in Peoria, Illinois, is among the most unabashedly modern you'll encounter. It is also the largest bourbon distillery in the world—but other things are produced here too—cordials, for instance—which makes this tour interesting even after you've seen all the rest. Tours cover the plant from top to bottom—from the thirteen-thousand-gallon pressure cookers in which the distiller's beer—the liquid that is then distilled to form alcohol—is produced, right down to the laboratories where people with faultless senses of taste and smell quality-control the products. For details on seeing the distillery and the town, contact the Peoria Association of Commerce, Convention and Visitors Department, 307 First National Bank Building, Peoria, Illinois 61614.

Most other distilleries that offer tours are located in Kentucky and Tennessee—and for the most part they're folksy places that play the southern heritage for all it's worth. But from this point of view, two distilleries have it head and shoulders over all the rest—the Jack Daniel Distillery near Lynchburg, Tennessee, in the southern part of the state, and the Maker's Mark Distillery at Star Hill Farm near Loretto, Kentucky. The Jack Daniel distillery, oldest registered distillery in the United States, is, for starters, in one of those quaint courthouse-in-the-center towns with not much more to recommend it than its country store on one side of the sidewalk that rings the square, and the saloon not far away where you can buy salads and sandwiches. The distillery itself is in a hollow just north of town. You can see the rickyard stacked with the sugar maple from which are made the charcoal chips through which the whiskey is filtered (and Jack Daniel's claim to being a Tennessee sippin' whiskey rather than an ordinary bourbon is assured); Jack Daniel's original office; and the limestone spring that, for all these years, has never failed to give its bounty of iron-free water. The Maker's Mark Distillery is not far from Bardstown, Kentucky, and the sites of Lincoln country in Kentucky, but it somehow seems very remote and very rural.

It's the sort of area where you don't have to try very hard to get lost. Distillery buildings are scattered around the pleasant small hills and fields; they're rusty looking, unpretentious. The bottling operation—which is usually the same everywhere—is distinguished by the final hand-dipping into hot sealing wax. For details on tours, contact the Western Marion County Chamber of Commerce, P. O. Box 45, Loretto, Kentucky 40037.

No tasting, though: The IRS men—who are provided with offices at each distiller's expense and who enforce the taxation on each and every bottle and keep the keys to the warehouses after hours to make sure that nobody cheats—won't permit it.

Whiskey History
Once upon a time there was a man named E. C. Booz, whose life was such that the only mark he left on society was a word—the slang word for liquor. His bottle is on display at the Barton Museum of Whiskey History in Bardstown, Kentucky. But it's only one of dozens and dozens and dozens of exhibits, which, all told, make this one of the most fascinating of small museums. As its founders will quickly tell you, the history of the United States is closely paralleled by the history of distilling. So when you tour the museum and look at the graphics and artifacts, you're actually getting a quick lesson in social studies. You'll see everything from medicine bottles—whose highly alcoholic contents provided ladies and religious zealots with their kicks in the old days—to photos of the Prohibition era, a collection of bottles, and Abraham Lincoln's retail permit. Bardstown is also the home of the grand brick mansion in which Stephen Foster wrote "My Old Kentucky Home," plus an outdoor drama that tells the story of the composer and his Jeanie with the light brown hair; a magnificent Cathedral; and a really nifty country inn, the Talbott Tavern, that serves up some of the best salty country ham and red eye gravy you'll find anywhere. The desserts are equally scrumptious. For details, contact the Bardstown Chamber of Commerce, P. O. Box 296, Bardstown 40004.

The National Park with an Operating Still
When the revenuers seized a fine moonshine still in the mountains around Cades Cove, Tennessee, they had little idea that it would end up in a National Park. Yet that's where it is today—cooking away at Catoctin Mountain Park, near Thurmont, Maryland, 65 miles north of Washington, D.C., and even closer to the

presidential retreat at Camp David. The Park Superintendent, who was responsible for getting the still from Tennessee and for coaxing operating instructions out of old-time Marylanders who suddenly turned ignorant when faced by a representative of the federal government, turns out 150 gallons of white lightning every weekend. For details about the park, contact National Capital Parks, c/o the National Park Service at 1100 Ohio Drive, S.W., Washington, D.C. 20242.

The World's Biggest Rum Distillery
Bacardi, near Dorado, Puerto Rico, on the north coast of the island just west of San Juan, gives free tours. The Puerto Rico Tourism Company, 1290 Avenue of the Americas, New York, New York 10019, can send you information about all the other things to do on this interesting island.

Breweries

Motors whir and scream. Bottles clank. The sweet smell of malt, barley, hops, and grits is in the air. And before you know it, you've got a bottle of beer. Brewery tours are fun from beginning to end—though bibulous types will probably like the end better than the beginning, for most breweries deposit guests who have toured the premises in hospitality rooms where all you can drink is the order of the day. Where better to experience brewing at its best than Milwaukee? Miller beer is made there at 4000 West State; Schlitz at 235 West Galena; and Pabst at 901 West Juneau. For details about hours, contact the Milwaukee Convention & Visitors Bureau, 828 North Broadway, Milwaukee 53202.

Flora and Fauna

Some Spectacular Gardens

The days in which a stroll in the public garden was *the* thing to do if you didn't stay home and read the Bible are long gone; the gardens that are left over from those days are too often overlooked as a vacation possibility. Yet gardens are works of art, just like paintings or musical compositions. They don't go out of style. If you've seen one garden, you most certainly have not seen them all, for there are colonial gardens, topiary gardens, landscape gardens, and more. The really grand gardens will speak to you, and touch you, as much as any other work of art.

The du Ponts' Showplaces
After you've seen Longwood Gardens, which Pierre S. du Pont established at Kennett Square, Philadelphia, it's hard to imagine that any other garden could be so beautiful: even in winter, when the fountains are shut down and the leaves are all off, it's a treat to roam through the soft woods, the Fountain Gardens (which in summer put on a display that rivals the best fountains in

Butchart Gardens, Victoria, British Columbia.

Europe), the Italian water gardens. There are some small, secret gardens devoted to a single flower—peony, for instance, or iris. There are rose gardens, herb gardens, vegetable gardens, gardens that grow plants that are used to make medicine. There are conservatories as well—four acres—cool and moist and full of the strangest types of insect-eating plants, tropical plants, desert plants, and the lushest varieties of the house plants you've tried to grow at home with considerably less success. (The Boston fern, for instance, has a root ball about two feet in diameter.) Spring is a wonderful time in the gardens. There are masses of azaleas, daffodils, magnolias, and dogwood; May apples, blood root, marsh marigolds, and trilliums are blooming in the wildflower wood. Perennials and tiny plants like anemones and red-and-white spotted fritillaria are like jewels in the rock garden. The main conservatories are sweetly scented by flowering cherries and apples, delphiniums, poppies and pansies. When you think that these will take you nearly an hour to breeze through—and that spring is only one of the beautiful seasons in the gardens—then you have some idea of how impressive the place is.

Nearby, there are sixty acres of gardens—landscaped by Henry Francis du Pont, who used to own the place, to look as if they'd been forever wild—on the grounds of Winterthur, the only museum completely devoted to American decorative arts in the United States. The Azalea Woods, completely banked by big bushes of pink, white, and lavendar flowers, is especially beautiful starting in about mid-May. At the same time, the forsythia and daffodils turn the hillsides nearly golden.

When you see what the du Ponts did with their money, you can't help but be glad they're sharing it.

For more information, write the Delaware State Visitors Service, 630 State College Road, Dover 19901; the Chester County Tourist Promotion Bureau, 33 West Market Street, West Chester, Pennsylvania 19380; Longwood Gardens, Kennett Square, Pennsylvania 19348.

The Largest Outdoor Collection of Cacti and Succulents in the World
It's at the Huntington Botanical Gardens in San Marino, California. Twelve acres of desert gardens are particularly impressive. The succulents—strange-looking plants, with strange names like milk barrel, cow's horn, elephant's foot, and living rock—come mainly from Africa, the cacti mainly from the United States.

But the Huntington Botanical Gardens don't end there. You'll also see a Japanese garden whose star is a vermilion-colored moon bridge, a Zen Garden of raked gravel with a few shrubs and trees, and a rose garden. Something is nearly always in bloom: camellias and forsythias in March, coral trees and wistaria in April, yellow-flowered cassia and roses in August.

For more information, write the gardens at 1151 Oxford Road in San Marino 91108.

Camellias in the Live Oaks
Three miles from the Pasadena Rose Bowl in La Canada, California, the Decanso Gardens flood into bloom in late winter and spring. It's a wondrous place. Newspaper publisher Manchester Boddy planted a hundred thousand camellias in all varieties and species in a grove of ancient live oaks. When they're out of bloom, iris, azaleas, rhododendron, and sweet-scented lilacs take over. Then, beginning in June, there are the roses. It's a grand parade indeed. For more information, contact the Southern California Visitors Council at 705 West Seventh, Los Angeles 90017.

Canada's Wonder Place
It may well be the most colorful place in the world. Butchart Gardens—in Victoria, British Columbia—is twenty-five acres of tulips, salvia, forget-me-nots, daffodils, dogwood, rhododendron, white and pink cherry, dahlias, zinnias, chrysanthemums, roses, begonias, fuchsias, and thousands of others spread out and around twenty-five acres that are divided up into an English rose garden, a stately formal Italian garden full of Florentine statuary, a Japanese garden complete with a tea-house, and a four-acre sunken garden, which you can stroll through on pathways or view from the top of a fifty-foot-high cliff. There are waterfalls, lacy fountains, trails and wisps of ivy, banks of marigolds, a lake. Butchart Gardens is a sea of pale pinks, purples, blues, bright reds, and yellows almost any time of the year you go.

And there are some special touches: the illumination at night—possible because of some four miles of underground wiring—when the gardens are quite at their best. The water coming out of the fountains is even more delicate and crystalline under lights. There are no "Do Not" do this-or-that signs, but instead, on one tree, a sign reads" "Please carve initials here." In the summer, there are musical variety shows on an outdoor stage at twilight, and sometimes magic shows or puppet shows or strolling musicians.

For more information, write the gardens at Box 4010, Station A, Victoria, British Columbia V8X 3X4.

Flowers You Can Grow Yourself
The Kingwood Center at Mansfield, Ohio, equidistant from Cleveland and Columbus off I-17, grows them: sixty thousand tulips bloom beginning in late April and peaking the first two weeks of May; dahlias in two hundred varieties, and day lilies in three hundred varieties start in July and bloom most of the fall until frost; fifty varieties of hostas; perennials from April to November gladiolus in August. And this is just a sampling of what goes on in the twelve gardens.

One of the amazing things about Kingwood Center is that each of the varieties is labeled and coded as to where the seeds to grow it were purchased—so that you can get the exact plants to grow at home.

For more information, write Kingwood Center in Mansfield 44901.

Cypress Gardens
Cypress Gardens, Florida, halfway between Orlando and Tampa, is not at all as hokey as you might expect but instead adds up to a tropical paradise: you see Italian fountains, palms, princess trees fairly dripping with bright purple blossoms (especially in May), allamandas, water lilies, bougainvillea, bird-of-paradise, and, January through April, azaleas, camellias. Year-round: roses. You can get more information by writing the gardens. The zip code is 33880.

The Charm Spot of the Deep South
Bellingrath Gardens, at Theodore, Alabama, is certainly one of the most memorable gardens in the United States: camellias bloom by the thousands from September until April, azaleas by the hundreds of thousands from mid-January into April. But there are dozens and dozens of other plants, some of which look exquisite and some of which smell exquisite, and some of which (like gardenias, which bloom in May) do both. This is a garden that has been designed as a feast for the nose as well as the eyes.

Other blossoms: mountain laurel and dogwood, in April; hydrangeas with the gardenias in May; crape myrtles in the summer; mums in fall—and Spanish moss, veiling the live oaks and making a muted gray green backdrop to set off the color show, year-round.

For more information, write the Gardens in Theodore 36582.

The Resort Gardens

Tucked away in the hills not far from Atlanta, Callaway Gardens at Pine Mountain, Georgia, occupy a land that in 1930, the local farmers were calling barren as a jenny mule. But you'd never know it to see the place today. Georgia textile magnate Cason J. Callaway came along and did a magical number on those twenty-five hundred acres, and today it flowers year round, with azaleas and wildflowers in the spring; roses, day lilies, and the rare plum-leaf azalea (rare because it blooms in July) in summer; and, in the fall, the camellias and the chrysanthemums.

Callaway Gardens is also a complete family outdoor recreation center, and so after you've hiked the flower trails, you can go on horseback rides, fish for bass and bluegills, play tennis, square dance, go canoeing. Golf is a very big deal indeed. And, the year round, there are all sorts of special events—garden workshops in bonsai, advanced bonsai, vegetable gardening, bulbs, propagation, wild flowers, terrariums. At Easter there's a big Easter Egg Hunt for kids under twelve.

For more information, write the gardens at Pine Mountain, Georgia 31822.

A Butterfly Garden

If it has ever occurred to you that you haven't seen any butterflies for a long time, it was probably because you haven't. Apparently the kind of scentless blooms that are grown in most gardens nowadays simply don't attract the butterflies the way the old English cottage gardens did. Bernard Jackson, the resident naturalist and manager of the Oxen Pond Botanic Park in St. John's, Newfoundland, is particularly interested in the problems of keeping butterflies in his garden. When you visit his establishment you'll see painted ladies and cosmopolite butterflies, red admirals, and the like sitting on Scabiosa and Buddleia and the like. It's an interesting place. For more information, write the Newfoundland Department of Tourism, Confederation Building, St. John's, Newfoundland.

Louisiana Gardens

The warm, moist climate of the state lends itself to gardens, and so it would be a surprise *not* to find several magnificent public gardens.

As it happens, there are five of exceptional interest.

Rosedown Plantation and Gardens, inspired by those at Versailles and studded by camellias so old and large that they're considered trees instead of shrubs, also contains sweet olive, gardenias, roses, azaleas, crape myrtles. Ancient oaks arch over the drive that leads to the house—it's what you might call super-South. Some of the

gardens are formal, some are close to natural, but it's all got a lush, almost untamed feel, as you'd expect of a garden in an area where plants grow like wildfire. March through June is the time to visit; the camellias are full starting in February, and the azaleas flower in March and April.

For more information, write the gardens at Drawer M, St. Francisville 70775.

Jungle Gardens

They sit on a submerged salt mountain eight miles deep and six miles around, the nesting place, in spring, of some hundred thousand snowy egrets, on Avery Island in the heart of the Louisiana Cajun Country.

The gardens started out at the end of the nineteenth century when Edward Avery McIlhenny—of the tobasco sauce family—started trapping young egrets in the area and bringing them up at his home on Avery Island in an effort to save them from the hunters who killed them to get their plumes, which were used on ladies' hats.

From March to July, the egrets are nesting in their bird city. However, there are always some around the property, and there are always the gardens: a thousand varieties of camellias including imported ones from Japan, China, France, blooming from November through March; azaleas, spectacular between February and April; wisteria, arranged in a delicately colored arch; an oriental holly called Ilex cornuta; waterfalls; African water lilies; and a temple garden. One of the most spectacular sections is the forest of sixty-foot-high Chinese Timber Bamboo; some sixty-four varieties of exotic

bamboos—from fern bamboos (lacy leafed) to huge timber canes—also grow on the island. And there is a rock garden, an iris garden, an alligator pool, and a lily pool. For more information about the gardens, write Avery Island, Louisiana 70513; for details on the area, contact the Chamber of Commerce, 108 West Main Street, New Iberia 70560.

New Orleans's Spanish Gardens

The Longue Vue Gardens outside New Orleans, Louisiana, were inspired by the Generalife gardens of Granada, a showplace created in the fifteenth century at the height of its Moorish civilization.

It's quite a lovely place—part stately formal gardens where sculpted hedges pattern emerald expanses of lawn, part more intimate courtyards. There are fountains everywhere—one in the form of dolphins, a hexagonal fountain mounted on a floor of delicately detailed patterns—and fragrance, from the wisteria, geraniums, sage, sweet olive, jasmine, citrus, roses. Boxwood, herbs, and myrtles were chosen for the fresh smell of their leaves. Lily-of-the-valley send more sweetness from behind a screen of shrubs. Longue Vue isn't one of those places where you're overwhelmed by color, but instead the flowers are "like jewels on a dress."

For more information, write Longue Vue, 7 Bamboo Road, New Orleans 70124.

An English Garden in a Tropical Setting

Rip Van Winkle's Live Oak Gardens at Jefferson Island, Louisiana, not far from Jungle Gardens and Avery Island is a series of somewhat informal gar-

Butchart Gardens, Victoria, British Columbia.

157

Longue Vue Gardens, New Orleans.

dens that have a sort of random feel; there are special Williamsii hydrid camellias from Wales (a special pride), hollies, copper plants, azaleas by the millions of blossoms, wisteria, jasmine, iris along an Azalea Trail. You can also walk a special summer trail—best during that season, when its crape myrtles, magnolias, gardenias, flamboyant hibiscus, bougainvillea, and oleander are at their best. Daffodil and narcissus bloom in late winter; camellias from Japan, China, Australia, England, France, and America blossom between October and March. For more information, write the gardens at Jefferson Island 70545.

Garden in the Forest

Hodges Gardens, forty-seven hundred acres near the town of Many, was built at an abandoned rock quarry, and so it has a sort of wild beauty: there are wildflowers, rocks covered with lichen, streams and waterfalls and pools.

When A. J. Hodges started working on the gardens in the 1940s, the landscape was scarcely disturbed: trees were not cut down, walkways were constructed along natural paths, and plantings were put onto the terraces of the natural hillsides. Each season is a delight: spring brings tulips, masses and masses of azaleas (some of them wild), roses, iris, jasmine, wisteria. The redbuds and dogwoods go crazy. Summer brings water lilies, roses, amaryllis, moss roses, crape myrtle, and salvias. Autumn has its chrysanthemums, camellias, angels' trumpets, and more—and the flowering continues even in winter.

Write Hodges Gardens at Box 921, Many 71449 for details.

More Louisiana Gardens

See the Pelican Guide to Louisiana Gardens, by Joyce YelDell LeBlanc, for information about other things to see and do in the area of all the major garden spots, plus brief accounts of the other flowery places in the state. Pelican Publishing, 630 Burmaster Street, Gretna, Louisiana 70053; $2.95.

The City of Gardens

Charleston, South Carolina, is a shrine to garden lovers, as any one of them will tell you; the city has not one horticultural paradise but three.

Cypress Gardens

The mood at this two-hundred-fifty-acre Eden—the grounds of Dean Hall Plantation on the Cooper River—is mystical, slightly spooky. The garden has been designed to capitalize on the feeling that one gets from the cypress forest at the core of the tract. The gardens are set around pathways over dikes built up to connect islands in a lake of cypress; you can explore them in boats or on foot. You can see the reflections of the masses of azaleas in the water—black because of leachings of the cypress roots—as well as of narcissus, daffodil, and daphne odora, and hundreds of others.

Magnolia Gardens

At the beginning of the twentieth century, a European guidebook gave its coveted two stars to just three spots in the United States: the Grand Canyon, Niagara Falls, and Charleston's Magnolia Gardens. More recently, John Galsworthy called it "the most beautiful garden in the world." An astonishing place, it is at its best in the spring, when some five hundred varieties of camellias, plus azaleas and wisterias, splotch a landscape of gray green cypress, lagoons, live oak, and Spanish moss with brilliant shades of pink, purple, white. The Reverend John Drayton, who created the gardens on his ancestral estate, had in mind the informal trend toward designing a landscape to look like nature—and the results were everything that the designers of those naturalistic landscape-garden theories would have wanted. You can see the gardens, then rent bikes or canoes or take electric boat tours for exploring the Waterfowl Wildlife Refuge, a 125-acre flooded area where you can see ducks and other waterfowl (as many as ten thousand during migrations in the late fall).

Middleton Place

This Charleston, South Carolina, establishment was the first landscaped garden in the United States, so the plants are all old and mature. The camellias are huge, more like trees than shrubs. They bloom from the beginning of winter through March. The azaleas, which flower at about the same time, are puffballs of color. There are wonderful lawns, a lake edged by bald cypresses; a giant oak that some say is a thousand years old. And you can tour the restored house. For details, write Middleton Place in Charleston 29407.

For more information

About Charleston, you can get details from the Charleston-Trident Chamber of Commerce, Box 975, Charleston 29402. The South Carolina Department of Parks, Recreation, and Tourism at Box 113, 1205 Pendleton Street, Columbia 29201 can send you a booklet about all of the state's gardens.

Some Arboretums

The Arnold Arboretum in Boston, Massachusetts, is one of the finest in the United States because of its two

hundred sixty-five acres of ornamental trees, flowers, and shrubs—all of which are labeled. It's spectacular in mid-May when lilacs, dogwoods, and rhododendrons bloom. For more information, write the Arboretum on the Arborway in Jamaica Plain, Boston, Massachusetts 02130.

In Cincinnati, Ohio, the Irvin M. Krohn Conservatory is not to be missed. It is one of the most important public greenhouses in the United States. For details, write the Cincinnati Park Board at 950 Eden Park Drive, Cincinnati 45202.

Caribbean Gardens

All the islands are lusher than the most splendid northern planting, so you can imagine what the public gardens and flowering places are like—full of bamboo, cinnamon, ilang ilang, and other strangely named plants.

In Mayagüez, Puerto Rico, the island's third largest city, there's the Federal Agricultural Experiment Station. It has the largest collection of tropical plants in the New World—quite something to see. Write the Puerto Rico Tourism Company at 1290 Avenue of the Americas, New York, New York 10019 for details on this area.

At the 63-acre Royal Botanic Gardens, founded in 1818 just north of the Queens Park Savannah in Port-of-Spain, Trinidad, guides take you around and tell you about the plants, which are strange and exotic enough that the tours are interesting even if you normally don't like tours. You'll see, for instance, lotus lilies, monkey pods, monkey puzzles, willows, orchids, frangipani, cocaine bushes, sapodillas, devil's ears, nutmeg trees, sausage trees, kola, butter nuts, the raw beef tree, and more. The Trinidad and Tobago Tourist Association at 400 Madison Avenue, New York, New York 10017 can send more information about the area.

Caribbean Wildlife

There are agoutis, turtledoves, thrushes, and raccoons at the 74,100-acre ferns-and-jungles Natural Park, which takes up most of the Basse-Terre wing of the island of Guadeloupe. The volcano Soufrière is in the Natural Area; you can walk to the top, where the heat coming out of the vents is so intense you can light a cigarette from it. There are also other hikes in the park; the French West Indies Tourist Board (610 Fifth Avenue, New York, New York 10020) can put you in touch with hiking groups and supply booklets and maps showing hiking trails in the area.

The Most Flamingos

The greatest number of flamingos that are easy to get to, anyway, are at Washington National Park on the tiny island of Bonaire, just a short hop from the northern coast of South America. The willowy pink birds thrive by the thousands in the park, which is at the northwestern end of the island not far from Goto Lake, where the birds build their mud-pie nests and care for their young, which usually hatch in March or April. The bird-watching is best in the late afternoon, for it's then that herons, tern, snipe, pelicans, parrots, parakeets, and other birds as brilliantly colored as the fish on the offshore reefs come out to feed. For details on watching the birds—and on the annual Flamingo Festival—contact the Bonaire Tourist Board at 685 Fifth Avenue, New York, New York 10022.

More Flamingos

On Great Inagua, in the Bahamas, there are some thirty thousand, and the government maintains much of the area around Windsor Lake, where the strange pink birds nest, as a wildlife park. In addition, you'll see wild donkeys and goats. Tourist development is practically nonexistent, but there are a couple of guest houses—Ford's Inagua Inn (six rooms) and the Main House, both in Matthew Town, which is the center of the main industry on the island, salt production. Rates at local hostelries start at about $12 MAP for *two* people and top off at about $30. The Out Islands Promotion Board (255 Alhambra Circle, Suite 450, Coral Gables, Florida 33134) can send you more information about wildlife and nature doings.

The Birds of Trinidad

This is one of the best spots in the Caribbean for animals: egrets, tanagers, potoos, blue-crowned motmot, tityras, parson birds, toucans, tufted coquettes, squirrel cuckoos, and some 400 other species as spectacular as the fish that swim around the Buccoo Reef not far away—plus 100 kinds of mammals, 55 kinds of snakes, and 617 kinds of butterflies—can all be seen at the Asa Wright Nature Center at Spring Hill Estate, east of Port-of-Spain in the Arima Valley. There are about thirty rooms—on the spartan side but comfortable—where you can spend the night, and there are special day- or week-long nature programs.

Seven miles outside Port-of-Spain there are more birds at the Caroni Bird Sanctuary—some ten thousand acres of marshland through which you can ride in boats and see egrets, ospreys, shrikes, herons, jaçanas, and maybe even the celebrated scarlet ibis. Tours are available; it's best to go early in the morning or late in the afternoon.

Also on Trinidad: the Guachano Caves, which you get to by wading along a narrow gorge through rapids and cascades and then crossing a long ladder that spans two boulders. What do you see when you get there? Oilbirds—big fat creatures named for the way they burned when the Indians used them as torches; they're rare.

Nearly half of Trinidad is forest preserve, so there's more to see. There are wild hogs (quencks), lappes and agoutis, mongooses, ocelots, deer, squirrels, raccoons, and armadillos in these thick forests. The rivers and swamps are full of crocodiles, the forests of parrots. And nineteen kinds of hummingbirds. The Trinidad and Tobago Tourist Board (400 Madison Avenue, New York, New York 10017) can send you more information about this wildlife wonderland.

The Wild Side of the Turks

The Turks and Caicos Islands, southeast of the Bahamas, are being developed—and this started only recently—along the lines of the British Virgin Islands, to retain the natural beauty and keep tourist facilities low-profile and sea-oriented. So far, however, not much has been done, and the islands are sandy, sunny, and full of wildlife—frigate birds nesting at Penniston Cay, noddy and sooty terns on Round and Gibb cays, spectacular reefs near South Caicos, Long Cay, and Providenciales. For more information, write the Turks and Caicos Tourist Association, c/o the Eastern Caribbean Tourist Board, 220 East 42nd Street, New York, New York 10017.

"Full fathom five thy father lies;
   Of his bones are coral made;
Those are pearls that were his eyes:
   Nothing of him that doth fade
But does suffer a sea-change
   Into something rich and strange."
   —William Shakespeare,
   The Tempest

Beneath the Seas of the West Indies

by Hans W. Hannau and Bernd H. Mock

"It is like a dream come true to float weightless in that warm, wet world from which all life came. . . . Fifteen feet under there is so much living color. Further down, those that always thought Heaven is blue find that blue. Divers riding an undersea sled in the Gulf Stream hardly know down from up, are literally bathed in that blessed, clear blue."

And if that's not enough to inspire you to sign up for a scuba course at your local Y, the pictures in this small, square coffee-table book will: there are reefs of elkhorn coral and gorgonians, and porkfish, trumpetfish, and angelfish floating in a peacock-blue sea. The corals look like feathers, or pine needles, or fans. Everything is incredibly delicate and lovely.

The text describes what you see, talks about treasure hunting (and finding), good diving spots, and reef ecology. A picture portfolio at the end identifies many varieties of fish and coral. Hastings House Publishers, 10 East 40th Street, New York, New York 10017; $5.95.

Undersea Life in the Caribbean

The fish—so brilliant that it's hard to believe they're real—are the principal and single most thrilling segment of the animal kingdom you'll see in the Caribbean islands. Some places that are particularly good for scuba diving and snorkeling:

Jamaica. Snorkeling is especially good off Negril, on the fine long strand at the west end of the island; and in coves around Ocho Rios, on the north coast. Scuba is best at offshore reefs, especially along the mile-long Chalet Caribe Reef near Montego Bay. The Chalet Caribe Hotel offers diving packages, as does the Teach Tour Diving Company (Box 390, Nazareth, Pennsylvania 18064).

The French West Indies. At Martinique and Guadeloupe you can get instruction at the Club Meds—information is available from 40 West 57th Street, New York, New York 10019.

The Bahamas. The Tongue of the Ocean—six thousand feet deep on one side and twelve feet deep on the other—makes for some really spectacular underwater sightseeing. The reef here, off Andros Island, is one of the world's most extraordinary. Diving and snorkeling are also big at Small Hope Bay, also on Andros; at the sea garden at Pelican Cay National Park; and at the Exuma National Land and Sea Park, in the Exumas. Teach Tour Diving Company (address above) sponsors diving weeks in the area; there are also hotels that highlight diving: the Underwater Explorers Club on Grand Bahama Island, the Stella Maris Inn on Long Island, and Small Hope Bay Lodge on Andros Island. For details, write the Bahamas Tourist Office (30 Rockefeller Plaza, New York, New York 10020) and the Out Islands Promotion Board (255 Alhambra Circle, Suite 450, Coral Gables, Florida 33134).

Bonaire. Everything from sharpnose puffers to stingrays can be seen along the reefs and wrecks, and the extra-clear waters, with a visibility of eighty to a hundred feet, make for quite an exceptional experience. Teach Tour Diving Company (address above) offers packages and programs, as does the Aquaventure Dive Center at the Hotel Bonaire. For details, write the Bonaire Tourist Board at 685 Fifth Avenue, New York, New York 10020.

The British Virgin Islands. The water is crystalline, the reefs spectacular. Dive B.V.I. on Virgin Gorda; the Aquatic Centre at Road Town, Tortola; and Marina Cay at Beef Island all have fine facilities and can provide more information—as can the B.V.I. Tourist Board, c/o J. S. Fones, 515 Madison Avenue, New York, New York 10022.

The Cayman Islands. Elkhorn coral forests, caves, coral heads, and wrecks—and a visibility of up to two hundred feet. There's good snorkeling off twelve-mile-long Cayman Brac, one of the Lesser Caymans. Bob Soto's Diving Lodge, at Pirate's Cove on Grand Cayman, is inexpensive and offers special diving plans; Spanish Bay Reef Resort, on the northwest point of Grand Cayman, is also big on diving and offers courses in underwater photography. For more information, write the Cayman Islands Department of Tourism, 420 Lexington Avenue, New York, New York 10017.

Buck Island Reef National Monument
Tropical fish, grottoes, coral, sea fans, gorgonias, and such make the underwater nature trail at this National Park Service facility off Buck Island (about

an hour's boat ride from Christiansted, St. Croix, U.S. Virgin Islands) quite an experience. The trail, marked with arrows, is easy to follow. On the shore, you can sometimes see green turtles and rookeries of pelicans and frigate birds. For more information, write the Superintendent, Virgin Islands National Park, Box 806, St. Thomas, Virgin Islands 00801.

Virgin Islands National Park
Snorkeling is to this area what hiking is in the Shenandoah; the underwater gardens—wonderlands of fish and coral and bright-colored formations in eerie, fascinating shapes—are even more spectacular than the brilliant jungles on shore. For more information, write the Superintendent, Virgin Islands National Park, Box 806, St. Thomas, Virgin Islands 00801.

Tobago's Buccoo
Though it's shallow enough for just about anybody, and even old women in support hose wade in and peer down at the fish, this reef contains one of the world's finest submarine gardens. It's filled with angelfish, purple damsels, autumn leaves, parrot fish, and more.

For information, write the Trinidad and Tobago Tourist Board, 400 Madison Avenue, New York, New York 10017.

Florida's Underwater Park
At John Pennekamp Coral Reef State Park, at Key Largo, Florida, you snorkel above a reef through forests of coral inhabited by angelfish, butterfly fish, snappers, and parrot fish; you go past yellow tube sponges and purple sea fans waving ever so slightly in the current. Porkfish, yellowtails, grunts, and wrasses glide by you in precise formation—and you're right there in the middle of it.

You can see it all with a snorkel and flippers—boats will take you out to Molasses Reef to find all the animals—or go on glass-bottom-boat tours. The tours might be a good idea even if you do snorkel, since a guide is available to identify the coral species and the fish, animals, and plants.

For more information, write the Florida Department of Commerce, Collins Building, Tallahassee, Florida 32304.

Snorkeling the Florida Sweet Water
In the Ocala National Forest at Alexan-

der Springs, Florida, a huge spring pours forth eighty million gallons of water every day. Until you've actually been there, it's hard to imagine just how soft the water feels, or just how crystal-clear it is. The rugged rock formations that line the walls of the pool take on an amazing clarity. And there are fish down there.

For more information, write the Florida Department of Commerce, Collins Building, Tallahassee, Florida 32304.

Organized Scuba Trips

For tour operators who will teach you on site, contact Teach Tour Diving Company (Box 390, Nazareth, Pennsylvania 18064); Life Bound (5631 Tennyson Street, Arvada, Colorado 80002); Sea & Sea Travel Service (680 Beach Street, Suite 340, San Francisco, California 94109); Atlantis Safaris (P. O. Box 303, Miami Shores, Florida 33153); Bay Travel, Inc. (2435 East Coast Highway, Corona del Mar, California 92625); or Kirk Anders Travel (P. O. Box 1418, Fort Lauderdale, Florida 92625).

Scuba Training

You can get information about instruction programs that will lead to certification (which is sometimes required in order to get air) from the National Association of Underwater Instructors (22809 Barton Road, Grand Terrace, Colton, California 92324) and the Professional Association of Diving Instructors (2064 North Bush Street, Santa Ana, California 92706).

Learn About the Ocean's Life

The Jean-Michel Cousteau Institute sponsors interesting Project Ocean Search programs to Hilton Head Island, South Carolina; Catalina Island, California; and Antigua, in the Caribbean. You can study the nature and diversity of life and man's relationship to his environment. On Hilton Head, you explore the wetlands and unpolluted marshes, study fiddler crabs, and discuss marine geology, continental drift, turtle ecology, plankton, and fish seining. On Antigua, in addition to discussing environmental problems, you examine the tropical jungle and desert communities, the coral reefs, and the ecology of the island's turtle grass community. You also study fundamental celestial navigation and sailing and visit archaeological digs of pre-Columbian Arawak Indian sites. On Catalina Island, you can study kelp-bed ecosystems, fish and invertebrate behavior, marine mammals, dolphins, tuna, underwater photography, and more. For details on all three, write the Institute at Drawer CC, Harbour Town, Hilton Head Island, South Carolina 29928.

Some Where-to-Go-Diving Guides

The Diving Guide to the U.S. and British Virgin Islands by Gail Glanville and Armando Jenik tells where the professional divers who make their homes in the area go during their time off. It also points out aspects of popular diving destinations that you might not have noticed before. There are some nice stories—like the one about the time author Armando Jenik, diving with a friend, ran into a herd of humpback whales near Frenchman's Cap, about a mile south of St. Thomas. The book discusses dozens of dive sites and lists diving facilities and their addresses.

Great Diving I by Judy and Dean May (Stackpole Books, Cameron & Kelker Streets, Harrisburg, Pennsylvania 17105; $3.95) tells you where to go all over the eastern United States: New England (Maine, New Hampshire, Vermont, and Massachusetts); the Middle Coastal States (Rhode Island, Connecticut, New York, and New Jersey); the Central Coastal States (Maryland, Delaware, Virginia, North Carolina); the Southern Atlantic States (South Carolina, Georgia, Florida, Alabama); the Inland Eastern States (Ohio, Pennsylvania, West Virginia, Kentucky); and the Gulf Coastal States (Louisiana, Mississippi, Texas). Not only are there coral reefs populated with colorful fish, as you'd expect, and where you'd expect, but there are also shipwrecks from the Civil War, the Revolution, and modern times; and submarine caves full of blind crayfish, albino catfish, mastodon bones. The sites and their locations are listed, along with information about local regulations and dive shops and services.

141 Dives in the Protected Waters of Washington and British Columbia by Betty Pratt-Johnson (The Writing Works, 7438 S.E. 40th Street, Mercer Island, Washington 98040; $11.95) offers a similar treatment of waters in the Pacific Northwest.

Butterfly Towns

Pacific Grove, California, on the coast, is a pleasant little town. Neighboring Carmel and Monterey are perhaps more interesting, but it's Pacific Grove that, every year about the middle of October, gets the visit of the monarch butterflies. As the people from the Chamber of Commerce will tell you, the swallows return to Capistrano and the monarchs come back to Butterfly Town U.S.A. (which is what the town calls itself). The butterflies don't flit here and there as much as you'd expect: for the most part, they rest on "butterfly trees" at George Washington Park, Pine and Alder, and Milar's Butterfly Grove Motel at 1073 Lighthouse Ave-

nue. When they're resting, you don't see the bright orange that is evident in flight but instead the buff-colored underparts, which look like dead leaves. But as many as a thousand will cluster on a three-foot branch—a sight that is reason enough to celebrate, as the town does with a Butterfly Pageant and a Children's Butterfly Parade. (The kids strap monarch wings onto their backs and carry signs "Welcome Monarchs" and "Mighty Oaks from Little Acorns Grow" down the main street in a single file presided over by assorted concerned or disinterested moms.) For more information, write the Pacific Grove Chamber of Commerce, P. O. Box 167, Pacific Grove 93950.

Ventura, California, can't claim the title Butterfly Town U.S.A., but the monarchs pay a visit there as well, and from October to March they're all over the place. For more information write the Visitors and Convention Bureau at 785 South Seaward Avenue, 93003.

Where to See Masses of American Wildlife

There are wildlife refuges and national parks where it's hard to believe that the wildlife situation isn't what it used to be—places where the buffalo graze as far as you can see, places where there are so many birds that the fields seem to be growing them and the sounds make the Hitchcock movie's soundtrack sound like a whisper. The U.S. Fish & Wildlife Service in Washington, D.C. 20240, has a wealth of material it can send about looking for wildlife in the United States and about the various refuges discussed below. For similar information about wildlife in Canada, contact the Information Service of Parks Canada, Department of Indian and Northern Affairs at 400 Laurier Avenue West, in Ottawa K1A 0H4, and the Canadian Government Travel Bureau, 150 Kent Street, Ottawa K1A 0H6.

A Hundred Thousand Birds

That's a conservative estimate on the population of geese that feeds at the Horicon National Wildlife Refuge in Waupun, Wisconsin, in the southeastern part of the state, and which drew so many Sunday drivers to the highway at the north end of the marsh that there were constant traffic jams in the fall and the road had to be widened. For details on other things to see and do in the area and on the refuge, write the headquarters, Route 2, Mayville 53050.

Horicon is along the central flyway, one of the great invisible highways in the sky along which all migratory birds make their way from north to south every year and back again. Along the Eastern or Atlantic flyway, the Montezuma National Wildlife Refuge, in the heart of the Finger Lakes region at Seneca Falls, New York, is one of the best places to see the birds—thousands of ducks and thousands of geese that nearly take over the yard at the refuge headquarters and make such a racket that the rangers can hardly hear themselves confer. But in addition, there are also pileated and red-bellied woodpeckers, ruby-throated hummingbirds, scarlet tanagers, and black-capped chickadees; this is about the best bird-watching area on the East Coast. To see it, you take a drive over the dike tops, stand at the top of an observation tower, or hike either of a couple of footpaths. Mid-October and early April are the times to come. For more information, write the refuge at RD 1, Box 323, Seneca Falls, New York 13148.

Farther south, visit the Brigantine National Wildlife Refuge in Oceanville, New Jersey, about eleven miles north of Atlantic City. Oceanville gets concentrations of up to one hundred fifty thousand in late October and November. The Bombay Hook National Wildlife Refuge, near Smyrna, Delaware, gets Canada geese by the thousands in November; and at the Blackwater National Wildlife Refuge, ten miles south of Cambridge, Maryland, populations of Canada geese peak at eighty-five thousand or even more sometime between November and early December. For more information, write the refuge headquarters in Oceanville (zip 08231), Smyrna (zip 19977), or Cambridge (zip 21613).

A Couple of Hundred Thousand Birds
At the J. Clark Salyer National Wildlife Refuge, about 40 miles northeast of Minot, North Dakota, you'll see a couple of hundred thousand Canada geese in the spring and fall; more will be nearby on the Upper Souris National Wildlife Refuge and the Des Lacs National Wildlife Refuge, where you can also watch the strange courtship performances of the western grebes.

A Half Million Birds
When you see the March-into-April flight of snow geese at the Sand Lake National Wildlife Refuge, twenty-eight miles northeast of Aberdeen, South Dakota, along the James River, you'll understand why countless photographers and bird-watchers have called it one of the most impressive sights in the United States. The fields are white—covered with a kind of spring snow, as it were. Beginning in August and peaking in September, a quarter of a million Franklin's gulls stop at the refuge on their flight south. Also in the

summer, as a matter of course, you can watch nesting cormorants and wading birds.

The Largest Concentration of Ducks and Geese on the Continent
You'll see it in October, usually, against a backdrop of low mountains in northern California near the town of Tulelake and the Tule Lake National Wildlife Refuge and adjacent public lands. The air vibrates with the beating of their wings when they take off; when they fly over, the sky is almost solid birds—as it well should be with a million and a half of them present. There are snow geese, white-fronted geese, Canada geese, whistling swans, almost any kind of duck you can name, and just about the world's entire population of Ross' geese. They all stay until cold weather ices over the lakes and marshes and ponds of the Klamath Basin—only to return again, in somewhat reduced numbers, in the spring. Why? Partly because the refuge is an important stop on the Pacific flyway, partly because of the isolation of the place, which also means that there aren't very many places in the area to stay or to eat in what you'd call high style. It doesn't much matter though: for a sight like this you could sleep in the car. To find out more, write the Tule Lake Wildlife Refuge, Route 1, Box 74, Tulelake, California 96134.

More Birds Along the Pacific Flyway
When the birds leave Tule Lake, they fly south, stopping next in somewhat lesser quantities—a million birds or so—at the Sacramento National Wildlife Refuge near Willows, California. Its ten thousand acres are the most important wintering area for waterfowl of the Pacific flyway, the great invisible highway in the western sky along which migratory fowl head north or south. Rice and other crops are grown on the refuge to provide food, which helps remove the threat the birds present to neighboring commercial rice crops. You can see pintails, snow geese, white-fronted geese, cackling geese, and mallards. For more information, write the Sacramento National Wildlife Refuge at Route 1, Box 311, Willows, California 95988.

Some Migratory Birds in the Pacific Northwest
On the 181,000-acre Malheur National Wildlife Refuge, thirty-two miles south of Burns, Oregon, in the southwest quarter of the state, snow geese congregate in the spring and fall (and pelicans in late summer), and rare sandhill cranes make their nests in the marshes, meadows, and sagebrush and juniper uplands. Write the refuge at Box 112, Burns 97720 for details.

A Day Trip to the Subtropics
On Bulls Island, South Carolina, the thirty-five-thousand-acre Cape Romain National Wildlife Refuge is a virgin forest of live oaks, magnolias, pines, and palmettos. To get there you've got to take a boat from the refuge headquarters at Moore's Landing. It's quite an experience—not just the vegetation, which is amazing, pristine, and thoroughly marvelous, but also the shorebirds: the brown pelicans, royal terns, herons, and oyster catchers that you see. For details, write the refuge manager at Moore's Landing 29369.

Brown Pelicans
These rare birds completely cover three-acre Pelican Island, near Sebastian, Florida, between April and July. They have nested here since 1903, when the refuge was established. You can get boats, and more information, from the headquarters of the Pelican Island National Wildlife Refuge in Sebastian 32958.

Gannets, Razorbills, Murres, Guillemots—and More—by the Thousand
Canada's Gasp Peninsula village of Perce Quebec is in many ways just an ordinary Gaspé Peninsula town—a little primitive, extremely French. But it is also the jumping-off point for trips to Bonaventure Island, out in the Gulf of the St. Lawrence.

The world's largest gannetry, and one of the most impressive sea-bird colonies anywhere, it earned bird-wizard Roger Tory Peterson's high praises. He believed the gannet ledges of Bonaventure "to be one of the greatest ornithological spectacles of the continent, more impressive even than the populous murre and auk colonies further north. The size and whiteness of the gannets give them a visual impact lacking in lesser fowl." You can see them by walking across the top of the ocean cliffs on the island, or circling it by boat and observing the nesting cliffs below.

For more information, write the Department of Tourism, Place de la Capitale, 150 St. Cyrille Boulevard East, Quebec City G1R 2B2.

The Biggest Eagle Concentration Known
It happens every year around the middle of November: two hundred to three hundred bald eagles and golden eagles congregate in Glacier National Park along Lower McDonald Creek and feed on the kokanee salmon that come up from Flathead Lake to spawn and die. From either of two bridges, you can watch the eagles soaring and sitting on trees along the creek. You need binoculars, but nonetheless, all these

big birds are an impressive sight. For more information, and to find out when the eagles are expected, contact the park superintendent at Glacier National Park, West Glacier, Montana 59936.

Elk

They're big rangy creatures, fascinating to watch—and you can watch them for hours on end at the National Elk Refuge, established in 1912 as a winter feeding ground outside Jackson, Wyoming. Five thousand to ten thousand of the animals come down from the mountains of adjacent Grand Teton National Park as soon as the first snowfall covers their food; thereafter, refuge personnel tow out bales of hay on sleds. Visitors can take sled tours December through March to watch the process. Write the refuge manager in Jackson, Wyoming 83001 for particulars.

Boulders, Mountains, and the United States' Largest Public Bison Herd

Oklahoma's Wichita Mountains, the remnants of the continent's oldest mountain range (now worn down to a mere two thousand feet), shelter valleys that are green with buffalo grass, named for the animals whose favorite food it is. A herd of some six hundred buffalo now live on a National Wildlife Refuge in the area. Some private parties own more, and there is a larger herd in Canada, but this is the largest herd on U.S. lands. Buffalo and longhorn cattle—of which one of the best U.S. herds is also here—can almost always be seen grazing by the roadways that run through the preserve; occasionally they'll even block your way.

In addition, there are deer and elk—especially in the meadows at sundown; prairie dogs; gray foxes; pack rats; armadillos; coyotes. One of the things that makes the Wichita Mountains so fine for wildlife watching is that almost all the animals are fairly easy to find. The bison that stay close to the roadside are just one example. There is also a prairie-dog town near the road, and tarantulas (harmless creatures despite their reputation) come out whenever a storm threatens, probably warned by a drop in the barometric pressure and acting on the instinctive knowledge that they'd drown otherwise. Wichita Mountains National Wildlife Refuge personnel also operate a good program of nature walks, which last about three hours each and concentrate on eagles, waterfowl, reptiles, creek-bottom life, and elk-bugling (trips in which rangers let out phony calls and the elk answer back). What you get to learn about depends on the season. For more in-

formation, write the Refuge at Box 448, Cache, Oklahoma 73527.

A National Bison Range

Dedicated primarily to the perpetuation of the American bison, this nineteen-thousand-acre grassland just north of Dixon, Montana, contains a big-game exhibition pasture where you can hang on the fence and watch the animals (and, in the spring, their young); a nineteen-mile self-guided tour route takes you through their most frequent stomping grounds. They're big and shaggy and so placid-looking that you might feel the urge to go up and touch them if you hadn't been warned repeatedly about how unpredictable they are. The refuge manager in Dixon (zip 59831) can send details.

In the winter, Yellowstone National Park also has a good herd; you can cross-country ski there or take tours in huge oversnow vehicles called snow coaches. Write the Yellowstone Park Company, Yellowstone National Park, Wyoming 82190, for more information.

Canadian Buffalo

Wood Buffalo National Park, in Alberta, shelters the largest herd of buffalo on the continent. For more information about this vast preserve—over seventeen thousand square miles—write Parks Canada, Department of Indian and Northern Affairs, 400 Laurier Avenue West, Ottawa K1A OH4. Parks Canada can also send you details about the fifteen hundred bison that graze Elk Island National Park, about thirty miles east of Edmonton.

Desert Wildlife

A million six hundred thousand acres of Arizona and California, reached from Yuma, Arizona, and encompassing five refuges—the Imperial, Havasu, Cibola, Kofa, and Cabeza Prieta—protect desert bighorn sheep and a variety of waterbirds on their way down the flyway. This is true desert country, so wild that it's sometimes difficult to get in and out.

Pogo's Swampy Haunt

At Okefenokee, you learn that a swamp is a spooky dark place where trees wreathed in Spanish moss tower over your head, a green place where shrubs tangled with vines are reflected in still waters, a place as wide-open and sunny-bright as a western prairie, and an incredible feeding ground for animals of all shapes and sizes—all interdependent, all fascinating. In Okefenokee, there are alligators by the score; snakes; birds large and small, pretty and incredibly ugly; green frogs. You learn to look closely—the gradations in color and vegetation in the swamp provide a thousand different kinds of camouflage for the animals.

The bumpy log suddenly becomes an alligator, as you'll see when it silently sinks below the surface as the boat conveying you through this wonderland gets close. Egrets and ibis are easy to spot, but other birds are harder to find, and the snakes are often almost impossible to see until you've hung around for a while and gotten the hang of *seeing* nature the way people used to see it when not everyone lived in cities.

For seeing animals and getting to know what they look like, the best place to start is the Okefenokee Swamp Park, an excellent establishment that you might put down as a tourist trap from the look of the signs on the roads. Actually, though, it's first-class—the setups that have animals in various buildings and areas around the grounds make it easy for you to pick up the facts you need to understand a little of what the swamp is all about. There are also boat tours—quite worthwhile, whether you go out for just half an hour or, better, for half a day. You can also spend extra money and hire a guide for a private day-long trip. At the headquarters of the National Wildlife Refuge—the second of three gateways to the swamp—you can rent canoes to go out on your own, and that's fun after you've learned a little of what the swamp is all about. You can overnight in the swamp at Stephen C. Foster State Park, near Fargo, Georgia, which is the third gateway. There are inexpensive cabins.

For more information, write the Suwannee Canal Recreation Area, Route 2, Folkston, Georgia 31537; the Stephen C. Foster State Park, Fargo, Georgia 31631; the Okefenokee Swamp Park, Waycross, Georgia 31501; and the Okefenokee National Wildlife Refuge, Box 117, Waycross, Georgia 31501.

Some more swamp prowls. The Corkscrew Swamp Sanctuary, a preserve owned by the National Audubon Society, protects one of the two largest remaining wood-stork rookeries in the United States. It's near Fort Myers, Florida. For more information, you can write the Society's Miles Wildlife Sanctuary at West Cornwall Road, Sharon, Connecticut 06069.

The Everglades National Park, equally fascinating, is full of snook, redfish, sea trout, and wildlife (including alligators). For details, write Box 279, Homestead, Florida 33030. The Natural History Association, at the same address, publishes a helpful guide that will tell you about boating on the Wilderness Waterway in the Park; you can also rent a houseboat. For information about that ultimate escape and wildlife trip, write the Flamingo Houseboat Corporation in the Park at Flamingo, Florida 33030.

More Spectacular Wildlife Watching

The U.S. Fish and Wildlife Service (Washington, D.C. 20240) can send you a fascinating eight-page writeup, "Outstanding Photographic Opportunities on National Wildlife Refuges." No addresses are given, but you are told what animals can be seen at each refuge, how many animals there are, and what the surrounding terrain is like. What else do you need?

Penning the Ponies at Chincoteague

This is one of those famous local customs that has been getting bigger and bigger for years, and it's one of the high points of the year for people who live on the Delmarva Peninsula, where it's held. What's all the fuss about? The descendants of some Spanish ponies that, back in the 1600s, somehow managed to get from a sinking Spanish ship to shore. The Pony Roundup, held annually the last Wednesday in July, starts out with ponies being herded together on the Chincoteague National Wildlife Refuge; across the channel, on Chincoteague Island, the colts are auctioned off as the highlight of the rousing Chincoteague Firemen's Carnival. The purpose of the roundup and auction is to keep the herd from exceeding about two hundred. For more information, write the Chincoteague Chamber of Commerce, Box 259, Chincoteague, Virginia 23336.

A Bird-Watching Ranch

American and Canadian birders come to the Bear Mountain Guest Ranch at Silver City, New Mexico, by the dozen to add to their life lists—the lists of all the birds they've seen in their lives—and to talk birds around the dinner table, which is next to a big window facing bird-feeding stations where birds are always flitting to and fro.

What do you see here? Hummingbirds, Scott's orioles and northern orioles, coppery-tailed trogons in May or early June, gambel's quails, brown towhees, Mexican jays, plain titmice, mountain chickadees, and more. Rates are remarkably low—about $35 per day for a couple *including* three meals. For more information, write the ranch in Silver City, New Mexico 88061.

Woodlands, Tall Grass Prairies, Cypress Swamps, Marshes, Rookeries, and Other Lands of the Nature Conservancy

The Nature Conservancy has been buying up and taking care of wild lands around the United States and some of the Caribbean islands for years, and some of the preserves (which are open at least to members) are the most beautiful wild areas on the continent. There are desert canyons, wet meadows of lush grass, desert streams, bare rocky peaks, forested ravines, boulder-strewn British Virgin Islands, and a beach in the American Virgins. The Katharine Ordway Preserve in central Minnesota is a 448-acre prairie, which, incredibly, has never been plowed, grazed, or mowed, so far as anybody knows. A complete listing of the Nature Conservancy preserves is available for $5 ($3 for members) from Department PD at the national headquarters, 1800 North Kent Street, Arlington, Virginia 22209.

Bird-Watching North of the Arctic Circle

You can do it at the Inuit-operated Bathurst Inlet Lodge on Victoria Island, at Cambridge Bay, Northwest Territories, between mid-June and mid-July. The bird life is some of the richest in Canada. For more information, write Glenn Warner at Box 820, Yellowknife, Northwest Territories XOE 1HO.

Dial-a-Bird

News of a rare sighting was spread by word of mouth in the old days; now the Telephone Company has taken over—recorded messages by dial-a-bird services provide data on unusual birds in a given area at any time. The Audubon Society (950 Third Avenue, New York, New York 10022) can send a listing of local dial-a-bird phone numbers for about 50c.

American Singers

Birds, that is: some of their owners, people who raise songbirds as a hobby, belong to an organization called the American Singers Club. Even if you haven't any intention of joining, you might consider the annual National Cage Bird Show as a sight to see if you're in the area. All those birds singing their heart out at an event that comes off something like a dog show, only with a different kind of noise, is quite something. To find out more, write the Club Secretary at 410-31 Barrington Road, Wauconda, Illinois 60084.

Tours and Camps for Wildlife Watching

The surest way to acquire a knack for spotting wild animals in their natural habitat is to go with someone who already has it. If you don't have a friend who can help out, a good bet is to contact one of the handful of nonprofit organizations that sponsor tours—with woods-wise guides—to areas where there will probably be quite a few animals. To wit: the National Audubon Society, Harwinton, Connecticut 06790; the National Wildlife Federation, 1412 Sixteenth Street, N.W., Washington, D.C. 20036; and the Sierra Club, 530 Bush Street, San Francisco, California 94108.

Caribou

When you visit Mount McKinley National Park in Alaska in July and August, bands of caribou are on the move and may pass you on the road. There's lots more to see—more wildlife, plus glaciers, rivers, forests, peaks. For details, write the Park Superintendent at Box 9, McKinley Park, Alaska 99755.

Whale Watching in California and Quebec

California gray whales, while not the largest species of whales, are nonetheless the most easily seen, for their annual migration from the Arctic Ocean to the warmer waters of Baja California takes them into shallow water. They're exciting to watch. When disturbed, they'll sometimes exhale steamy clouds through their blowholes. And, inexplicably, they do other things. They blow. They undulate. They dive. They perform a great, graceful water ballet. It's not surprising that whale watching is a big deal on the West Coast from late December to early February. For information about whale-watching in the San Diego area, write the Convention and Visitors Bureau at 1200 Third Avenue, Suite 824, San Diego, California 92101. For details on the Los Angeles area, write the

Cabrillo Beach Marine Museum, 3720 Stephen White Drive, San Pedro, California 90731; or the Southern California Visitors Council, 705 West Seventh Street, Los Angeles, California 90017. The American Cetacean Society (P. O. Box 22305, San Diego, California 92122) can tell you about whale-watching expeditions along the entire California coast.

In Quebec, you can often see pods of finback, humpback, and pilot whales passing close by Forillon National Park's coastline, on the Gaspé Peninsula. For details on the park, write its headquarters at Box 1220, Gaspé, Quebec GOC 1RO.

The Zoological Society of Montreal sponsors whale-watching weekends to Tadoussac, up the St. Lawrence, where passengers go out and look for blue, fin, sei, minke, and white beluga whales from twenty-passenger fishing boats. For details, write the Projects Committee of the Zoological Society of Montreal, P. O. Box 80, Victoria Station, Montreal H2Z 2V4.

Clyde, the World's Largest Kodiak Bear

This sixteen-hundred-pound fellow can be visited at the Dakota Zoo in Sertoma-Riverside Park in Bismarck, North Dakota. Not a big zoo, it nonetheless displays a big collection of animals native to the area as well as a flock of rabbits that kids can pick up and hug. For more information about the area, write the Mandan Chamber of Commerce in the Lewis and Clark Hotel, Mandan, North Dakota 58554.

Polar-Bear Watching in the Wild

When the ice goes out of the Churchill River in early June, the belugas come in. You can fish for trout, northern pike, char, and grayling—and visit one of the world's largest polar-bear denning areas, forty miles south of the town of Churchill. The Port of Churchill Commission (P. O. Box 275, Churchill, Manitoba) and the Manitoba Government Travel office (200 Vaughan Street, Winnipeg R3C 0V8) can send more information.

The World's Largest Alligator Farm

The St. Augustine Alligator Farm may be a classic tourist trap, but there's no arguing the fact that all those alligators—from infants to adults, and all sizes in between—are worth seeing. Big ones rest on the sands like big lumps, or surface suddenly in the ponds of the preserve. Little ones heap themselves on top of each other when they doze. When one at the bottom

squirms out from under, the whole mass wiggles.

St. Augustine has some nice old restored houses, working craftsmen, a fort, and fine beaches. The St. Augustine and St. Johns County Chamber of Commerce (10 Castillo Drive, St. Augustine, Florida 32084) can send you more information about the area.

The International Worm-Fiddling Contest

This annual Caryville, Florida, event has nothing at all to do with playing a stringed instrument to please the earthworms. Instead, it features an ancient method of getting worms for fishing bait, a method that is also known as "grunting." The prospective angler drives a stake into the ground, then rubs it with some other object, causing vibrations that reach the earthworms in the ground and prompt them to crawl out into the open.

In the contest, whoever gets the most worms in the allotted time wins the trophy. It's a good show, with all those oldsters on all fours, hammering and sawing away. More information: the Town of Caryville, P. O. Box 206, Caryville, Florida 32427.

Rattlesnake Roundups

Part of the culture of the Southwest in recent years, rattlesnake roundups feature men, women, children poking the brush for the creatures every spring, while the snakes are still slightly groggy from hibernation. Then they're brought back to town and penned up in a pit, where, often, there will be a snake handler to entertain the crowds gathered for the other goings-on: rattlesnake meat, deep-fried, for meals and a bazaar where you can buy rattles, preserved snakes, scorpions, and tarantulas. Whether or not you find these roundups brutal (as some critics do) remains to be seen—but if you want to try one out, check into those held in Waurika, Oklahoma; Mangum, Oklahoma (both in April); Valdosta, Georgia; San Antonio, Florida; Okeene, Oklahoma; Gainesville, Texas; and Sweetwater, Texas. The state tourist-development agencies can give you dates.

Frog Jumps

If you've heard about the frog-jumping contests that have perpetuated themselves on the model set up by Jim Smiley, Mark Twain's fictional character from "The Celebrated Jumping Frog of Calaveras County," you might well have wondered how the kids who handle the animals get their frogs to

jump. Wonder no more: bull frogs and leopard frogs alike are tickled with feathers, sprinkled with water, exhorted; sometimes they jump, sometimes they don't. Sometimes, instead of taking three giant jumps forward, they'll jump around in circles, or lose yardage by jumping backward, or hop off the table into the crowd, where they risk being trampled. The idea is for the frog to jump, in three consecutive leaps, farther than any other contestant.

Where can you see such goings-on? One of the older frog jumps is held every year at Nook Farm, once a one-hundred-forty-acre literary colony where Mark Twain lived for a while in a sprawling old Victorian house (now restored) as did Harriet Beecher Stowe. The frog jump is ordinarily held in June; it's open to frog handlers between six and seventeen. For more information, write Nook Farm at 77 Forest Street in Hartford, Connecticut (06105).

And, of course, there are frog-jumping contests at Angels Camp, California, site of the original contest. Every year, frogs from foreign countries and from all over the United States are shipped in for the competition. In the old days, miners, who on working days pursued the elusive yellow metal, found the training of frogs a good break from the continuous round of work and life in the saloons and dance halls. Of course, they regularly staged frog jumps, and wagered small fortunes on the hops of their frogs. But the Angels Camp event, fifty years old in 1978, got its start as a celebration of the paving of the city streets. It's a good time in the gold country. For more information, you can write the Calaveras County Chamber of Commerce, Box 177, San Andreas 95249. Sunset Books' *Gold Rush Country* is the best guide you'll find to the inns and historic sites and pretty back roads of this interesting area. The book is nearly as much fun to read as the area is to visit. (Lane Publishing, Menlo Park, California 94025; $2.95.)

The International Burro Race

Since Bishop, California, is the Mule Capital of the World, it's only fitting that it should be the site of this big event, and of a half dozen others—a Mule Days Parade featuring nearly two hundred immaculately groomed pack strings from the area and comedy entries in which mules carry beds or outhouses, a mule shoeing contest, and barrel racing, calf roping, pole bending, jumping, and a One Mile Mule Run, and the Mule Sale (just in case, by this time, you decide you've got to have one). There's also a braying contest in which local citizens do their darnedest to sound more like a mule than their neighbors. All this takes place in the neighborhood of June Lake, Mt. Whitney, Kings Canyon National Park, Yosemite, and the ancient bristlecone pine forest, so there's plenty to do should you stubbornly refuse to get into the spirit of the event. Write the Bishop Chamber of Commerce, 690 North Main Street, Bishop 93514, for more information.

Stubborn creatures are popular, and there are a couple of other similar events in Colorado. These include the World's Championship Pack Burro Race in Fairplay, which features a race every year the last weekend in July, and the Leadville Boom Days' International Burro Race. They're not exactly what you'd call speedy runs: mules take their time and finish the twenty-three miles usually in three to four hours—though in 1949, the Fairplay winner took five hours and ten minutes, and in 1972, the winner did it in two hours and fifty minutes. However, there's a good deal of clowning to make up for the pace. For details, write the chambers of commerce in Fairplay (zip 80440) and Leadville (Box 861, zip 80461).

The World Championship Turkey Races

They're part of the annual mid-September Turkey Trot Festival in Daviess County, Indiana, in the hilly southwestern part of the state. The Indiana Department of Commerce (Room 336 State House, Indianapolis 46204) can send more information.

Now turkey calling, that's something else again. Pennsylvania has its annual Potter County Championship Turkey Calling Contest in May in the town of Coudersport. For information and entry blanks, write Potter County Recreation, Inc., P. O. Box 245, Coudersport 16915.

Rooster Day

Once a year in May, the people of Broken Arrow, Arizona, celebrate an old tradition—of farmers that came to town to trade their old roosters for better chick producers—with a settlers' dinner, a rodeo, and a beauty queen

(the victor is called "Miss Chick") contest. For more information, write the Broken Arrow Chamber of Commerce, 110 East Commercial Street, 74012.

A Chicken Museum

In Sterling, Michigan, chicks hatch before your eyes in twenty-one special incubators that let you watch the day-by-day development of the chick from the time the egg is laid until the chicken appears. It's amazing to see how hard the creature has to work to get into the world, and fascinating to see how fast the eggs develop. For details, write the museum in Sterling 48469.

Sunday, Buzzard Sunday

Hinckley, Ohio, is a small town and to see it you wouldn't get especially excited about it. However, it *is* Buzzard Town, U.S.A. (or so the town fathers have decreed), and it does honor the feathered friends with their own day in much the same way that the rest of the world talks about groundhogs, on the first Sunday after March 14. The big event is a pancakes-and-sausages breakfast; but there is also a bazaar where you can buy milk-chocolate buzzards with red icing on their beaks, buzzard T-shirts, buzzard bumper stickers, buzzard cookie cutters, black-and-orange frosted buzzard cookies, and more—and they go fast. However, sooner or later, everybody wanders over to the Buzzard Roost, in the Hinckley Nature Reservation, where every year for the past century and a half (or so it's said) a flock of fifty of the big birds has arrived for the spring and summer from winter quarters in the Great Smokies.

For up-to-date information, write the Ohio Department of Economic and Community Development, Box 1001, Columbus, Ohio 43216.

Watery Spots

Some Perfect Beaches

Some strands are short crescents of sand bounded by rocks at either end; some are endless affairs where you can jog along for mile upon sea-pounded mile without meeting a single impediment. An assortment of the great beauties follows.

Some Caribbean Sands

Haiti is not much for beaches—you go there for the sensual exoticism of the place and for the bright colors and the rugged green mountains. But there are fine beaches almost everywhere else in the Caribbean.

The Caymans, for instance. Grand Cayman is flat and generally well built up with hotels. But if you don't mind that, there's Seven Mile Beach, named for its length, and excellent for rambles.

Negril, Jamaica, has one of those seemingly endless powdery white strands, about seven miles long. There's some development, but not as much as on the rest of the island.

St. John in the U.S. Virgin Islands has spectacular and unspoiled beaches, especially fine because there's nothing in the area except mountains, forests, and sea-grape trees. Check out the U.S. Virgin Islands National Park (Box 806, St. Thomas, Virgin Islands 00801) and Caneel Bay Plantation, the expensive Rockefeller resort. There are *seven* beaches—Caneel, Hawksnest, Little Caneel, Scott, and Turtle Bay among them—all of them about as close to perfect as beaches can be. The resort manager (Box 1091, St. Thomas, Virgin Islands 00801) can send more information.

Palm Island, in the Grenadines, one of those islands where the island *is* the hotel, has a wonderful mile-and-a-half-long beach, and since the Palm Island Club has only twenty rooms, there aren't going to be too many other people on it. Palm Island's palms, some three thousand of them, bend and sway over the beach, which also makes the

beach rather special. The Palm Island Club (St. Vincent, Grenadines, West Indies) can send details.

In Sint Maarten and St. Martin nearly every rutted bumpy road ends at the beach or a seaside cove. Boatmen in the villages on the east coast of St. Martin can take you out to still quieter beaches on the offshore islands.

Tobago, seven miles wide and twenty-six miles long, has such powdery white sand that Trinidadians come over for weekends. The Trinidad and Tobago Tourist Board (400 Madison Avenue, New York, New York 10017) can send more information about this quiet island.

Antigua is famous for beaches—it claims to have one for every day of the year—and its dependency Barbuda is practically nothing but beach. Write the Antigua Tourist Board (101 Park Avenue, New York, New York 10017) for information.

In Barbados, Crane Beach, backed by high cliffs, is spectacular—long, wide, and surf-pounded because it's on the Atlantic coast of this easternmost Caribbean isle. The beach at Sam Lord's Castle, also on the Atlantic, is a perfect crescent—wide, white, palm-dotted. The beaches on the Caribbean side of the island—platinum-white, soft—are long but narrow. For more information: the Barbados Board of Tourism, 800 Second Avenue, New York, New York 10017.

Beaches in the British Virgin Islands are white and soft as talcum powder. Moreover, there are lots of them, so if the one you visit first is overpopulated (with maybe half a dozen people), you can hunt up another without much trouble. For more information, contact the B.V.I. Tourist Board, c/o J. S. Fones, 515 Madison Avenue, New York, New York 10022.

In Aruba, Palm Beach is glorious and blinding white (with not a huge amount of greenery to soften its brilliance, for this is an arid island), but lined with high-rise hotels. For more information about the island and its other quite exceptional strands, write the Aruba Tourist Information Office, 576 Fifth Avenue, New York, New York 10036.

In the Bahamas there are miles of spectacular sand strips: Cat Island's are untouched; Eleuthera's beaches go

on forever; and the beaches on Harbour Island are nearly pink. Many of the Out Islands are uninhabited, with fine beaches. For details: the Bahamas Tourist Office at 30 Rockefeller Center, New York, New York 10020, or the Out Islands Promotions Board, 255 Alhambra Circle, Suite 450, Coral Gables, Florida 33134.

The Pacific Rim

Snow-capped peaks soften to rain forests, which drop off to fourteen miles of driftwood-cluttered beaches at British Columbia's Pacific Rim National Park. The Long Beach section, where you'll see all this, is also the most popular; offshore you can see sea-lion-covered rocks, harbor seals, dolphins. For more information, write the park headquarters at Box 280, Ucluelet, British Columbia VOR 3A0.

The Florida-As-It-Used-to-Be Beach

Head northwards in Florida until you get to the armpit. Pass all the big beach cities along the coast, and keep going until you hit Apalachicola. Then prepare yourself for wonderful surprises.

The white-as-sugar sand for which Panama City is so famous extends all the way to Apalachicola, and in the process takes in some sand extravaganzas: the superb strand at St. Joseph Beach State Park, which slips gently out under the turquoise waters, and which is generally uncrowded even on weekends and holidays—one of those state parks that simply has not been discovered; the thirteen miles of beach, a favorite nesting ground of sea turtles, at St. Vincent National Wildlife Refuge nearby; and, also in the area, St. George Island, whose miles of beach are destined to be fringed with tract houses as a result of some mischief of zoning laws.

The wonderful things about the beaches, apart from their pristine whiteness and the absolute absence of crowds, are the dunes at their backs and the vine-twined jungles not far away. For more information, contact the Chamber of Commerce at 90 Avenue E, in Apalachicola 32320; the St. Vincent National Wildlife Refuge, Box 447, Apalachicola 32320; the Port St. Joe-Gulf County Chamber of Commerce at P. O. Box 964, Port St. Joe 32456; and, for cottage rentals on St. George Island, H. G. Smith, Box 2, St. George Island 32328.

Walk-Forever Beaches of the Atlantic Coast

The entire East Coast of the United States, from Cape Cod to Florida, is one long series of magnificent strands that protect the mainland from the lashings of the Atlantic. Barrier islands, they're called. Now *these* are beaches. Mainly, they're wide, hard, and they go on forever, scarcely broken up by boulders or coves. The sands are soft (but not powdery) and, as a rule, white to golden in color. If you were to travel the world searching out beautiful beaches to walk, you would find none to compare with these. Quite a bit of this long strand has been built upon; the foundations of hotels in Miami Beach are nearly licked by the ocean. However, there are quite a number of beaches that are now in the protectorship of the National Park Service, and there are visitor centers and naturalist programs dedicated to telling you what these barrier islands are all about: how the ecology works, how the land and the ocean are one harmonious whole, neither part of which can be touched in any way without affecting the rest. Whether or

not you take advantage of the offerings—though if you're a dedicated beach person you will probably want to—you can have a fine time on your walks. The character of your vacation will depend on how much settlement there is in the surrounding areas and how far south you go. Both aspects also affect the kind of people you find and the kind of vegetation.

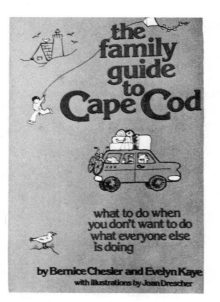

Starting north and working south, you encounter such wonders as the following:

The Cape Cod National Seashore preserves some forty miles of beach, the Province Lands (one section) has some of the most spectacular dunes in the East. Offshore there are kelp, clam, rockweed; on the land, marshes that you can visit with the enlightening company of naturalists of the National Park Service. The little towns between the Atlantic shore and the Bay are full of clapboard houses, winding roadways, forests, and summer theaters; population centers and shopping centers have grown up in recent years but still don't spoil this most wonderful place. For information about the shore, write the park superintendent in South Wellfleet, Massachusetts 02663. To find out about accommodations and resorts, contact the Cape Cod Chamber of Commerce in Hyannis 02601; reserve well in advance.

The Family Guide to Cape Cod, by Bernice Chesler and Evelyn Kaye (Barre Publishing, Barre, Massachusetts 01005; $6.95) talks about, as the subtitle says, "what to do when you don't want to do what everyone else is doing" and gives you details, in the process, on bird-watching, beaches, surfing; skin diving, swimming in the ponds, clam digging, crafts, tuna

fishing, biking and bike rentals, country stores, historical societies and museums, seeing the Kennedy compound, going to the town dump in Barnstable, renting boats, and on and on.

Other informative tomes: *Short Walks on Cape Cod and the Vineyard*, by Paul and Ruth Sadlier (Pequot Press, Old Chester Road, Chester, Connecticut 06412; $3.50) details twenty-five walks through woods, marshes, swamps, seashores, dunes, kettle holes, drumlins, ponds, streams, and wildlife sanctuaries and tells you about sunsets, vistas across sand and marsh, blossoming shad bush, beach plums, wildlife—everything from cottontail rabbits to ospreys and herring gulls and fiddler crabs. *The Visitor's Guide to the Cape Cod National Seashore* talks about the National Park Service activities and neighboring communities of the Nauset area, the Marconi Area and Great Island, the Pilgrim Heights area, and the Province Lands —the four principal parts of the Seashore (Chatham Press, 15 Wilmot Lane, Riverside, Connecticut 06878; $1.95).

Also helpful and inexpensive is the *Cape Cod Guide* (Guide Publications, 23 Middle Street, Plymouth 02360; 50c).

Fire Island National Seashore, off the shore of Long Island, has nineteen thousand acres of beach grass, wild rose, poison ivy, beach plum, dunes, and magnificent beach and wetlands; the Seashore protects the largest remaining barrier beach in the area. You can swim, fish, walk, go bicycling. Eight state parks are within an hour's drive. For further information, write Box 229, Patchogue, Long Island, New York 11772. Walks on other beaches on Long Island—Westhampton, Quogue-Tiana Beach, Southampton, Wainscott, East Hampton, Amagansett, Napeague, and Montauk beaches (all of which are similarly wide and long and surf-pounded)—are discussed in *Short Walks on Long Island*, by Rodney and Priscilla Albright (Pequot Press, Old Chester Road, Chester, Connecticut 06412; $2.95). *The Fire Island Guide*, available from the Eastern National Park and Monument Association, c/o the Seashore headquarters for $2.14, gives you information about the communities on the island.

Assateague National Seashore, off the coast of Maryland and Virginia, stretches thirty-seven miles without a break. You can comb the beaches and surf-fish and swim and sunbathe to your heart's content. Camping is at Assateague Island State Park, in Maryland. At Chincoteague National Wildlife Refuge, which takes up ten miles of the southern part of Assateague, you can see enormous flocks of geese, duck, and swan in the winter and during migrations in April and May;

wild Chincoteague ponies, which also inhabit the refuge, are rounded up the last week in July. For more information, write Route 2, Box 294, Berlin, Maryland 21811.

Cape Hatteras National Seashore—all seventy miles of it—offers more beach than you'd be able to prowl if you spent your life at it. This first National Seashore covers twenty-eight thousand acres between Nags Head and Ocracoke, and takes in several quaint old villages where it's easy to remember the days of Blackbeard the Pirate. (*Blackbeard the Pirate*, by Robert E. Lee, $8.95 from John F. Blair, Publisher, 1406 Plaza Drive, Winston-Salem, North Carolina 27103, tells the story.) It is a countryside of spooky legends and superstitions; until a few years ago the people who lived here were so isolated that they spoke with the slight Elizabethan accent of the area's earliest settlers. At Ocracoke Village, a small fishing town, there are sandy lanes lined with live oaks, an interesting cemetery, and a free ferry. There are lighthouses at Ocracoke and Diamond Shoals. For more information, write Box 457, Manteo, North Carolina 27954. For particulars about local resorts, write the Dare County Tourist Bureau, also in Manteo.

As it happens, North Carolina has still more untrammeled shoreline. Just south of Cape Hatteras National Seashore lies Cape Lookout National Seashore, established in 1966 along fifty-eight miles of strand on Portsmouth Island, Core Banks, and Shackleford Banks. For details on what facilities may have been recently established, write the superintendent at Box 690, Beaufort, North Carolina 28516.

Cumberland Island National Seashore, off the coast of St. Mary's, Georgia, just north of the Florida line, is a white-beach-fringed jungle of live oak and palmetto and longleaf and slash pines and wonderful marshes. There are biking, hiking, horseback riding, and beach-sitting. For more information, write the superintendent at P. O. Box 806, St. Mary's, Georgia 31558. Georgia's Golden Isles—Sea Island, Jekyll, St. Simons Islands—are immediately north. There are pleasant resorts like the King and Prince (genteel, well-mannered, but informal and not at all stuffy; write c/o Arnold Road, St. Simons 31522) and various still more unpretentious establishments on Jekyll Island. Write the Georgia Bureau of Industry and Trade, Trinity-Washington Building, Box 38097, in Atlanta 30334, for more information.

Robinson Crusoe Islands
On the Gulf Islands National Seashore, near Biloxi, Mississippi, you'll find

wilderness beach on three offshore islands: Horn, Ship, and Petit Bois.

Ship Island, the home of what's left of Fort Massachusetts, can be reached by excursion boats that leave from Biloxi and Gulfport twice daily. The boats are not very big, but they're usually crowded, and when you get on you get a sinking feeling in your stomach; you can't help thinking your first time around that the beach is going to be crowded. No need to worry. Ship Island has plenty of beach, and most of the people on the boat stick to the strand near the boardwalk where the boat lands. Walk down the beach even five minutes and you won't see

another soul except perhaps a diehard beach-jogger. Walk fifteen minutes and even he (or she) might not catch up with you. Spread your towel in a sheltered spot among · the beach grasses that make up most of the island's vegetation and you can make yourself pretty much invisible.

Horn and Petit Bois—which you can get to only by private boat or charter craft available in Gulfport and Biloxi—are more remote than Ship Island and, because of their tall pines, they're even more beautiful. You can ship out there and camp for as long as you want, and you won't encounter another soul except the fish.

For more information, write the Gulf Islands National Seashore at Box T, Ocean Springs, Mississippi 39564.

For more information about quiet islands, see Norman Ford's *Utopia Is an Island* (Harian Publications, Greenlawn, New York 11740; $2.50). While not brand-new—the fourth edition was published in 1971—the islands described are still pleasant, if somewhat more developed than they were when the manuscript went to press. Some of Ford's offerings: the Mag-Magdalen Islands, Quebec; Grand Manan Island, New Brunswick; Campobello and Deer islands, also in New Brunswick; Vinalhaven and Monhegan and Chebeague islands, in Maine; Cuttyhunk Island, Massachusetts; Block Island, Rhode Island; Prudence Island, Rhode Island; Smith Island, Maryland, and Tangier Island, Virginia—both in Chesapeake Bay; Bull's Island, South Carolina; Dog Island and Cedar Keys, Florida; and a score of exotics scattered around the Caribbean. For each, there are brief descriptions of the area as a whole and the things to see and do, as well as of the retirement scene—for Ford is telling you what it would be like to live in the areas he describes as well as to vacation there. After you've read what he has to say about them, you may well want to do just that.

A Subtropical Island Beach
Edisto Beach State Park, fifty miles southeast of Charleston, South Carolina, at Edisto Beach, is filled with thousands of palmetto trees; there are sand dunes and seashells and petrified fossils along its two-and-a-half-mile strand, which is probably the best in the state for collecting shells. You can camp or hire cabins in the park. For details, write the South Carolina Department of Parks, Recreation, and Tourism at Box 113, Columbia, South Carolina 29201.

A Lake Superior Island Wilderness
You can get to Isle Royale National Park only by plane or boat; once there, you've got to boil your water for drinking. But it's quite an empty, northwoods place—vast, lonely, with some wonderful strands for strolls. For details, write the park superintendent at 87 North Ripley Street, Houghton, Michigan 49931.

For an entertaining description of the other things to see and do in the park, see Ruth Rudner's *Off and Walking* (Holt, Rinehart and Winston, 383 Madison Avenue, New York, New York 10017; $4.95). The Isle Royale Natural History Association (P. O. Box 27, Houghton, Michigan 49931) can send you a list of inexpensive publications dealing with fishes and forests, birds, trees and trails, wildflowers and wolves.

A Pacific Wilderness Beach
The only section of wilderness beach on the U.S. Pacific Coast is at Olympic National Park, near Port Angeles, Washington. Near the Indian village of LaPush, you can get trails to Second Beach, which winds through lush rain forests to a crescent of sand guarded by giant wave-eroded rocks. Third Beach, accessible by another trail, leads to another sweep of sand bounded by immense headlands. Getting to the beaches involves fairly short walks, but you can walk up to twenty miles along the beach, to Lake Ozette or to the Hoh River. For more information, write the park superintendent at Olympic National Park, in Port Angeles 98362.

One Man's Beach

Todd Ballentine, an environmentalist who lives around Hilton Head Island, South Carolina, talks about his beach, which is about twelve miles long and up to six hundred feet wide at low tide. What he says should give you some idea of why beaches can be so fascinating aside from the constant roar of the waves:

"The beach is constantly changing. Due to a north-to-south alongshore current, the island is undergoing a process known as littoral drift, the eroding of sand at the north end of the island and the building up of sand at the south end. The estimated net gain at the south end is one hundred yards during the past century.

"The above drift takes place more in the storms and northeasters of winter than in summer. The beach, to me, feels like this year-round:

"Spring: changing weather fronts push up waves, push around sand, deposit beach treasures.

"Summer: gentle waves, even tides, a slow-down in the food chain. Most stable beach.

"Fall: hurricane watch. Occasional storms. Migrating birds and butterflies.

"Winter: good shelling (though fair to poor compared to places like Sanibel Island). Strong waves tear loose treasures like sand dollars, sponges, corals, cockles and whelks. Rafts of surf ducks by the hundreds. Quite windy."

You can get more information about the beach and the island from the Chamber of Commerce at Box 5647, Hilton Head Island 29928.

Nude Beaches

Guadeloupe and the Isles des Saintes surrounding it are among the first of the West Indies to have officially designated public nudist beaches. Another is the no-clothes beach near Le Galion Hotel on Sint Maarten in the Netherlands Antilles near Philipsburg, the Dutch capital. In Hawaii, you can skinny dip on Kauai's deserted northern NaPali coast (though you have to get dropped off by a helicopter).

For more information about these islands, write their tourist information offices: the French West Indies Tourist Board, 610 Fifth Avenue, New York, New York 10020; the Sint Maarten Tourist Office, c/o Sontheimer & Company, 4 West 58th Street, New York, New York 10019; and the Hawaii Visitors Bureau, 2270 Kalakaua Avenue, Honolulu 96815.

Also see *Nude Resorts and Beaches* (Popular Library, 600 Third Avenue, New York, New York 10022; $1.25).

Black Beaches

They're as soft as the white or gold or pink variety, but they're eerie. Where to see them?

In the Caribbean on the islands of Dominica, Nevis, Martinique and Guadeloupe, Haiti (at Jacmel), Montserrat, on St. Vincent (especially along the west and northeast coasts). In Hawaii on the island of Maui's eastern coast near Hana. Along with the beaches, there are soaring vistas, isolated fishing villages, old lava flows, and that incredible dense jungle growth that seems all the greener against the black. Same goes for the black beaches on the island of Molokai, near Kaunakakai; the Black Sand Beach near Kalapana, on the Big Island, and down the coast at Punaluu.

Sand Castles

Every year on the first Saturday in May, the Sheraton Sandcastle at Lido Beach in Sarasota, Florida, sponsors its International Sand Castle Building Contest. Men with beer bellies, little kids, old women in terrycloth beach robes and young ones in the skimpiest bikinis, and assorted other specimens of humanity come out in droves to look at the bizarre assortment of sand creations sculpted for the occasion: a crocodile fifty feet long; a sprawl of an octopus; a perfectly smooth pyramid as high as a man is tall; a fagged-out beach bum, complete with curly hair, sprawling on a lounge chair. For information about entering, write the hotel at Lido Beach, Sarasota, Florida 33577.

There are more contests at Oceanside, California, north of San Diego. The Southern California Visitors Council (705 West Seventh, Los Angeles, California 90017) can provide information.

Beach Camping

There are dozens of places where you can do it, but surely one of the most spectacular is the Padre Island National Seashore strand, off the Texas Gulf Coast. Padre Island, which is 113 miles long (only 81 miles are National Seashore, though) is almost entirely uninhabited. You can drive an ordinary car along most of the beach, but it can be tricky, so not many people do. Wherever you set up your tent you can pretty much count on having the area to yourself. There's usually a good stiff breeze; the ocean rolls away, comber after comber. You couldn't be any closer to nature.

For more information, write the Superintendent of the National Seashore at 9405 South Padre Island Drive, Corpus Christi, Texas 78418; the Cameron County Park Board, Box 666, Port Isabel, Texas 78578; and the Corpus Christi Area Tourist Bureau, Box 1147, Corpus Christi, Texas 78403.

In Alaska's National Forests

The Forest Supervisors (at Box 757, Sitka, Alaska 99835; Box 2278, Ketchikan, Alaska 99901; and Box 309, Petersburg, Alaska 99833—all in the Tongass National Forest) can send you information about beach camping in their districts. You can collect wildflowers, edible greens, and such. These beaches are empty and lonely as the land—quite something.

Shells

Two good field guides come from the Golden Press: *Seashells of North America, a Guide to Field Identification* ($4.95), and *Seashells of the World: A Guide to the Better-Known Species* ($1.95). Both are written by R. Tucker Abbott, of the Delaware Museum of Natural History (which has one of the United States' best seashell collections). The former book is good if you're collecting on the continent; if you're in the Caribbean, you want the smaller guide. Both are full of pictures and as clearly written as all Golden Guides. The North America book also contains a good deal of information about how mollusks live. Golden Press, Western Publishing, 1220 Mound Avenue, Racine, Wisconsin 53404.

A Shell Collector's Dream

At Sanibel and Captiva Islands, Florida, shells wash up with storms, or just as a matter of course with the Gulf tides. The fame of the region has spread fast, and magazine articles are always talking about the "Sanibel stoop"—which is what you get after you've bent over for an hour trying to spot a rare item in the middle of all the flotsam of co-

quinas and cockles. Shell collecting on the beach is popular just about anywhere you go, so the tales of heaps upon heaps of prize specimens, and of the low-key atmosphere on the island, were bound to draw crowds.

And indeed they did draw crowds—Sanibel is no longer the remote, idyllic place it used to be. Instead, it has become a woodsier version of some of the more built-up beach cities. However, it's still quite pleasant, and the beaches are indeed spectacular—and there are enough varieties of interesting shells, even when the hordes have picked over the heaps, to keep anybody but a fanatical malacologist happy.

For more information, write the Chamber of Commerce at P. O. Box 166, Sanibel, Florida 33957.

Shell-Collecting Tours

They go to Andros Island, Antigua, Bonaire, the Virgin Islands, British Honduras—not to the busy sections, but to the more remote parts where the shelling is better. Diving is part of the game. The sponsor: Kirk Anders Travel, Box 1418, Fort Lauderdale, Florida 33302.

Shore Life

More than a book about shells, *Seashores* will also tell you about the algae, flowering plants of the dunes, the sponges, corals, worms, crustacea, starfish and their kin, and other interesting life you encounter on rambles along the beach. If you don't have a shore-wise companion to identify these items as you walk, this little book is great to have.

Golden Books, Western Publishing, 1220 Mound Avenue, Racine, Wisconsin 53404; $1.95.

The Ultimate Swimming Hole

The ultimate swimming hole is, perhaps, River Country at Walt Disney World at Lake Buena Vista, Florida, near Orlando. You can jump out of rope swings into the water, twist and turn through a series of small waterfalls, body surf through a two-hundred-sixty-foot-long flume. There are swimming pools and beaches and lakes. Just about anything that was ever wet and splashy and delighted kids is presented in its most perfect form at Disney's River Country—a real live Magic Kingdom. For more information, write the Guest Relations Office, P. O. Box 40, Lake Buena Vista, Florida 32830.

Swimming in Hawaiian Waterfall Pools and an Underground Cave

On the northeast coast of Maui, at

Waianapanapa State Park, you dive into the pool and swim underwater to get into the grotto, where you can sit on a rocky ledge. West of there, you can paddle upstream from the ocean between spiky cliffs, feathered with ferns and ginger, and soak in a pool pounded by a waterfall. Or, at Kipahulu, swim in one of seven pools where the mother of Maui, the demigoddess, used to wash and bleach her tapa-cloth clothes. For more information, contact the Maui Department of Parks and Recreation, County Building, High Street, Wailuku, Hawaii 96793, or the Hawaii Visitors Bureau, 2270 Kalakaua Avenue, Honolulu 96815.

Pools in the Black River

They're formed by huge rock outcroppings, at Johnson's Shut-Ins State Park near Lesterville, Missouri. Kids splash around and have a great time, and the river keeps flowing through, making a little current. For more information about the area, write the East Ozark Travel Association, Box 287, Bonne Terre, Missouri 63628.

The Indian Bathtub

This is an indentation into which pours steaming water from Hot Creek, near Bruneau Canyon, in Idaho. You're in the middle of miles and miles of rocky sagebrush wilderness—quite a place for an old swimming hole. The Idaho Division of Tourism & Industrial Development, Capitol Building, Boise 83720, can send more information about the area.

World's Largest Man-Made Ocean

Big Surf, right in the middle of the desert near Tempe, Arizona, is a man-made lagoon with a four-acre man-made beach and a man-made machine that churns up three-to-five-foot waves at the flick of a man-made switch. It's eerily unlike the ocean, but the concession stand does a big business in surf-board rentals. Another amusement at this slick swimming hole is the three-hundred-foot-long Surf Slide, something like a log flume minus the log. You skitter and whirl all over the place. You can get more information about the place from the manager at 1500 North Hayden Road, Tempe 85281.

The World's Largest Open-Air Hot Springs Swimming Pool

You'll find it in Glenwood Springs, Colorado, and it's open year round; in winter clouds of steam wrap you up and make it seem as if you're almost alone in the fog. The Chamber of Commerce in Glenwood Springs 81601 can send you more information.

World's Largest Free Concrete Municipal Swimming Pool

It's in Garden City, Kansas, in Finnup

Park. The town is also the home of the largest buffalo herd in Kansas, and of a famous hotel, the Windsor. You can get more information about the place from the Kansas Department of Economic Development, Travel Division, State Office Building, Topeka 66612.

Floating in an Inland Ocean
The Salton Sea, a mountain-ringed lake about ninety miles due east of San Diego, is not just any lake. A quirk in its formation has left it saltier than the Pacific Ocean—and when you go swimming, *you float*. The water that runs into the sea—drained off by farmers who habitually flood their fields and orchards in order to dissolve the salts built up in the soil—soaks up the salts at the bottom of the lake, which is consequently getting so saline that the fish in the lake (orange-mouthed corvina, Gulf croaker, and Gulf sargo, brought in from the Gulf of California by the California Parks Department) may not be able to produce viable eggs. Meanwhile, back-stroking is fun because you're so buoyant, and the water is warm (up to 90 degrees Fahrenheit in the summer). You can also camp on the lakeshore. For more information, write the Salton Sea State

Recreation Area, General Delivery, North Shore, California 92254.

"Finding, or cooking up some world's first is a special American talent hardly known elsewhere. We all practically flip at the news that the new Columbia River Bridge at Astoria has the 'longest continuous three-span through truss series of any bridge in the world.' How would we react to . . . 'Norway, world's narrowest Scandinavian country' or 'Egypt: locust capital of the world'?"

—Roy Bongartz
Holiday Magazine

Great Surfing

In Hawaii—a mecca for surfers worth their salt—the waves come in all shapes and sizes. There are waves you can catch without a board, waves you can catch on an air mattress, waves you can catch on a belly board, waves you can catch on a regular surfboard, and each kind of wave has its beach. In winter, on beaches like Sunset, Waimea Bay, Yokohama Bay, Maili, Makaha, Haleiwa, waves reach *thirty* feet—hard to believe until you've seen them.

The Hawaii Surfing Association, Box

8125, Honolulu 96815, can send you some information and/or answer questions. Sunset's *Hawaii: A Guide to All the Islands* also does a good job of putting you in touch with places where you can meet the surf at whatever level you choose (Lane Publishing, Menlo Park, California 94025; $2.95).

The Coney Island Icebergers

The Iceberg Athletic Club, New York City's Oldest Winter Bathing Club, was founded in 1918, and, though there's another similar organization in the area, it's one of the few groups of its kind in the country. It's fairly easy to see why: Iceberg Athletes go for winter swims in the ocean, whether it's warm, snowy, or 60 below zero. The club has had only two presidents since its founding, Detective George O'Connor of the Missing Persons Bureau of the New York City Police Department and the present chief, David M. Cory (2048 East 14th Street, Brooklyn, New York 11229), who can send you more information. The club is open to men of all ages interested in winter bathing—and visitors can come and watch them swim.

173

Running Some Rivers

The best and most comprehensive guide to what's doing is *Adventure Travel U.S.A.* (Adventure Guides, 36 East 57th Street, New York, New York 10022; $5 postpaid). You also get a rundown on sailing, cycling, riding, walking, ballooning, skiing, and vacation sites and outfitters.

Tubing

Slipping along in an inner tube is one of the most peaceful ways to spend an afternoon, but good streams to tube on—clean water, some current, and no underwater obstructions—are hard to find. The Ichetucknee River, near Fort White, Florida, meets all three criteria, and it's also particularly pretty. Jungly vegetation grows on both sides of the river, the bottom is white and sandy, and superbly clear waters boil up out of the springs you pass over. Inner tubes are for rent all around Fort White; on weekends the river is jammed with students from the nearby University of Florida. For details, contact the Department of Natural Resources, Crown Building, Tallahassee, Florida 32304.

Then there's the Apple River, in northwest Wisconsin, where tubing is so popular that Terrace Tubes, one of three rental agents in Somerset, tubing headquarters, installed a 1,900-foot-long chair lift so that floaters could yo-yo up and down the river all afternoon if they wanted. Reserve ahead for your tubes, with Somerset Camp (Box 217A, Somerset, Wisconsin 54025; 715/247-3728); River's Edge (Box 30; Somerset, Wisconsin 54025; 715/247-3305); or Terrace Tubes (Somerset, Wisconsin 54025; 715/247-5262).

In Minnesota, you can tube on the Cannon River, in the southern part of the state about forty-five minutes out of the Twin Cities. There are deciduous trees all along the way, sandbars every now and then, a couple of small rapids, and a ten-foot-high dam you slither over at the end. Tubes can be rented from the Nelsons (Welch, Minnesota 55089; 612/258-4530), or from Paul's Landings (Box 355, Cannon Falls, Minnesota 55009; 507/263-3525).

The Rum River, north of the Twin Cities, is slow-moving, fifty feet wide, and wooded on either side; you can always see the bottom. Rentals are available from the Sports Forest Rum River Village Campground (Route 2, Onamia, Minnesota 56359), and Ramblin' Rum (22022 Lake George Boulevard, Anoka, Minnesota 55303; 612/753-2211).

Long Canoe Trips Beginners Can Handle

Not all of those vast unspoiled lakelands and free-flowing streams are wild-water torrents. Even if you're not a champion paddler, you can experience real wilderness. All the rivers mentioned in this section are serviced by liveries or outfitters, all are manageable by everyone but rank beginners, and all are extensive enough to give you time to absorb the peace of the back country.

The Delaware River. From the Catskill foothills in southern New York State to the Delaware Water Gap, this river coasts through 120 miles of the kind of lush forest land you would not expect to find a mere two hours away from Philadelphia or New York. Rentals: from Kittatinny Canoes (Dingmans Ferry, Pennsylvania 18328) and Abbott's (Titusville, New Jersey 08560). South Branch Canoe Cruises (Box 173, Lebanon, New Jersey 08833) sponsors guided trips (about $45 per person for two days) as well as unusual three-day whitewater instruction programs.

The Allagash. On its northerly ninety-mile course from near Maine's Moosehead Lake and Mount Katahdin, the Allagash River links seven lakes as it sweeps and swirls through some of the East's wildest woodlands. Countless other lakes (glassy-surfaced, loon-haunted) and streams—some tunneling through dense thickets of black spruce and occasionally so shallow you've got to tow your canoe through the icy waters—are accessible by portages of anywhere from a few hundred yards to a mile and a half: "the Allagash" is a region as well as a river. For a complete list of outfitters, write the State Park & Recreation Commission, Augusta, Maine 04330. Greenville, Maine, is a gateway town.

The Adirondack Canoe Routes. Paddling this hundred-mile-long chain of river- and portage-connected lakes in upstate New York makes you feel like a nineteenth-century woodsman. The countryside is rocky, forested, and practically undeveloped except for a scattering of three-sided log lean-tos. When you canoe, you can usually camp on islands accessible only by boat and therefore utterly private. For details, contact the New York State Department of Environmental Conservation, 50 Wolf Road, Albany, New York 12233.

The Okefenokee Swamp. These south Georgia waters, stained black as a moonless night by the leachings of decaying vegetation, camouflage snakes and alligators and, smooth as glass, turn upside-down a magical, mysterious world of lofty moss-veiled cypress, tangled brush, and vast grassy prairies. The U.S. Fish & Wildlife Service (P. O. Box 117, 411 Pendleton Street, Waycross, Georgia 31501) has a strict limited-permit system, so you can be sure of getting the most of the experience. Write well in advance for permits; canoe reservations should also be obtained early from the Suwannee Canal Recreation Area (Route 2, Folkston, Georgia 31537). Trips are best in spring and fall, when temperatures are mild, insect problems minimal, and the birds and animals that inhabit this National Wildlife Refuge most active.

The Buffalo River. Like many other rivers in the south-central part of the country, this 130-mile-long stream in northern Arkansas is a series of long pools alternating with rapids and riffles. It is speckled by gravel bars that make for great camping and has fine smallmouth fishing, swimming holes, and shores full of waterfalls, caves, natural arches, and fernfalls. Because of the concentration of features, it has been named a National River. For a list of liveries, write the Buffalo National River, 115 West Central Avenue, P. O. Box 1173, Harrison, Arkansas 72601.

Northern Minnesota. There's enough lake-dotted river-ribboned north-country woodland up here to keep you paddling for a couple of months without backtracking. The brand-new and still largely undeveloped Voyageurs National Park is at the western end of the Minnesota-Canada border; the Superior National Forest, with its famous Boundary Waters Canoe Area, lies to the east. Wherever you go, fishing for walleye, bass, and northern pike is excellent, especially in spring and fall. For details, write the Superior National Forest (Box 338, Duluth, Minnesota 55801) and the Voyageurs National Park (P. O. Box 50, International Falls, Minnesota 56649). Hibbing, Minnesota, is the best access to the Superior National Forest; International Falls is closest to the Voyageurs National Park.

The Missouri River. Along one 150-mile stretch in central Montana, the stark beauty of this sagebrush-and-sandstone-cliff wilderness, almost treeless except for occasional cottonwoods and willows and patchy stands of spruce and fir, still looks the way it did when Lewis and Clark came through here nearly two hundred years ago. For a canoe trip out West, where most streams are experts-only torrents (when they're canoeable at all), the Missouri can't be beat. Missouri River Cruises (Box 1212, Fort Benton, Montana 59442) provides rental canoes as well as outfitting services. The biggest town near the put-in is Great Falls.

For more canoeing. See Robert Colwell's *Introduction to Water Trails in America* (Stackpole Books, Cameron & Kelker Streets, Harrisburg, Pennsylvania 17105; $2.95). Several trips are outlined in detail in each state, and brief information is provided for other canoeable streams in the area, including names of the U.S.G.S. quadrangles applicable to the area and any local publications on the stream. However, since the book was published in 1973, you can expect some of the information to be out of date—particularly the names and addresses of the canoeing clubs, which are your principal sources for information on across-the-U.S. canoeing.

More up-to-date is the canoeing guidebooks section of Cliff Jacobson's *Wilderness Canoeing & Camping* (E. P. Dutton, 201 Park Avenue South, New York, New York 10003; $6.95). It will put you in touch with publications dealing with canoe trails in Wisconsin, Minnesota, Missouri and the Ozarks, New England, New York State, New Jersey, the Appalachians, and Upper Michigan.

Kayaking

What you feel most strongly in a kayak are the vulnerability of your own life and the surge and the strength of the river—especially when the river is Idaho's Salmon, the "River of No Return." Wilderness Encounters, Inc. (P. O. Box 3417, Boise, Idaho 83703) takes groups of learners and guides (safely) onto the Main Salmon starting at the Shepp Ranch, to which you return every night after a day of learning. *Adventure Travel U.S.A.* can tell you about other kayakking opportunities. Order it from Adventure Guides, Inc., 36 East 57th Street, New York, New York 10022; $5 postpaid.

You-Paddle Whitewater Rafting Trips

When you join up with a commercial outfitter on whitewaters as wild as the ones on the New River between Thurmond and Fayette Station, West Virginia, you might not expect to be asked to do anything except stay out of the way. But here, you're handed a paddle—and your efforts count. The fact that you're paddling just to get through in good shape adds to the excitement provided by the river itself, which offers Class Five and Six rapids and ten- to twenty-foot rollers that crash over the bow of the boat like tidal waves. The danger is actually minimal, because New River guides know what they're doing. You will not, however, come out dry. There are several outfitters on the river; Wildwater Expeditions Unlimited (P. O. Box 55, Thurmond, West Virginia 25936) is one of the best.

Along the same lines are trips on the Chattooga, the river James Dickey described in *Deliverance*. Along its forty-mile run down the Georgia-South Carolina border to Lake Tugaloo, the Chattooga works itself up into some of the most challenging whitewater east of the Mississippi. In one seven-mile stretch, for example, there are eight Class Five and higher rapids; the last half-mile consists of five Class Five and Six rapids *back to back*. You wouldn't want to tackle this in a canoe unless you were superhuman with your paddles, but Wildwater, Ltd. (Long Creek, South Carolina 29658) will take you down in rafts even if you've never even fiddled around in a rowboat before.

Rafting a Tropical River

There are those who call Jamaica's interior the most beautiful landscape in all the West Indies—and they don't get too much argument. There are mountains. And there are palm-fringed beaches. And waterfalls that cascade through lush green vegetation from the mountains to rivers where the waters meet the ocean. It's on one of these rivers, the fern-, palm-, and bamboo-fringed Rio Grande, that you can take a tropical raft ride. Action-packed it isn't (unless you call bobbing through some occasional riffles "action"), but it is one of the most pleasant raft rides around for the lovely scenery and the Gauguin feeling of riding in a strange-looking thirty-foot-long bamboo craft.

Most tourists don't go east or south of the Rio Grande, but it's beautiful country, and cottages are available for rent through the Jamaica Association of Villas and Apartments at 200 Park Avenue, New York, New York 10017. For more information about the raft trips, write the Jamaica Tourist Board at 2 Dag Hammarskjold Plaza, New York, New York 10017.

Contacts for States, Provinces, and the Caribbean Islands

ALABAMA
Bureau of Publicity and Information
State Highway Building
Montgomery 36104

ALASKA
Division of Tourism
Department of Commerce and
　Economic Development
Pouch E
Juneau 99811

ALBERTA
Travel Alberta
10065 Jasper Avenue
Edmonton
Canada T5J 3B1

ANGUILLA
Eastern Caribbean Tourist Board
220 East 42nd Street
New York, New York 10017

ANTIGUA
Antigua Tourist Board
101 Park Avenue
New York, New York 10017

ARIZONA
Office of Economic Planning and
　Development
Visitor Development Section
1645 West Jefferson Street
Phoenix 85007

ARKANSAS
Arkansas Department of Parks and
　Tourism
State Capitol
Little Rock 72201

ARUBA
Aruba Tourist Information Office
576 Fifth Avenue
New York, New York 10036

BARBADOS
Barbados Board of Tourism
800 Second Avenue
New York, New York 10017

BERMUDA
Bermuda Board of Tourism
630 Fifth Avenue
New York, New York 10020

BONAIRE
Bonaire Tourist Board
685 Fifth Avenue
New York, New York 10022

BRITISH COLUMBIA
Tourism British Columbia
1117 Wharf Street
Victoria V8W 2Z2

BRITISH VIRGIN ISLANDS
British Virgin Islands Tourist Board
515 Madison Avenue
New York, New York 10022

CALIFORNIA
State Office of Tourism
1400 Tenth Street
Sacramento 95814

CARIBBEAN
Caribbean Tourism Association
20 East 46th Street
New York, New York 10017

THE CAYMAN ISLANDS
Cayman Islands Department of
　Tourism
420 Lexington Avenue
New York, New York 10017

COLORADO
Colorado Division of Commerce and
　Development
500 State Centennial Building
Denver 80203

CONNECTICUT
State of Connecticut
Department of Commerce
210 Washington Street
Hartford 06106

CURAÇAO
Curaçao Tourist Board
30 Rockefeller Center
New York, New York 10020

DELAWARE
Delaware State Visitors Service
630 State College Road
Dover 19901

DOMINICA
Eastern Caribbean Tourist Board
220 East 42nd Street
New York, New York 10017

DOMINICAN REPUBLIC
Dominican Republic Government
　Tourist Office
64 West 50th Street
New York, New York 10020

FLORIDA
State of Florida Department of
　Commerce
Visitor Inquiry Section
Division of Tourism
107 West Gaines Street
Tallahassee 32304

GEORGIA
Georgia Bureau of Industry and Trade
Trinity-Washington Building
P. O. Box 38097
Atlanta 30334

GRENADA
Grenada Tourist Board
866 Second Avenue
New York, New York 10017

GUADELOUPE
French West Indies Tourist Board
610 Fifth Avenue
New York, New York 10020

HAITI
Haitian Office of Tourism and
　Public Relations
30 Rockefeller Plaza
New York, New York 10020

HAWAII
Hawaii Visitors Bureau
2270 Kalakaua Avenue
Honolulu 96815

IDAHO
Division of Tourism and
Industrial Development
Capitol Building
Boise 83720

ILLINOIS
Department of Business and Economic
Development
205 West Wacker Drive
Chicago 60606

INDIANA
Department of Commerce
336 State House
Indianapolis 46204

IOWA
Development Commission, Travel and
Tourism Division
250 Jewett Building
Des Moines 50309

JAMAICA
Jamaica Tourist Board
2 Dag Hammarskjold Plaza
New York, New York 10017

KANSAS
Department of Economic Development
Travel Division
State Office Building
Topeka 66612

KENTUCKY
Department of Public Information
Advertising and Travel Production
Capitol Annex
Frankfort 40601

LOUISIANA
Tourist Commission
P. O. Box 44291
Baton Rouge 70804

MAINE
Department of Commerce and Industry
State House
Augusta 04330

MANITOBA
Manitoba Government Travel Office
200 Vaughan Street
Winnipeg R3C 0V8

MARTINIQUE
French West Indies Tourist Board
610 Fifth Avenue
New York, New York 10020

MARYLAND
Department of Economic and
Community Development
Division of Tourism
1748 Forest Drive
Annapolis 21401

MASSACHUSETTS
Department of Commerce and
Development
100 Cambridge Street
State Office Building
Boston 02202

MICHIGAN
Tourist Council
300 South Capitol Avenue
Lansing 48926

MINNESOTA
Department of Economic Development
480 Cedar Street
Hanover Building
St. Paul 55101

MISSISSIPPI
Agricultural and Industrial Board
P. O. Box 849
Jackson 39205

MISSOURI
Division of Tourism
308 East High Street
P. O. Box 1055
Jefferson City 65101

MONTANA
Department of Highways
Helena 59601

MONTSERRAT
Eastern Caribbean Tourist Board
220 East 42nd Street
New York, New York 10017

NEBRASKA
Department of Economic Development
P. O. Box 94666
State Capitol
Lincoln 68509

NEVADA
Department of Economic Development
Travel-Tourism Division
Carson City 89701

NEW BRUNSWICK
Department of Tourism
P. O. Box 12345
Fredericton E3B 5C3

NEWFOUNDLAND
Department of Tourism
Confederation Building
St. John's A0L 3E0

NEW HAMPSHIRE
Division of Economic Development
Vacation Travel Promotion
P. O. Box 856
Concord 03301

NEW JERSEY
Division of Economic Development
Department of Labor and Industry
P. O. Box 2766
Trenton 08625

NEW MEXICO
Department of Development
Travel Bureau
113 Washington Avenue
Santa Fe 87501

NEW YORK
State Department of Commerce
Travel Bureau
99 Washington Avenue
Albany 12210

NORTH CAROLINA
Department of Natural and Economic
Resources
Travel and Promotion
P. O. Box 27685
Raleigh 27611

NORTH DAKOTA
Highway Department
Capitol Grounds
Bismarck 58501

NORTHWEST TERRITORIES
Division of Tourism
Yellowknife X1A 2L9

NOVA SCOTIA
Department of Tourism
P. O. Box 456
Halifax B3J 2R5

OHIO
Department of Economic and
Community Development
P. O. Box 1001
Columbus 43216

OKLAHOMA
Tourism and Recreation Division
500 Will Rogers Building
Oklahoma City 73105

ONTARIO
Ministry of Industry and Tourism
Queen's Park
Toronto M7A 2E5

OREGON
Travel Information Section
Oregon State Highway Department
Salem 97310

PENNSYLVANIA
Department of Commerce
Bureau of Travel Development
431 South Office Building
Harrisburg 17120

PRINCE EDWARD ISLAND
Tourist Information Division
Department of the Environment and
Tourism
Box 940
Charlottetown CIA 7N5

PUERTO RICO
Tourism Development Company
1290 Avenue of the Americas
New York, New York 10019

QUEBEC
Department of Tourism
Place de la Capitale
150 St. Cyrille Boulevard
Quebec City G1R 2B2

RHODE ISLAND
Department of Economic Development-Tourism
One Weybosset Hill
Providence 02903

SABA
c/o Sontheimer & Company
4 West 58th Street
New York, New York 10019

ST. BARTH—ELEMY
French West Indies Tourist Board
610 Fifth Avenue
New York, New York 10020

ST. KITTS-NEVIS
St. Kitts-Nevis Tourist Board
39 West 55th Street
New York, New York 10020

ST. LUCIA
St. Lucia Tourist Board
c/o Eastern Caribbean Tourist Board
220 East 42nd Street
New York, New York 10017

ST. MARTIN
French West Indies Tourist Board
610 Fifth Avenue
New York, New York 10020

ST. VINCENT
St. Vincent Tourist Board
c/o Eastern Caribbean Tourist Board
220 East 42nd Street
New York, New York 10017

SASKATCHEWAN
Department of Tourism
Box 7105
Regina S4P 3N2

SINT MAARTEN
c/o Sontheimer & Company
4 West 58th Street
New York, New York 10019

SOUTH CAROLINA
Department of Parks, Recreation and Tourism
P. O. Box 113
1205 Pendleton Street
Columbia 29201

SOUTH DAKOTA
Department of Economic and Tourism Development
Division of Tourism
Pierre 57501

TENNESSEE
Tourism Development
1007 Andrew Jackson State Office Building
Nashville 37211

TEXAS
Travel and Information Division
Highway Department
Austin 78701

TRINIDAD AND TOBAGO
Tourist Board
400 Madison Avenue
New York, New York 10017

TURKS AND CAICOS ISLANDS
Caribbean Tourism Association
20 East 46th Street
New York, New York 10017

UNITED STATES VIRGIN ISLANDS
Government Information Center
10 Rockefeller Plaza
New York, New York 10020

UTAH
Travel Council
Council Hall
Salt Lake City 84114

VERMONT
Agency of Development and Community Affairs
61 Elm Street
Montpelier 05602

VIRGINIA
State Travel Service
6 North Sixth Street
Richmond 23219

WASHINGTON
Department of Commerce and Economic Development
General Administration Building
Olympia 98504

WEST VIRGINIA
Department of Commerce
Travel Development Division
1900 Washington Street, East
Charleston 25305

WISCONSIN
Department of Business Development
P. O. Box 7606
Madison 53707

WYOMING
Travel Commission
2320 Capitol Avenue
Cheyenne 82002

YUKON TERRITORY
Government of the Yukon Territory
Box 2703
Whitehorse Y1A 2C3

INDEX